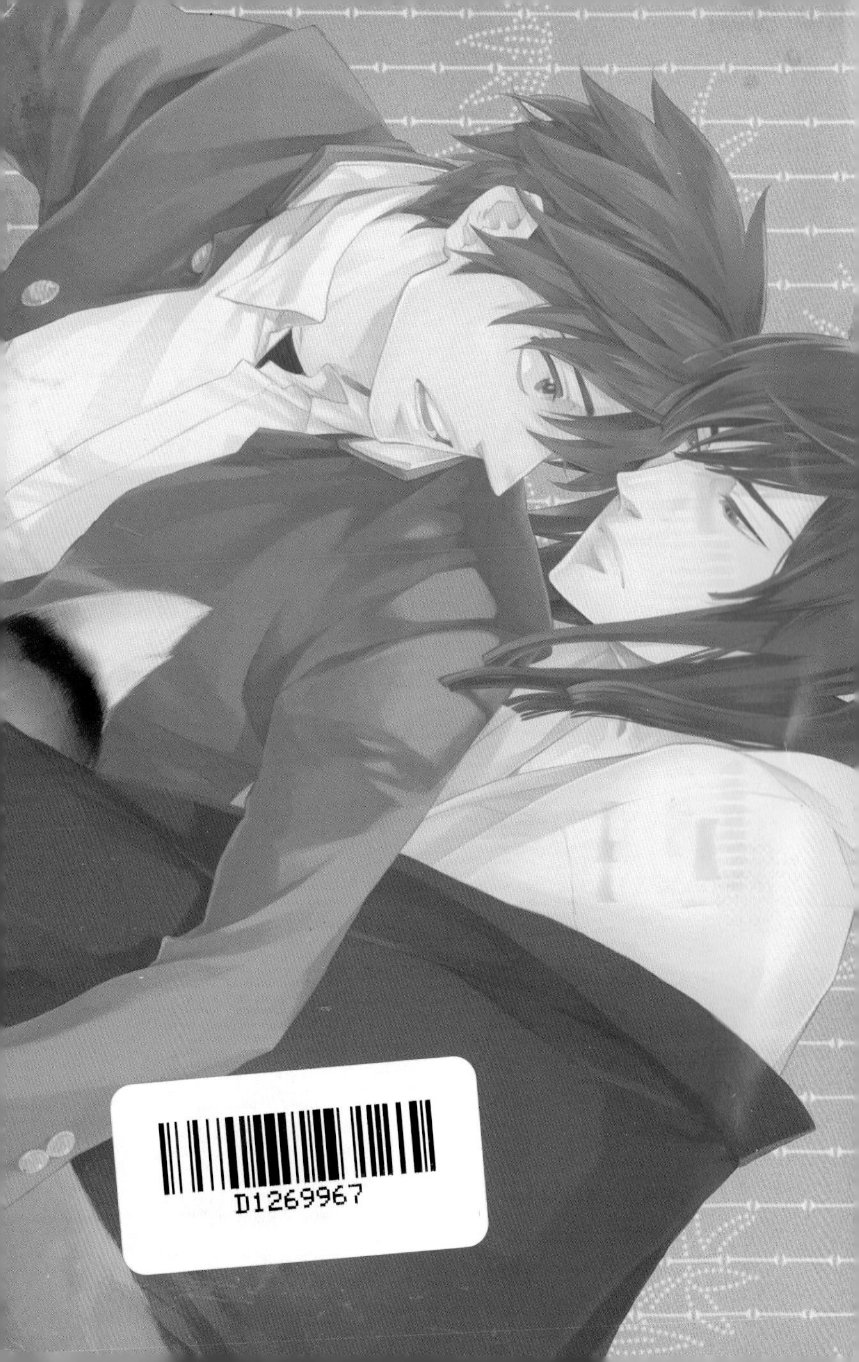

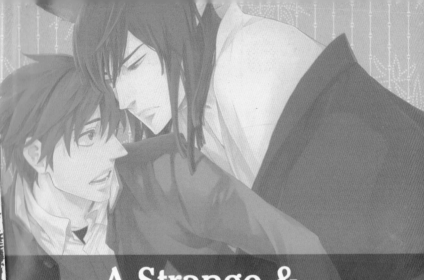

A Strange & Mystifying Story

Story and Art by **Tsuta Suzuki**   volume **3**

CONTENTS

SUBLIME
SuBLime Manga Edition

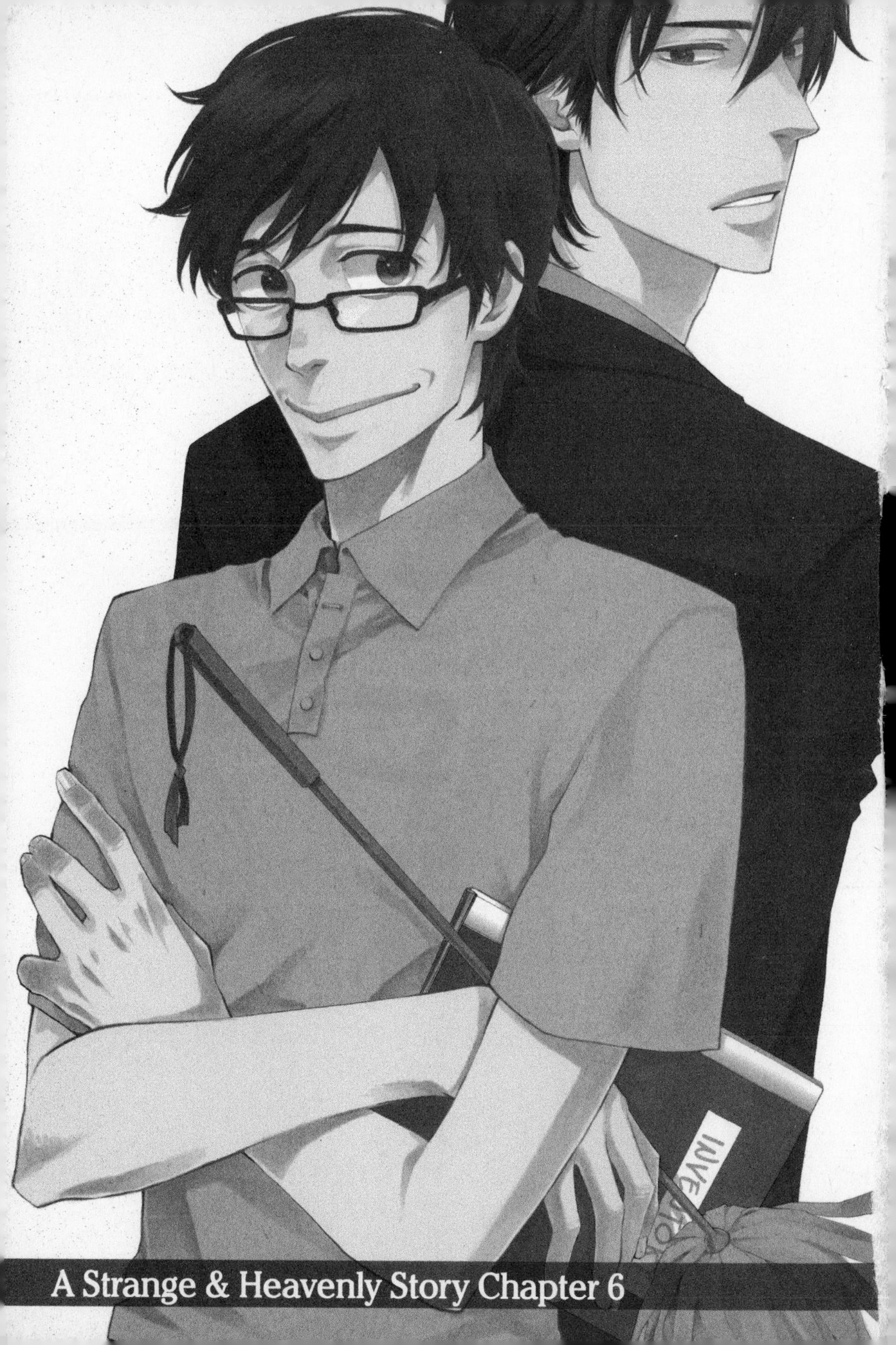

A Strange & Heavenly Story Chapter 6

A Strange &
Mystifying Story

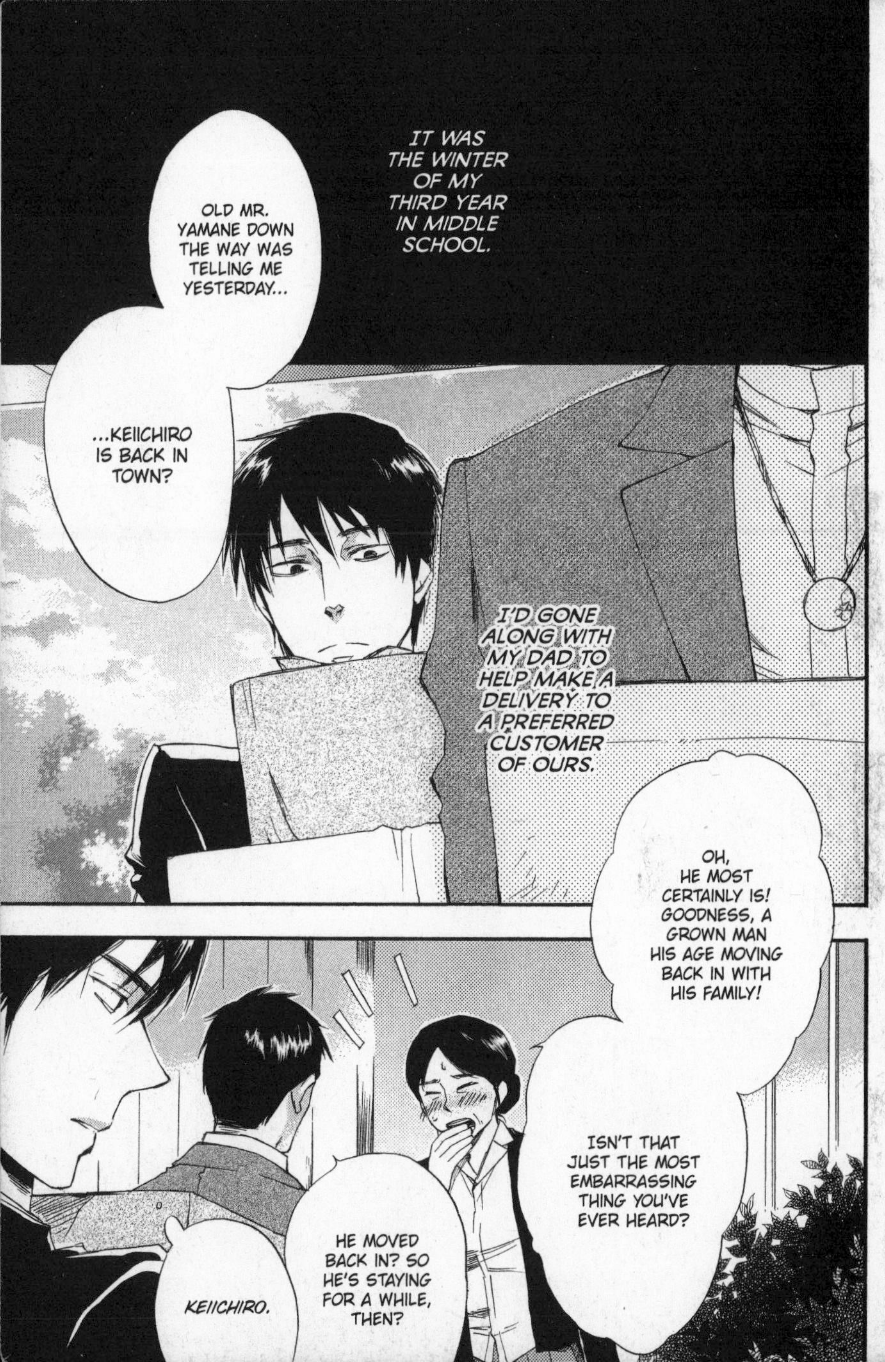
IT WAS THE WINTER OF MY THIRD YEAR IN MIDDLE SCHOOL.
OLD MR. YAMANE DOWN THE WAY WAS TELLING ME YESTERDAY...
...KEIICHIRO IS BACK IN TOWN?
I'D GONE ALONG WITH MY DAD TO HELP MAKE A DELIVERY TO A PREFERRED CUSTOMER OF OURS.
OH, HE MOST CERTAINLY IS! GOODNESS, A GROWN MAN HIS AGE MOVING BACK IN WITH HIS FAMILY!
ISN'T THAT JUST THE MOST EMBARRASSING THING YOU'VE EVER HEARD?
HE MOVED BACK IN? SO HE'S STAYING FOR A WHILE, THEN?
KEIICHIRO.

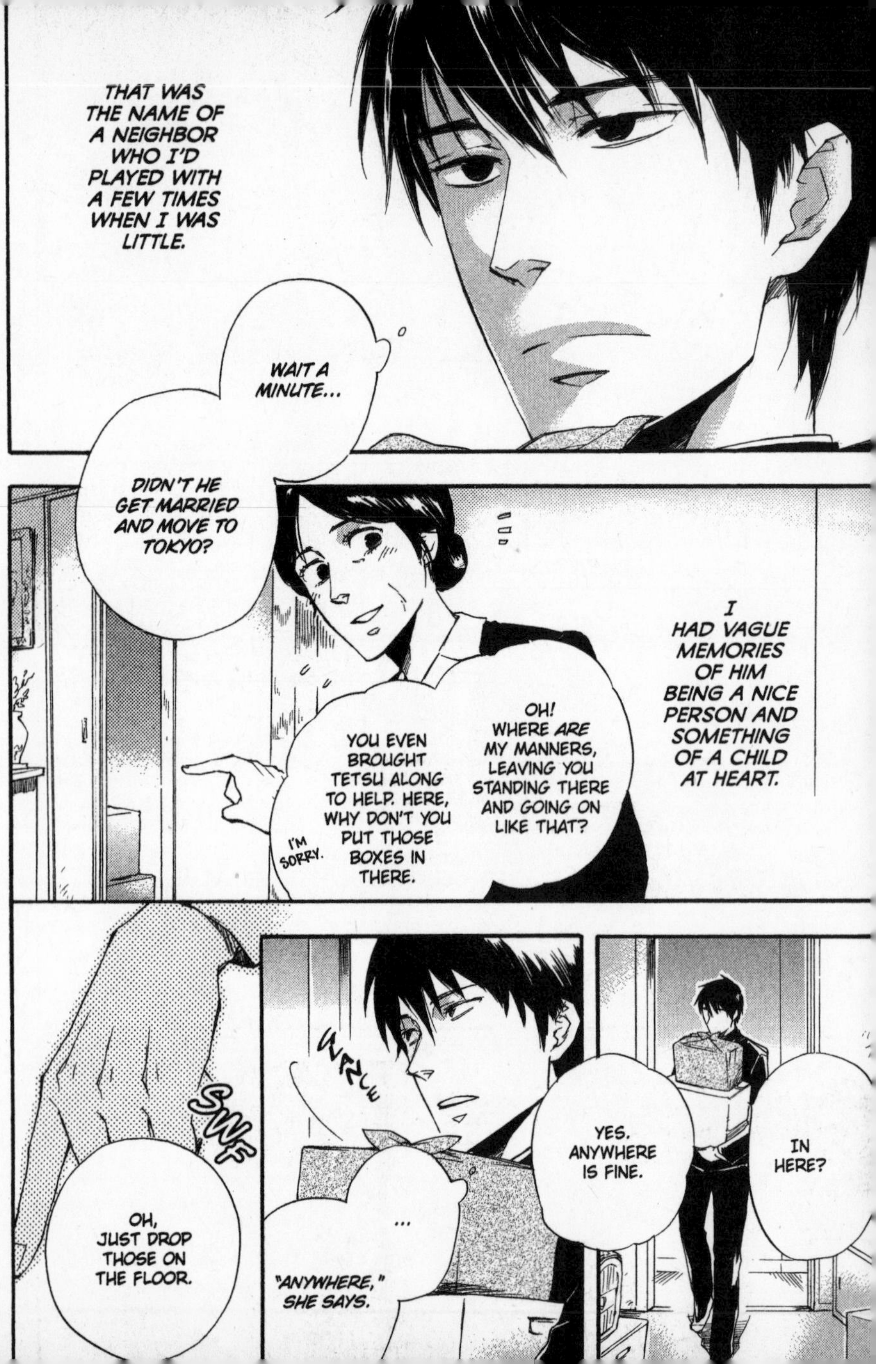
THAT WAS THE NAME OF A NEIGHBOR WHO I'D PLAYED WITH A FEW TIMES WHEN I WAS LITTLE.
WAIT A MINUTE...
DIDN'T HE GET MARRIED AND MOVE TO TOKYO?
I HAD VAGUE MEMORIES OF HIM BEING A NICE PERSON AND SOMETHING OF A CHILD AT HEART.
OH! WHERE *ARE* MY MANNERS, LEAVING YOU STANDING THERE AND GOING ON LIKE THAT?
YOU EVEN BROUGHT TETSU ALONG TO HELP. HERE, WHY DON'T YOU PUT THOSE BOXES IN THERE.
I'M SORRY.
IN HERE?
YES. ANYWHERE IS FINE.
...
"ANYWHERE," SHE SAYS.
OH, JUST DROP THOSE ON THE FLOOR.

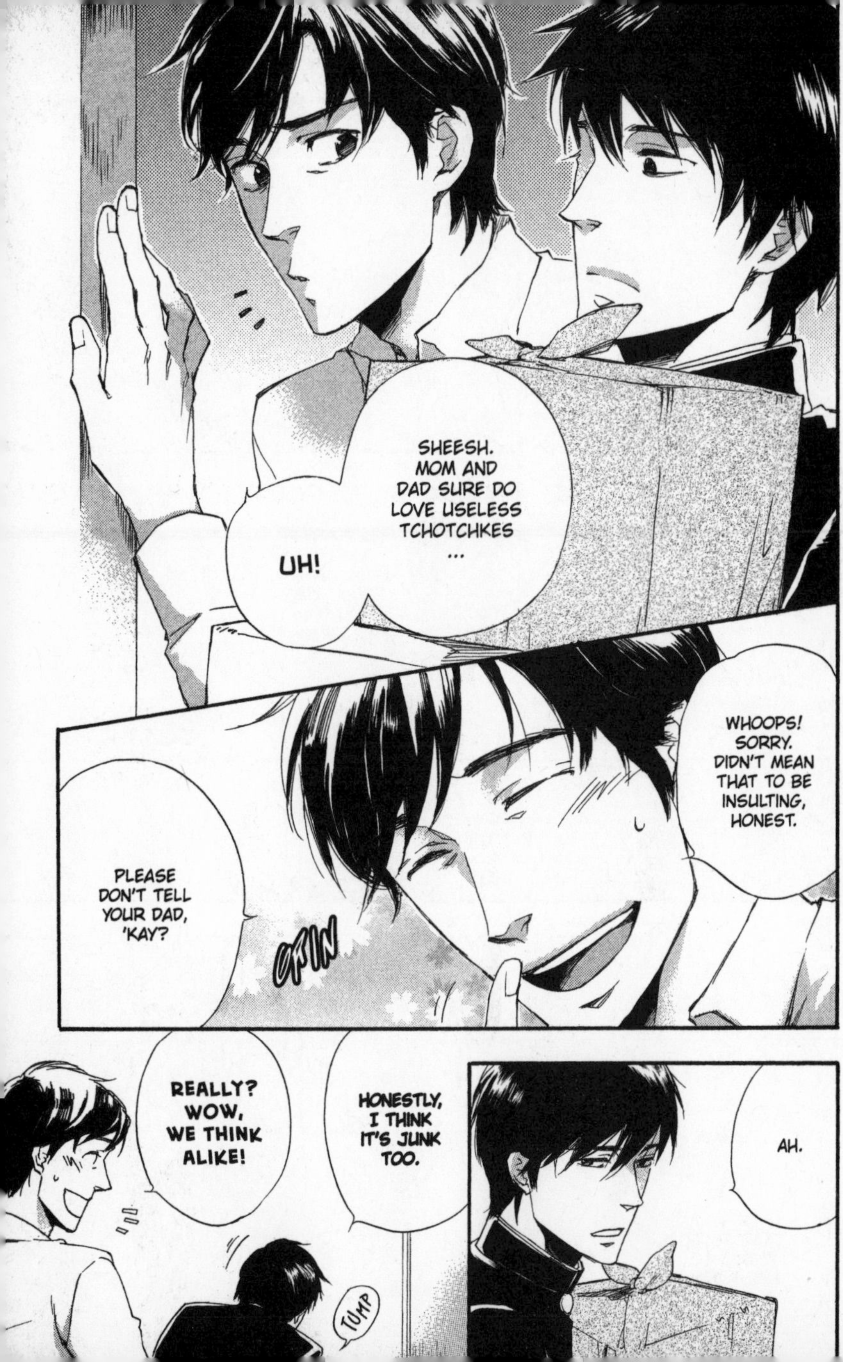
SHEESH. MOM AND DAD SURE DO LOVE USELESS TCHOTCHKES ...
UH!
WHOOPS! SORRY. DIDN'T MEAN THAT TO BE INSULTING, HONEST.
PLEASE DON'T TELL YOUR DAD, 'KAY?
AH.
HONESTLY, I THINK IT'S JUNK TOO.
REALLY? WOW, WE THINK ALIKE!
TUMP

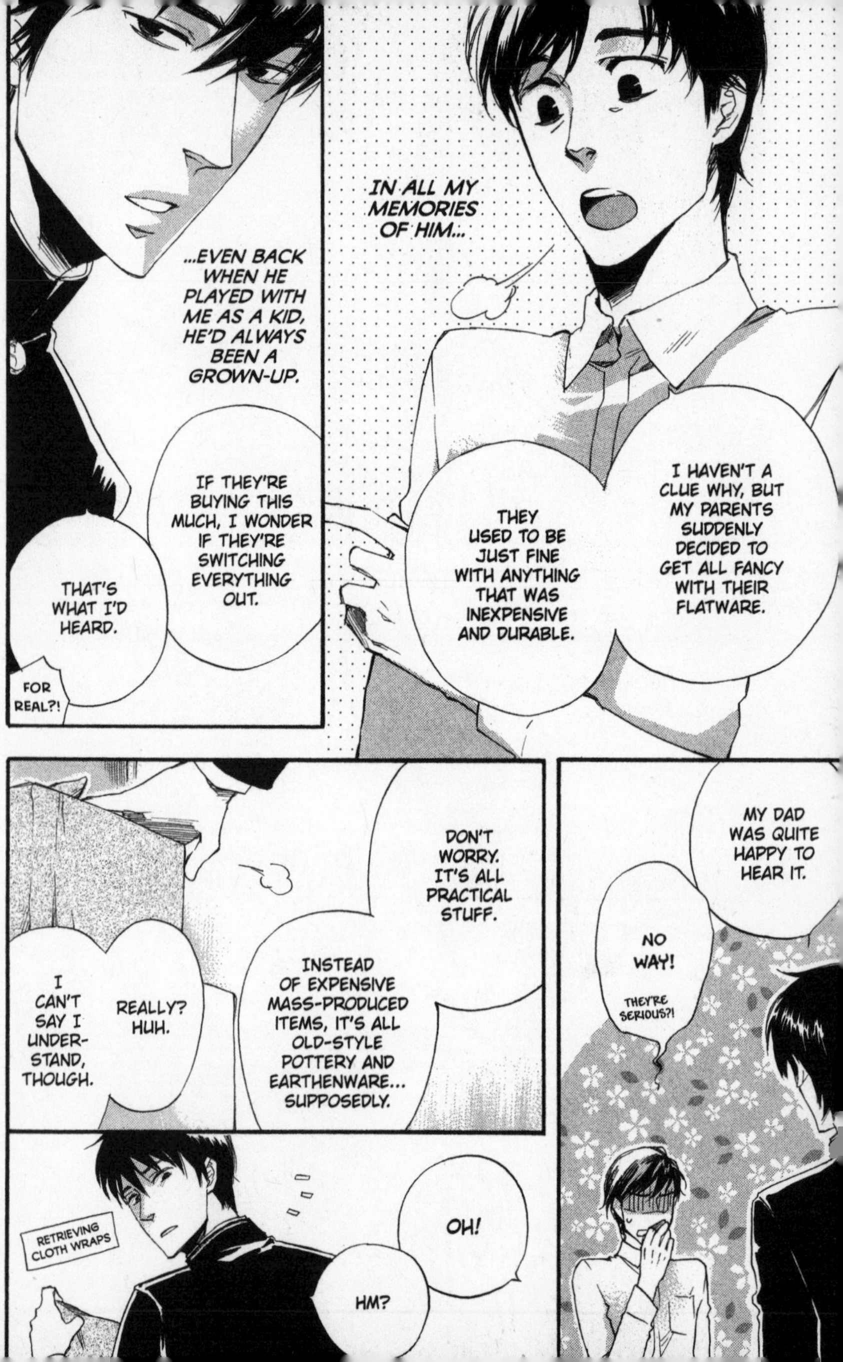
I HAVEN'T A CLUE WHY, BUT MY PARENTS SUDDENLY DECIDED TO GET ALL FANCY WITH THEIR FLATWARE.
THEY USED TO BE JUST FINE WITH ANYTHING THAT WAS INEXPENSIVE AND DURABLE.
IN ALL MY MEMORIES OF HIM...
...EVEN BACK WHEN HE PLAYED WITH ME AS A KID, HE'D ALWAYS BEEN A GROWN-UP.
IF THEY'RE BUYING THIS MUCH, I WONDER IF THEY'RE SWITCHING EVERYTHING OUT.
THAT'S WHAT I'D HEARD.
FOR REAL?!
MY DAD WAS QUITE HAPPY TO HEAR IT.
NO WAY!
THEY'RE SERIOUS?!
DON'T WORRY. IT'S ALL PRACTICAL STUFF.
INSTEAD OF EXPENSIVE MASS-PRODUCED ITEMS, IT'S ALL OLD-STYLE POTTERY AND EARTHENWARE... SUPPOSEDLY.
REALLY? HUH.
I CAN'T SAY I UNDER-STAND, THOUGH.
OH!
HM?
RETRIEVING CLOTH WRAPS

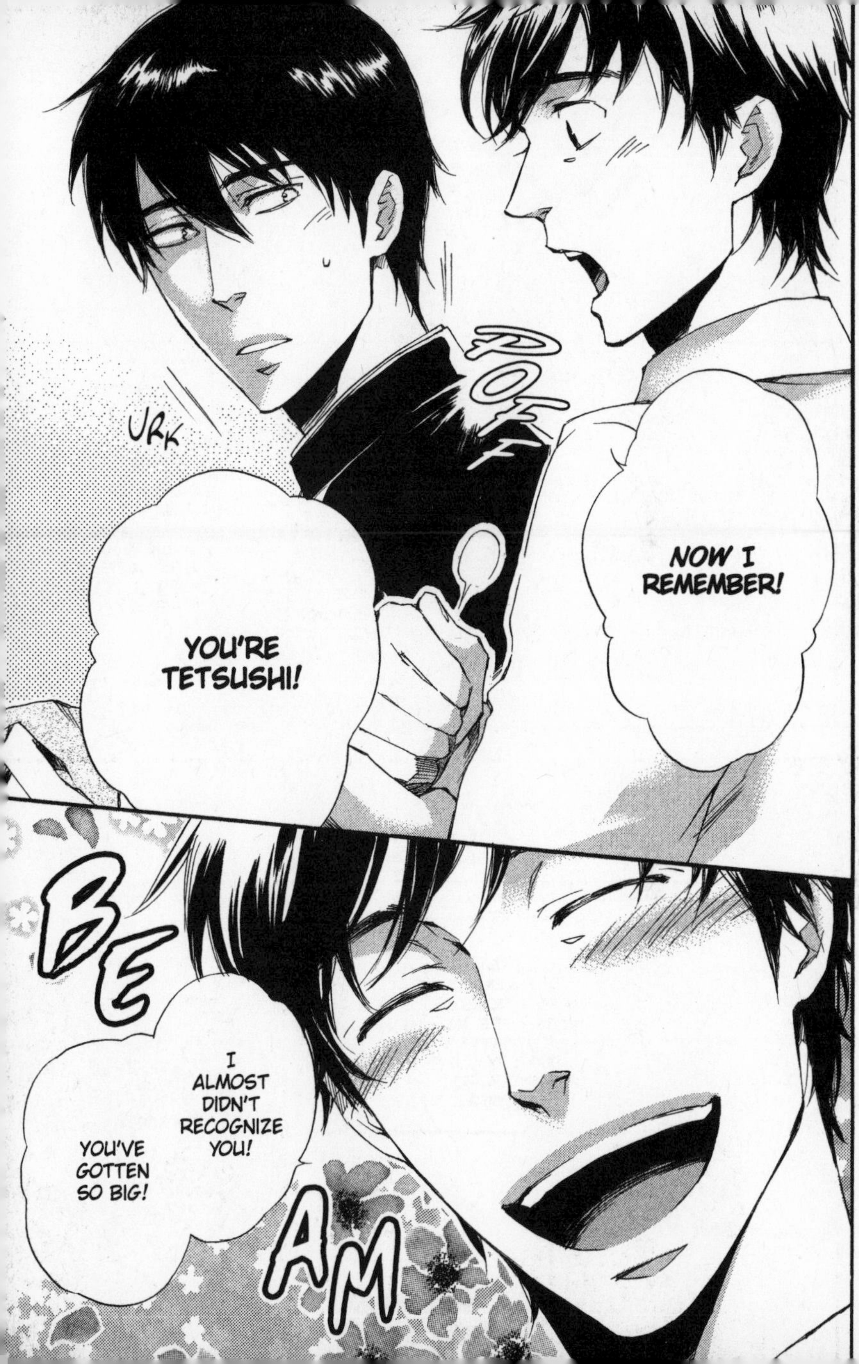
NOW I REMEMBER!
POFF
URK
YOU'RE TETSUSHI!
BEAM
I ALMOST DIDN'T RECOGNIZE YOU!
YOU'VE GOTTEN SO BIG!

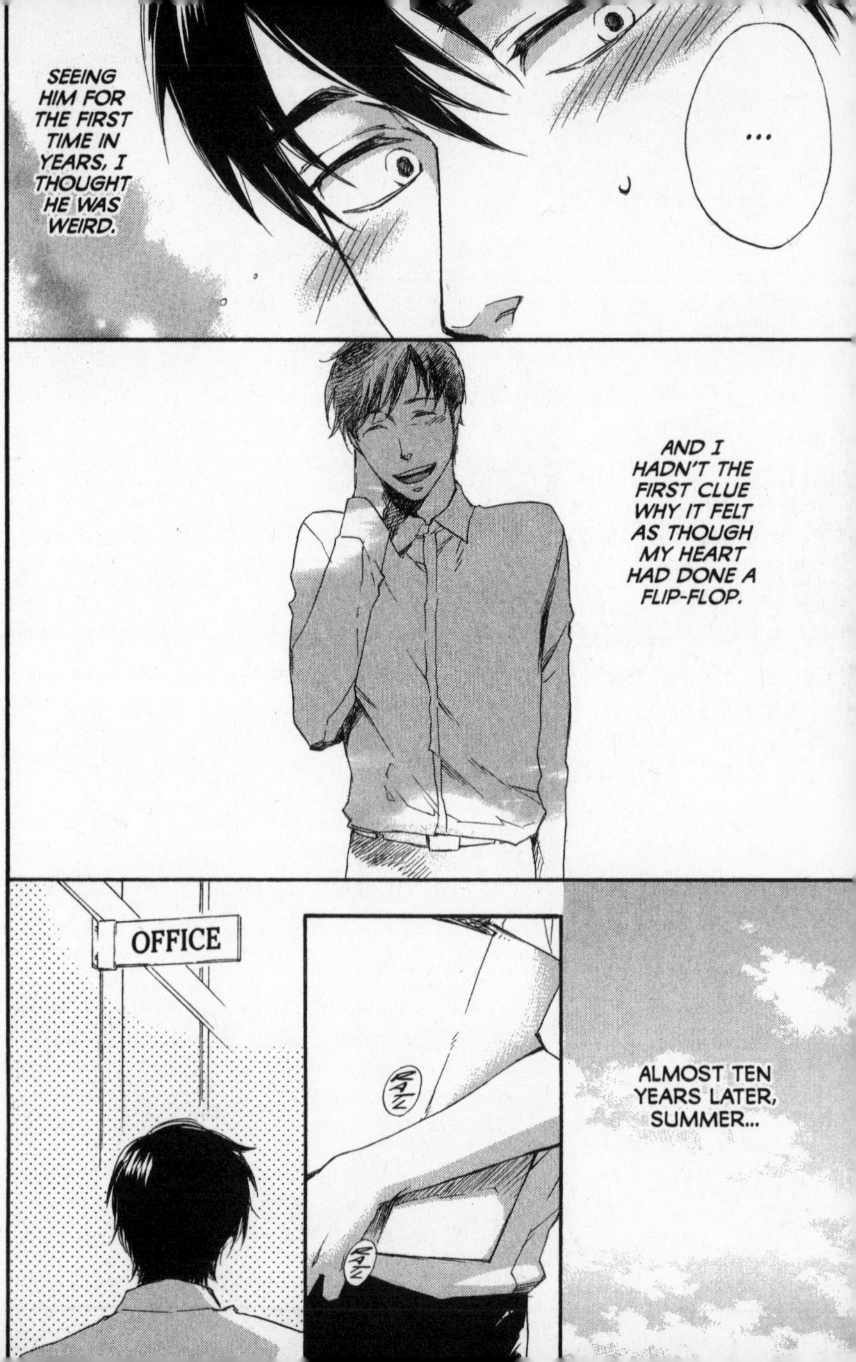
...
SEEING HIM FOR THE FIRST TIME IN YEARS, I THOUGHT HE WAS WEIRD.
AND I HADN'T THE FIRST CLUE WHY IT FELT AS THOUGH MY HEART HAD DONE A FLIP-FLOP.
ALMOST TEN YEARS LATER, SUMMER...
OFFICE

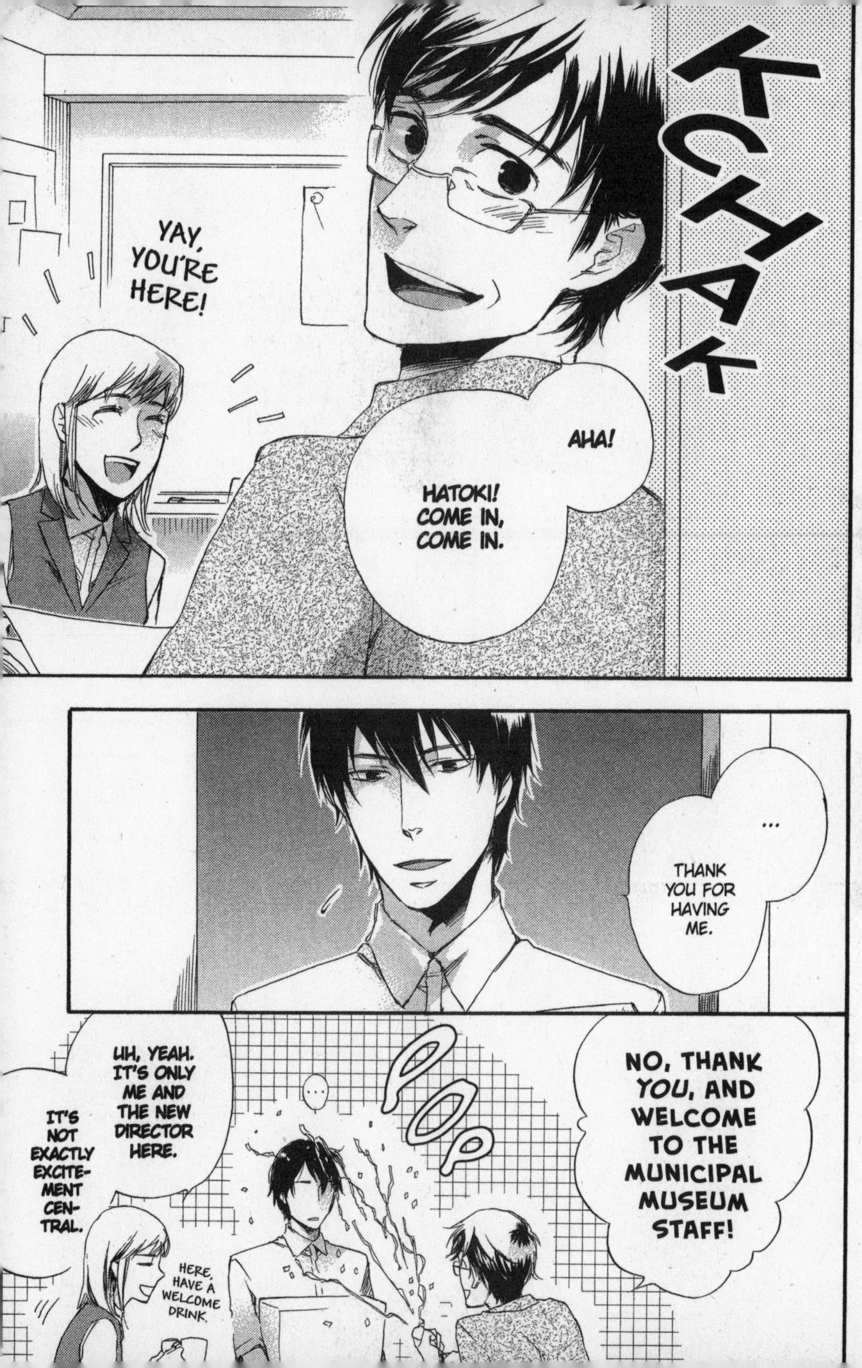
KCHAK
AHA! HATOKI! COME IN, COME IN.
YAY, YOU'RE HERE!
... THANK YOU FOR HAVING ME.
NO, THANK YOU, AND WELCOME TO THE MUNICIPAL MUSEUM STAFF!
POP
...
UH, YEAH. IT'S ONLY ME AND THE NEW DIRECTOR HERE.
IT'S NOT EXACTLY EXCITE-MENT CEN-TRAL.
HERE, HAVE A WELCOME DRINK.

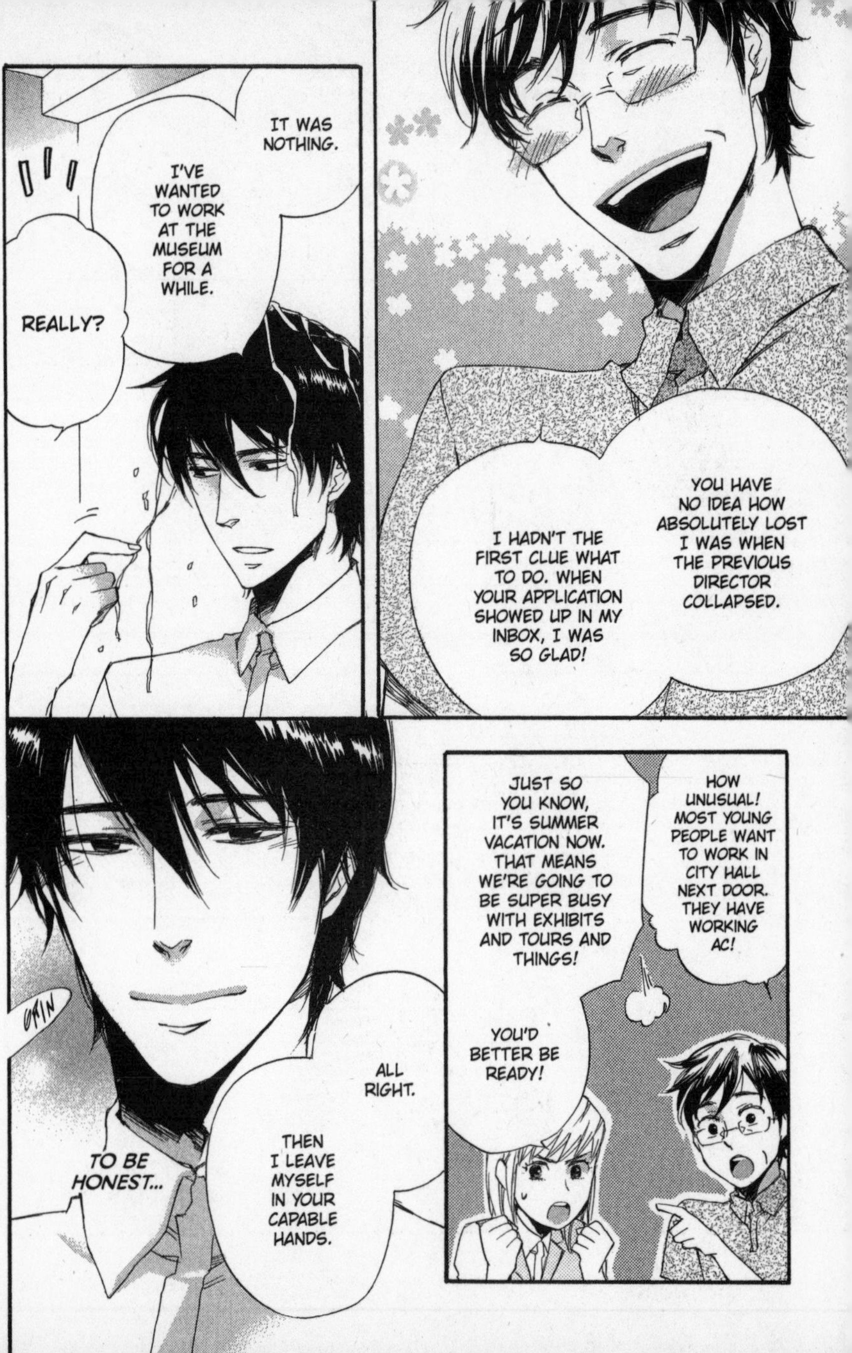
YOU HAVE NO IDEA HOW ABSOLUTELY LOST I WAS WHEN THE PREVIOUS DIRECTOR COLLAPSED.
I HADN'T THE FIRST CLUE WHAT TO DO. WHEN YOUR APPLICATION SHOWED UP IN MY INBOX, I WAS SO GLAD!
IT WAS NOTHING.
I'VE WANTED TO WORK AT THE MUSEUM FOR A WHILE.
REALLY?
HOW UNUSUAL! MOST YOUNG PEOPLE WANT TO WORK IN CITY HALL NEXT DOOR. THEY HAVE WORKING AC!
JUST SO YOU KNOW, IT'S SUMMER VACATION NOW. THAT MEANS WE'RE GOING TO BE SUPER BUSY WITH EXHIBITS AND TOURS AND THINGS!
YOU'D BETTER BE READY!
ALL RIGHT.
THEN I LEAVE MYSELF IN YOUR CAPABLE HANDS.
TO BE HONEST...
GRIN

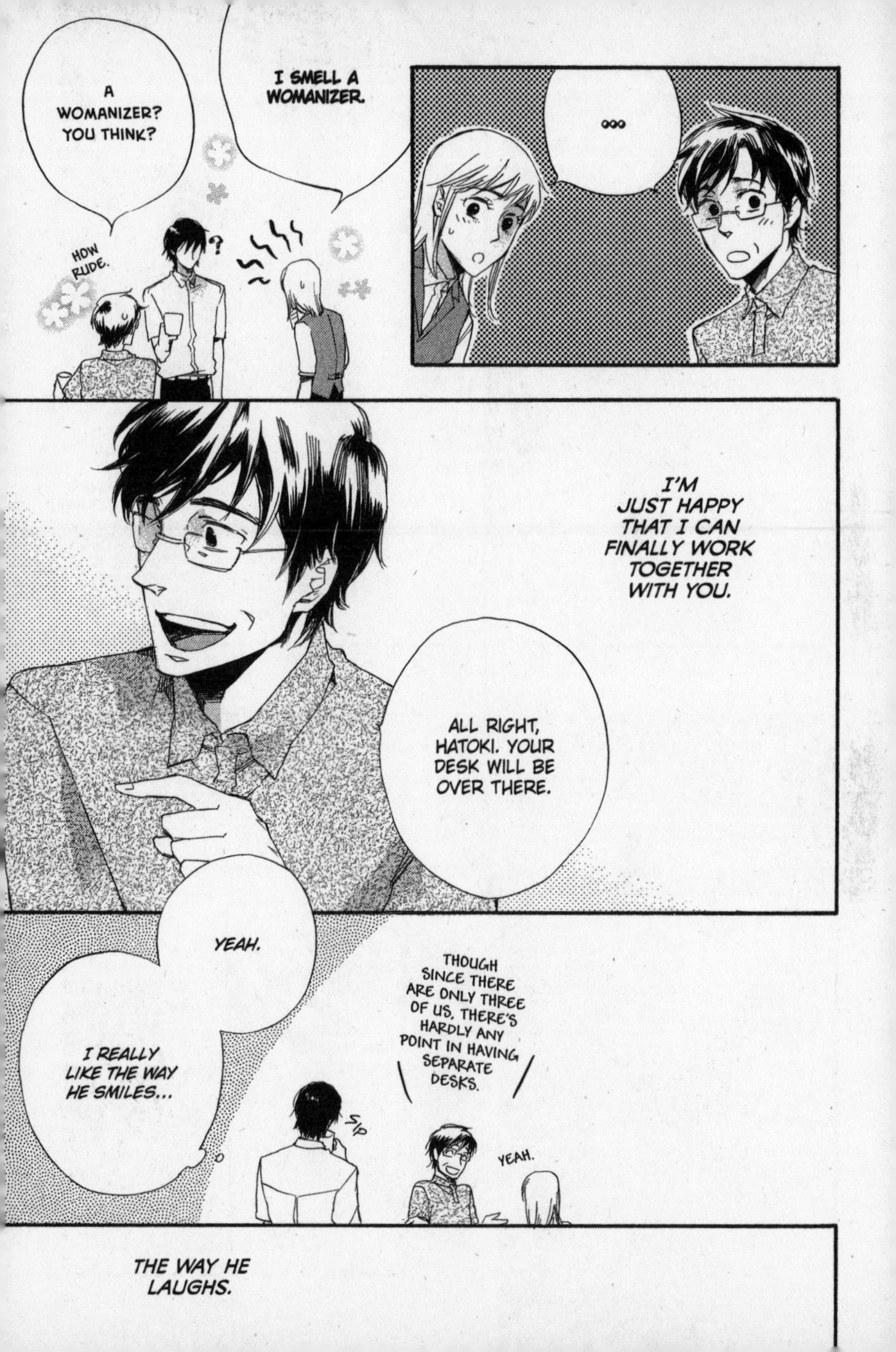
...
I SMELL A WOMANIZER.
A WOMANIZER? YOU THINK?
HOW RUDE.
I'M JUST HAPPY THAT I CAN FINALLY WORK TOGETHER WITH YOU.
ALL RIGHT, HATOKI. YOUR DESK WILL BE OVER THERE.
THOUGH SINCE THERE ARE ONLY THREE OF US, THERE'S HARDLY ANY POINT IN HAVING SEPARATE DESKS.
YEAH.
SIP
YEAH.
I REALLY LIKE THE WAY HE SMILES...
THE WAY HE LAUGHS.

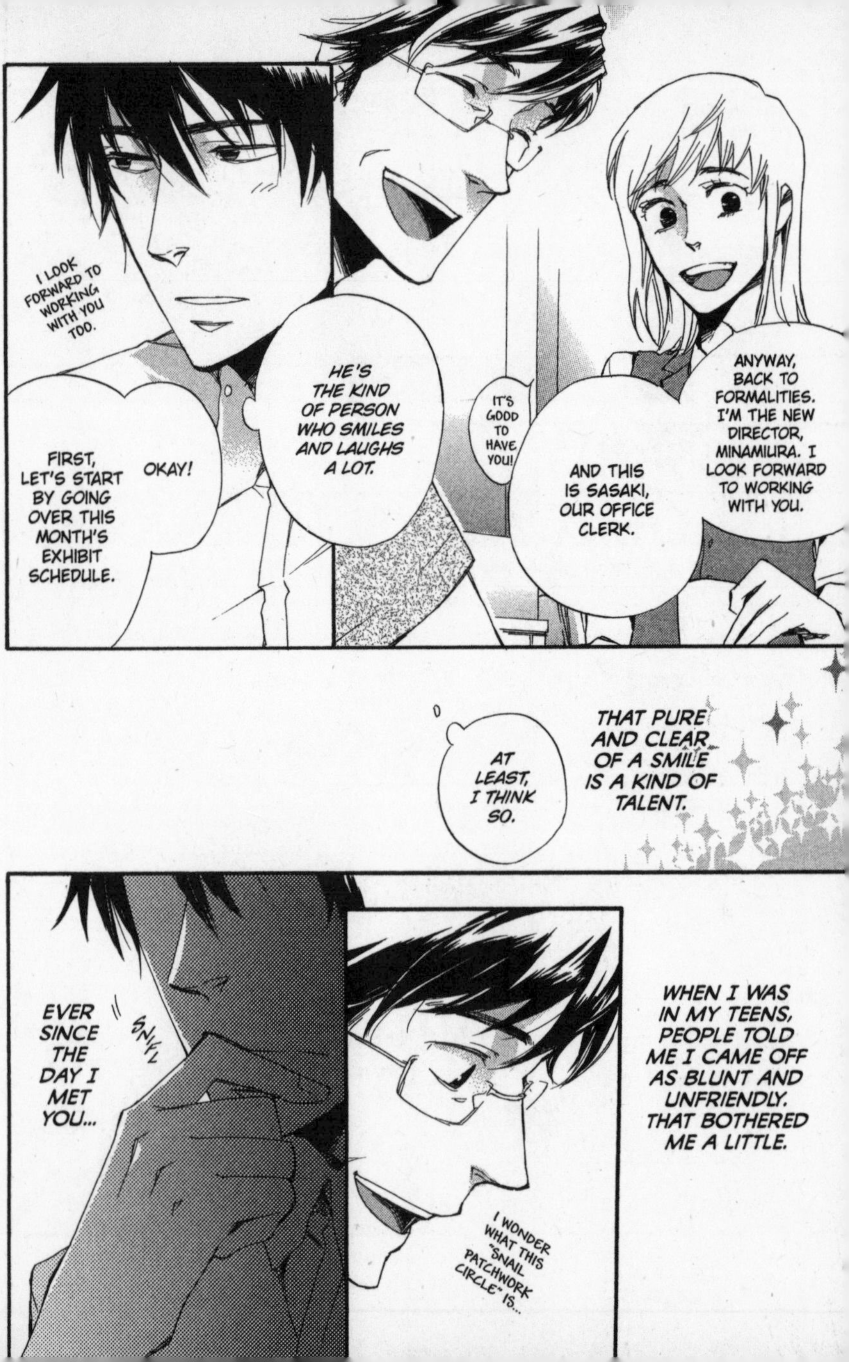
ANYWAY, BACK TO FORMALITIES. I'M THE NEW DIRECTOR, MINAMIURA. I LOOK FORWARD TO WORKING WITH YOU.
AND THIS IS SASAKI, OUR OFFICE CLERK.
IT'S GODD TO HAVE YOU!
HE'S THE KIND OF PERSON WHO SMILES AND LAUGHS A LOT.
OKAY!
FIRST, LET'S START BY GOING OVER THIS MONTH'S EXHIBIT SCHEDULE.
I LOOK FORWARD TO WORKING WITH YOU TOO.
THAT PURE AND CLEAR OF A SMILE IS A KIND OF TALENT.
AT LEAST, I THINK SO.
WHEN I WAS IN MY TEENS, PEOPLE TOLD ME I CAME OFF AS BLUNT AND UNFRIENDLY. THAT BOTHERED ME A LITTLE.
I WONDER WHAT THIS "SNAIL PATCHWORK CIRCLE" IS...
SNIFL
EVER SINCE THE DAY I MET YOU...

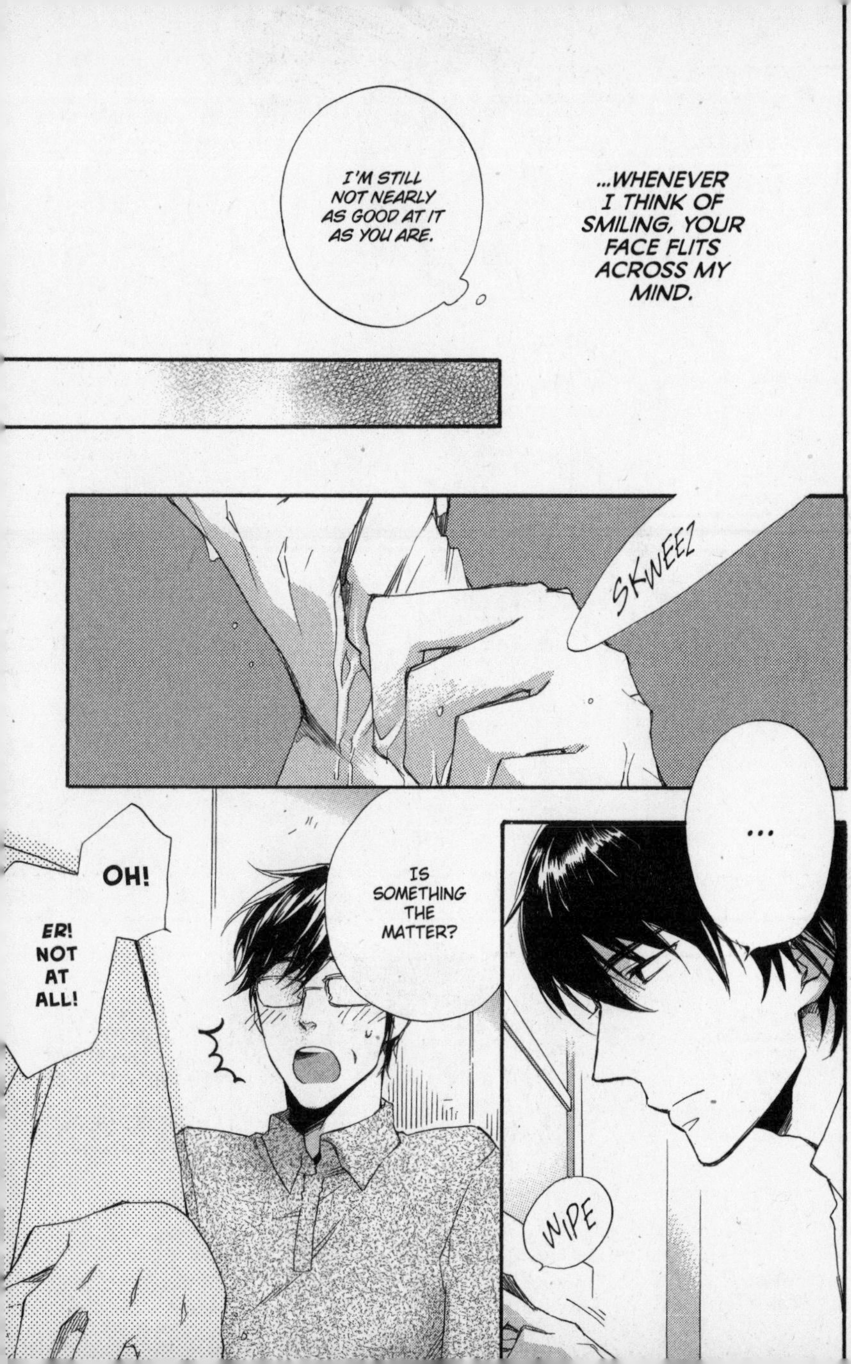
...WHENEVER I THINK OF SMILING, YOUR FACE FLITS ACROSS MY MIND.
I'M STILL NOT NEARLY AS GOOD AT IT AS YOU ARE.
SKWEEZ
...
WIPE
IS SOMETHING THE MATTER?
OH!
ER! NOT AT ALL!

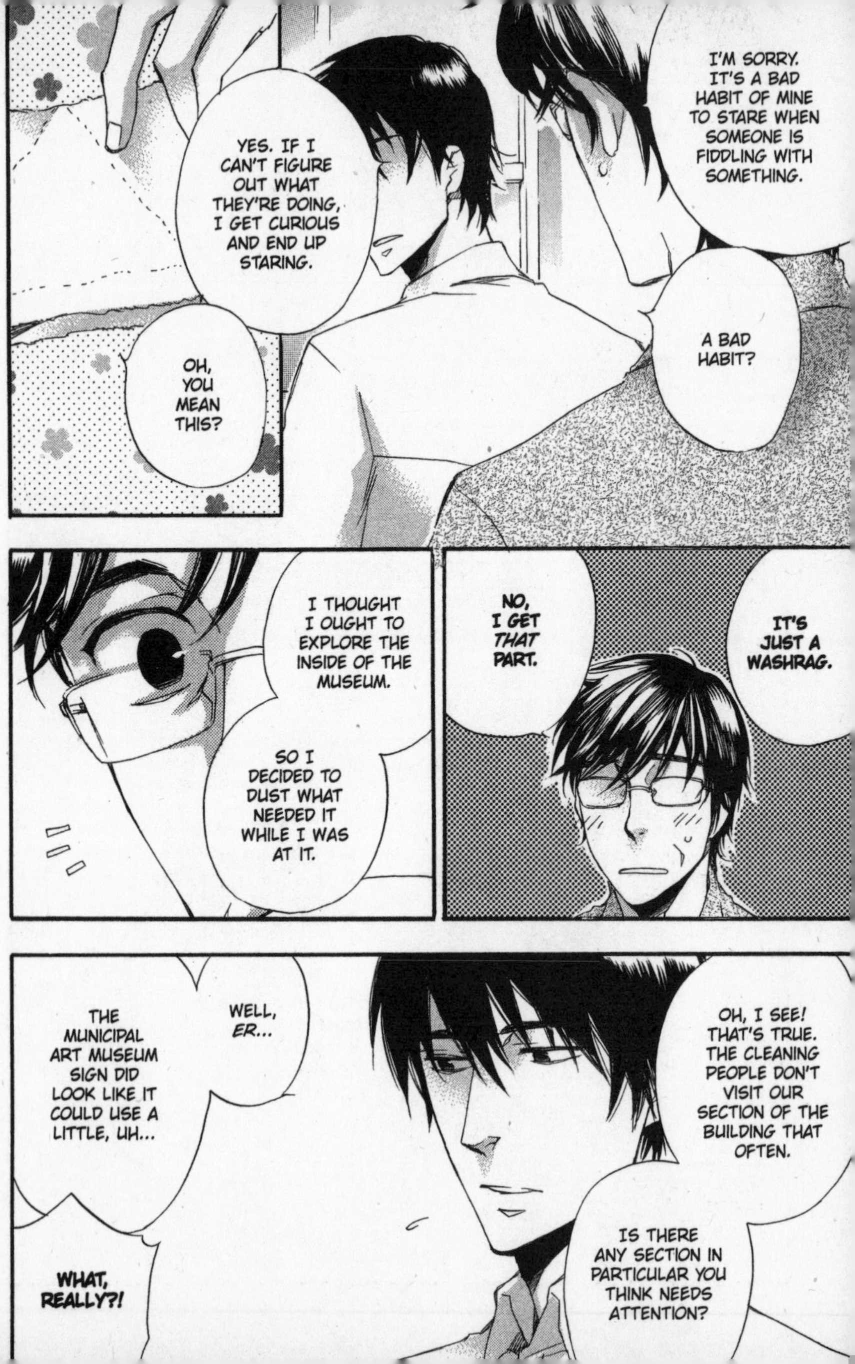
I'M SORRY. IT'S A BAD HABIT OF MINE TO STARE WHEN SOMEONE IS FIDDLING WITH SOMETHING.
A BAD HABIT?
YES. IF I CAN'T FIGURE OUT WHAT THEY'RE DOING, I GET CURIOUS AND END UP STARING.
OH, YOU MEAN THIS?
IT'S JUST A WASHRAG.
NO, I GET *THAT* PART.
I THOUGHT I OUGHT TO EXPLORE THE INSIDE OF THE MUSEUM.
SO I DECIDED TO DUST WHAT NEEDED IT WHILE I WAS AT IT.
OH, I SEE! THAT'S TRUE. THE CLEANING PEOPLE DON'T VISIT OUR SECTION OF THE BUILDING THAT OFTEN.
IS THERE ANY SECTION IN PARTICULAR YOU THINK NEEDS ATTENTION?
WELL, ER...
THE MUNICIPAL ART MUSEUM SIGN DID LOOK LIKE IT COULD USE A LITTLE, UH...
WHAT, REALLY?!

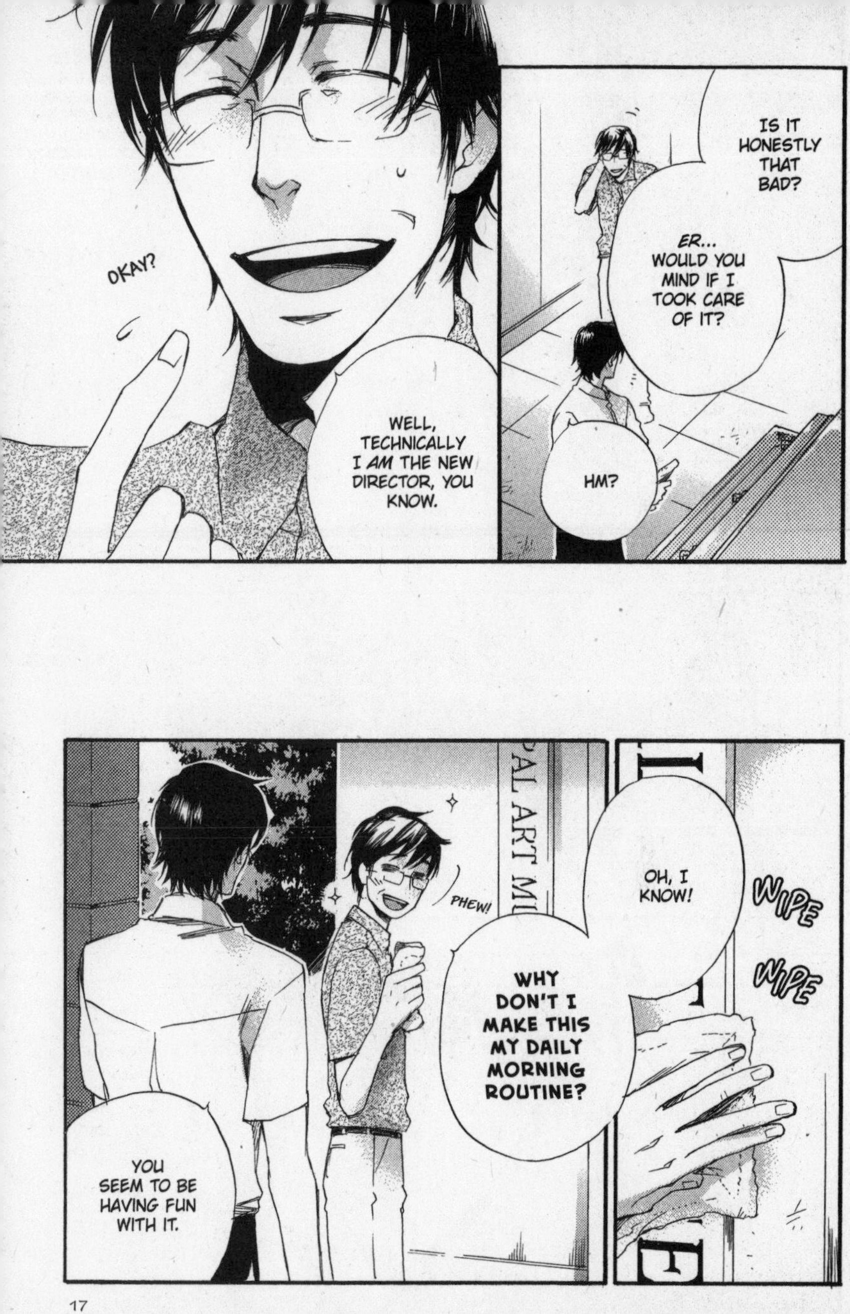
IS IT HONESTLY THAT BAD?
ER... WOULD YOU MIND IF I TOOK CARE OF IT?
HM?
WELL, TECHNICALLY I *AM* THE NEW DIRECTOR, YOU KNOW.
OKAY?
WIPE
WIPE
OH, I KNOW!
WHY DON'T I MAKE THIS MY DAILY MORNING ROUTINE?
PHEW!
YOU SEEM TO BE HAVING FUN WITH IT.

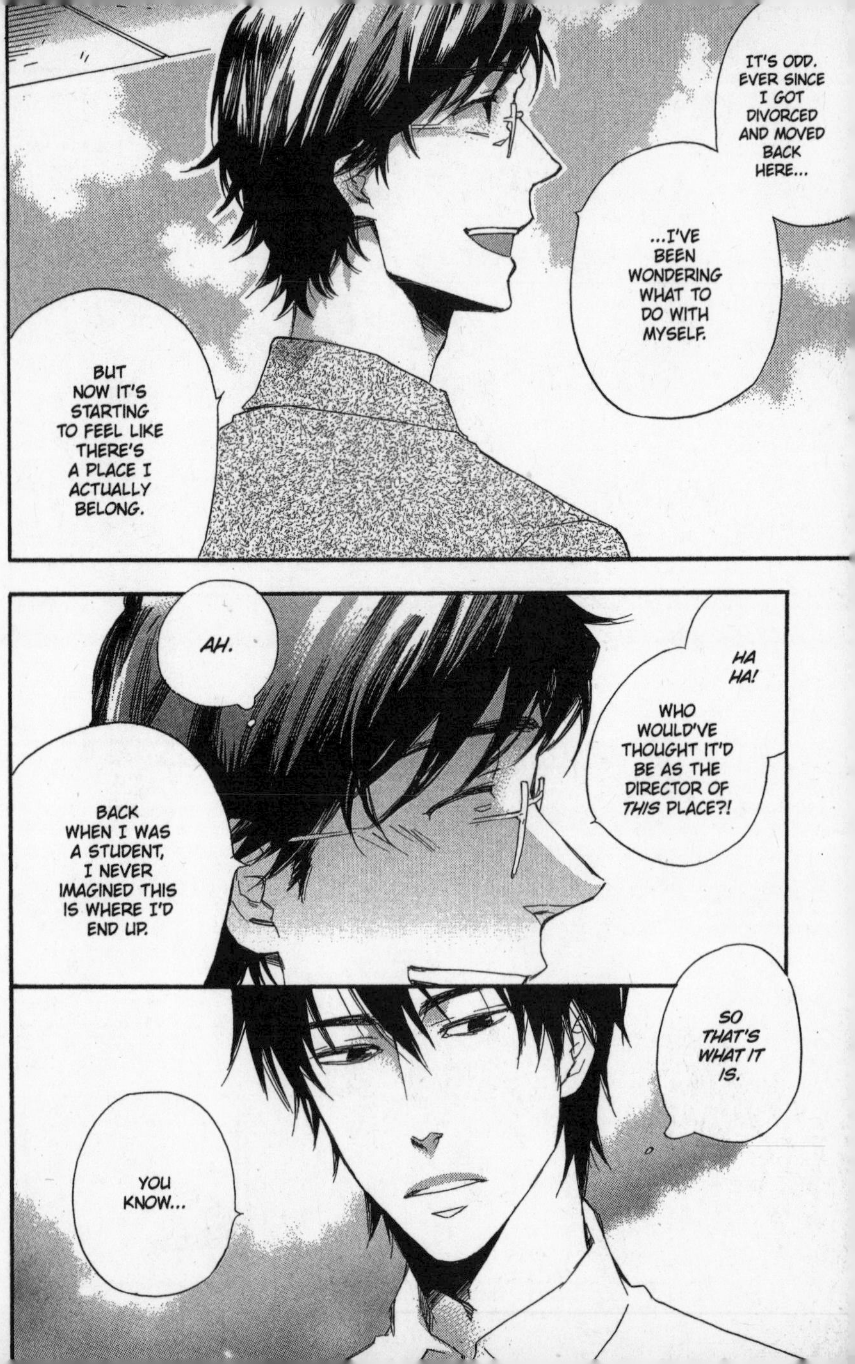
IT'S ODD. EVER SINCE I GOT DIVORCED AND MOVED BACK HERE...
...I'VE BEEN WONDERING WHAT TO DO WITH MYSELF.
BUT NOW IT'S STARTING TO FEEL LIKE THERE'S A PLACE I ACTUALLY BELONG.
HA HA!
WHO WOULD'VE THOUGHT IT'D BE AS THE DIRECTOR OF *THIS* PLACE?!
AH.
BACK WHEN I WAS A STUDENT, I NEVER IMAGINED THIS IS WHERE I'D END UP.
SO THAT'S WHAT IT IS.
YOU KNOW...

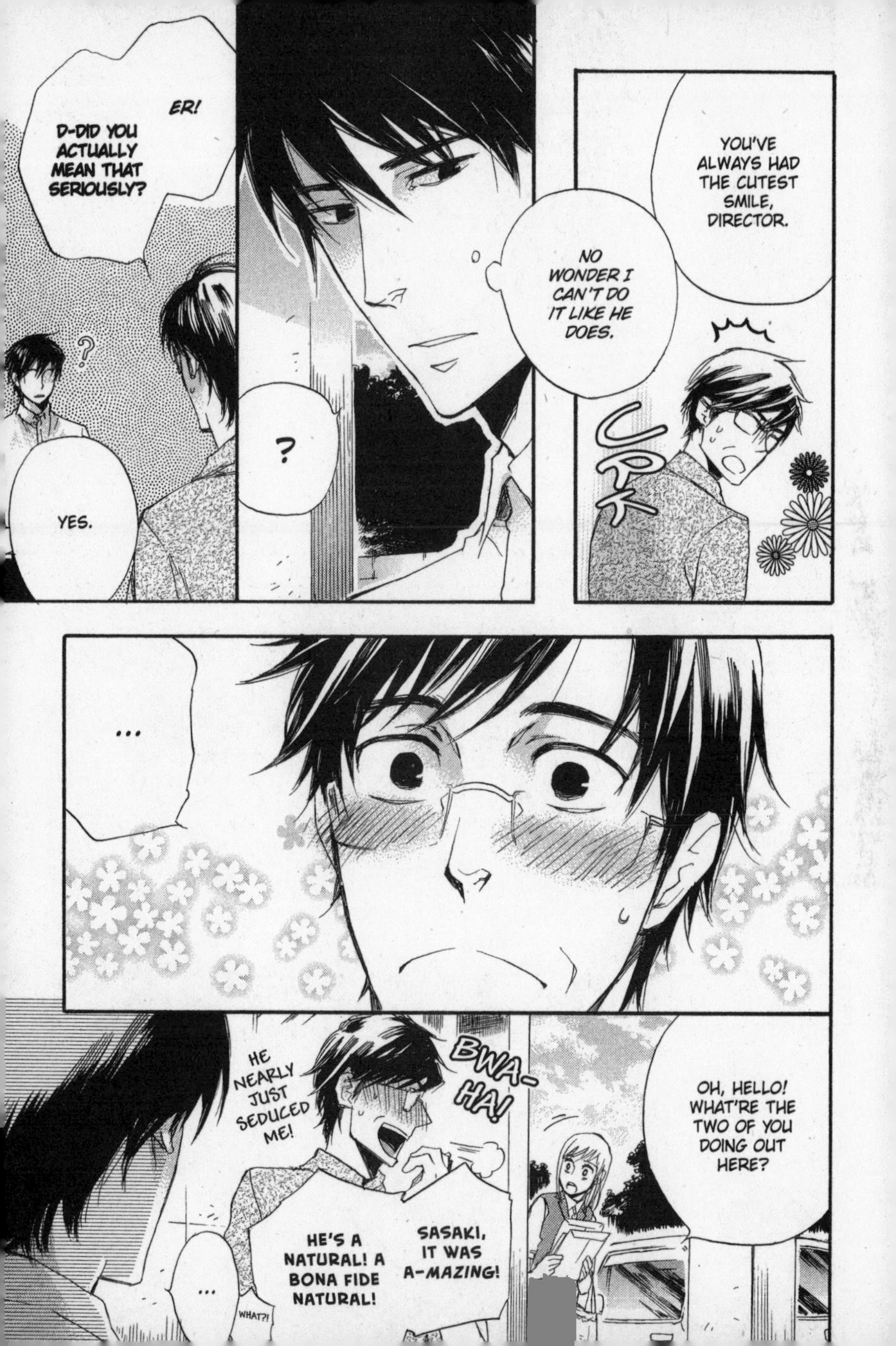
YOU'VE ALWAYS HAD THE CUTEST SMILE, DIRECTOR.
URK
NO WONDER I CAN'T DO IT LIKE HE DOES.
?
ER!
D-DID YOU ACTUALLY MEAN THAT SERIOUSLY?
YES.
...
OH, HELLO! WHAT'RE THE TWO OF YOU DOING OUT HERE?
BWA-HA!
HE NEARLY JUST SEDUCED ME!
SASAKI, IT WAS A-MAZING!
HE'S A NATURAL! A BONA FIDE NATURAL!
WHAT?!
...

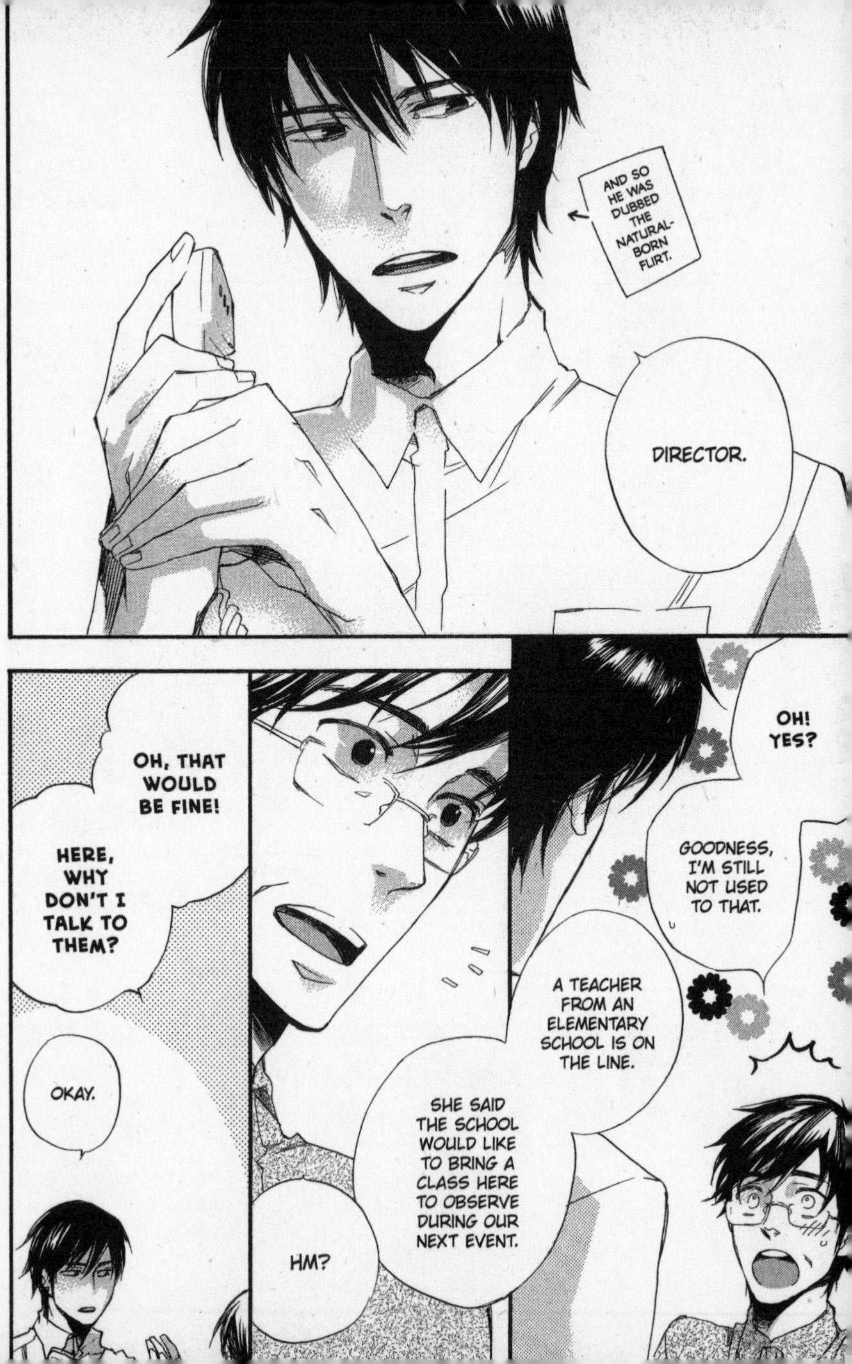
AND SO HE WAS DUBBED THE NATURAL-BORN FLIRT.
DIRECTOR.
OH! YES?
GOODNESS, I'M STILL NOT USED TO THAT.
A TEACHER FROM AN ELEMENTARY SCHOOL IS ON THE LINE.
SHE SAID THE SCHOOL WOULD LIKE TO BRING A CLASS HERE TO OBSERVE DURING OUR NEXT EVENT.
HM?
OH, THAT WOULD BE FINE!
HERE, WHY DON'T I TALK TO THEM?
OKAY.

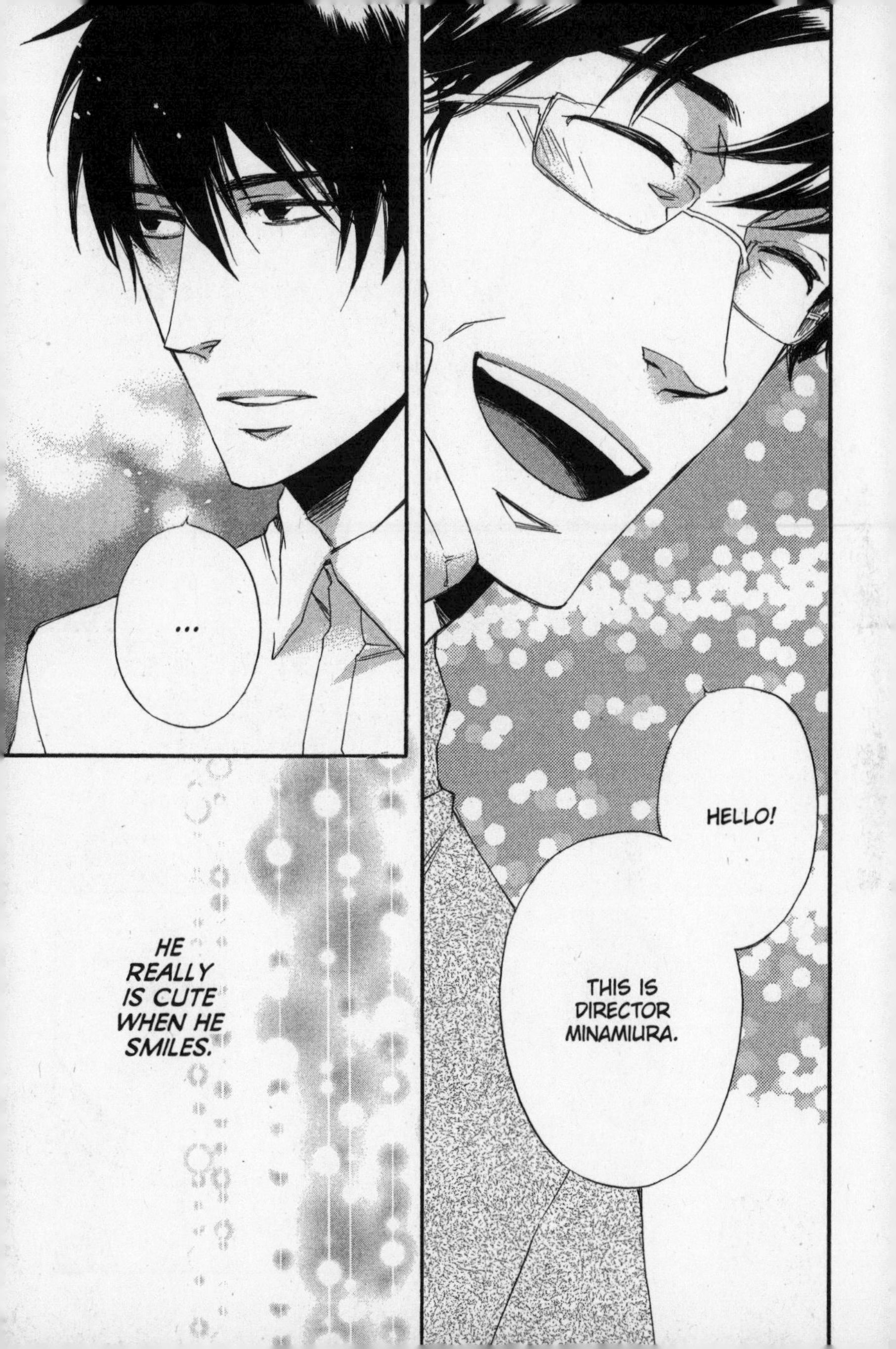
HELLO!
THIS IS DIRECTOR MINAMIURA.
...
HE REALLY IS CUTE WHEN HE SMILES.

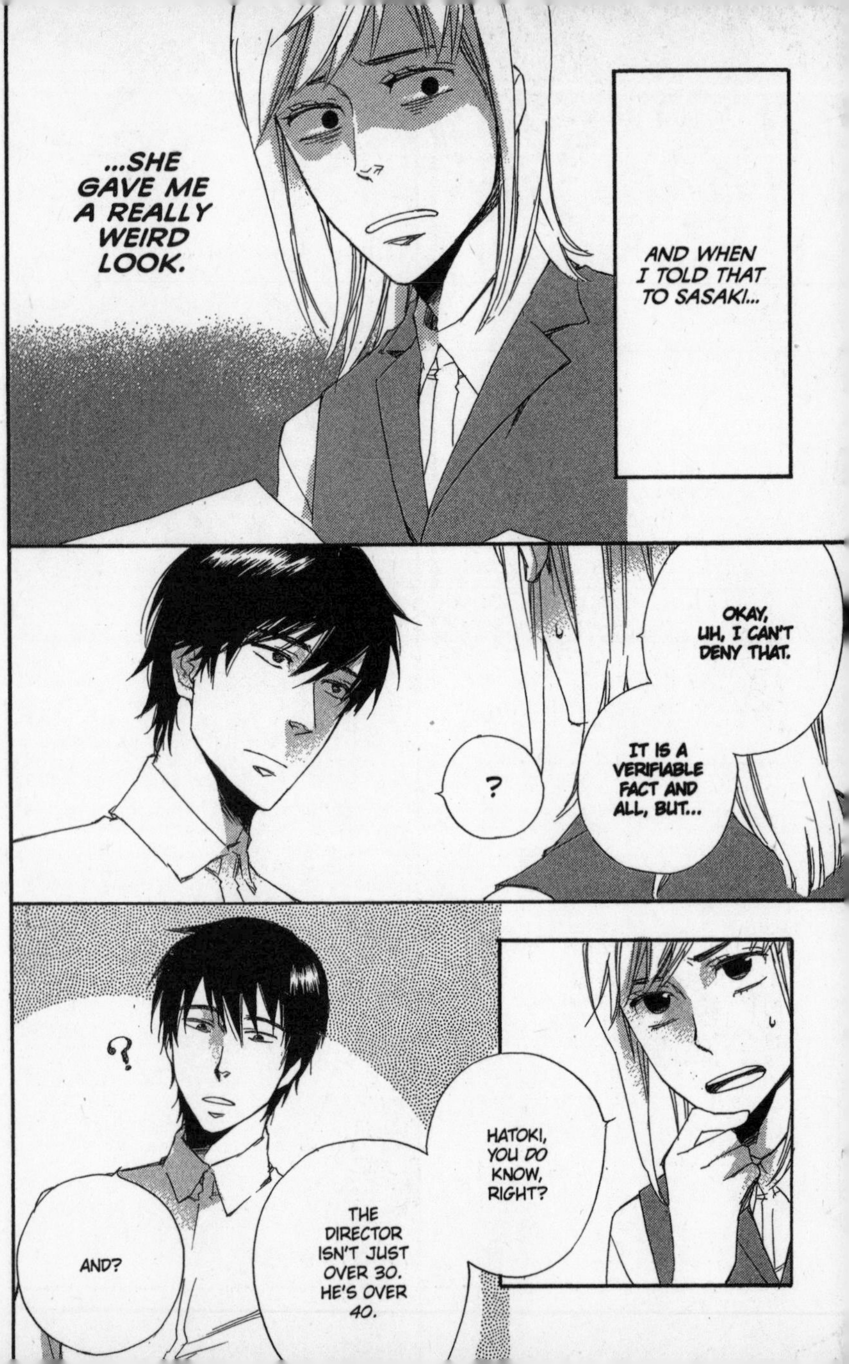
AND WHEN I TOLD THAT TO SASAKI...
...SHE GAVE ME A REALLY WEIRD LOOK.
OKAY, UH, I CAN'T DENY THAT.
IT IS A VERIFIABLE FACT AND ALL, BUT...
?
HATOKI, YOU DO KNOW, RIGHT?
THE DIRECTOR ISN'T JUST OVER 30. HE'S OVER 40.
?
AND?

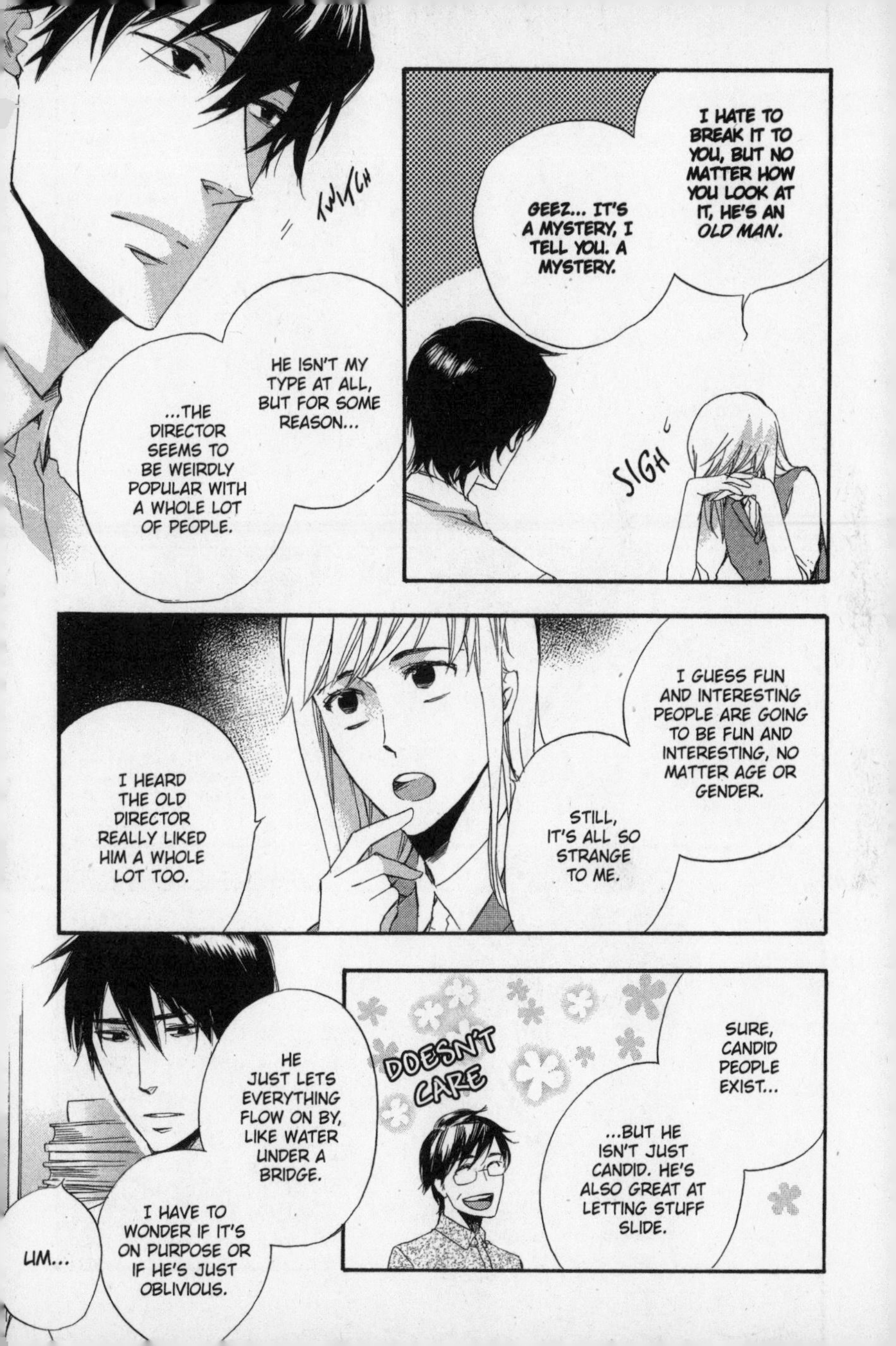
I HATE TO BREAK IT TO YOU, BUT NO MATTER HOW YOU LOOK AT IT, HE'S AN *OLD MAN*.
GEEZ... IT'S A MYSTERY, I TELL YOU. A MYSTERY.
SIGH
TWITCH
HE ISN'T MY TYPE AT ALL, BUT FOR SOME REASON...
...THE DIRECTOR SEEMS TO BE WEIRDLY POPULAR WITH A WHOLE LOT OF PEOPLE.
I GUESS FUN AND INTERESTING PEOPLE ARE GOING TO BE FUN AND INTERESTING, NO MATTER AGE OR GENDER.
STILL, IT'S ALL SO STRANGE TO ME.
I HEARD THE OLD DIRECTOR REALLY LIKED HIM A WHOLE LOT TOO.
SURE, CANDID PEOPLE EXIST...
...BUT HE ISN'T JUST CANDID. HE'S ALSO GREAT AT LETTING STUFF SLIDE.
DOESN'T CARE
HE JUST LETS EVERYTHING FLOW ON BY, LIKE WATER UNDER A BRIDGE.
I HAVE TO WONDER IF IT'S ON PURPOSE OR IF HE'S JUST OBLIVIOUS.
UM...

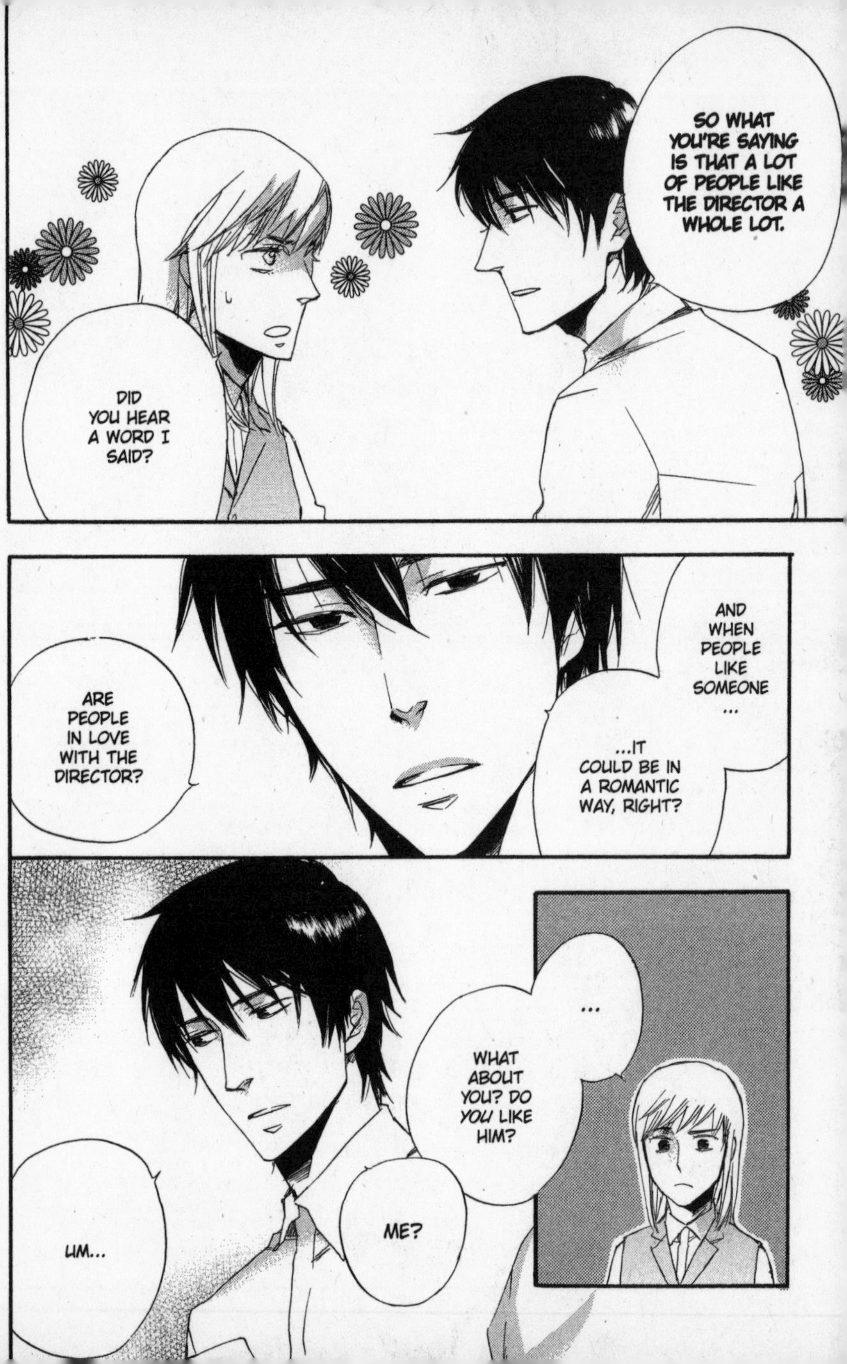
SO WHAT YOU'RE SAYING IS THAT A LOT OF PEOPLE LIKE THE DIRECTOR A WHOLE LOT.
DID YOU HEAR A WORD I SAID?
AND WHEN PEOPLE LIKE SOMEONE ...
...IT COULD BE IN A ROMANTIC WAY, RIGHT?
ARE PEOPLE IN LOVE WITH THE DIRECTOR?
...
WHAT ABOUT YOU? DO *YOU* LIKE HIM?
ME?
UM...

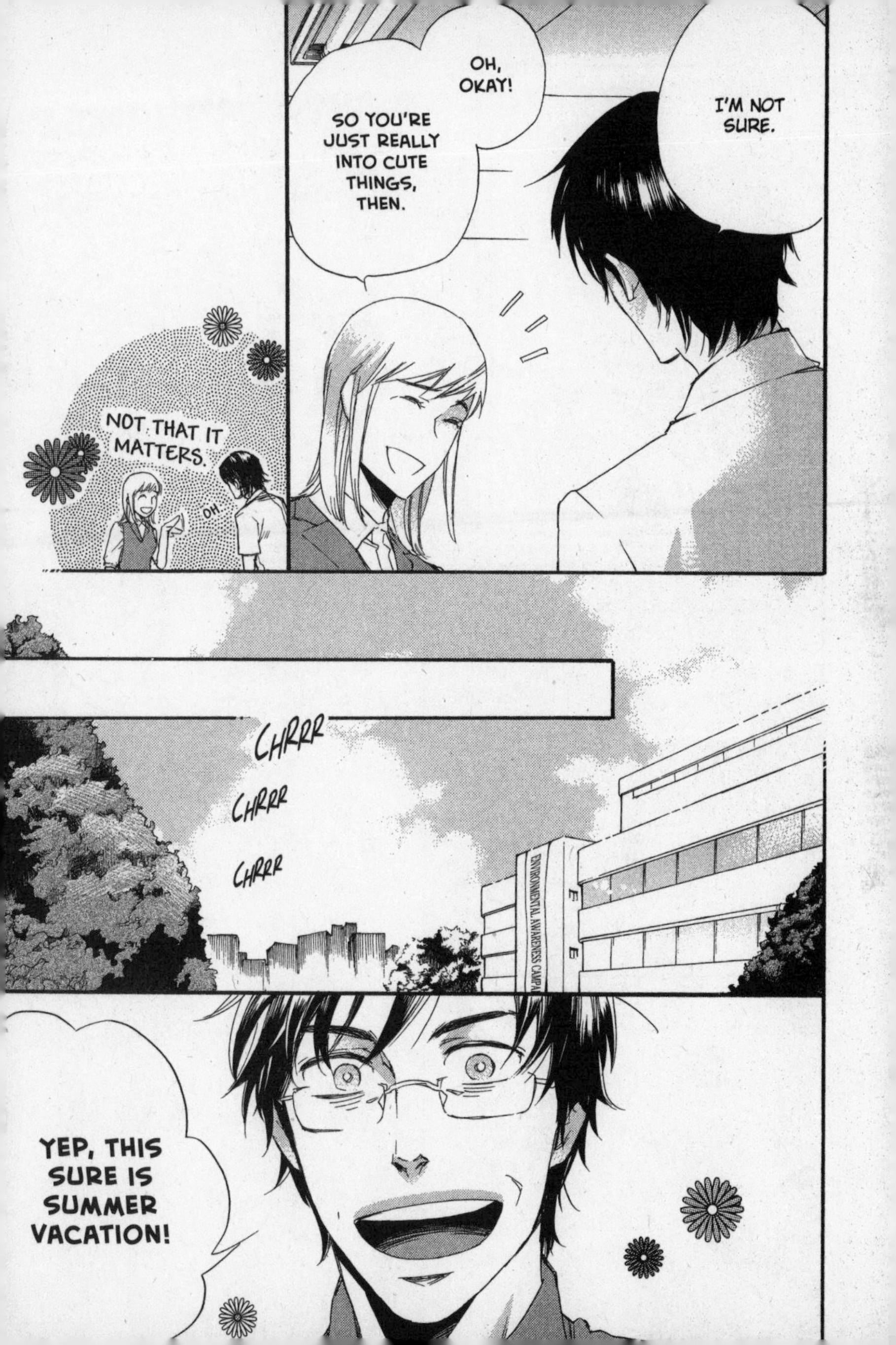
I'M NOT SURE.
OH, OKAY! SO YOU'RE JUST REALLY INTO CUTE THINGS, THEN.
NOT THAT IT MATTERS.
OH.
CHRRR
CHRRR
CHRRR
YEP, THIS SURE IS SUMMER VACATION!

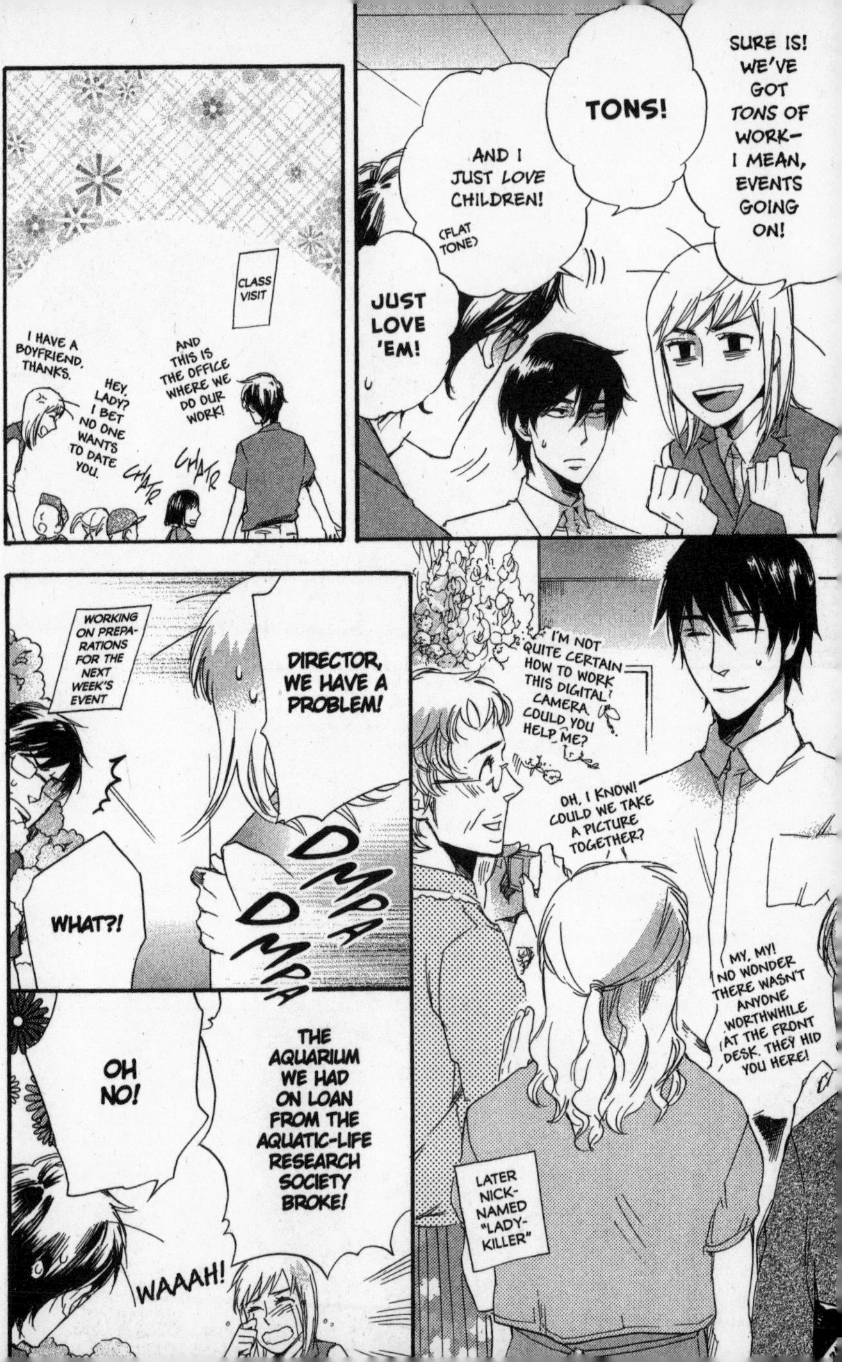
SURE IS! WE'VE GOT TONS OF WORK— I MEAN, EVENTS GOING ON!
TONS!
AND I JUST LOVE CHILDREN!
(FLAT TONE)
JUST LOVE 'EM!
CLASS VISIT
AND THIS IS THE OFFICE WHERE WE DO OUR WORK!
HEY, LADY? I BET NO ONE WANTS TO DATE YOU.
I HAVE A BOYFRIEND, THANKS.
CHATTER
CHATTER
I'M NOT QUITE CERTAIN HOW TO WORK THIS DIGITAL CAMERA. COULD YOU HELP ME?
OH, I KNOW! COULD WE TAKE A PICTURE TOGETHER?
MY, MY! NO WONDER THERE WASN'T ANYONE WORTHWHILE AT THE FRONT DESK. THEY HID YOU HERE!
LATER NICK-NAMED "LADY-KILLER"
WORKING ON PREPA-RATIONS FOR THE NEXT WEEK'S EVENT
DIRECTOR, WE HAVE A PROBLEM!
WHAT?!
DMPA DMPA DMPA
THE AQUARIUM WE HAD ON LOAN FROM THE AQUATIC-LIFE RESEARCH SOCIETY BROKE!
OH NO!
WAAAH!

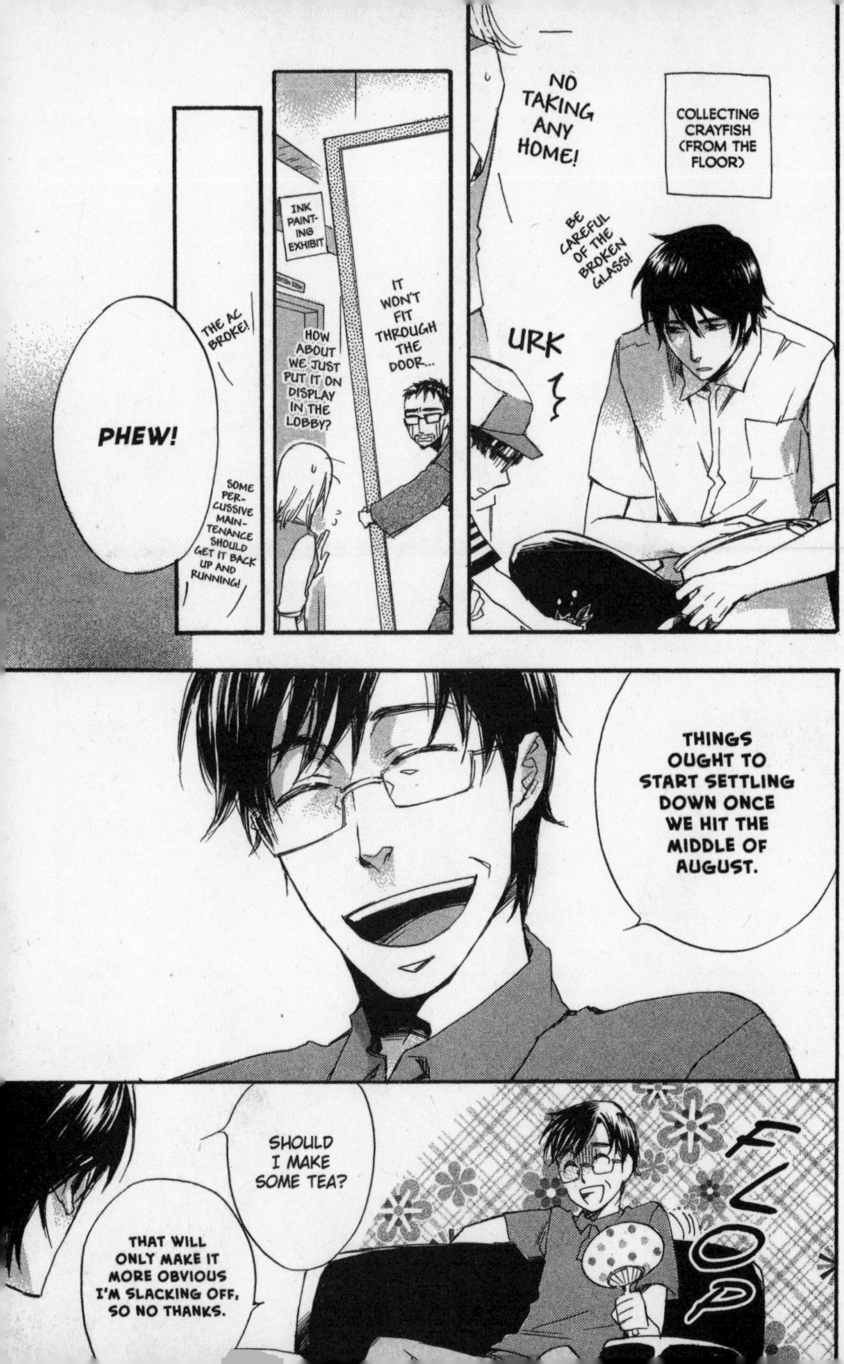
COLLECTING CRAYFISH (FROM THE FLOOR)
NO TAKING ANY HOME!
BE CAREFUL OF THE BROKEN GLASS!
URK
IT WON'T FIT THROUGH THE DOOR...
HOW ABOUT WE JUST PUT IT ON DISPLAY IN THE LOBBY?
INK PAINTING EXHIBIT
THE AC BROKE!
SOME PERCUSSIVE MAINTENANCE SHOULD GET IT BACK UP AND RUNNING!
PHEW!
THINGS OUGHT TO START SETTLING DOWN ONCE WE HIT THE MIDDLE OF AUGUST.
FLOP
SHOULD I MAKE SOME TEA?
THAT WILL ONLY MAKE IT MORE OBVIOUS I'M SLACKING OFF, SO NO THANKS.

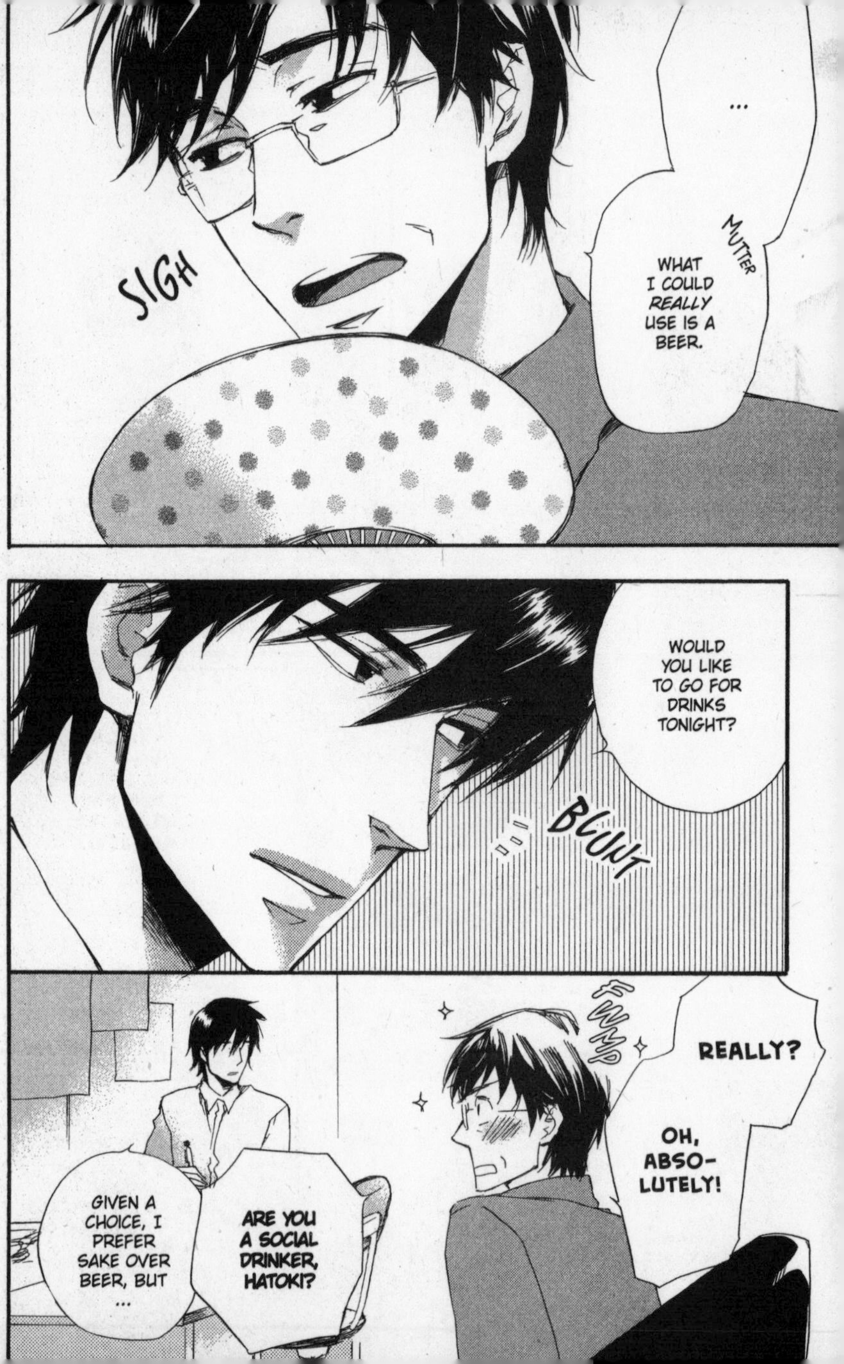
...
MUTTER
WHAT I COULD REALLY USE IS A BEER.
SIGH
WOULD YOU LIKE TO GO FOR DRINKS TONIGHT?
BLUNT
REALLY?
OH, ABSO-LUTELY!
FWMP
ARE YOU A SOCIAL DRINKER, HATOKI?
GIVEN A CHOICE, I PREFER SAKE OVER BEER, BUT ...

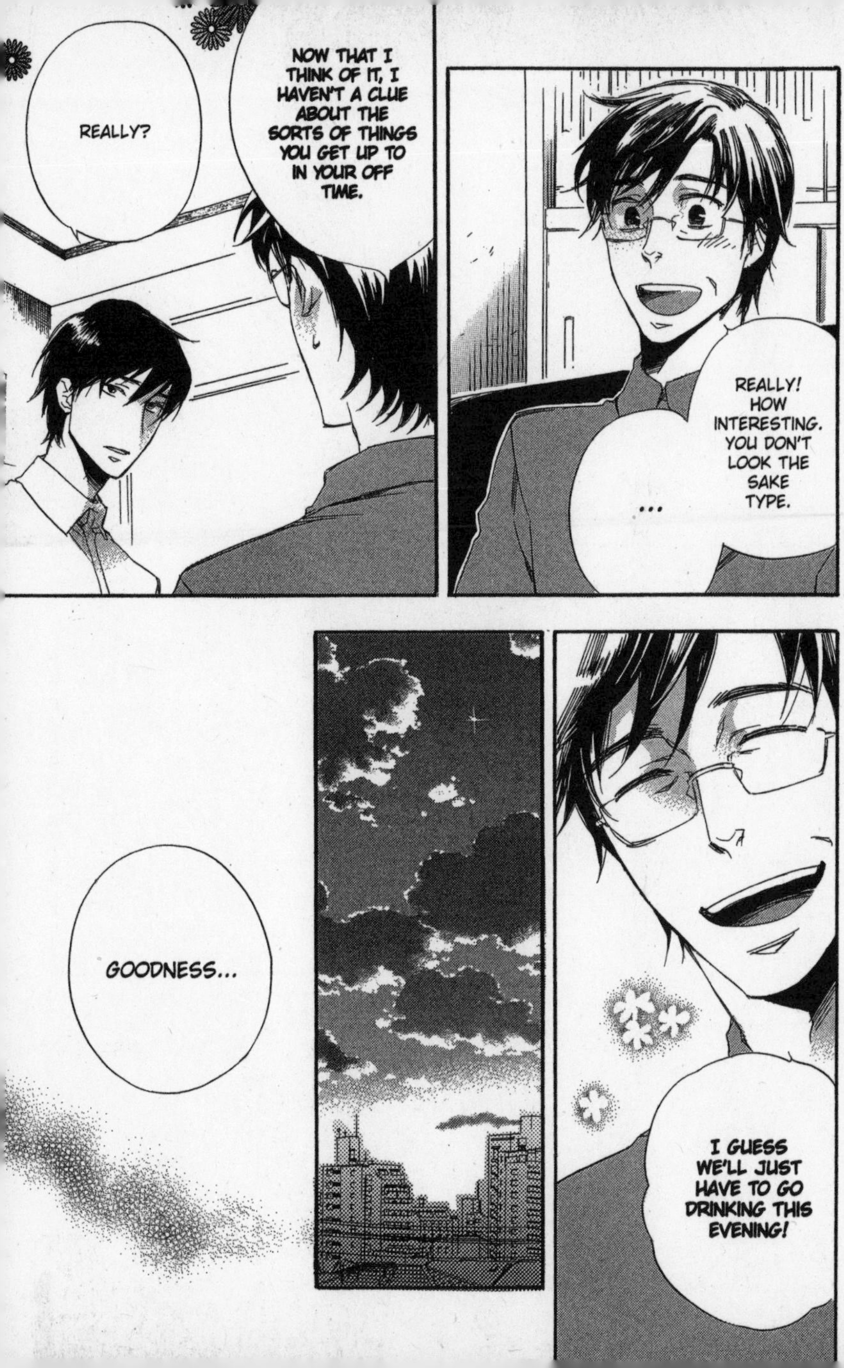
REALLY! HOW INTERESTING. YOU DON'T LOOK THE SAKE TYPE.
...
NOW THAT I THINK OF IT, I HAVEN'T A CLUE ABOUT THE SORTS OF THINGS YOU GET UP TO IN YOUR OFF TIME.
REALLY?
I GUESS WE'LL JUST HAVE TO GO DRINKING THIS EVENING!
GOODNESS...

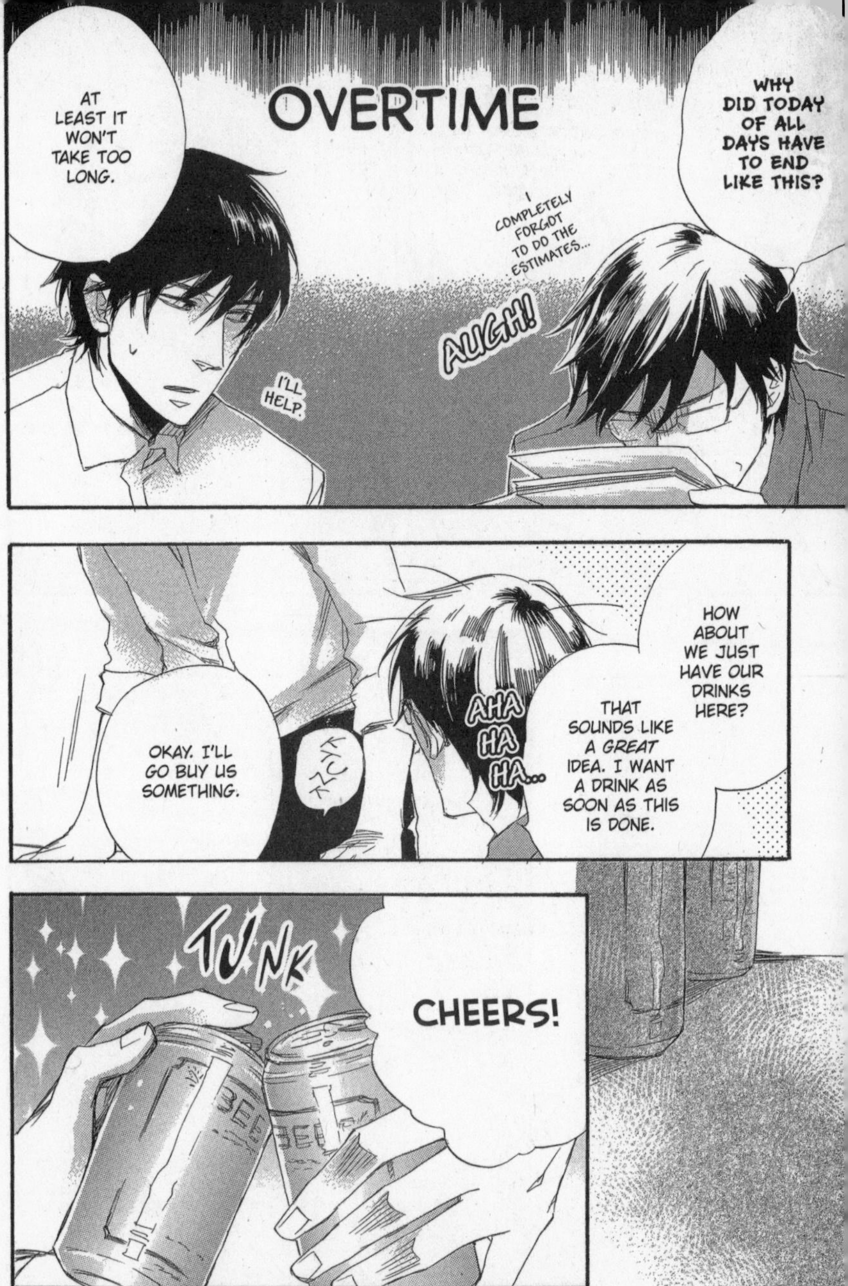
OVERTIME
WHY DID TODAY OF ALL DAYS HAVE TO END LIKE THIS?
I COMPLETELY FORGOT TO DO THE ESTIMATES...
AUGH!
I'LL HELP.
AT LEAST IT WON'T TAKE TOO LONG.
HOW ABOUT WE JUST HAVE OUR DRINKS HERE?
THAT SOUNDS LIKE A *GREAT* IDEA. I WANT A DRINK AS SOON AS THIS IS DONE.
AHA HA HA...
OKAY. I'LL GO BUY US SOMETHING.
CHEERS!
TINK

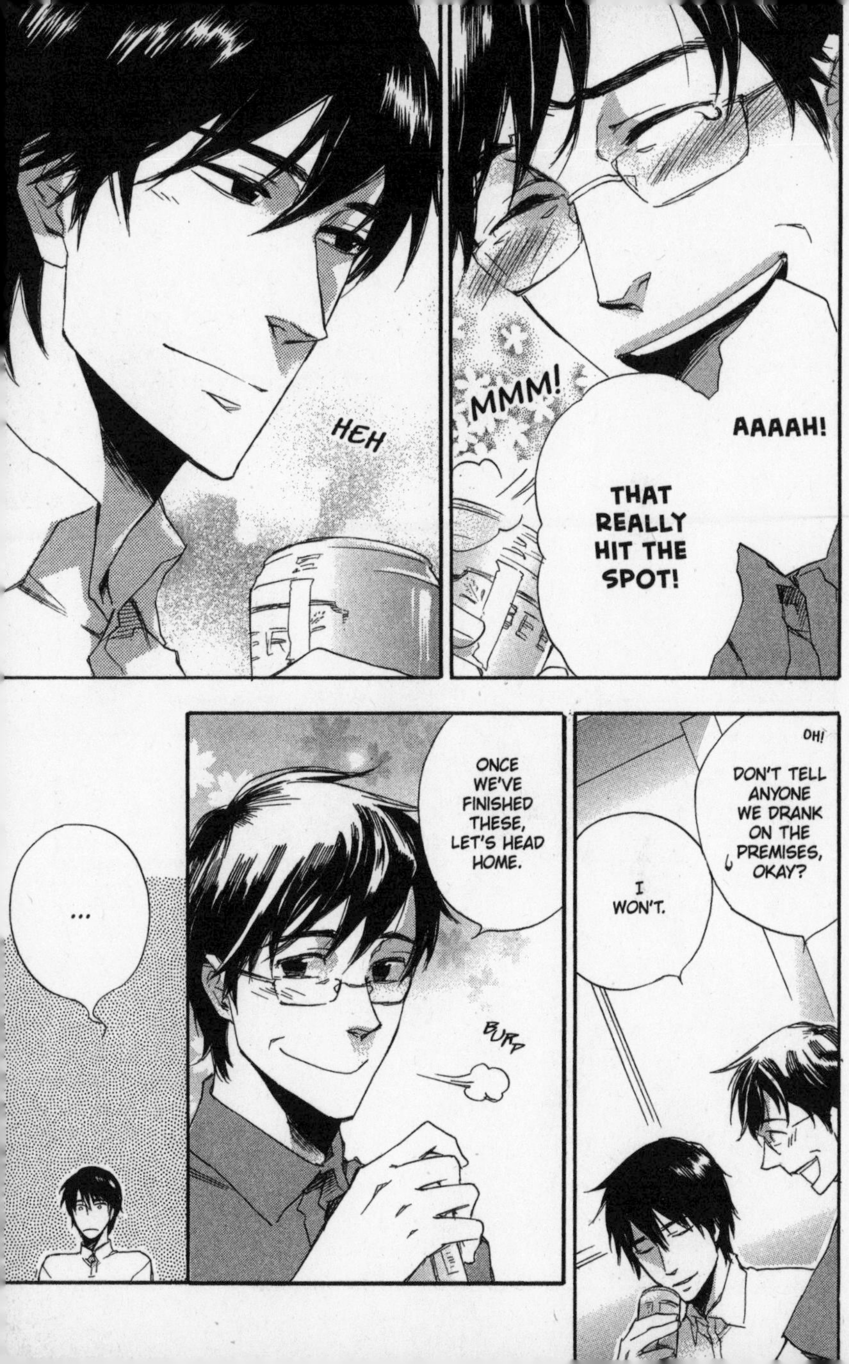
MMM!
AAAAH!
THAT REALLY HIT THE SPOT!
HEH
OH!
DON'T TELL ANYONE WE DRANK ON THE PREMISES, OKAY?
I WON'T.
ONCE WE'VE FINISHED THESE, LET'S HEAD HOME.
BURP
...

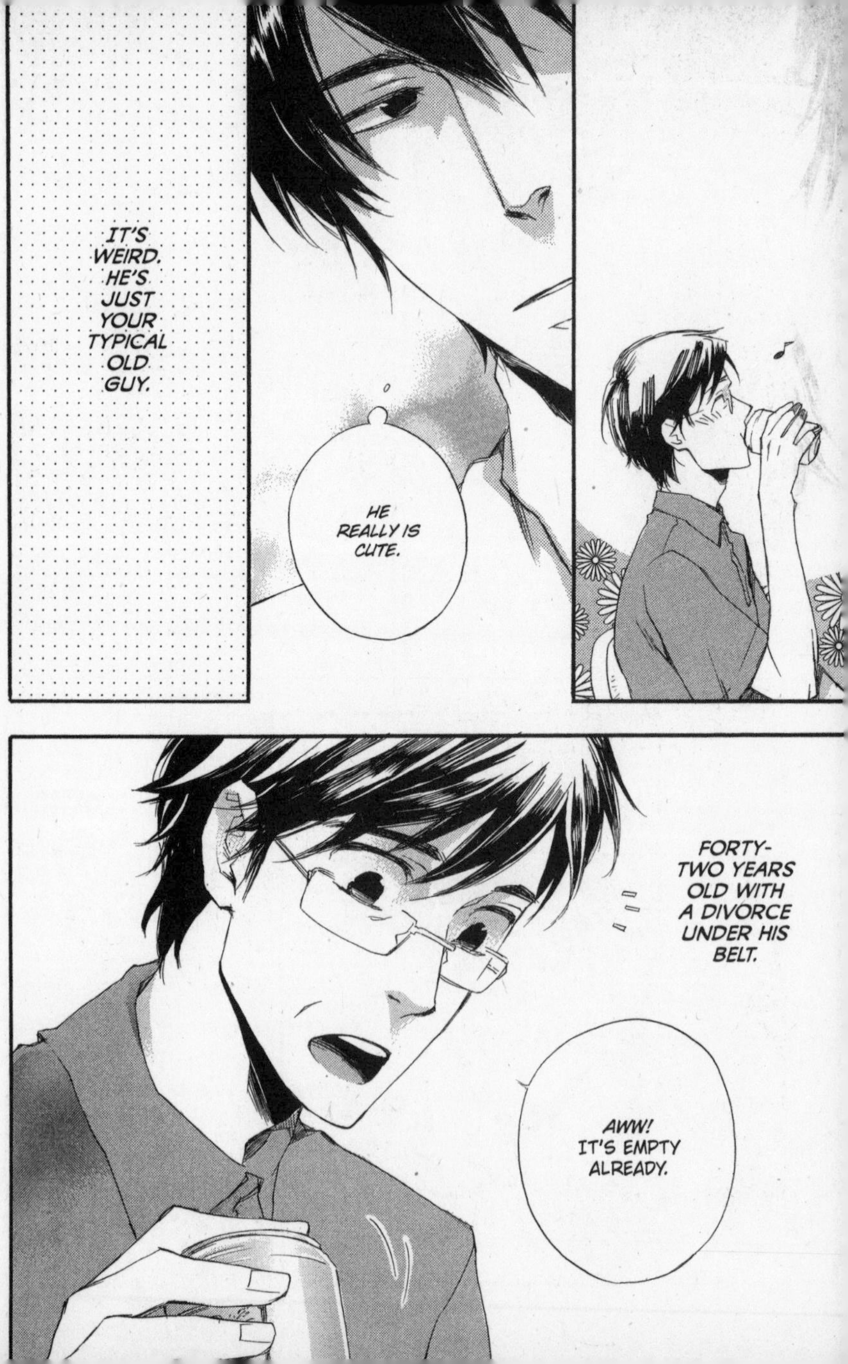
HE REALLY IS CUTE.
IT'S WEIRD. HE'S JUST YOUR TYPICAL OLD GUY.
FORTY-TWO YEARS OLD WITH A DIVORCE UNDER HIS BELT.
AWW! IT'S EMPTY ALREADY.

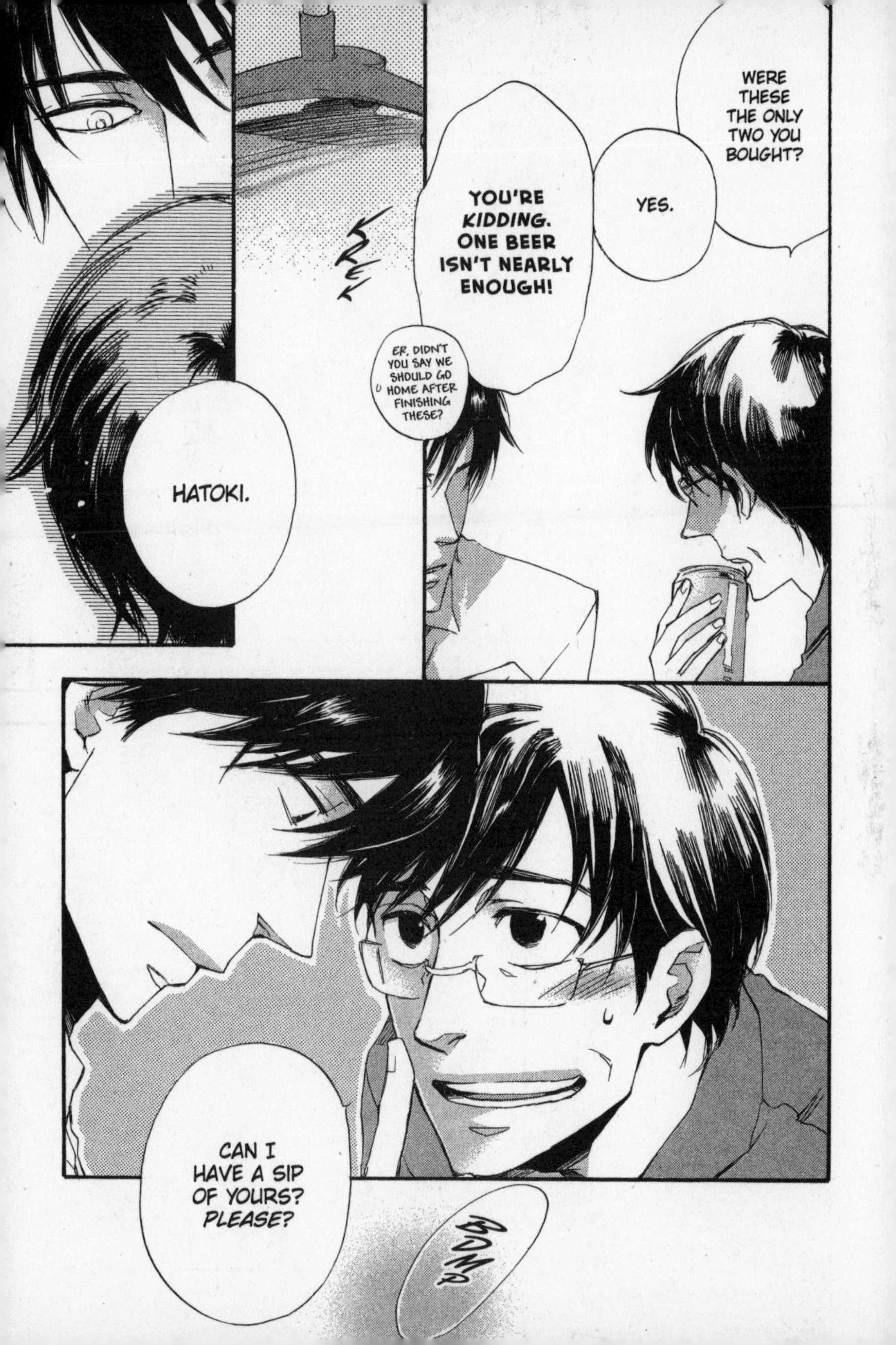
WERE THESE THE ONLY TWO YOU BOUGHT?
YES.
YOU'RE *KIDDING.* ONE BEER ISN'T NEARLY ENOUGH!
ER, DIDN'T YOU SAY WE SHOULD GO HOME AFTER FINISHING THESE?
KREK
HATOKI.
CAN I HAVE A SIP OF YOURS? *PLEASE?*
BOMP

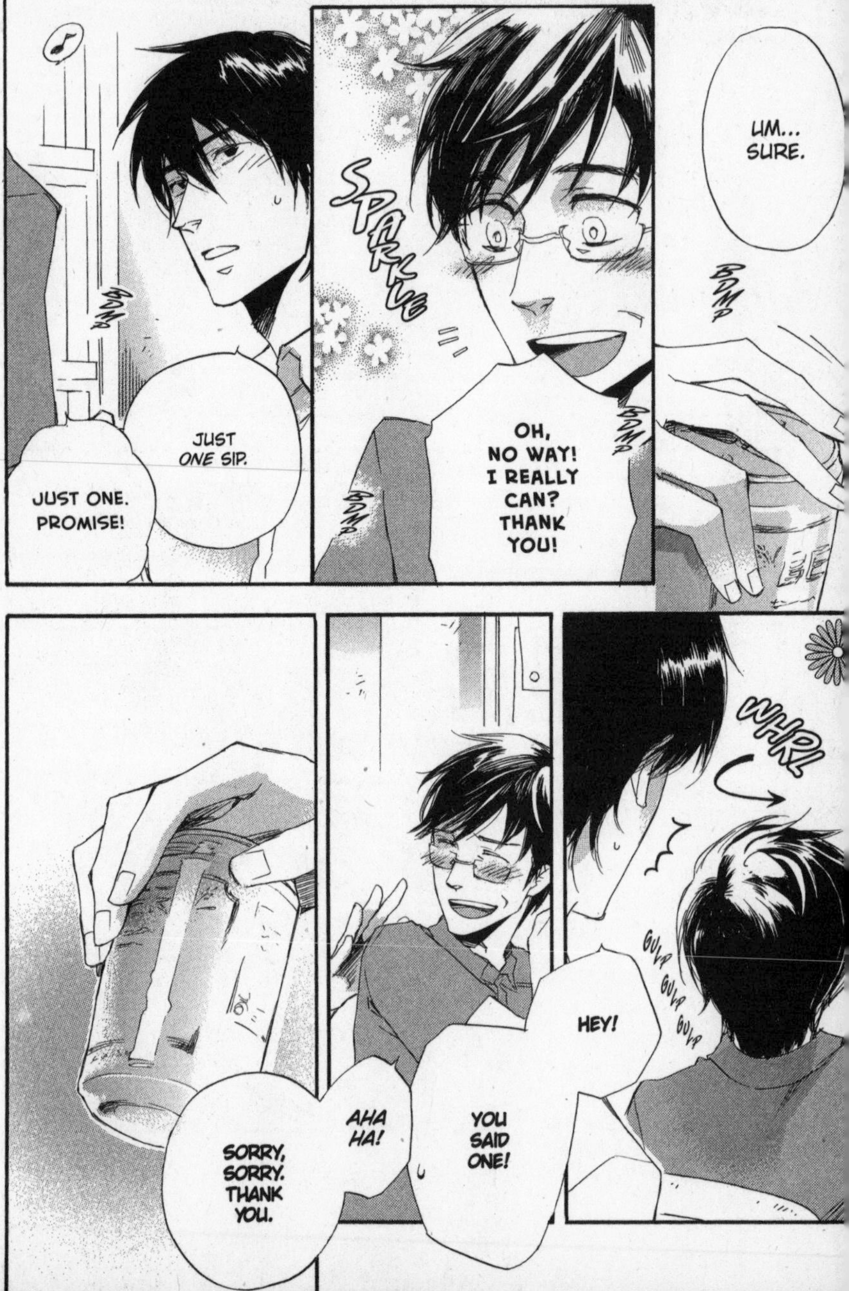
UM... SURE.
BDMP
SPARKLE
OH, NO WAY! I REALLY CAN? THANK YOU!
BDMP
BDMP
JUST ONE SIP.
JUST ONE. PROMISE!
BDMP
WHRL
HEY!
GULP GULP GULP
YOU SAID ONE!
AHA HA!
SORRY, SORRY. THANK YOU.

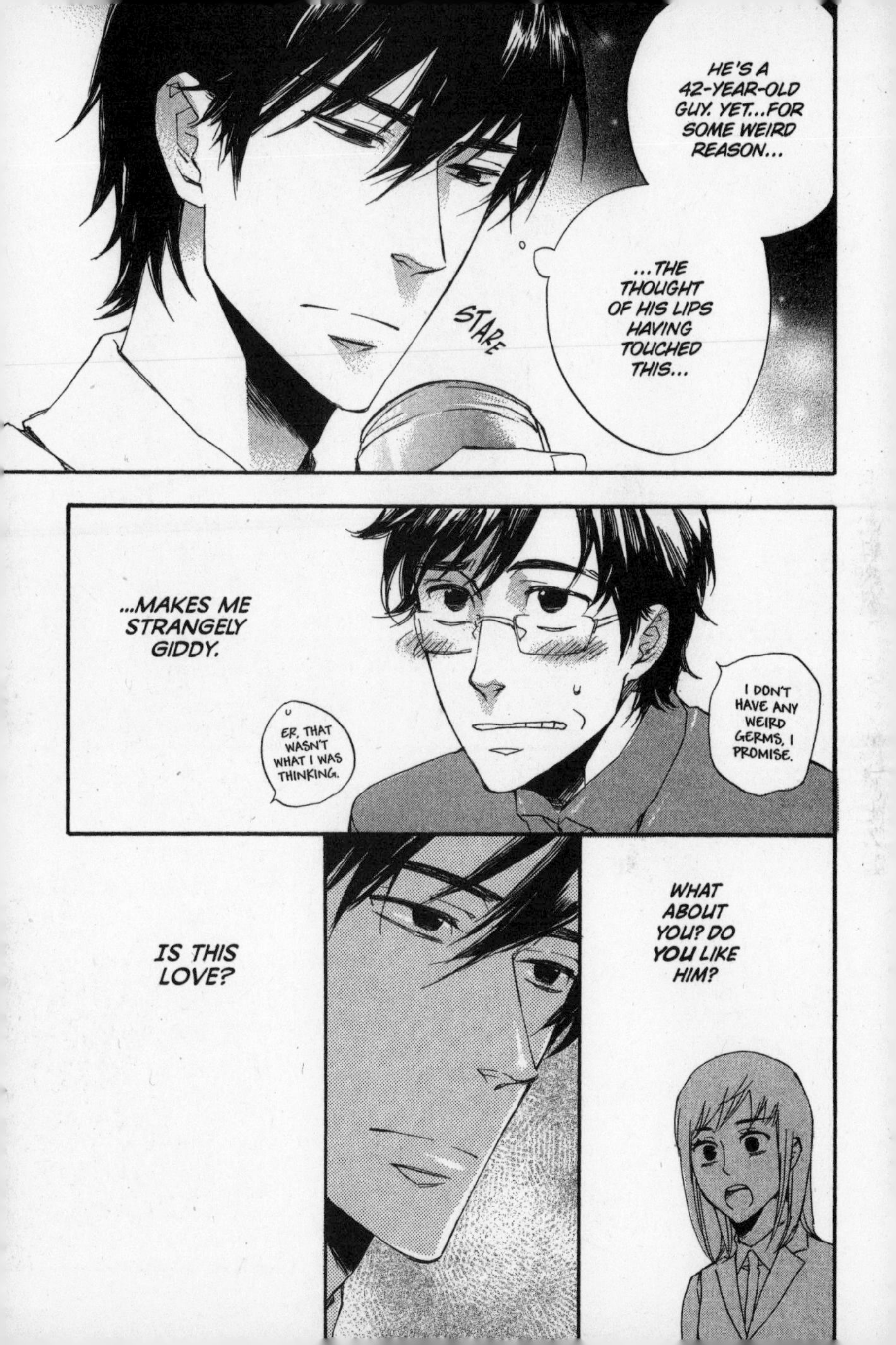
HE'S A 42-YEAR-OLD GUY. YET...FOR SOME WEIRD REASON...
...THE THOUGHT OF HIS LIPS HAVING TOUCHED THIS...
STARE
...MAKES ME STRANGELY GIDDY.
I DON'T HAVE ANY WEIRD GERMS, I PROMISE.
ER, THAT WASN'T WHAT I WAS THINKING.
WHAT ABOUT YOU? DO YOU LIKE HIM?
IS THIS LOVE?

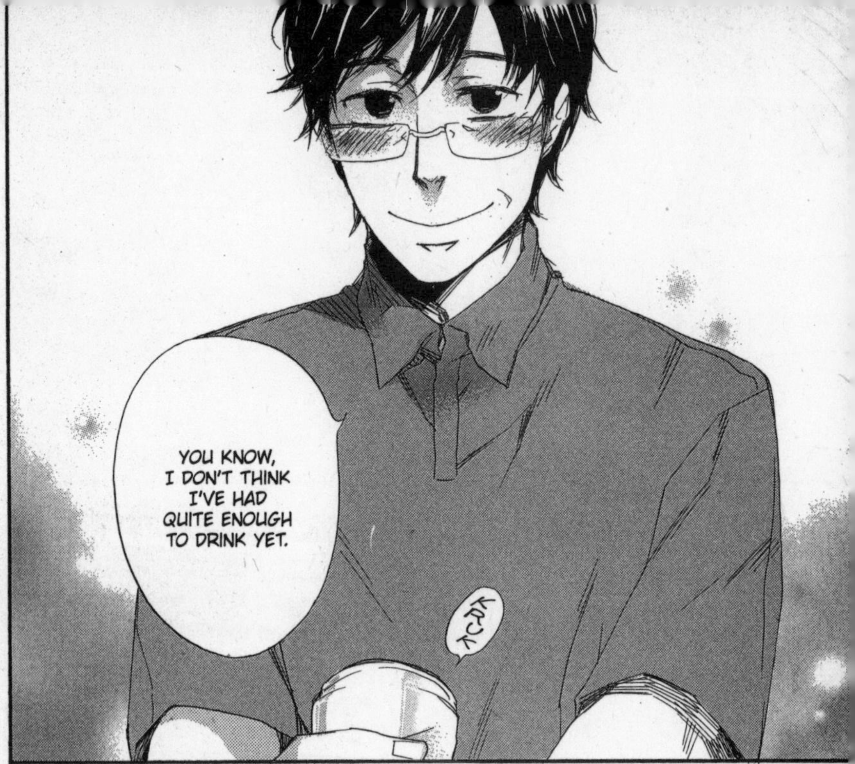
YOU KNOW, I DON'T THINK I'VE HAD QUITE ENOUGH TO DRINK YET.
KRJK

LOVE, EH?

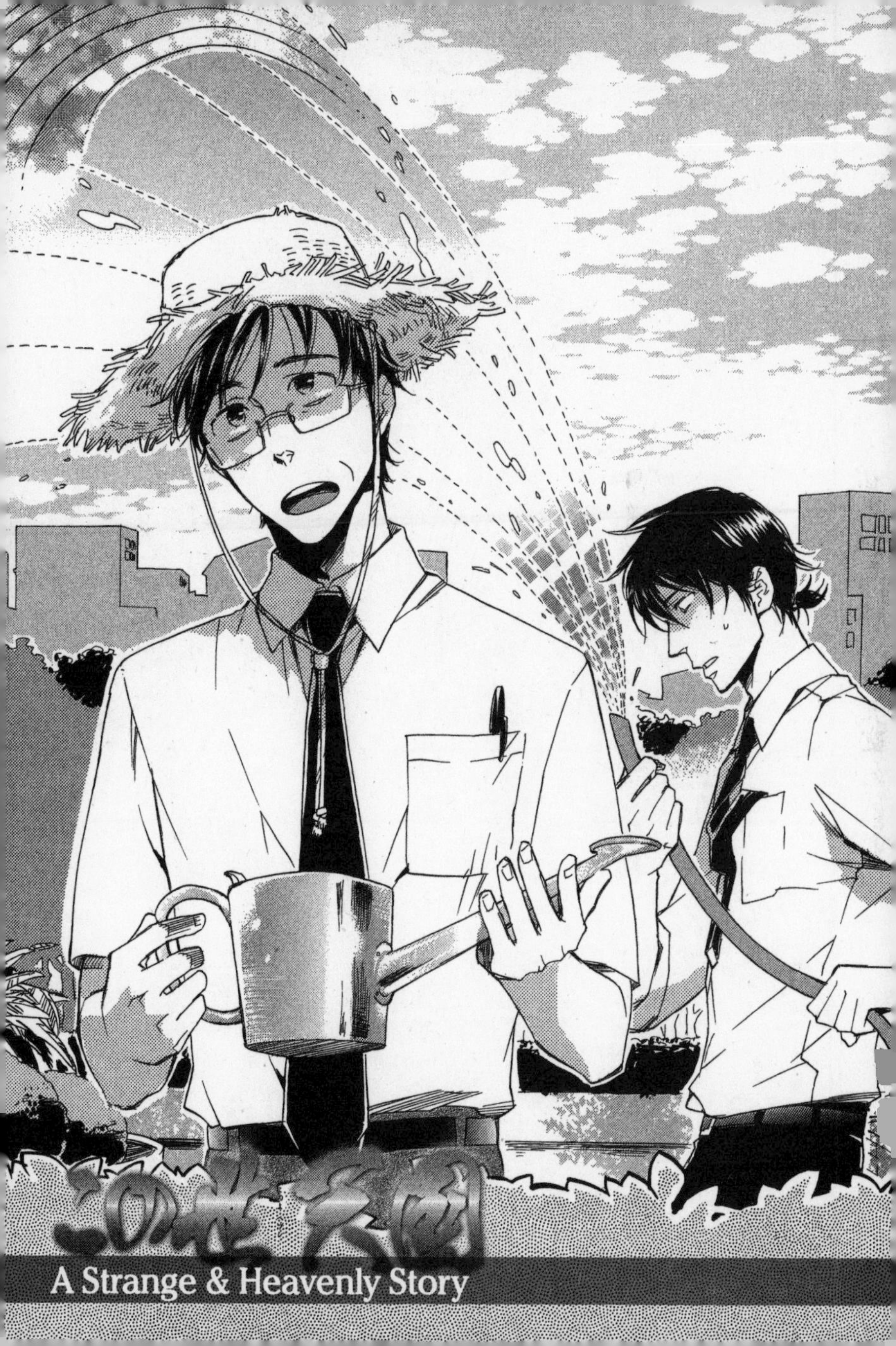
A Strange & Heavenly Story

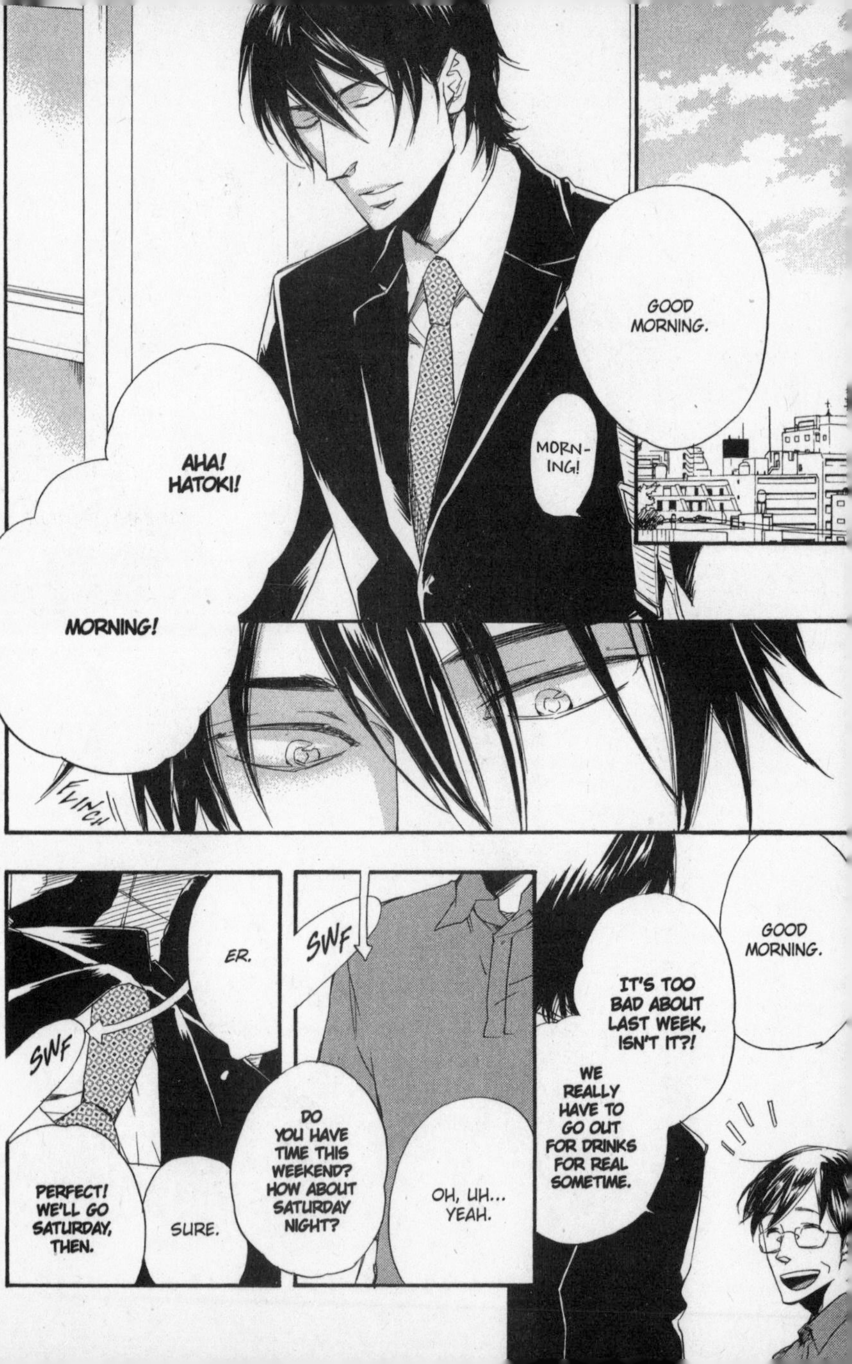
GOOD MORNING.
MORN-ING!
AHA! HATOKI!
MORNING!
FLINCH
GOOD MORNING.
IT'S TOO BAD ABOUT LAST WEEK, ISN'T IT?!
WE REALLY HAVE TO GO OUT FOR DRINKS FOR REAL SOMETIME.
SWF
OH, UH... YEAH.
DO YOU HAVE TIME THIS WEEKEND? HOW ABOUT SATURDAY NIGHT?
ER.
SWF
SURE.
PERFECT! WE'LL GO SATURDAY, THEN.

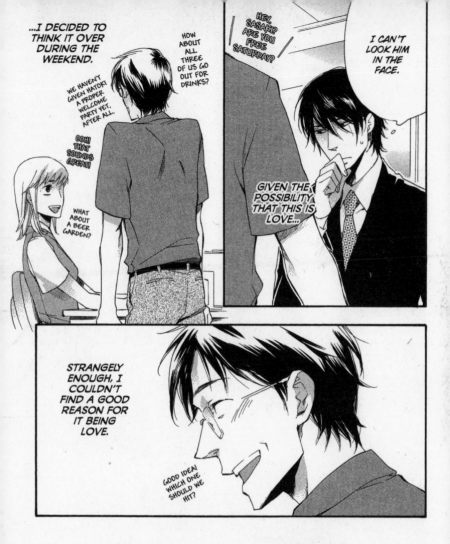

HEY, SASAKI? ARE YOU FREE SATURDAY?
I CAN'T LOOK HIM IN THE FACE.
GIVEN THE POSSIBILITY THAT THIS IS LOVE...
...I DECIDED TO THINK IT OVER DURING THE WEEKEND.
HOW ABOUT ALL THREE OF US GO OUT FOR DRINKS?
WE HAVEN'T GIVEN HATOKI A PROPER WELCOME PARTY YET, AFTER ALL.
OOH! THAT SOUNDS GREAT!
WHAT ABOUT A BEER GARDEN?
STRANGELY ENOUGH, I COULDN'T FIND A GOOD REASON FOR IT BEING LOVE.
GOOD IDEA! WHICH ONE SHOULD WE HIT?

"BECAUSE HE SMILES A LOT AND I THINK IT'S CUTE" IS THE VAGUE AND RATHER ARBITRARY REASON I FELL IN LOVE WITH HIM.

I THINK I DID, ANYWAY.

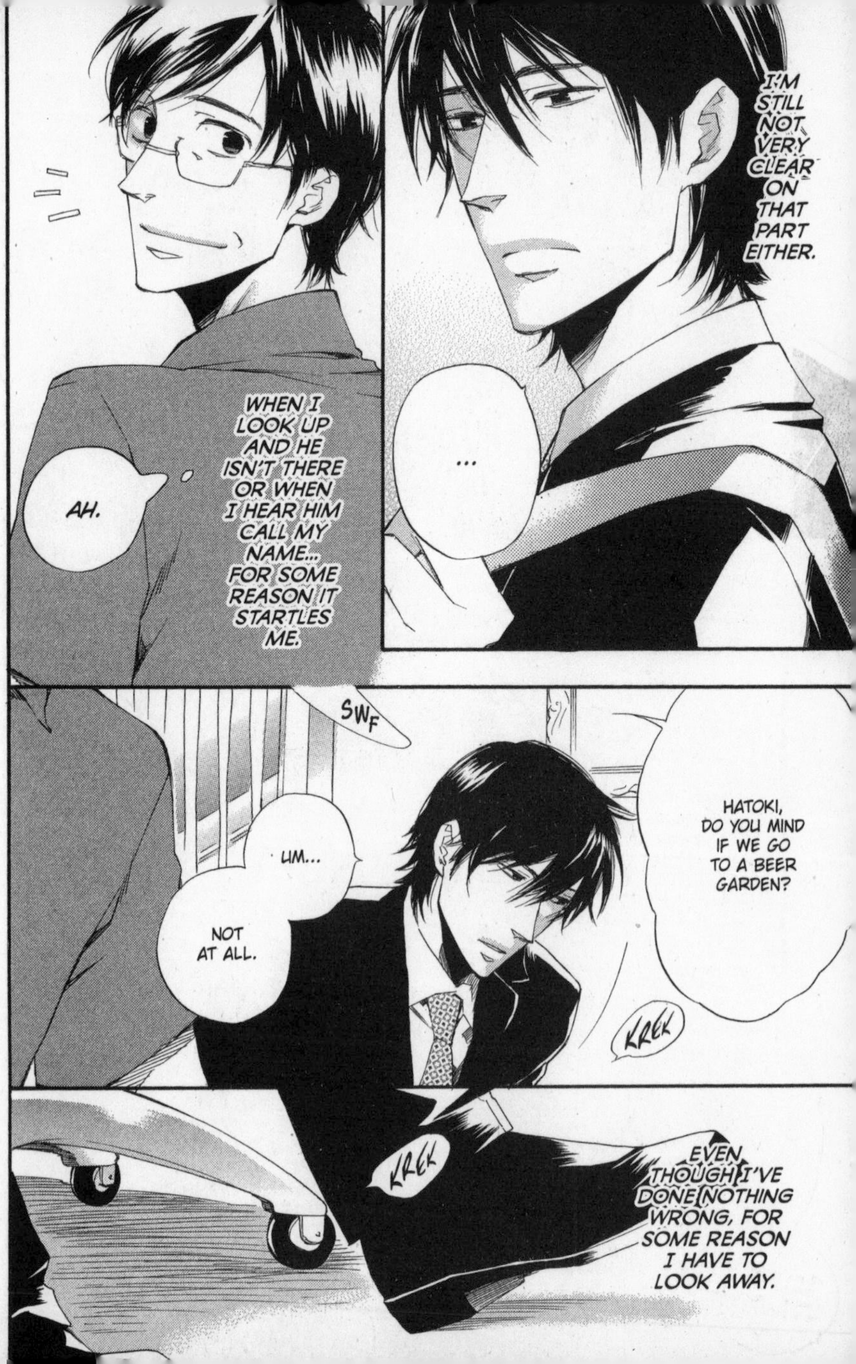
I'M STILL NOT VERY CLEAR ON THAT PART EITHER.
...
WHEN I LOOK UP AND HE ISN'T THERE OR WHEN I HEAR HIM CALL MY NAME... FOR SOME REASON IT STARTLES ME.
AH.
HATOKI, DO YOU MIND IF WE GO TO A BEER GARDEN?
KREK
UM...
NOT AT ALL.
SWF
EVEN THOUGH I'VE DONE NOTHING WRONG, FOR SOME REASON I HAVE TO LOOK AWAY.
KREK

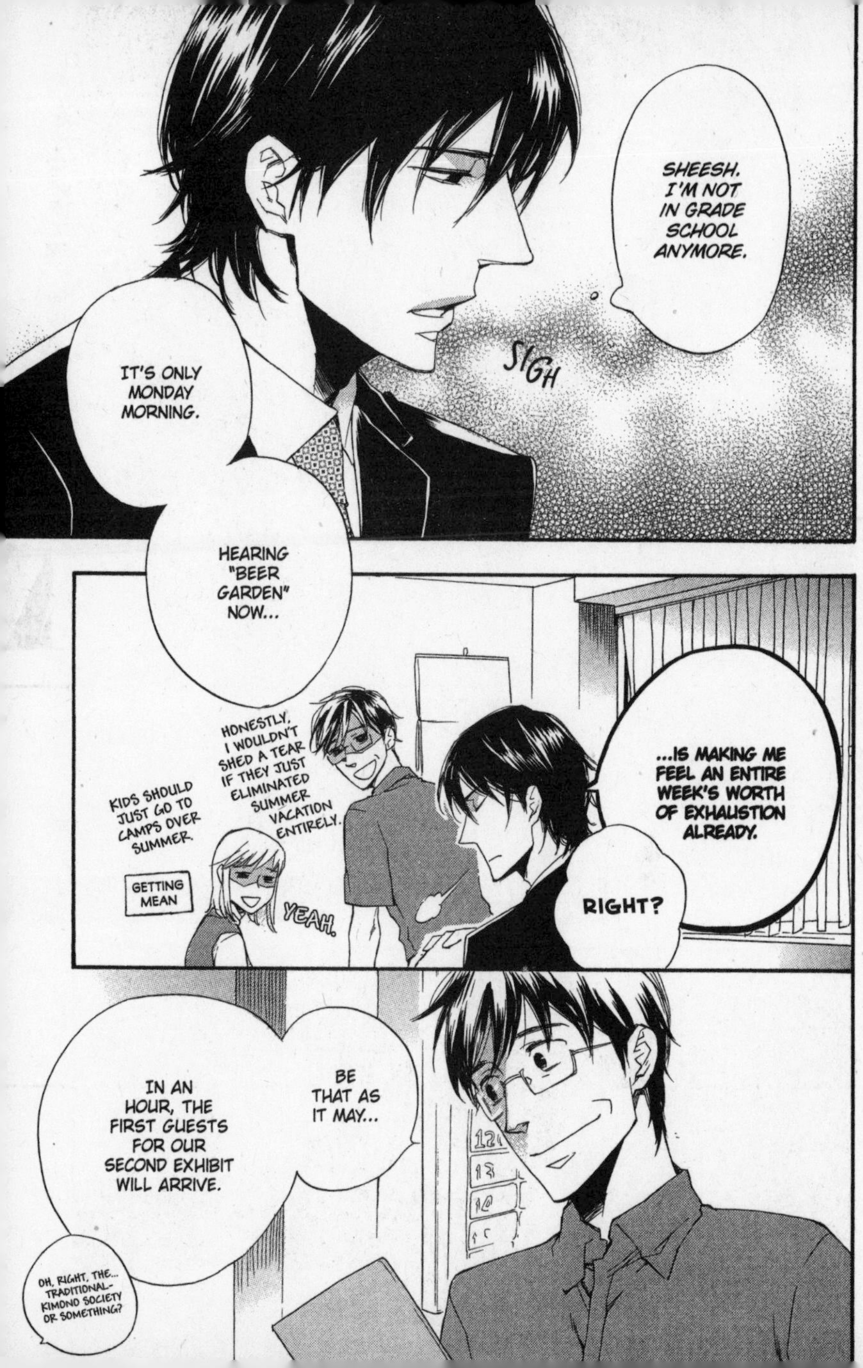
SHEESH. I'M NOT IN GRADE SCHOOL ANYMORE.
SIGH
IT'S ONLY MONDAY MORNING.
HEARING "BEER GARDEN" NOW...
...IS MAKING ME FEEL AN ENTIRE WEEK'S WORTH OF EXHAUSTION ALREADY.
RIGHT?
HONESTLY, I WOULDN'T SHED A TEAR IF THEY JUST ELIMINATED SUMMER VACATION ENTIRELY.
KIDS SHOULD JUST GO TO CAMPS OVER SUMMER.
YEAH.
GETTING MEAN
BE THAT AS IT MAY...
IN AN HOUR, THE FIRST GUESTS FOR OUR SECOND EXHIBIT WILL ARRIVE.
OH, RIGHT, THE... TRADITIONAL-KIMONO SOCIETY OR SOMETHING?

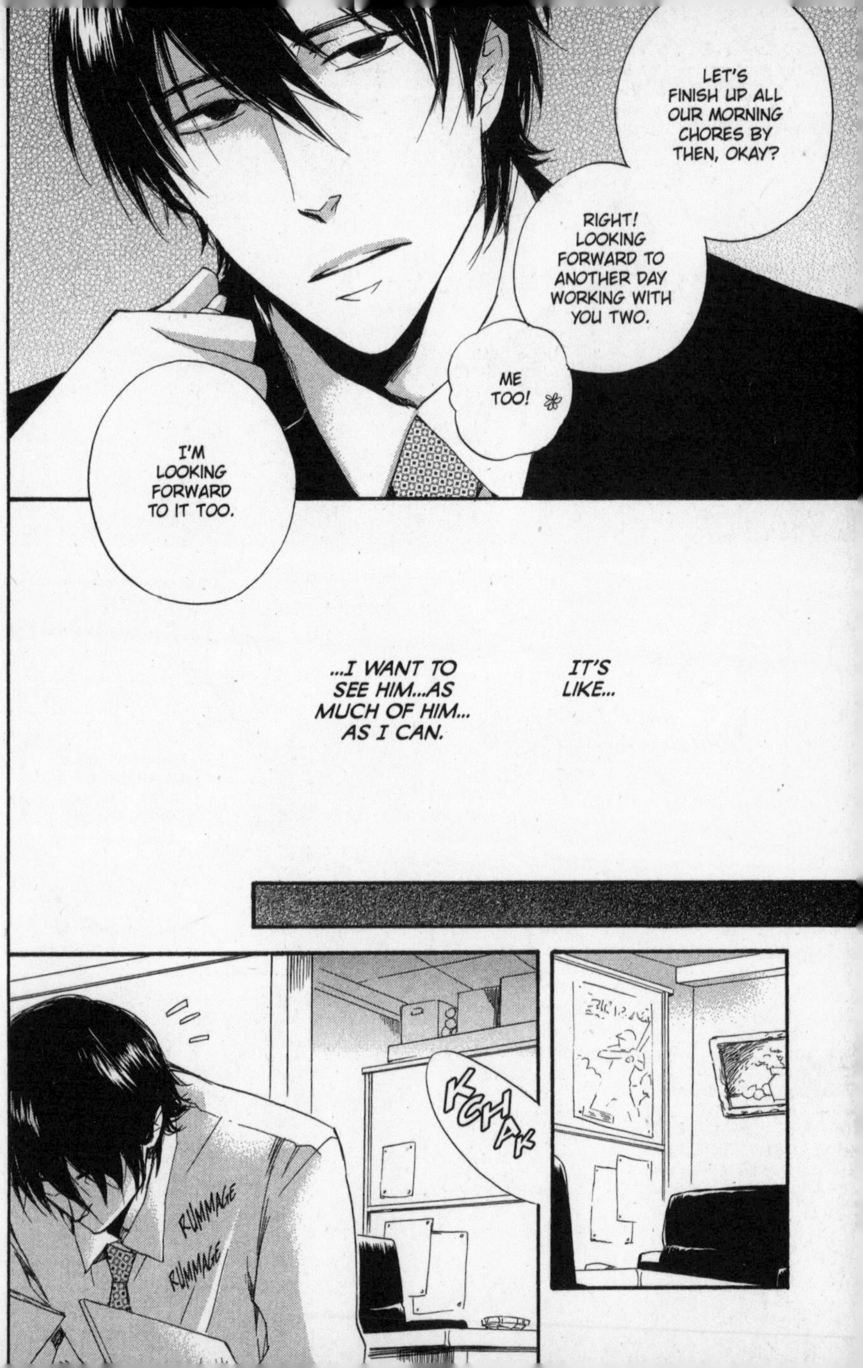

LET'S FINISH UP ALL OUR MORNING CHORES BY THEN, OKAY?
RIGHT! LOOKING FORWARD TO ANOTHER DAY WORKING WITH YOU TWO.
ME TOO!
I'M LOOKING FORWARD TO IT TOO.
IT'S LIKE...
...I WANT TO SEE HIM...AS MUCH OF HIM... AS I CAN.
KCHAK
RUMMAGE
RUMMAGE

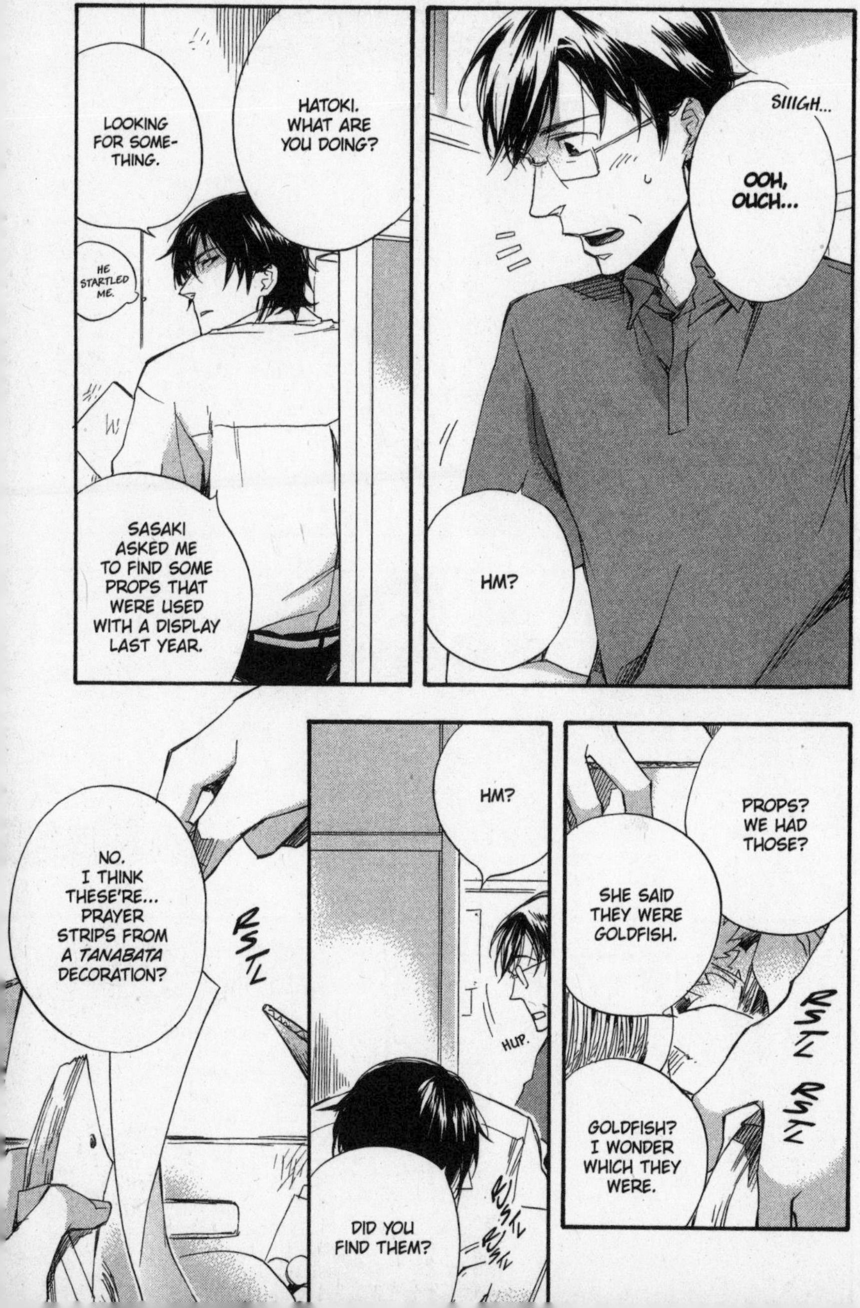
SIIIGH...
OOH, OUCH...
HM?
HATOKI. WHAT ARE YOU DOING?
LOOKING FOR SOME-THING.
HE STARTLED ME.
SASAKI ASKED ME TO FIND SOME PROPS THAT WERE USED WITH A DISPLAY LAST YEAR.
PROPS? WE HAD THOSE?
SHE SAID THEY WERE GOLDFISH.
RSTL
RSTL
GOLDFISH? I WONDER WHICH THEY WERE.
HM?
HUP.
RSTL
RSTL
DID YOU FIND THEM?
RSTL
NO. I THINK THESE'RE... PRAYER STRIPS FROM A *TANABATA* DECORATION?

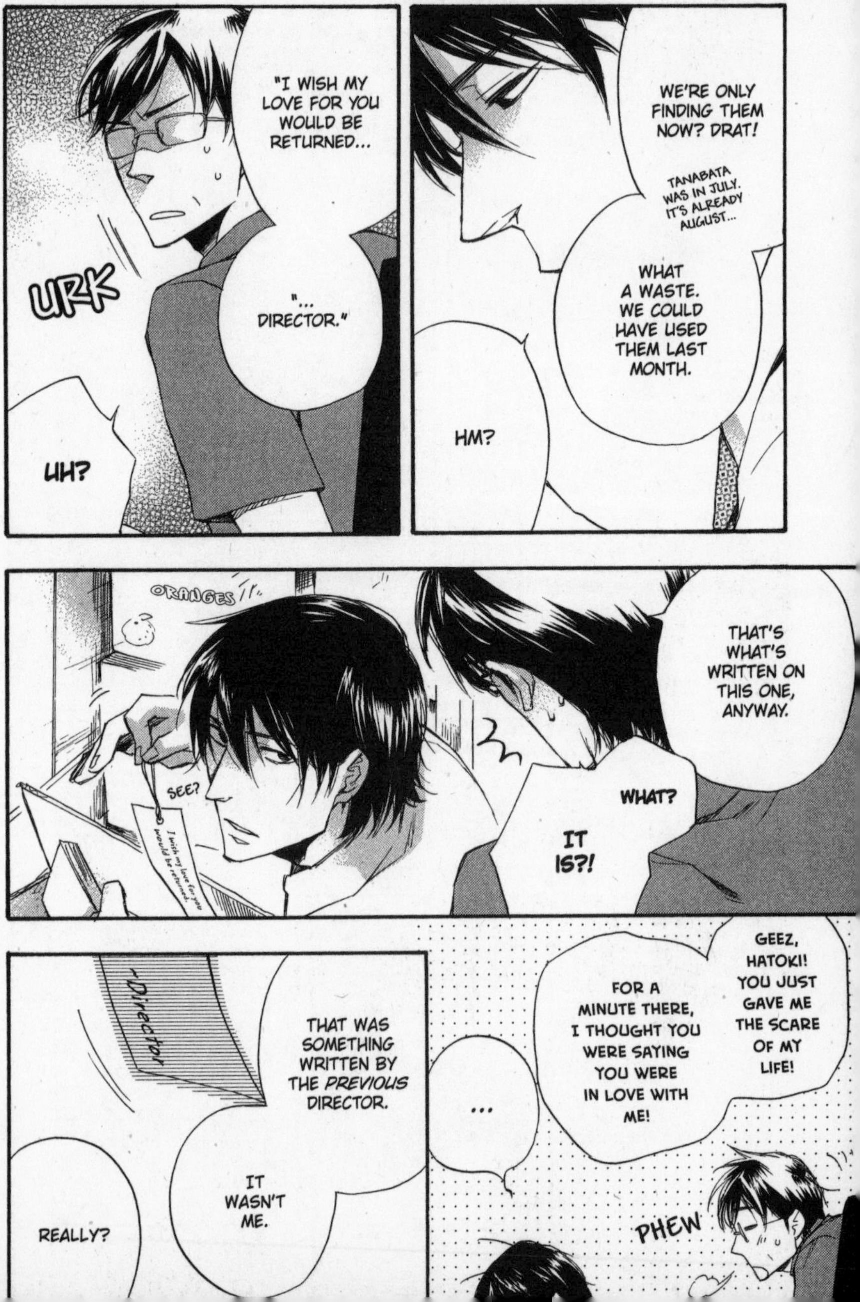
WE'RE ONLY FINDING THEM NOW? DRAT!
TANABATA WAS IN JULY. IT'S ALREADY AUGUST...
WHAT A WASTE. WE COULD HAVE USED THEM LAST MONTH.
HM?
"I WISH MY LOVE FOR YOU WOULD BE RETURNED...
URK
"... DIRECTOR."
UH?
THAT'S WHAT'S WRITTEN ON THIS ONE, ANYWAY.
WHAT?
IT IS?!
ORANGES
SEE?
I wish my love for you would be returned.
GEEZ, HATOKI! YOU JUST GAVE ME THE SCARE OF MY LIFE!
FOR A MINUTE THERE, I THOUGHT YOU WERE SAYING YOU WERE IN LOVE WITH ME!
...
PHEW
-Director
THAT WAS SOMETHING WRITTEN BY THE *PREVIOUS* DIRECTOR.
IT WASN'T ME.
REALLY?

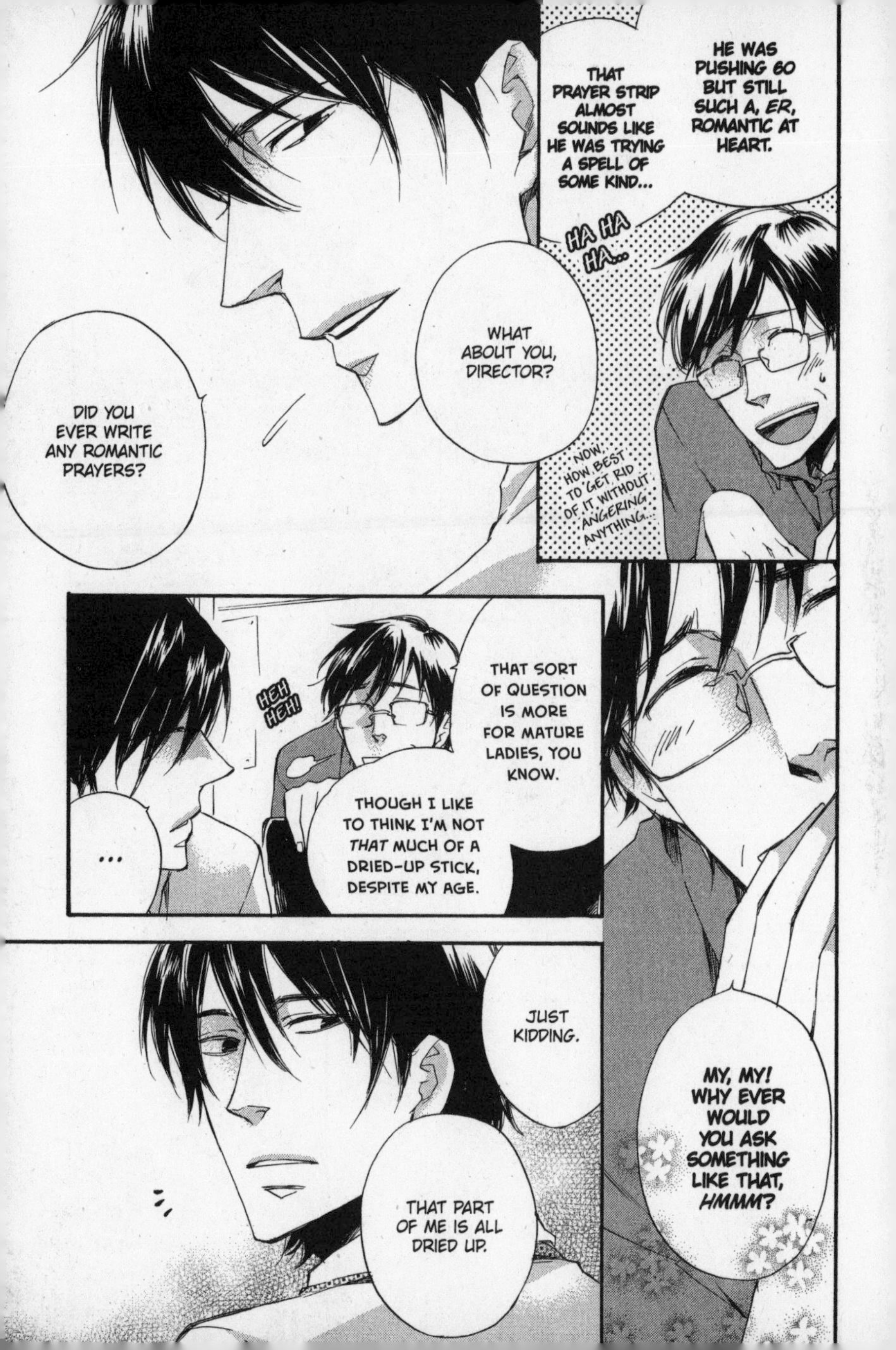

HE WAS PUSHING 60 BUT STILL SUCH A, *ER*, ROMANTIC AT HEART.
THAT PRAYER STRIP ALMOST SOUNDS LIKE HE WAS TRYING A SPELL OF SOME KIND...
HA HA HA...
NOW, HOW BEST TO GET RID OF IT WITHOUT ANGERING ANYTHING...
WHAT ABOUT YOU, DIRECTOR?
DID YOU EVER WRITE ANY ROMANTIC PRAYERS?
MY, MY! WHY EVER WOULD YOU ASK SOMETHING LIKE THAT, *HMMM*?
THAT SORT OF QUESTION IS MORE FOR MATURE LADIES, YOU KNOW.
HEH HEH!
THOUGH I LIKE TO THINK I'M NOT *THAT* MUCH OF A DRIED-UP STICK, DESPITE MY AGE.
...
JUST KIDDING.
THAT PART OF ME IS ALL DRIED UP.

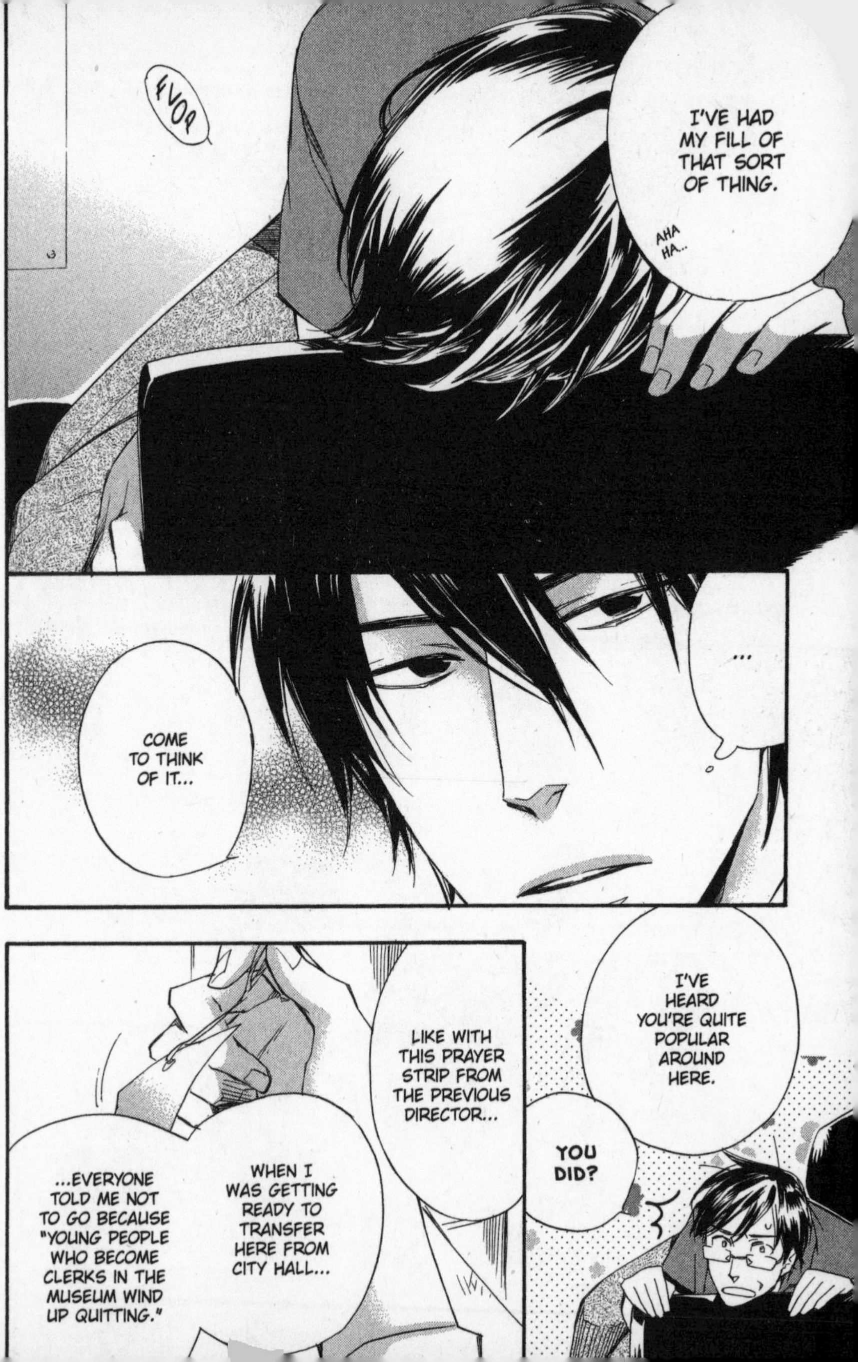
I'VE HAD MY FILL OF THAT SORT OF THING.
AHA HA...
FVOP
...
COME TO THINK OF IT...
I'VE HEARD YOU'RE QUITE POPULAR AROUND HERE.
YOU DID?
LIKE WITH THIS PRAYER STRIP FROM THE PREVIOUS DIRECTOR...
WHEN I WAS GETTING READY TO TRANSFER HERE FROM CITY HALL...
...EVERYONE TOLD ME NOT TO GO BECAUSE "YOUNG PEOPLE WHO BECOME CLERKS IN THE MUSEUM WIND UP QUITTING."

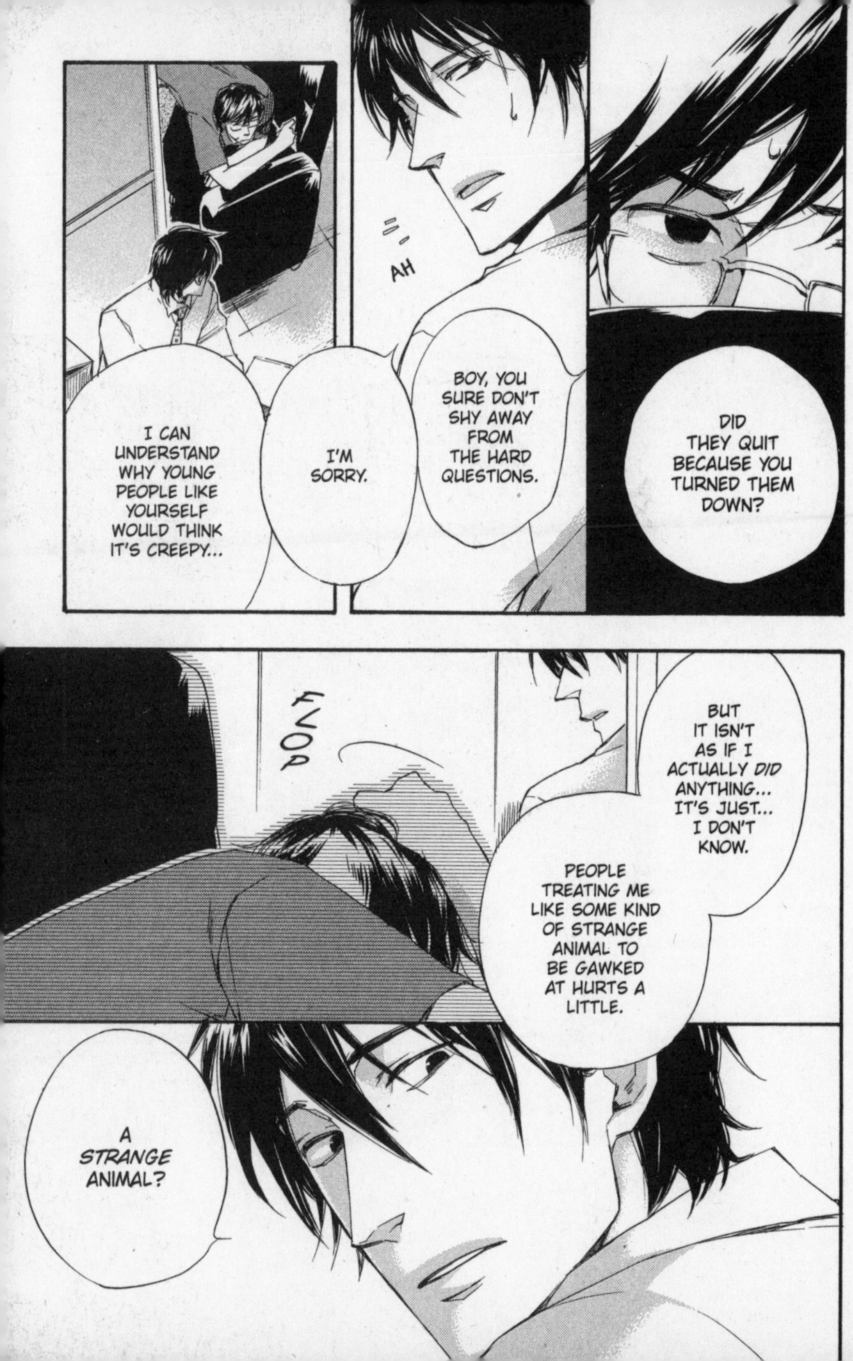
DID THEY QUIT BECAUSE YOU TURNED THEM DOWN?
AH
BOY, YOU SURE DON'T SHY AWAY FROM THE HARD QUESTIONS.
I'M SORRY.
I CAN UNDERSTAND WHY YOUNG PEOPLE LIKE YOURSELF WOULD THINK IT'S CREEPY...
BUT IT ISN'T AS IF I ACTUALLY *DID* ANYTHING... IT'S JUST... I DON'T KNOW.
PEOPLE TREATING ME LIKE SOME KIND OF STRANGE ANIMAL TO BE GAWKED AT HURTS A LITTLE.
FLOP
A *STRANGE* ANIMAL?

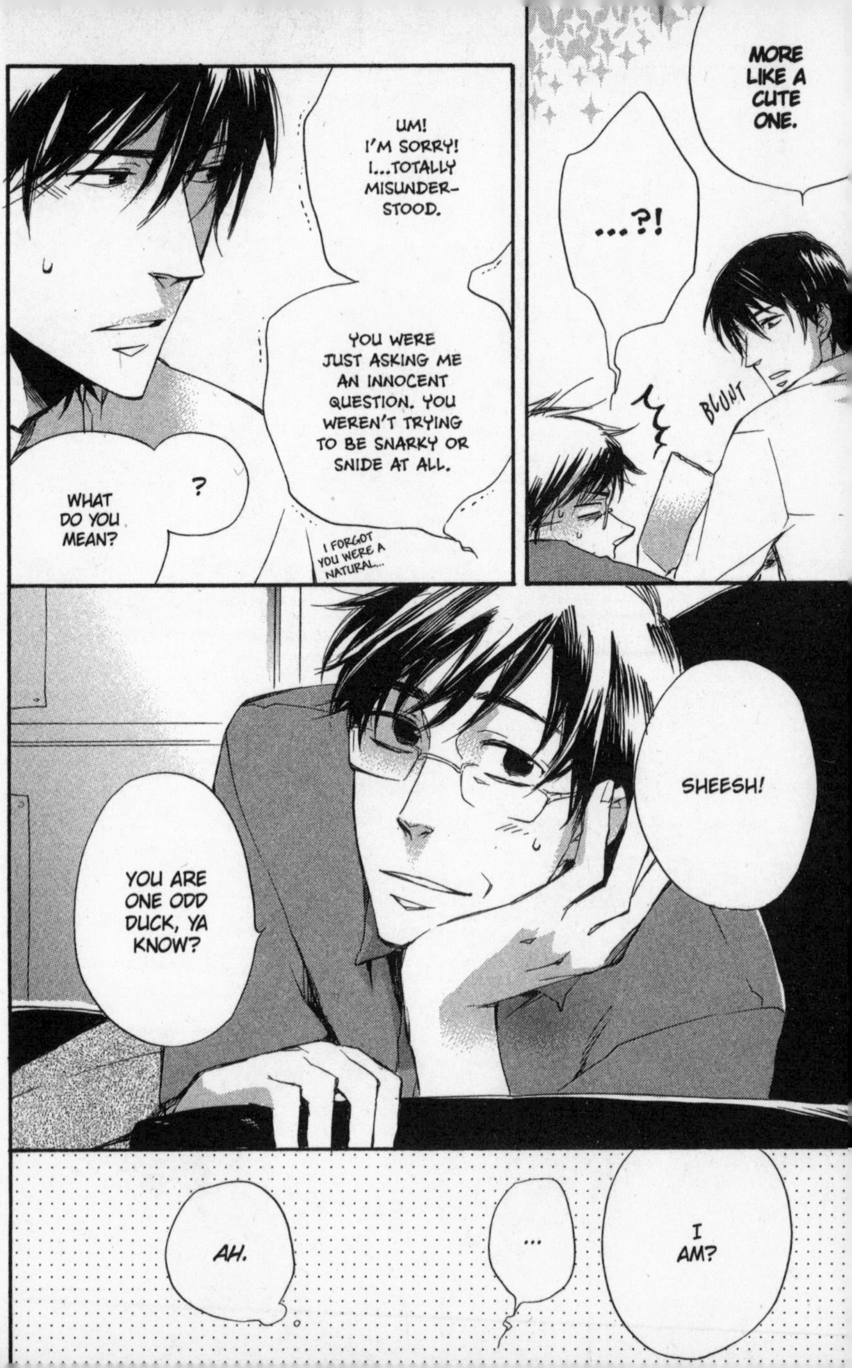
MORE LIKE A CUTE ONE.
...?!
BLUNT
UM! I'M SORRY! I...TOTALLY MISUNDER-STOOD.
YOU WERE JUST ASKING ME AN INNOCENT QUESTION. YOU WEREN'T TRYING TO BE SNARKY OR SNIDE AT ALL.
I FORGOT YOU WERE A NATURAL...
?
WHAT DO YOU MEAN?
SHEESH!
YOU ARE ONE ODD DUCK, YA KNOW?
I AM?
...
AH.

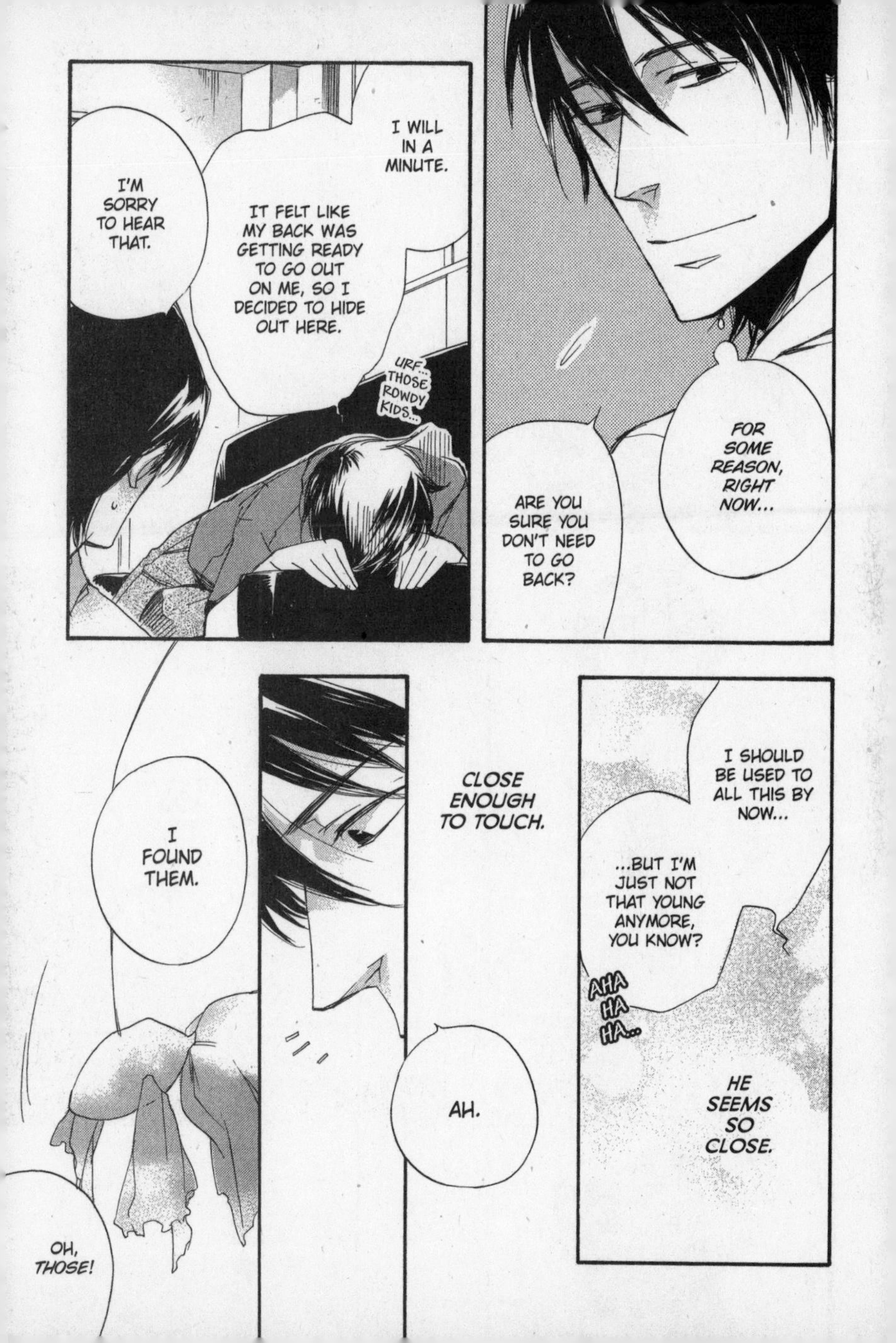
FOR SOME REASON, RIGHT NOW...
ARE YOU SURE YOU DON'T NEED TO GO BACK?
I WILL IN A MINUTE.
IT FELT LIKE MY BACK WAS GETTING READY TO GO OUT ON ME, SO I DECIDED TO HIDE OUT HERE.
URF... THOSE ROWDY KIDS...
I'M SORRY TO HEAR THAT.
I SHOULD BE USED TO ALL THIS BY NOW...
...BUT I'M JUST NOT THAT YOUNG ANYMORE, YOU KNOW?
AHA HA HA...
HE SEEMS SO CLOSE.
CLOSE ENOUGH TO TOUCH.
AH.
I FOUND THEM.
OH, THOSE!

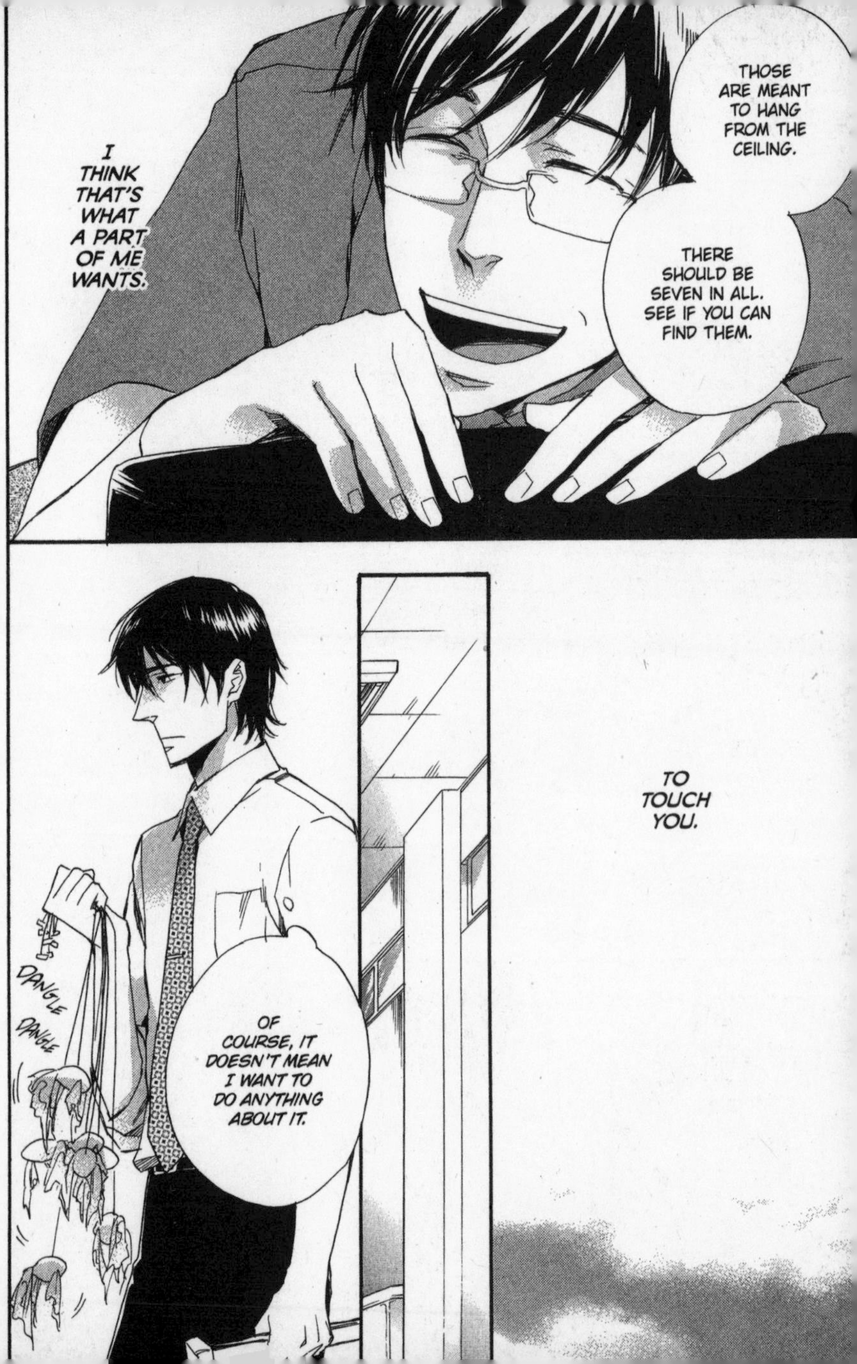
THOSE ARE MEANT TO HANG FROM THE CEILING.
THERE SHOULD BE SEVEN IN ALL. SEE IF YOU CAN FIND THEM.
I THINK THAT'S WHAT A PART OF ME WANTS.
TO TOUCH YOU.
OF COURSE, IT DOESN'T MEAN I WANT TO DO ANYTHING ABOUT IT.
DANGLE
DANGLE

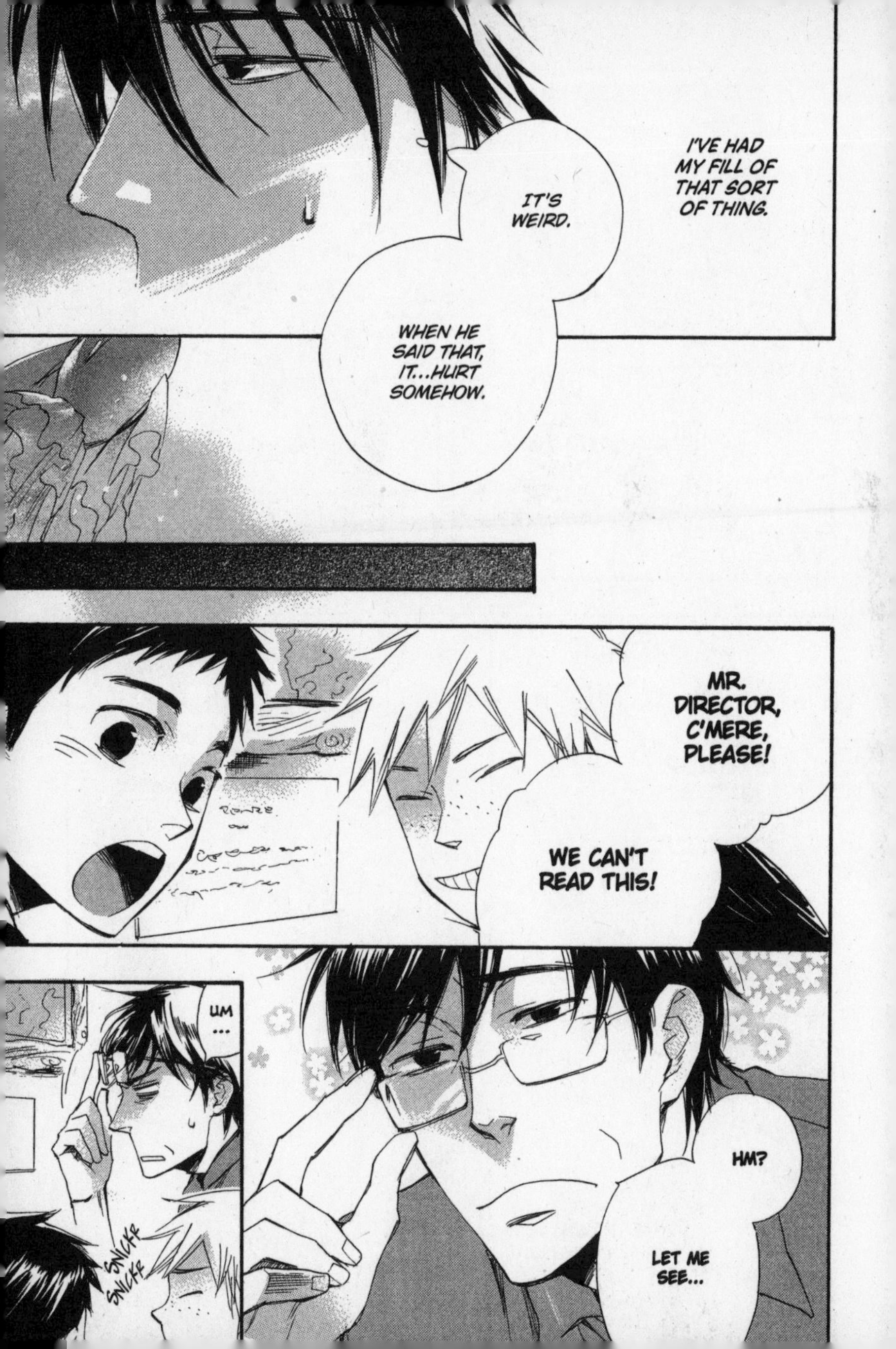
I'VE HAD MY FILL OF THAT SORT OF THING.
IT'S WEIRD.
WHEN HE SAID THAT, IT...HURT SOMEHOW.
MR. DIRECTOR, C'MERE, PLEASE!
WE CAN'T READ THIS!
HM?
LET ME SEE...
UM ...
SNICKR SNICKR

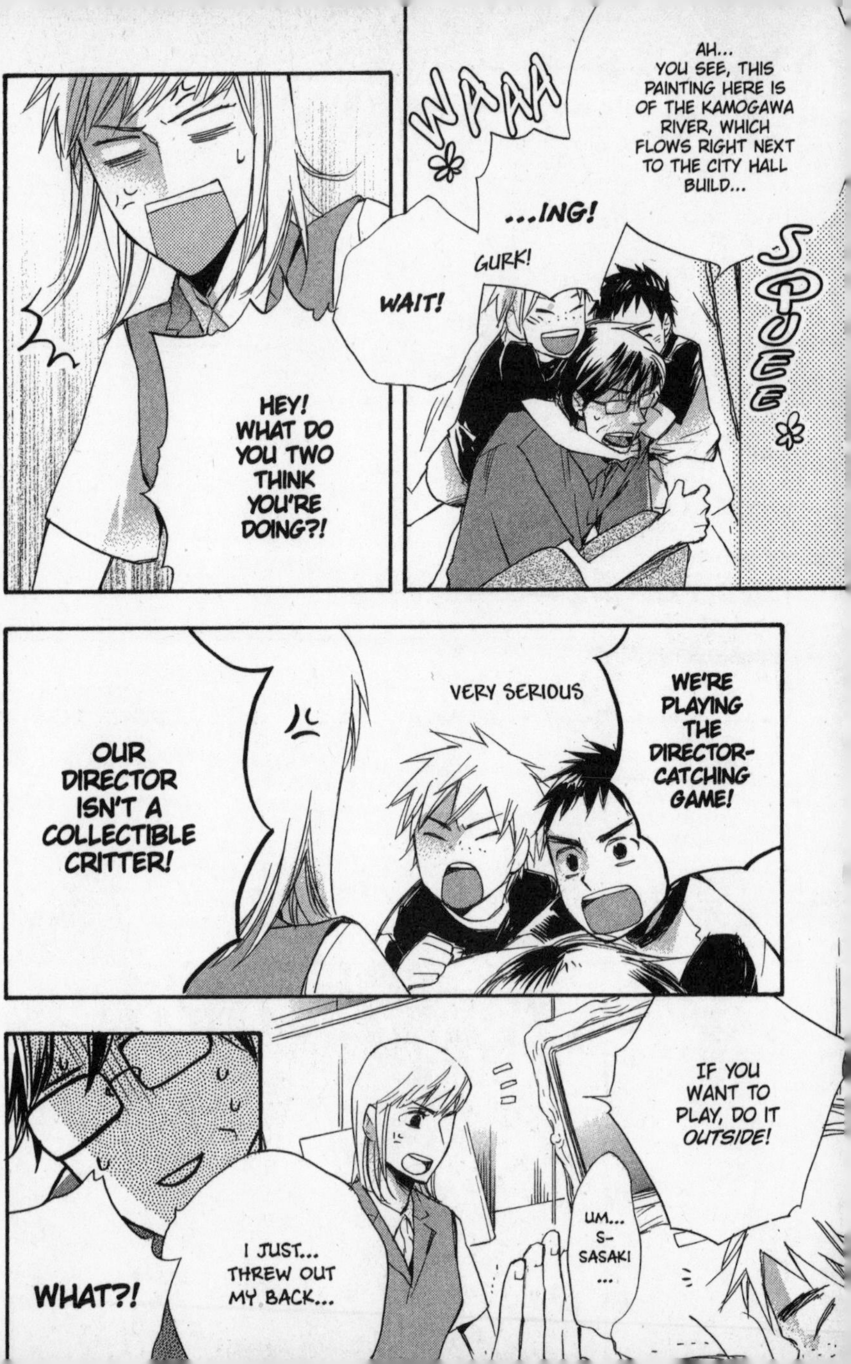
AH... YOU SEE, THIS PAINTING HERE IS OF THE KAMOGAWA RIVER, WHICH FLOWS RIGHT NEXT TO THE CITY HALL BUILD...
WAAA
...ING!
SQUEE
GURK!
WAIT!
HEY! WHAT DO YOU TWO THINK YOU'RE DOING?!
VERY SERIOUS
WE'RE PLAYING THE DIRECTOR-CATCHING GAME!
OUR DIRECTOR ISN'T A COLLECTIBLE CRITTER!
IF YOU WANT TO PLAY, DO IT *OUTSIDE*!
UM... S-SASAKI ...
I JUST... THREW OUT MY BACK...
WHAT?!

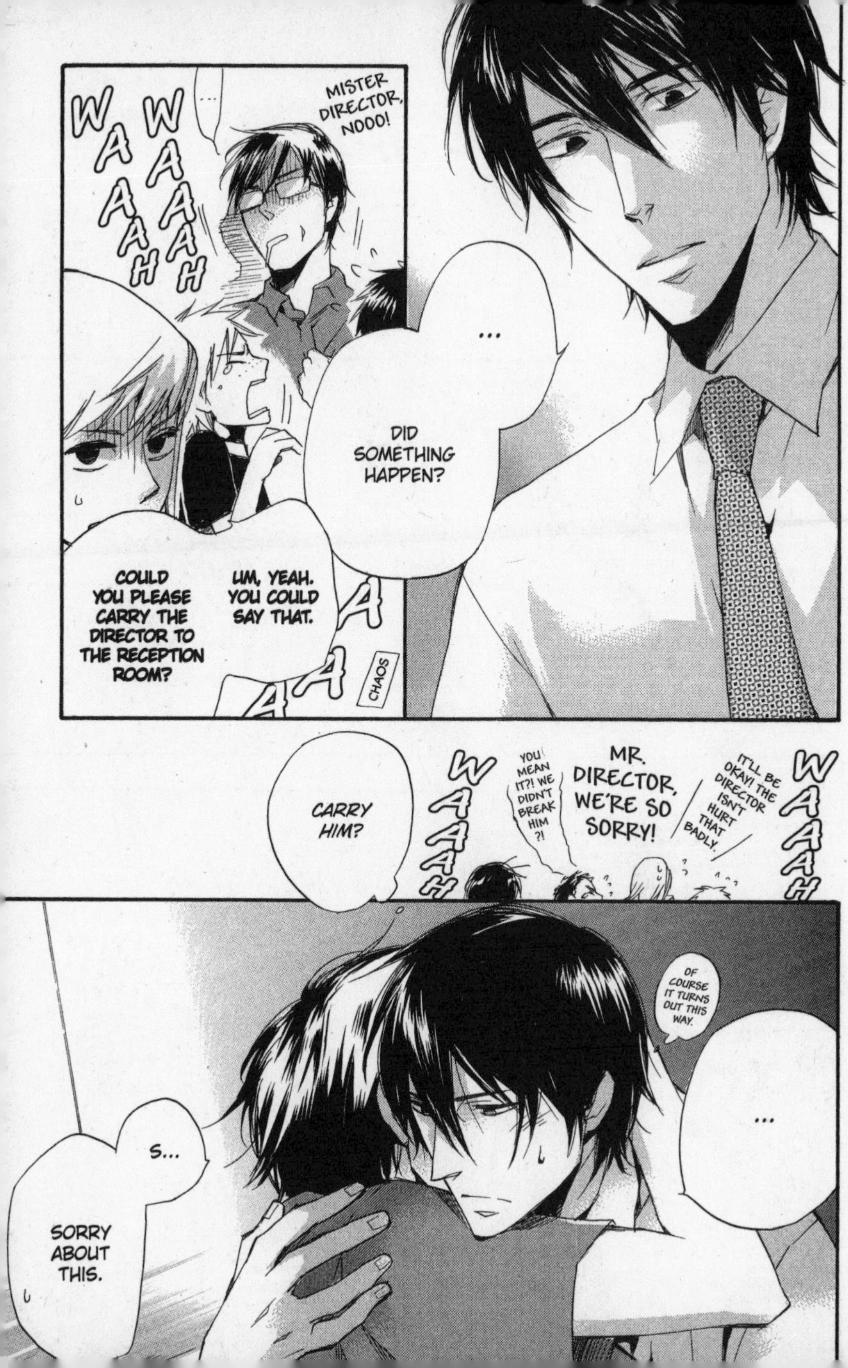
...
DID SOMETHING HAPPEN?
MISTER DIRECTOR, NOOO!
WAAAAH
WAAAAH
...
UM, YEAH. YOU COULD SAY THAT.
COULD YOU PLEASE CARRY THE DIRECTOR TO THE RECEPTION ROOM?
CHAOS
WAAAAH
IT'LL BE OKAY! THE DIRECTOR ISN'T HURT THAT BADLY.
MR. DIRECTOR, WE'RE SO SORRY!
YOU MEAN IT?! WE DIDN'T BREAK HIM ?!
WAAAAH
CARRY HIM?
...
OF COURSE IT TURNS OUT THIS WAY.
S...
SORRY ABOUT THIS.

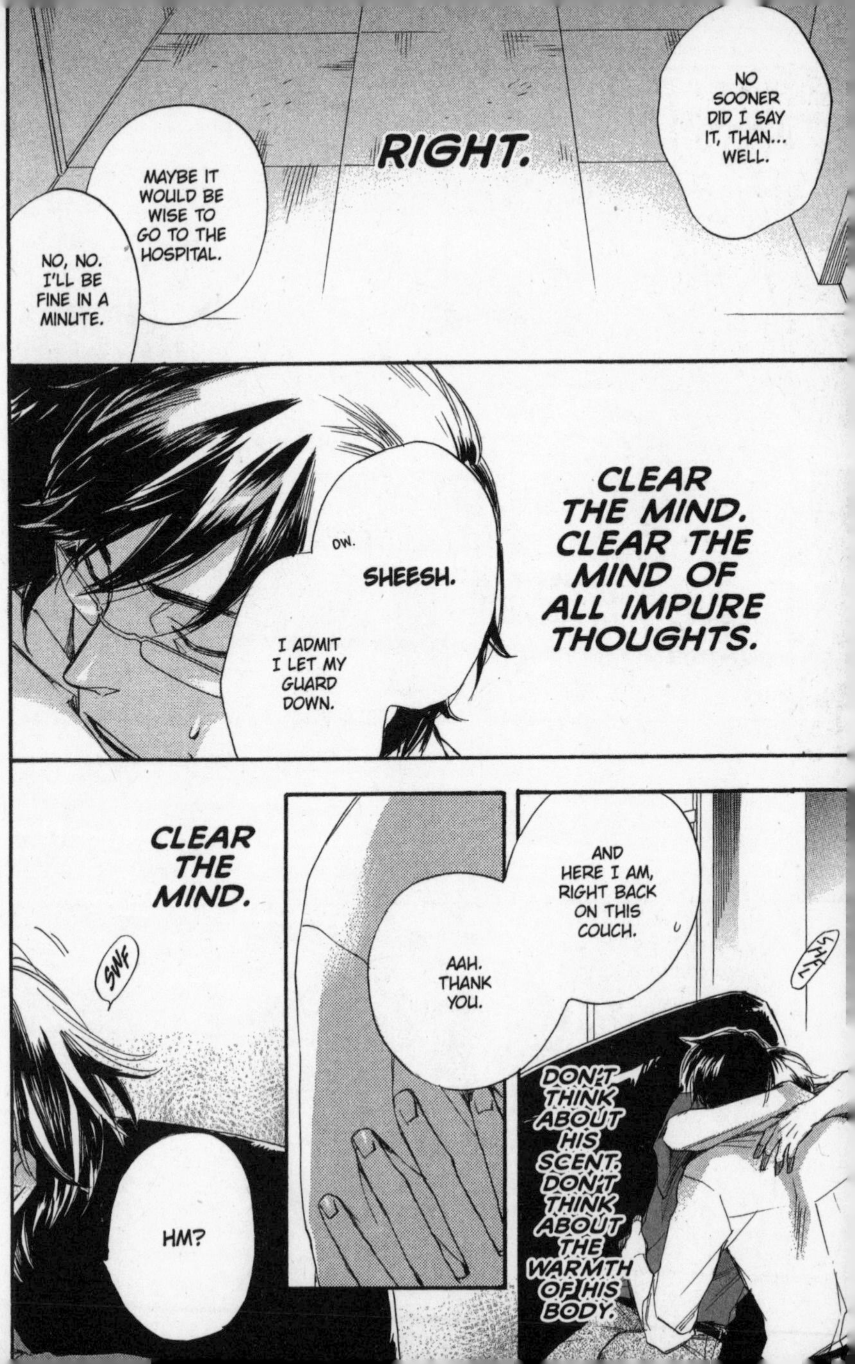
NO SOONER DID I SAY IT, THAN... WELL.
RIGHT.
MAYBE IT WOULD BE WISE TO GO TO THE HOSPITAL.
NO, NO. I'LL BE FINE IN A MINUTE.
CLEAR THE MIND. CLEAR THE MIND OF ALL IMPURE THOUGHTS.
OW.
SHEESH.
I ADMIT I LET MY GUARD DOWN.
AND HERE I AM, RIGHT BACK ON THIS COUCH.
AAH. THANK YOU.
DON'T THINK ABOUT HIS SCENT. DON'T THINK ABOUT THE WARMTH OF HIS BODY.
CLEAR THE MIND.
SNF
HM?

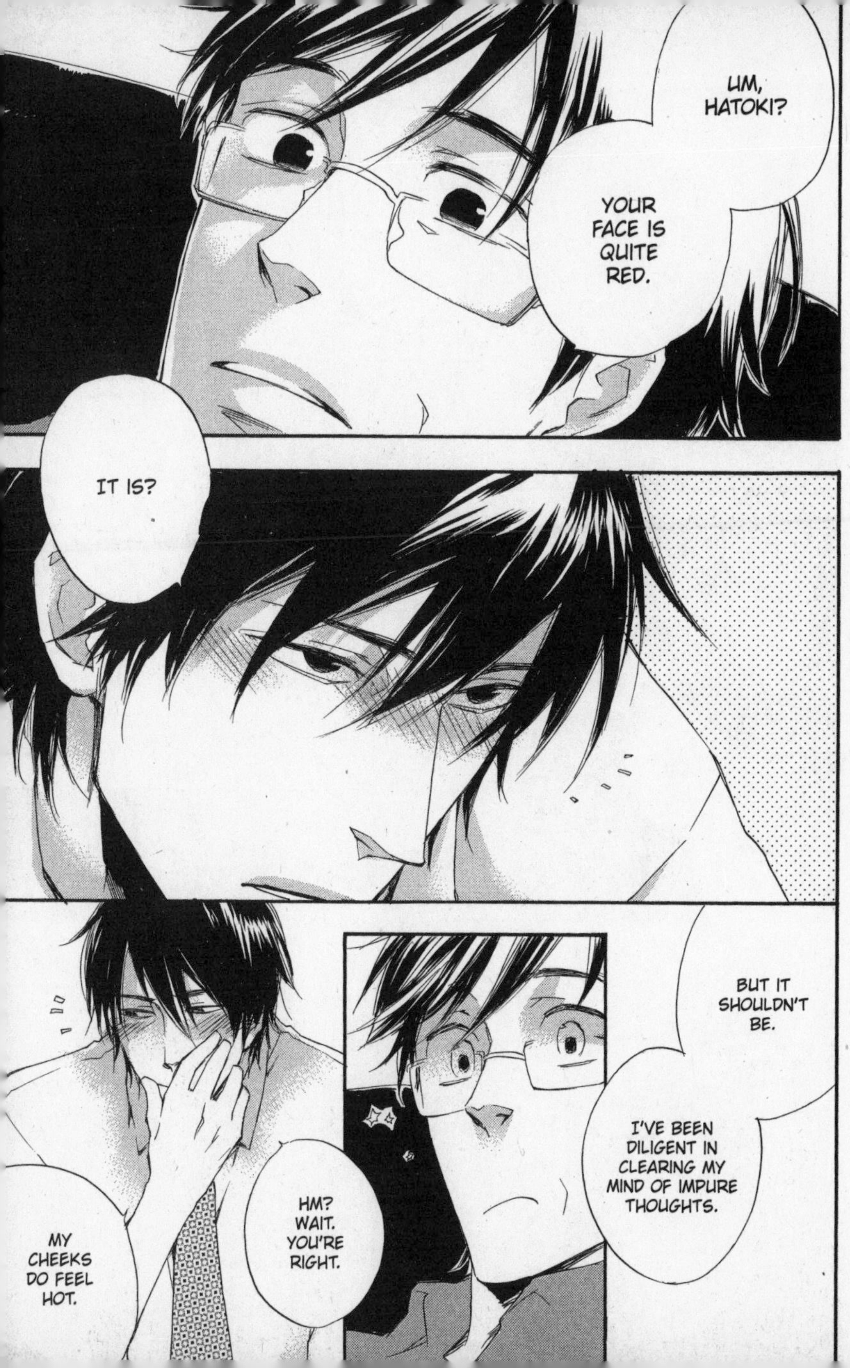
UM, HATOKI?
YOUR FACE IS QUITE RED.
IT IS?
BUT IT SHOULDN'T BE.
I'VE BEEN DILIGENT IN CLEARING MY MIND OF IMPURE THOUGHTS.
HM? WAIT. YOU'RE RIGHT.
MY CHEEKS DO FEEL HOT.

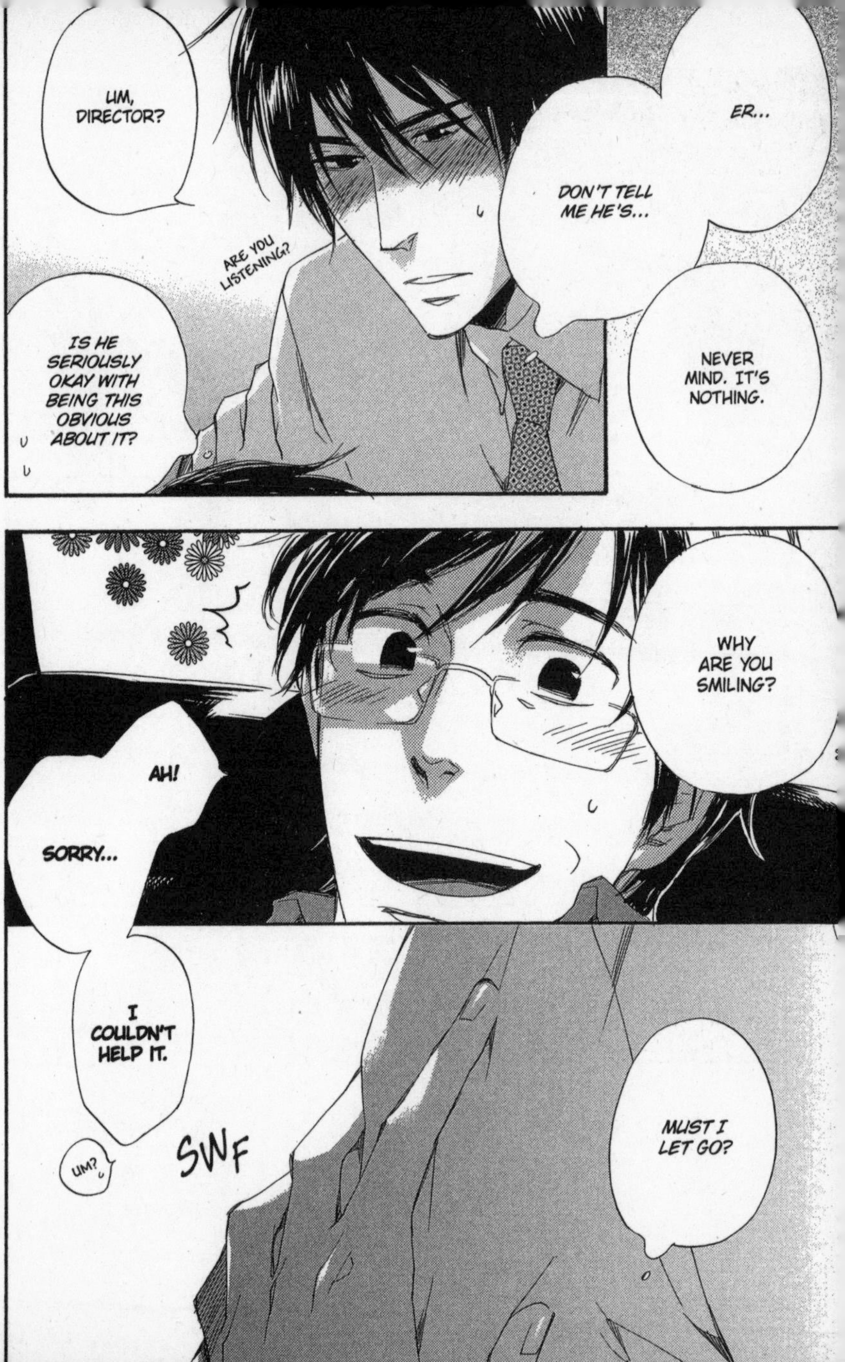
ER... DON'T TELL ME HE'S...
UM, DIRECTOR?
ARE YOU LISTENING?
NEVER MIND. IT'S NOTHING.
IS HE SERIOUSLY OKAY WITH BEING THIS OBVIOUS ABOUT IT?
WHY ARE YOU SMILING?
AH! SORRY... I COULDN'T HELP IT.
MUST I LET GO?
SWF
UM?

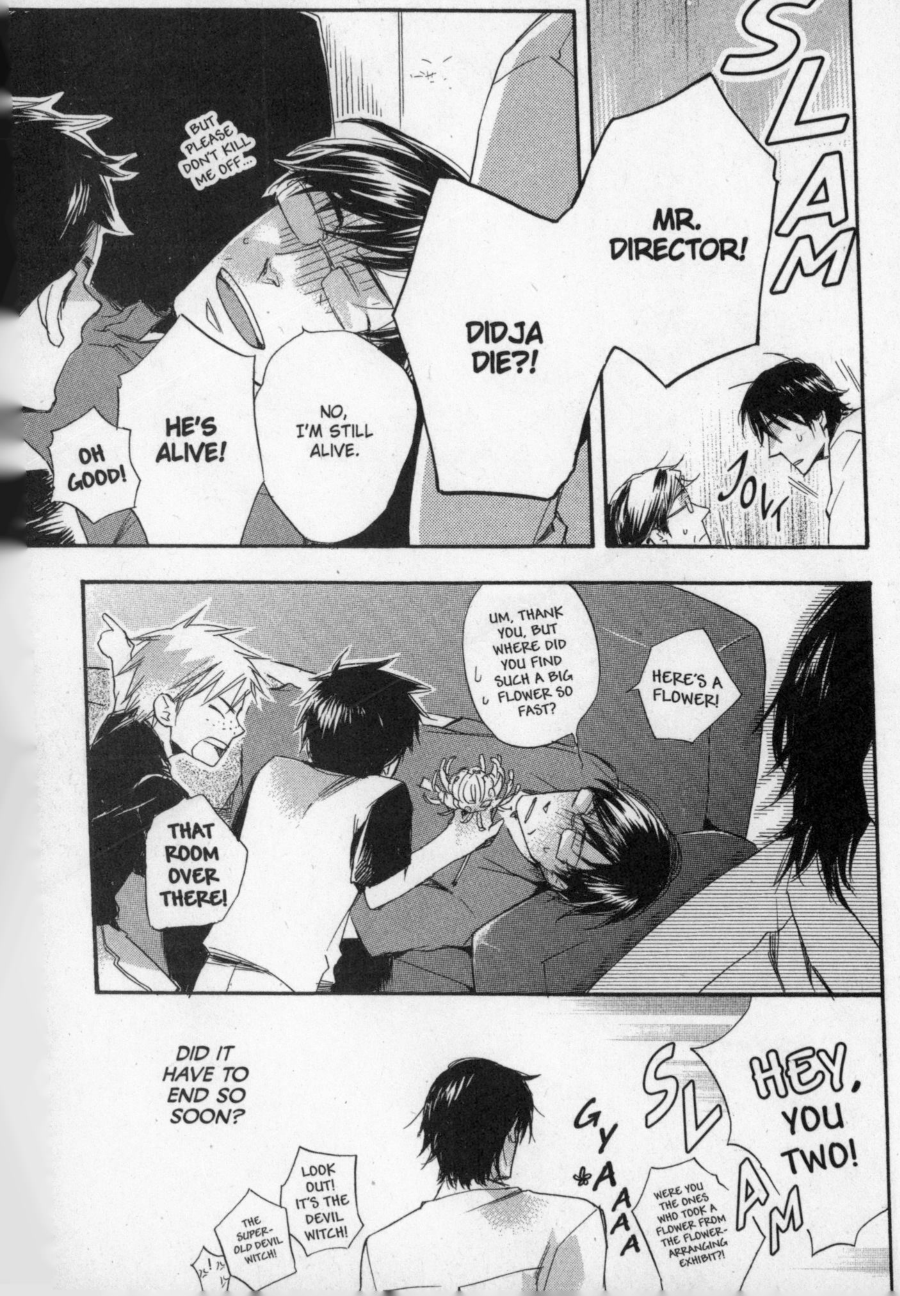
SLAM
MR. DIRECTOR!
DIDJA DIE?!
JOLT
NO, I'M STILL ALIVE.
HE'S ALIVE!
OH GOOD!
BUT PLEASE DON'T KILL ME OFF...
HERE'S A FLOWER!
UM, THANK YOU, BUT WHERE DID YOU FIND SUCH A BIG FLOWER SO FAST?
THAT ROOM OVER THERE!
HEY, YOU TWO!
SLAM
WERE YOU THE ONES WHO TOOK A FLOWER FROM THE FLOWER-ARRANGING EXHIBIT?!
GYAAAA
LOOK OUT! IT'S THE DEVIL WITCH!
THE SUPER-OLD DEVIL WITCH!
DID IT HAVE TO END SO SOON?

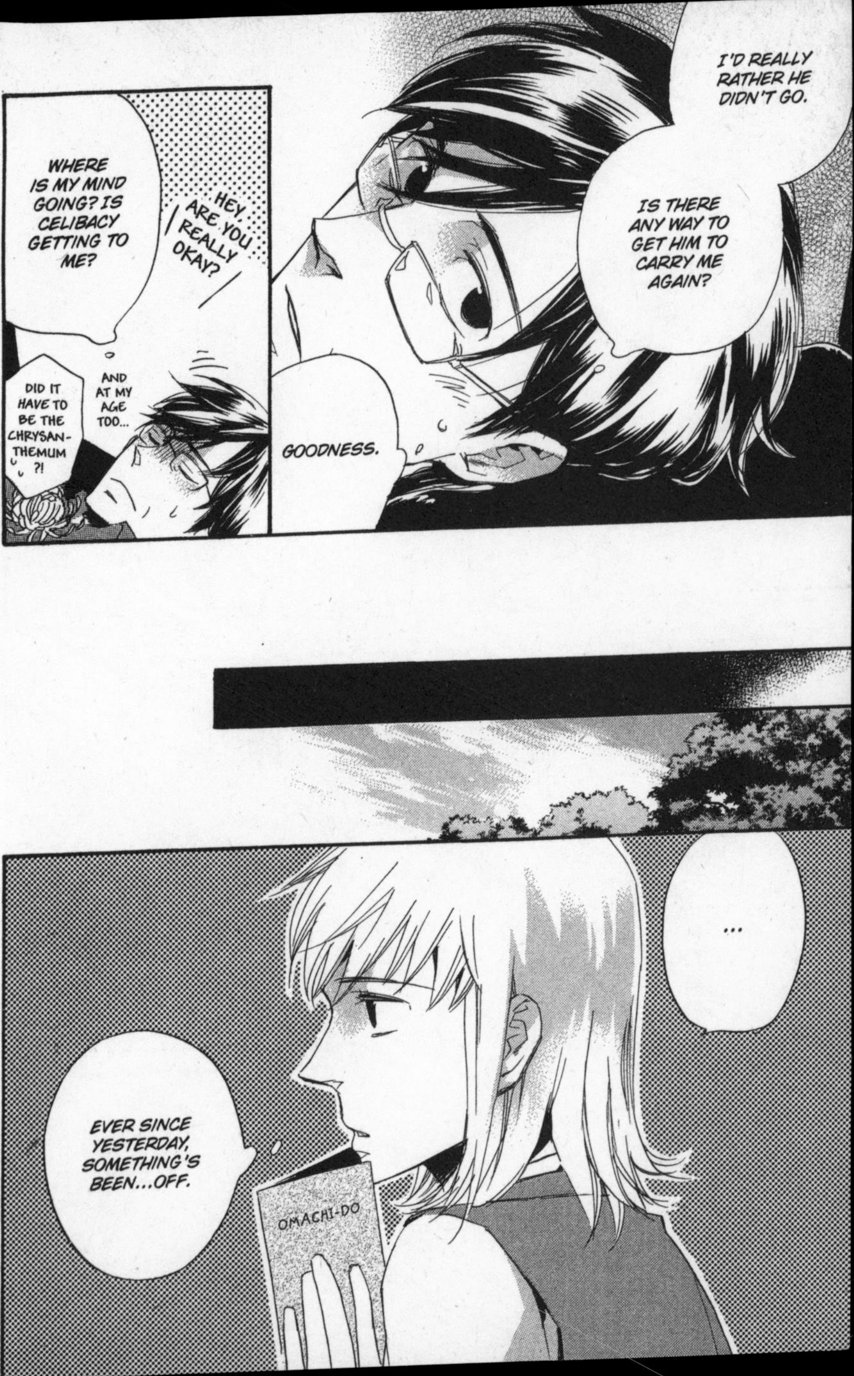
I'D REALLY RATHER HE DIDN'T GO.
IS THERE ANY WAY TO GET HIM TO CARRY ME AGAIN?
GOODNESS.
HEY, ARE YOU REALLY OKAY?
WHERE IS MY MIND GOING? IS CELIBACY GETTING TO ME?
AND AT MY AGE TOO...
DID IT HAVE TO BE THE CHRYSANTHEMUM?!
...
EVER SINCE YESTERDAY, SOMETHING'S BEEN...OFF.
OMACHI-DO

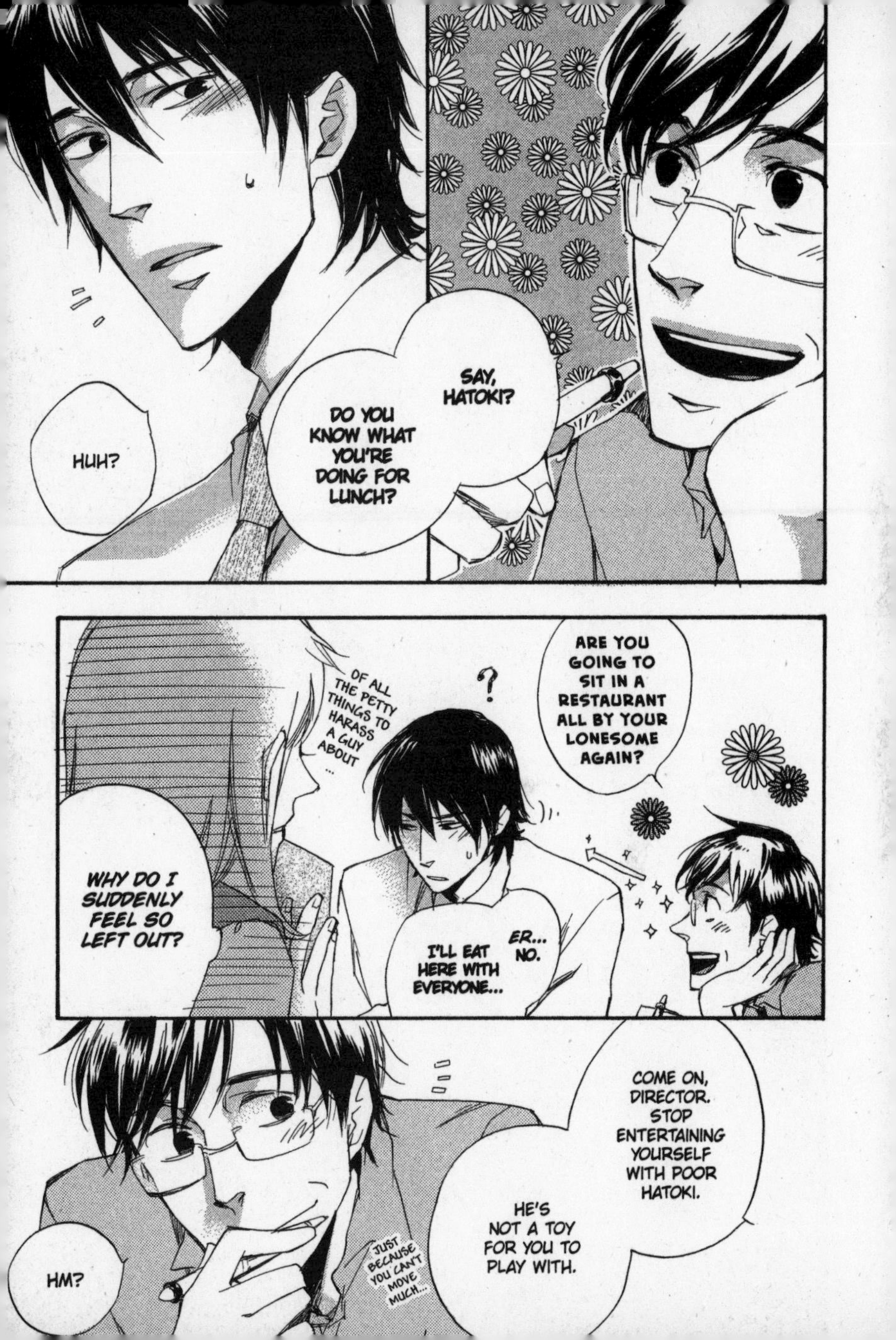
SAY, HATOKI?
DO YOU KNOW WHAT YOU'RE DOING FOR LUNCH?
HUH?
ARE YOU GOING TO SIT IN A RESTAURANT ALL BY YOUR LONESOME AGAIN?
ER... NO.
I'LL EAT HERE WITH EVERYONE...
OF ALL THE PETTY THINGS TO HARASS A GUY ABOUT ...
WHY DO I SUDDENLY FEEL SO LEFT OUT?
COME ON, DIRECTOR. STOP ENTERTAINING YOURSELF WITH POOR HATOKI.
HE'S NOT A TOY FOR YOU TO PLAY WITH.
JUST BECAUSE YOU CAN'T MOVE MUCH...
HM?

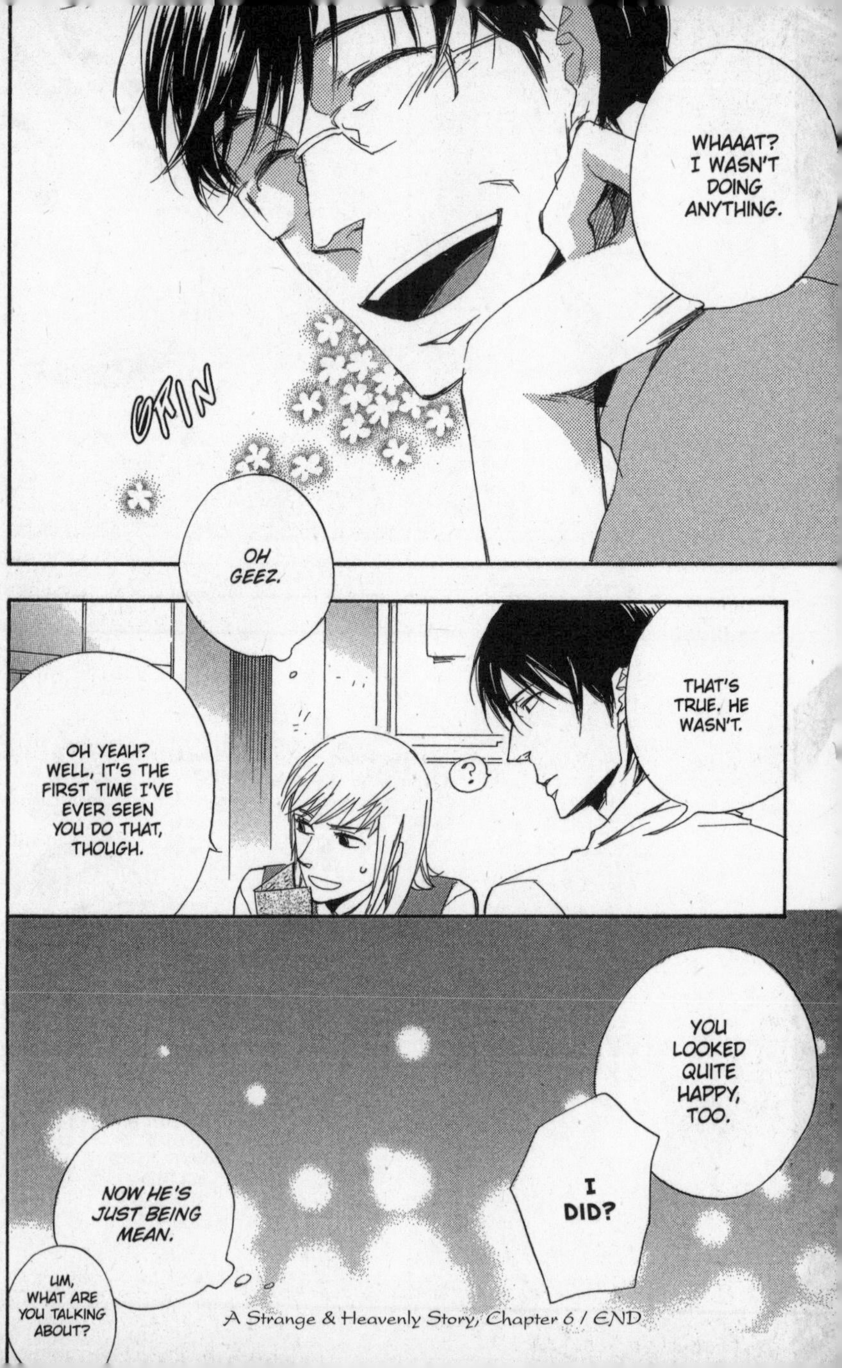
WHAAAT? I WASN'T DOING ANYTHING.
OH GEEZ.
THAT'S TRUE. HE WASN'T.
?
OH YEAH? WELL, IT'S THE FIRST TIME I'VE EVER SEEN YOU DO THAT, THOUGH.
YOU LOOKED QUITE HAPPY, TOO.
I DID?
NOW HE'S JUST BEING MEAN.
UM, WHAT ARE YOU TALKING ABOUT?
A Strange & Heavenly Story, Chapter 6 / END

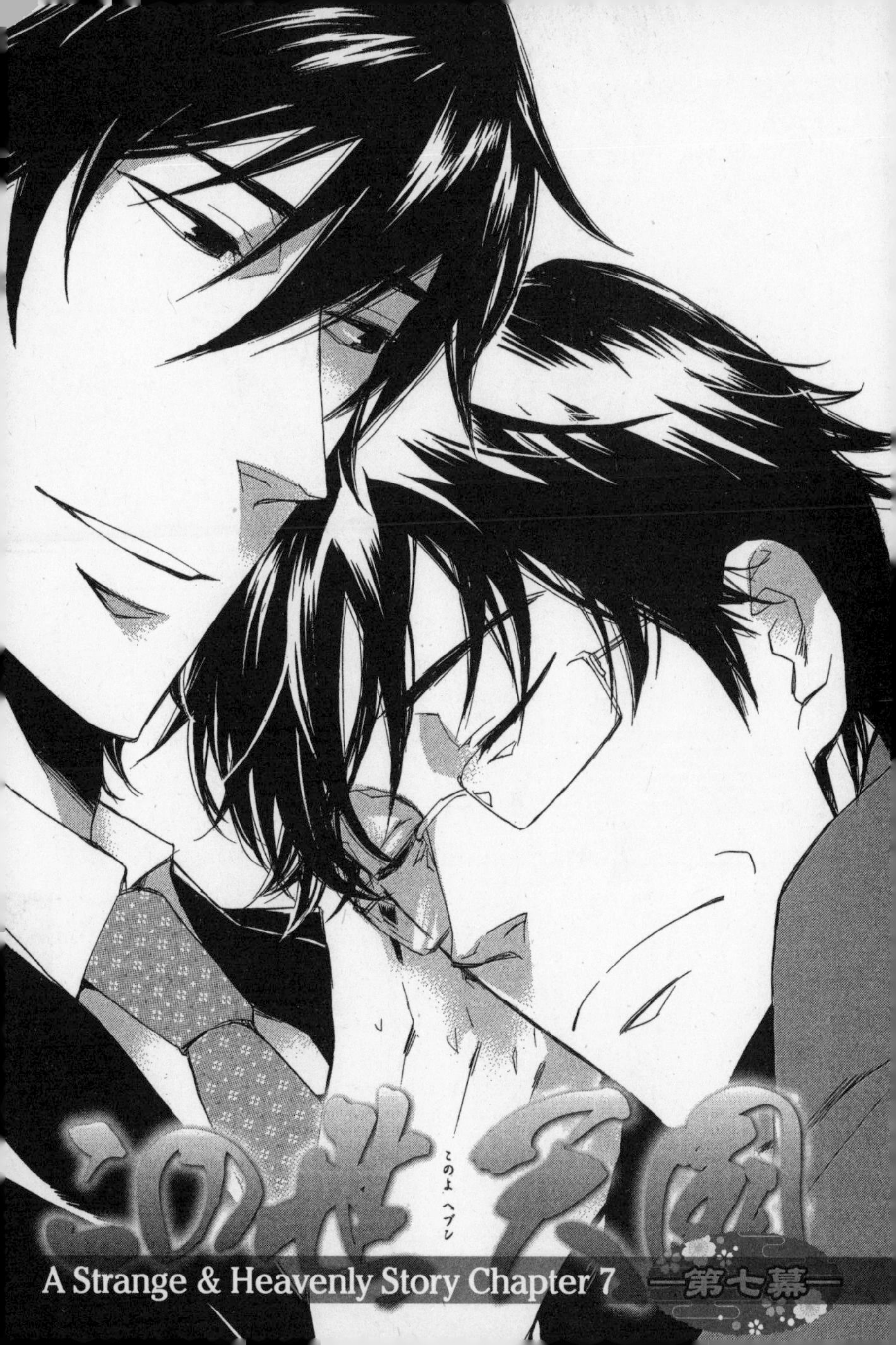

このよ
A Strange & Heavenly Story Chapter 7
—第七幕—

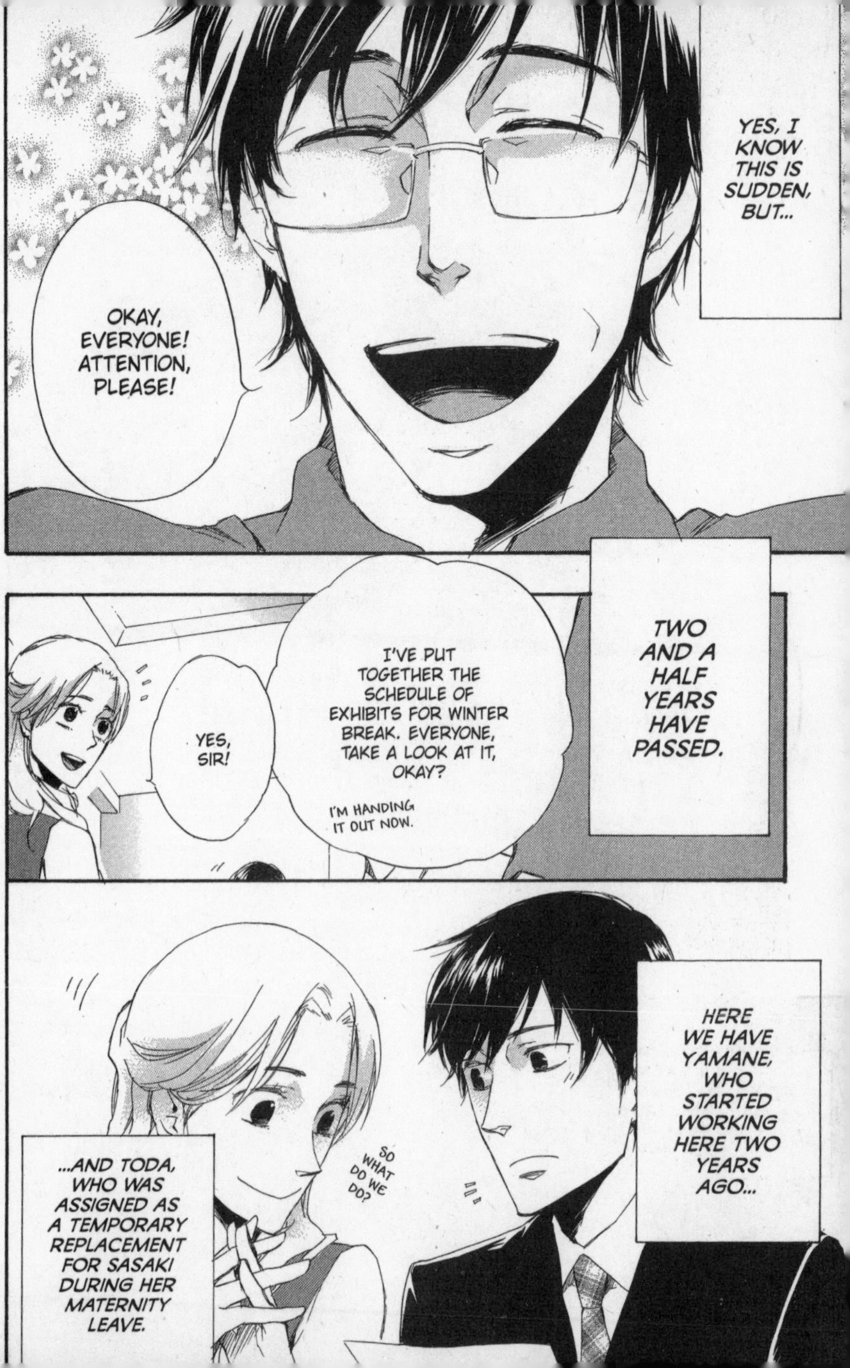
YES, I KNOW THIS IS SUDDEN, BUT...
OKAY, EVERYONE! ATTENTION, PLEASE!
TWO AND A HALF YEARS HAVE PASSED.
I'VE PUT TOGETHER THE SCHEDULE OF EXHIBITS FOR WINTER BREAK. EVERYONE, TAKE A LOOK AT IT, OKAY?
I'M HANDING IT OUT NOW.
YES, SIR!
HERE WE HAVE YAMANE, WHO STARTED WORKING HERE TWO YEARS AGO...
SO WHAT DO WE DO?
...AND TODA, WHO WAS ASSIGNED AS A TEMPORARY REPLACEMENT FOR SASAKI DURING HER MATERNITY LEAVE.

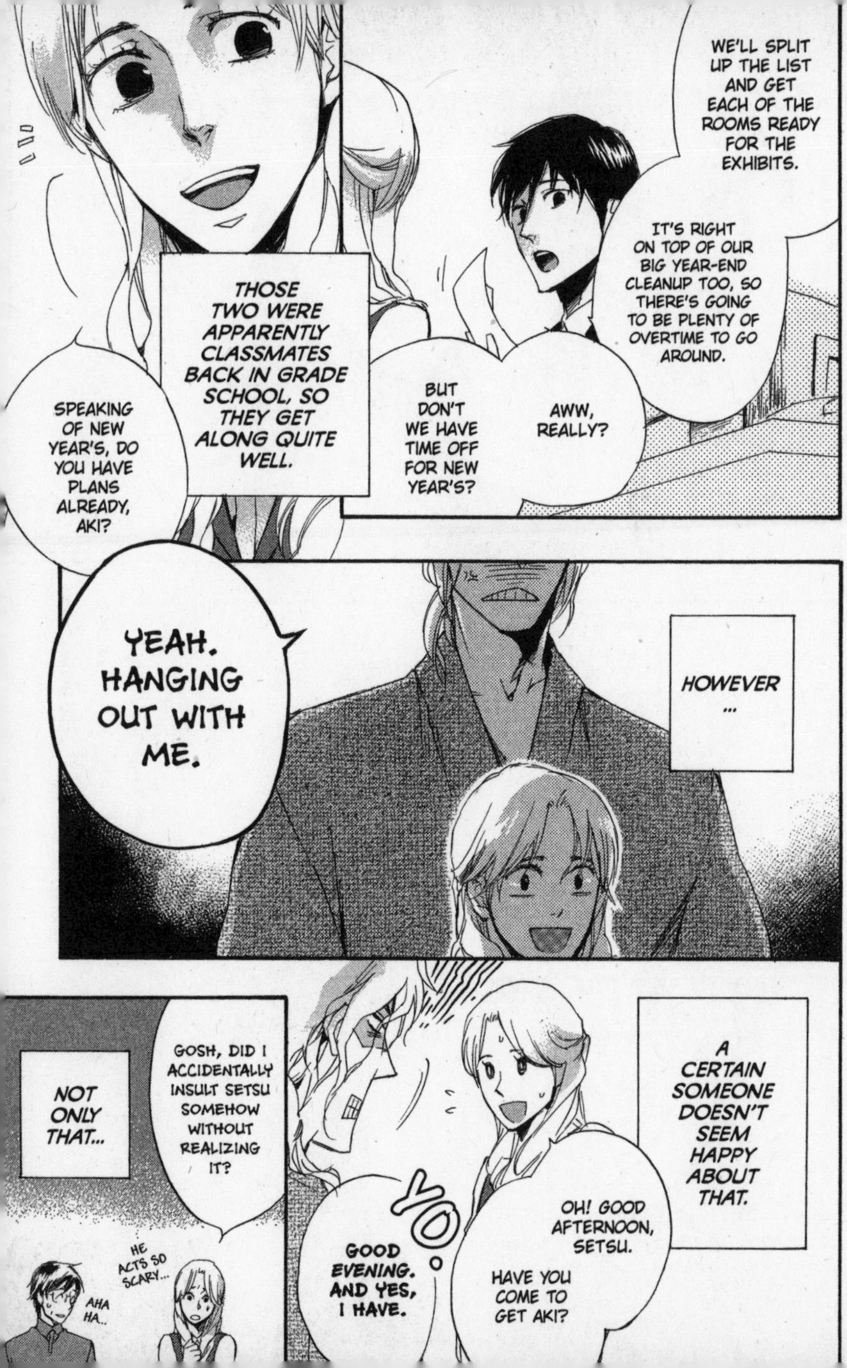
WE'LL SPLIT UP THE LIST AND GET EACH OF THE ROOMS READY FOR THE EXHIBITS.
IT'S RIGHT ON TOP OF OUR BIG YEAR-END CLEANUP TOO, SO THERE'S GOING TO BE PLENTY OF OVERTIME TO GO AROUND.
AWW, REALLY?
BUT DON'T WE HAVE TIME OFF FOR NEW YEAR'S?
THOSE TWO WERE APPARENTLY CLASSMATES BACK IN GRADE SCHOOL, SO THEY GET ALONG QUITE WELL.
SPEAKING OF NEW YEAR'S, DO YOU HAVE PLANS ALREADY, AKI?
HOWEVER...
YEAH. HANGING OUT WITH ME.
A CERTAIN SOMEONE DOESN'T SEEM HAPPY ABOUT THAT.
OH! GOOD AFTERNOON, SETSU.
HAVE YOU COME TO GET AKI?
YO.
GOOD EVENING. AND YES, I HAVE.
GOSH, DID I ACCIDENTALLY INSULT SETSU SOMEHOW WITHOUT REALIZING IT?
NOT ONLY THAT...
HE ACTS SO SCARY...
AHA HA...

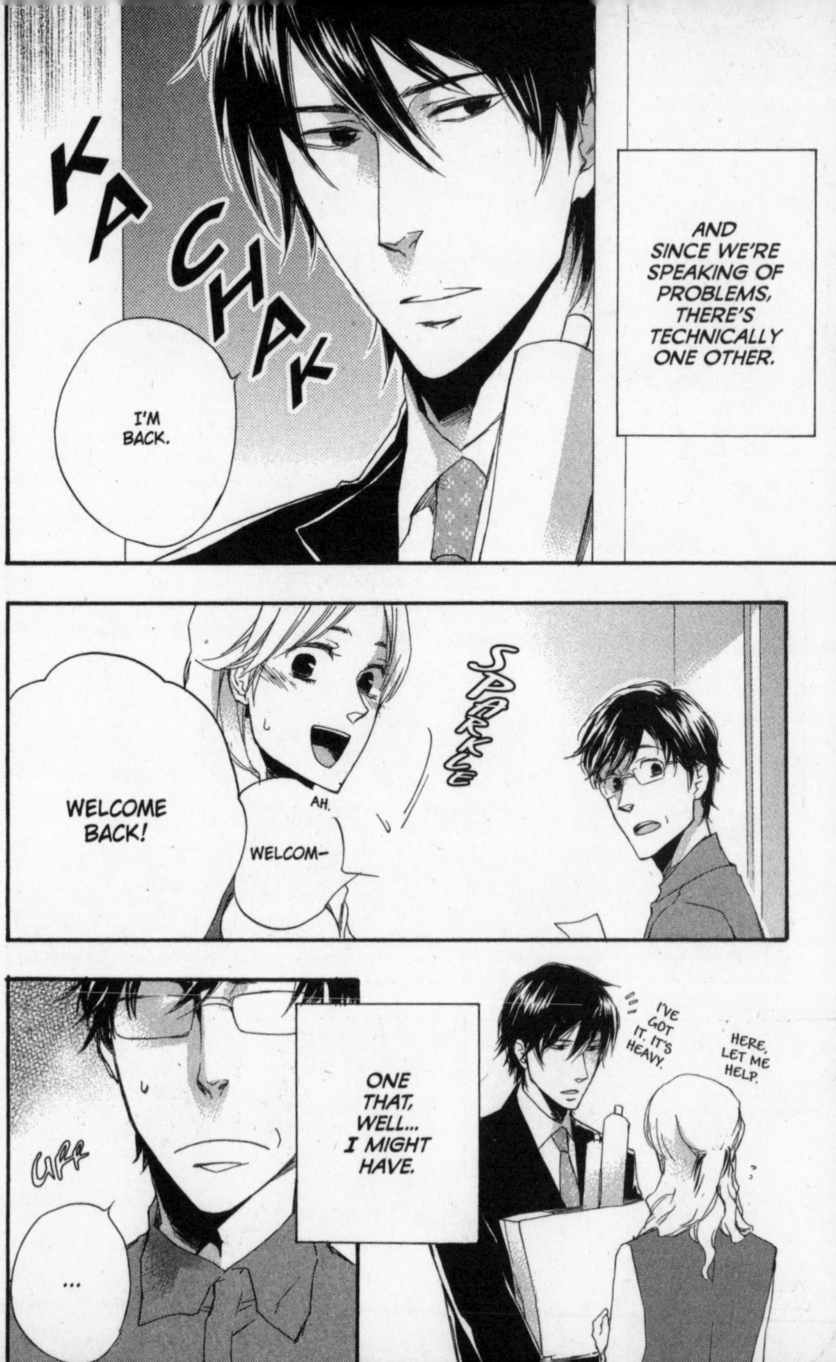
AND SINCE WE'RE SPEAKING OF PROBLEMS, THERE'S TECHNICALLY ONE OTHER.
KA CHAK
I'M BACK.
SPARKLE
AH.
WELCOM-
WELCOME BACK!
HERE, LET ME HELP.
I'VE GOT IT. IT'S HEAVY.
ONE THAT, WELL... I MIGHT HAVE.
UFF
...

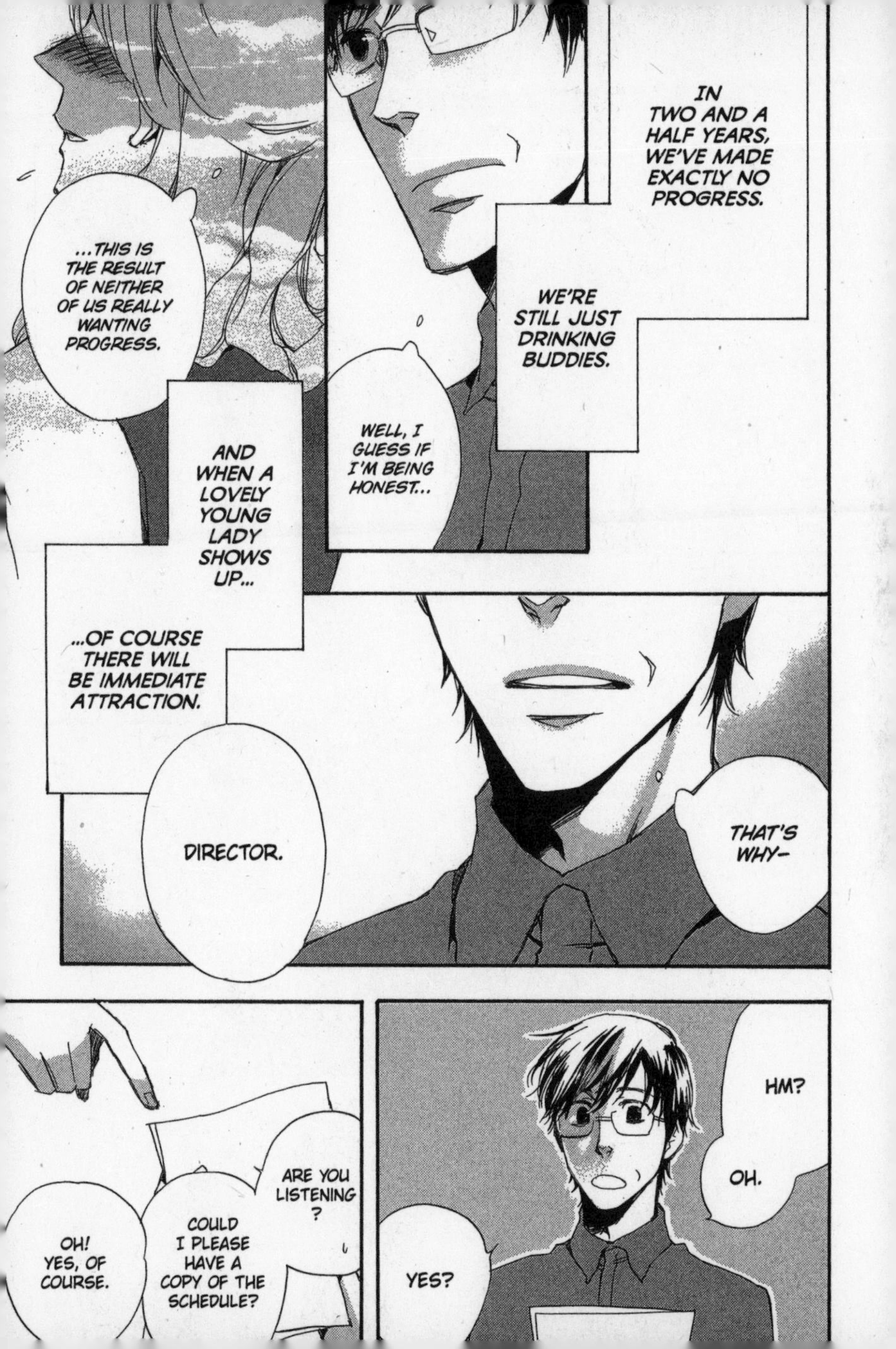
IN TWO AND A HALF YEARS, WE'VE MADE EXACTLY NO PROGRESS.
WE'RE STILL JUST DRINKING BUDDIES.
WELL, I GUESS IF I'M BEING HONEST...
...THIS IS THE RESULT OF NEITHER OF US REALLY WANTING PROGRESS.
AND WHEN A LOVELY YOUNG LADY SHOWS UP...
...OF COURSE THERE WILL BE IMMEDIATE ATTRACTION.
THAT'S WHY-
DIRECTOR.
HM?
OH.
YES?
ARE YOU LISTENING?
COULD I PLEASE HAVE A COPY OF THE SCHEDULE?
OH! YES, OF COURSE.

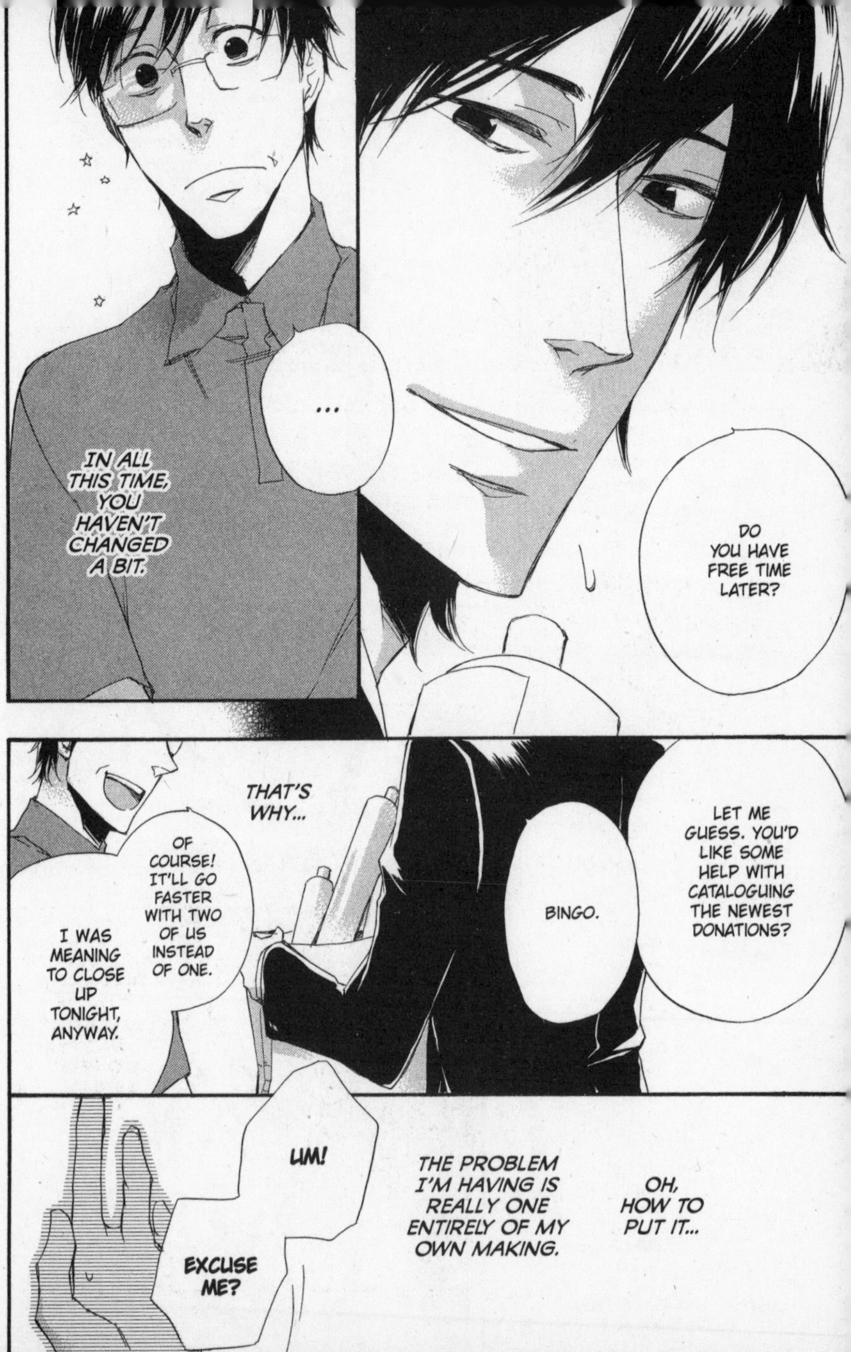
DO YOU HAVE FREE TIME LATER?
...
IN ALL THIS TIME, YOU HAVEN'T CHANGED A BIT.
LET ME GUESS. YOU'D LIKE SOME HELP WITH CATALOGUING THE NEWEST DONATIONS?
BINGO.
THAT'S WHY...
OF COURSE! IT'LL GO FASTER WITH TWO OF US INSTEAD OF ONE.
I WAS MEANING TO CLOSE UP TONIGHT, ANYWAY.
OH, HOW TO PUT IT...
THE PROBLEM I'M HAVING IS REALLY ONE ENTIRELY OF MY OWN MAKING.
UM!
EXCUSE ME?

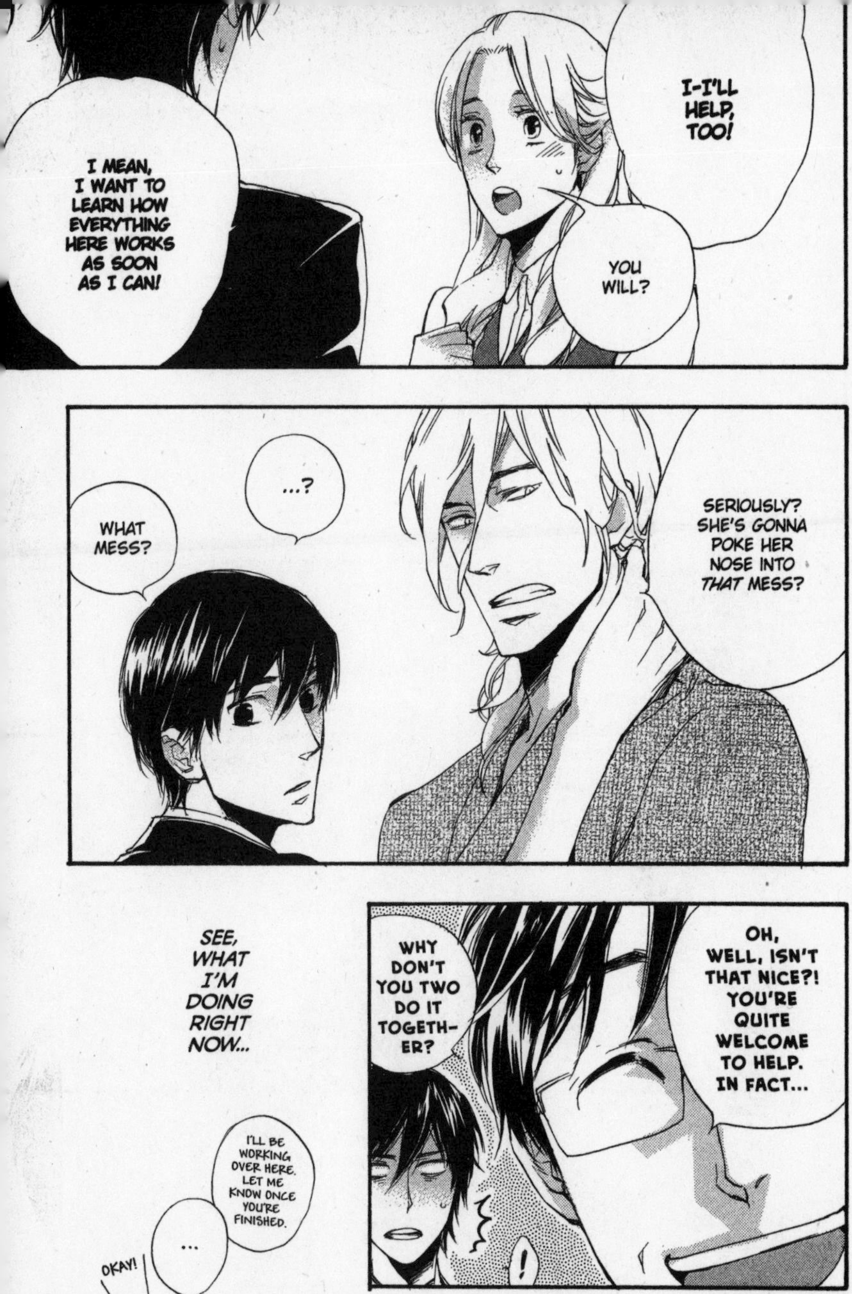
I-I'LL HELP, TOO!
YOU WILL?
I MEAN, I WANT TO LEARN HOW EVERYTHING HERE WORKS AS SOON AS I CAN!
SERIOUSLY? SHE'S GONNA POKE HER NOSE INTO *THAT* MESS?
...?
WHAT MESS?
OH, WELL, ISN'T THAT NICE?! YOU'RE QUITE WELCOME TO HELP. IN FACT...
WHY DON'T YOU TWO DO IT TOGETH-ER?
!
SEE, WHAT I'M DOING RIGHT NOW...
I'LL BE WORKING OVER HERE. LET ME KNOW ONCE YOU'RE FINISHED.
...
OKAY!

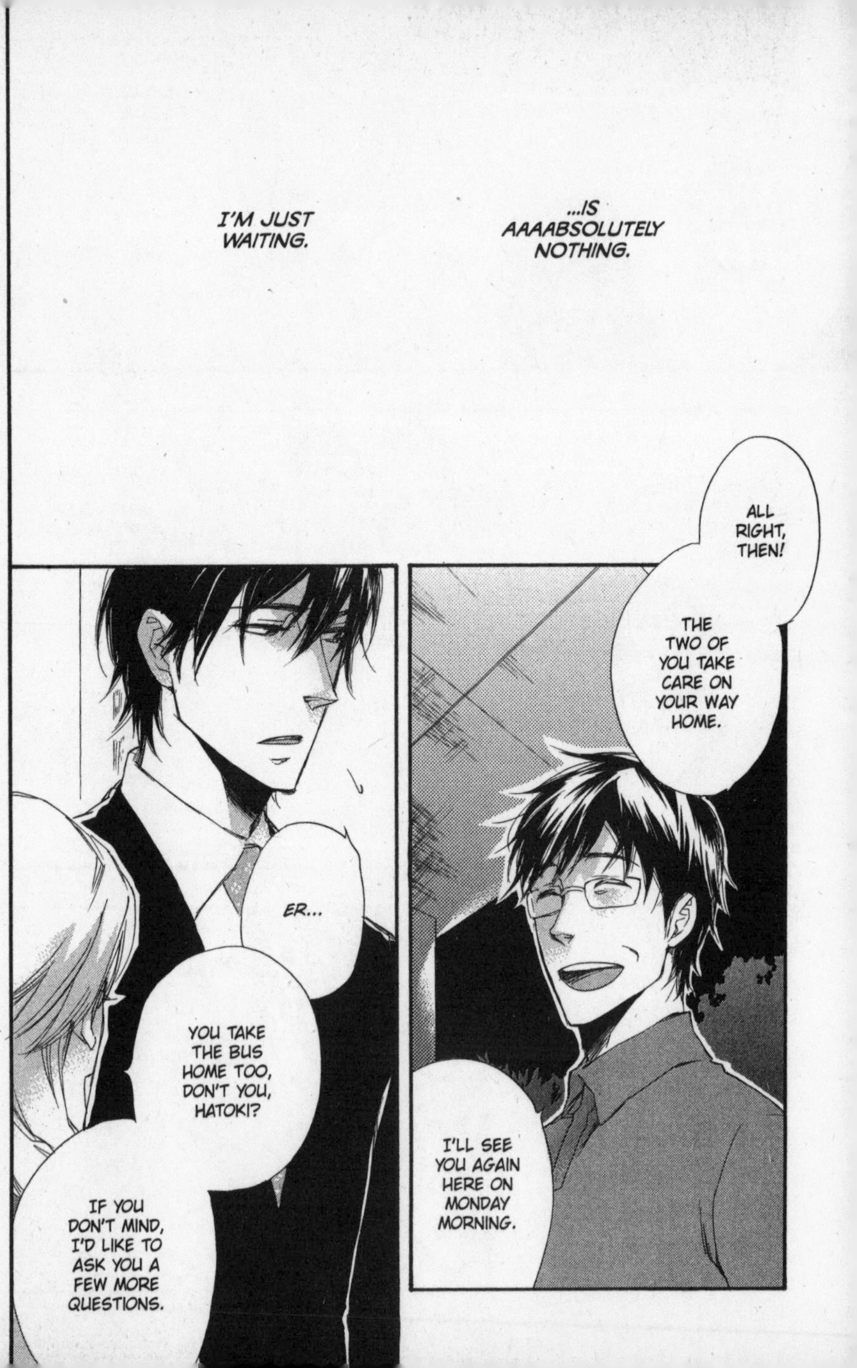
...IS AAAABSOLUTELY NOTHING.
I'M JUST WAITING.
ALL RIGHT, THEN!
THE TWO OF YOU TAKE CARE ON YOUR WAY HOME.
I'LL SEE YOU AGAIN HERE ON MONDAY MORNING.
ER...
YOU TAKE THE BUS HOME TOO, DON'T YOU, HATOKI?
IF YOU DON'T MIND, I'D LIKE TO ASK YOU A FEW MORE QUESTIONS.

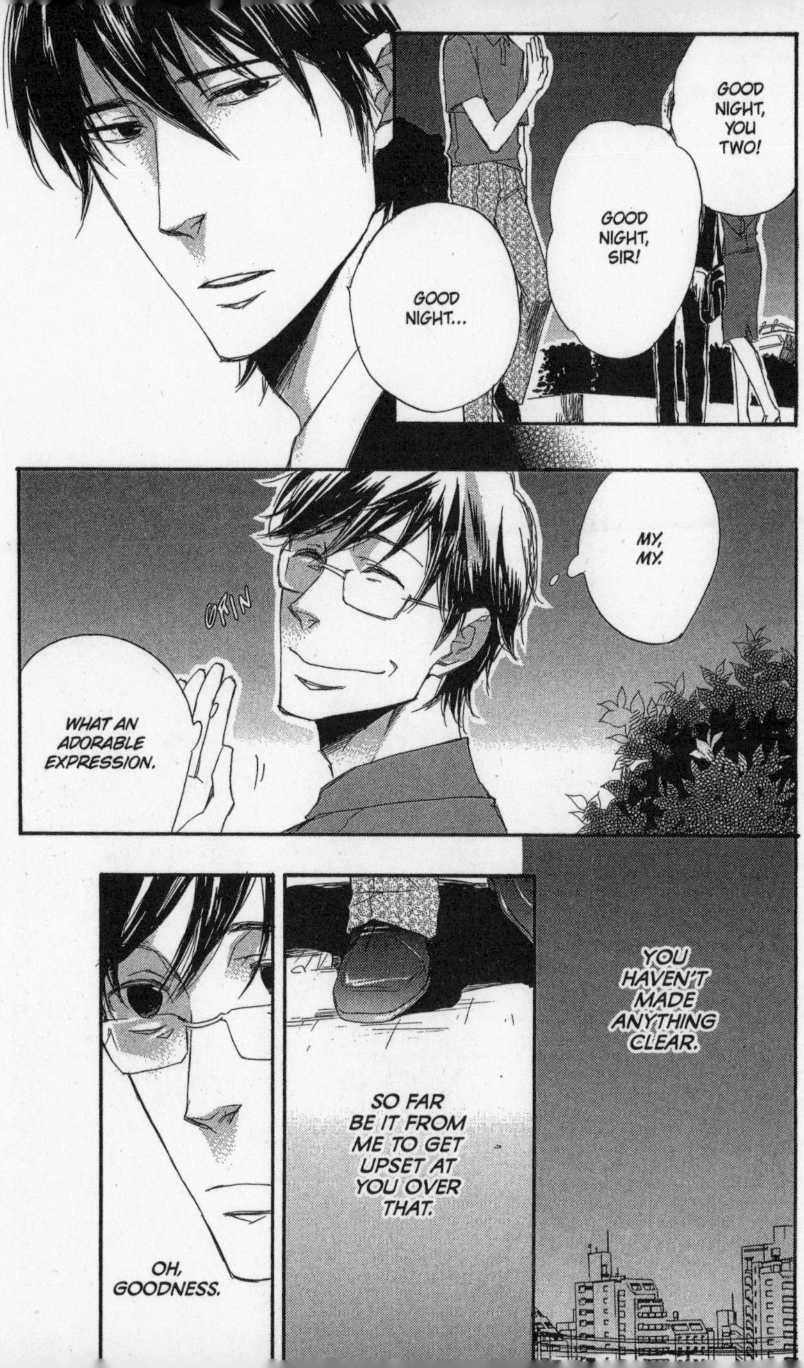
GOOD NIGHT, YOU TWO!
GOOD NIGHT, SIR!
GOOD NIGHT...
MY, MY.
GRIN
WHAT AN ADORABLE EXPRESSION.
YOU HAVEN'T MADE ANYTHING CLEAR.
SO FAR BE IT FROM ME TO GET UPSET AT YOU OVER THAT.
OH, GOODNESS.

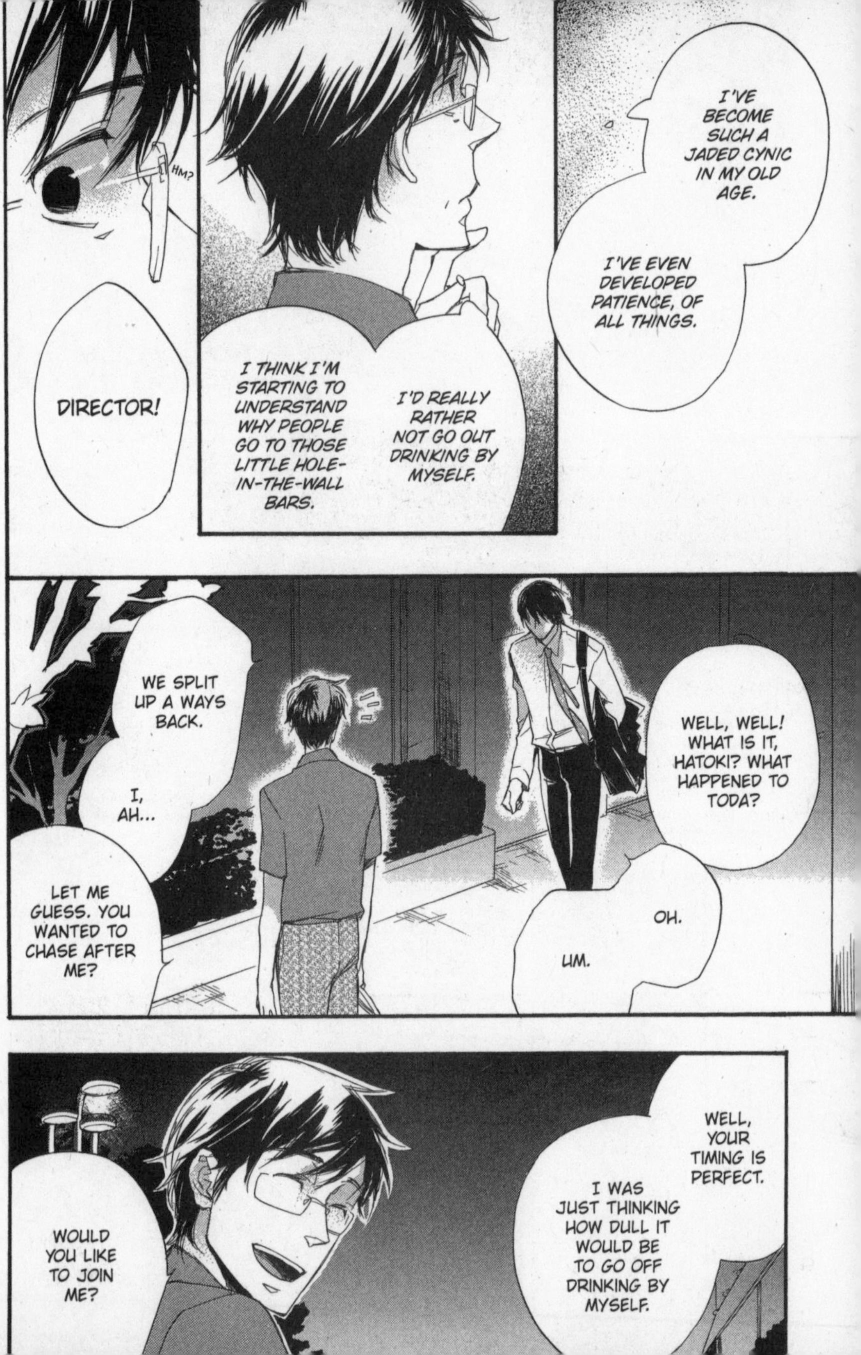
I'VE BECOME SUCH A JADED CYNIC IN MY OLD AGE.
I'VE EVEN DEVELOPED PATIENCE, OF ALL THINGS.
I'D REALLY RATHER NOT GO OUT DRINKING BY MYSELF.
I THINK I'M STARTING TO UNDERSTAND WHY PEOPLE GO TO THOSE LITTLE HOLE-IN-THE-WALL BARS.
HM?
DIRECTOR!
WELL, WELL! WHAT IS IT, HATOKI? WHAT HAPPENED TO TODA?
OH.
UM.
WE SPLIT UP A WAYS BACK.
I, AH...
LET ME GUESS. YOU WANTED TO CHASE AFTER ME?
WELL, YOUR TIMING IS PERFECT.
I WAS JUST THINKING HOW DULL IT WOULD BE TO GO OFF DRINKING BY MYSELF.
WOULD YOU LIKE TO JOIN ME?

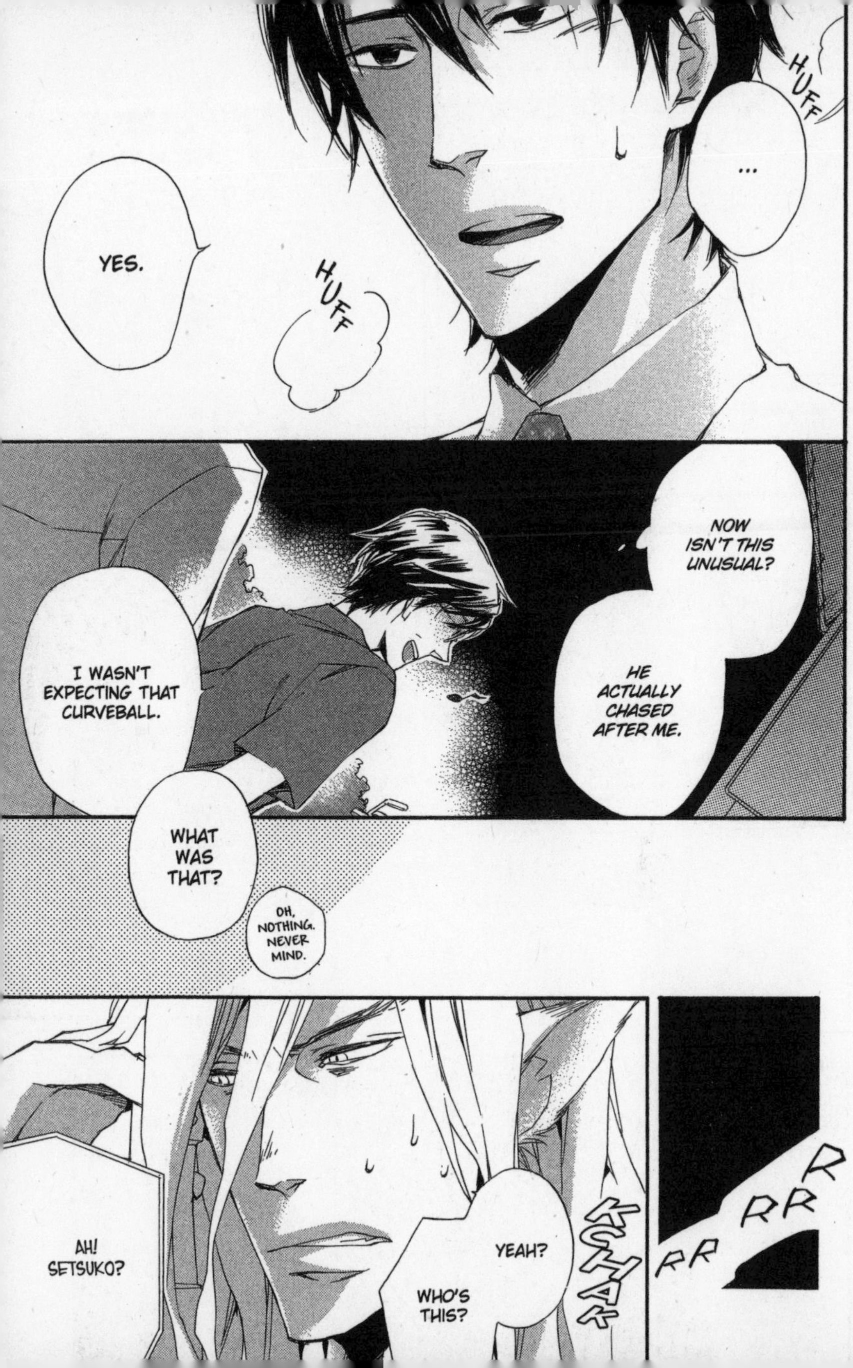
HUFF
...
HUFF
YES.
NOW ISN'T THIS UNUSUAL?
HE ACTUALLY CHASED AFTER ME.
I WASN'T EXPECTING THAT CURVEBALL.
WHAT WAS THAT?
OH, NOTHING. NEVER MIND.
RRRRR
KCHAK
YEAH?
WHO'S THIS?
AH! SETSUKO?

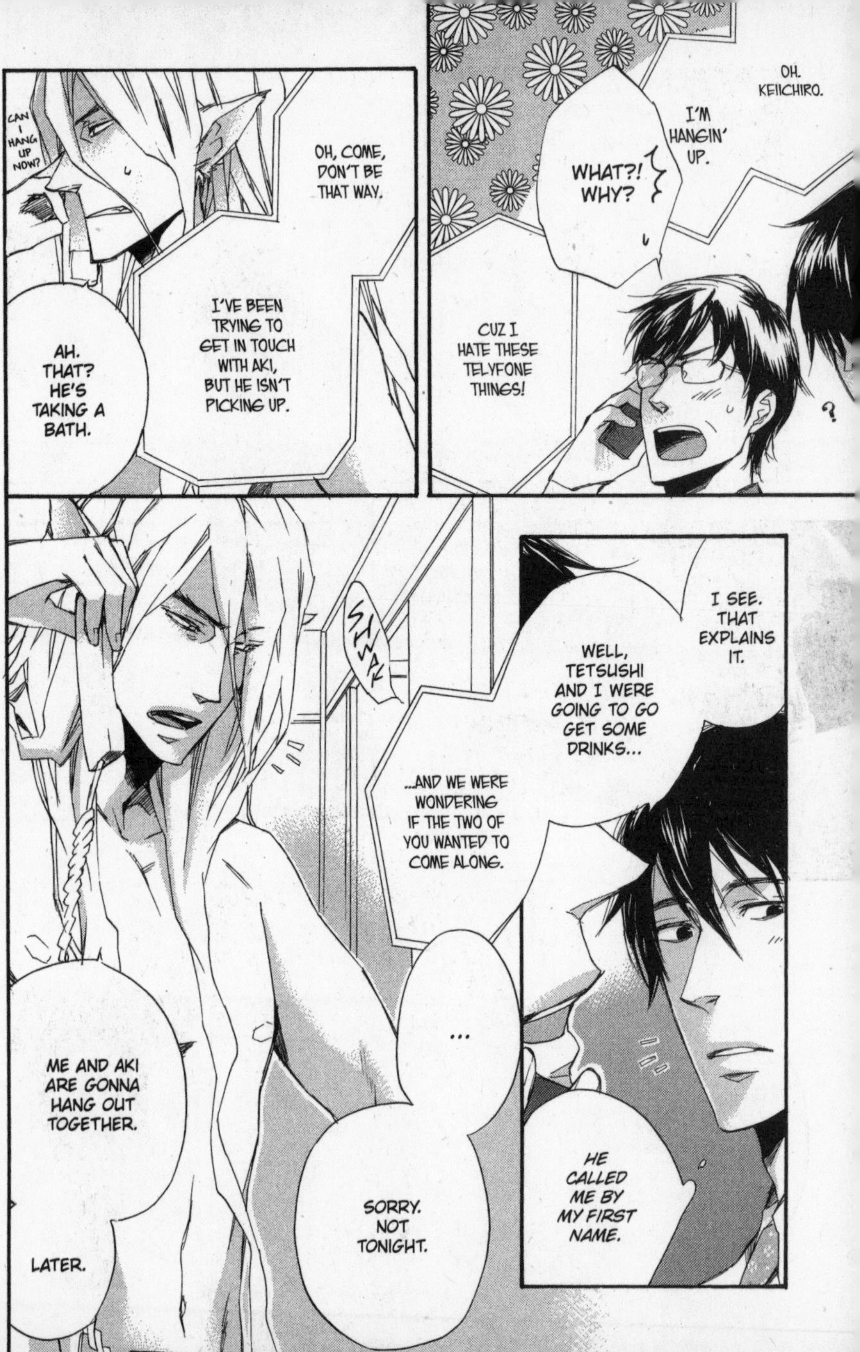
OH. KEIICHIRO.
I'M HANGIN' UP.
WHAT?! WHY?
CUZ I HATE THESE TELYFONE THINGS!
OH, COME, DON'T BE THAT WAY.
CAN I HANG UP NOW?
I'VE BEEN TRYING TO GET IN TOUCH WITH AKI, BUT HE ISN'T PICKING UP.
AH. THAT? HE'S TAKING A BATH.
I SEE. THAT EXPLAINS IT.
WELL, TETSUSHI AND I WERE GOING TO GO GET SOME DRINKS...
...AND WE WERE WONDERING IF THE TWO OF YOU WANTED TO COME ALONG.
HE CALLED ME BY MY FIRST NAME.
SHWAK
...
SORRY. NOT TONIGHT.
ME AND AKI ARE GONNA HANG OUT TOGETHER.
LATER.

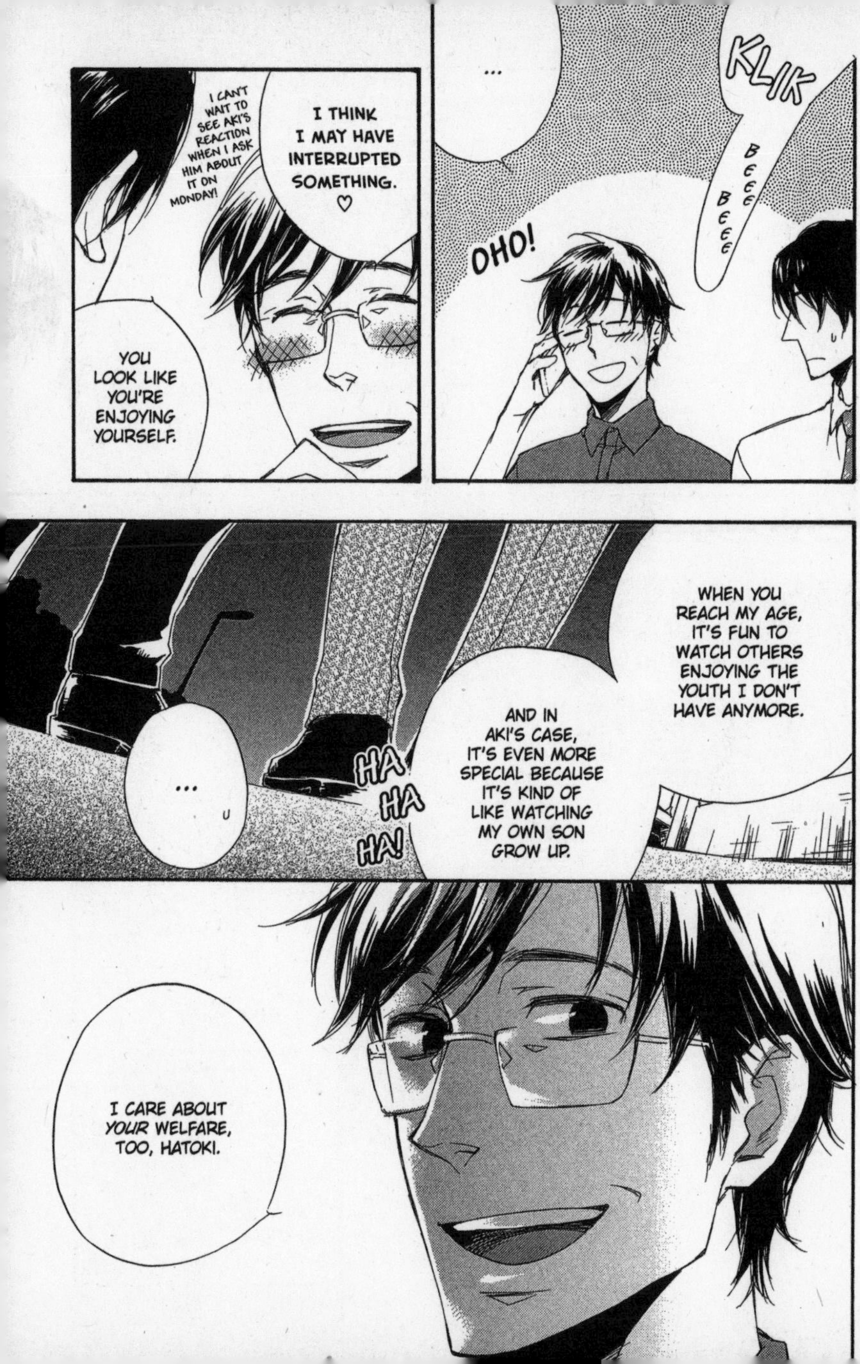
KLIK
BEEE BEEE
...
OHO!
I THINK I MAY HAVE INTERRUPTED SOMETHING. ♡
I CAN'T WAIT TO SEE AKI'S REACTION WHEN I ASK HIM ABOUT IT ON MONDAY!
YOU LOOK LIKE YOU'RE ENJOYING YOURSELF.
WHEN YOU REACH MY AGE, IT'S FUN TO WATCH OTHERS ENJOYING THE YOUTH I DON'T HAVE ANYMORE.
AND IN AKI'S CASE, IT'S EVEN MORE SPECIAL BECAUSE IT'S KIND OF LIKE WATCHING MY OWN SON GROW UP.
HA HA HA!
...
I CARE ABOUT *YOUR* WELFARE, TOO, HATOKI.

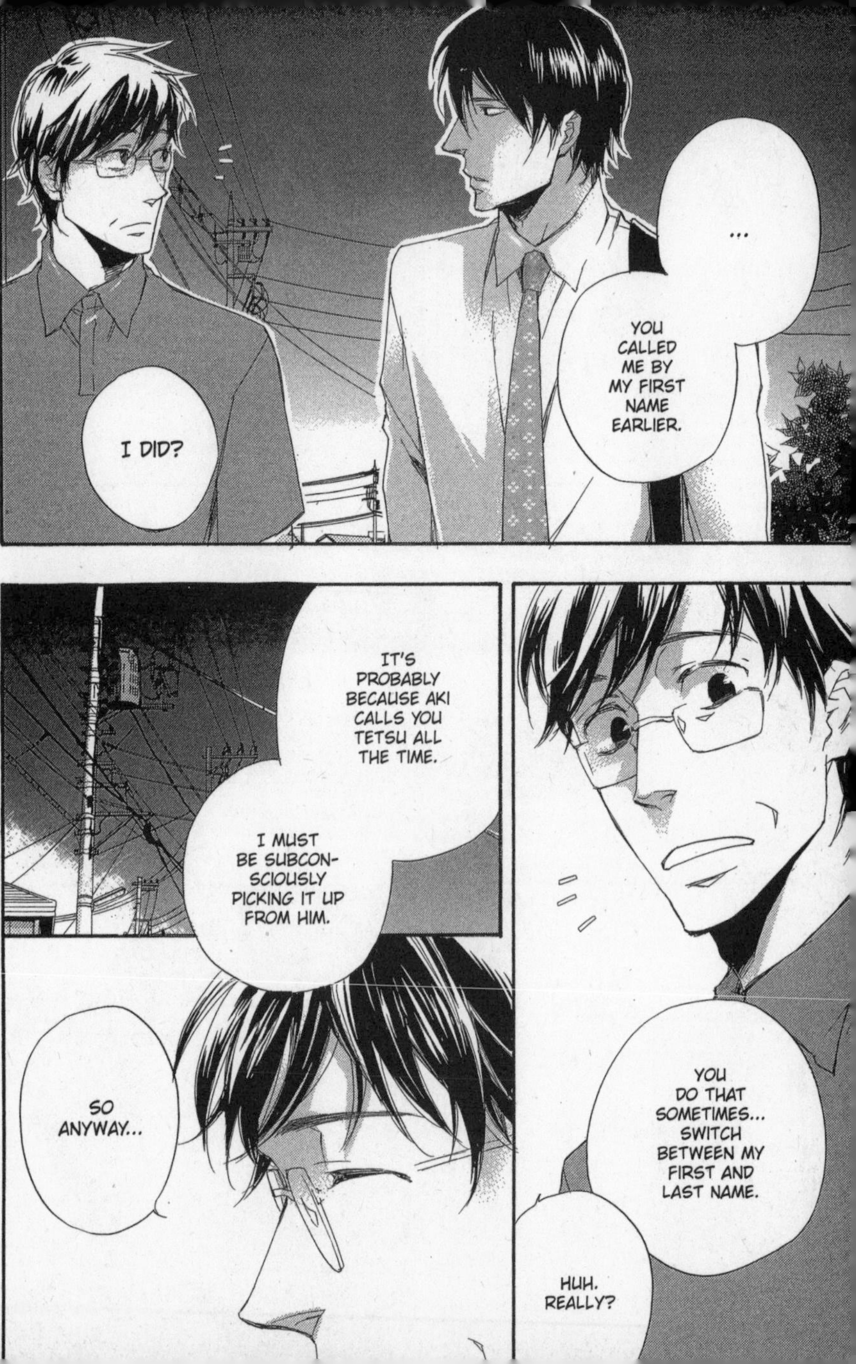
...
YOU CALLED ME BY MY FIRST NAME EARLIER.
I DID?
IT'S PROBABLY BECAUSE AKI CALLS YOU TETSU ALL THE TIME.
I MUST BE SUBCONSCIOUSLY PICKING IT UP FROM HIM.
YOU DO THAT SOMETIMES... SWITCH BETWEEN MY FIRST AND LAST NAME.
HUH. REALLY?
SO ANYWAY...

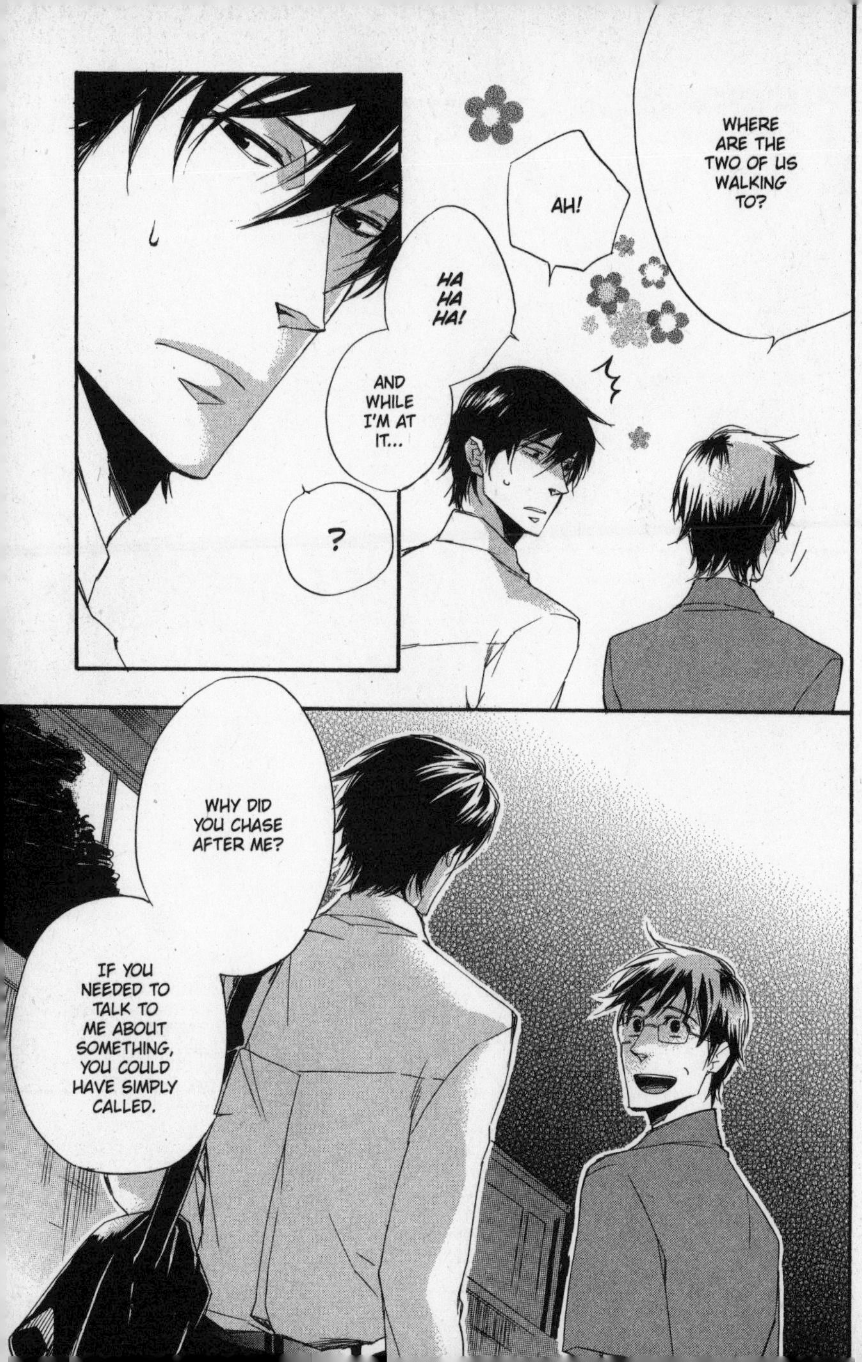
WHERE ARE THE TWO OF US WALKING TO?
AH!
HA HA HA!
AND WHILE I'M AT IT...
?
WHY DID YOU CHASE AFTER ME?
IF YOU NEEDED TO TALK TO ME ABOUT SOMETHING, YOU COULD HAVE SIMPLY CALLED.

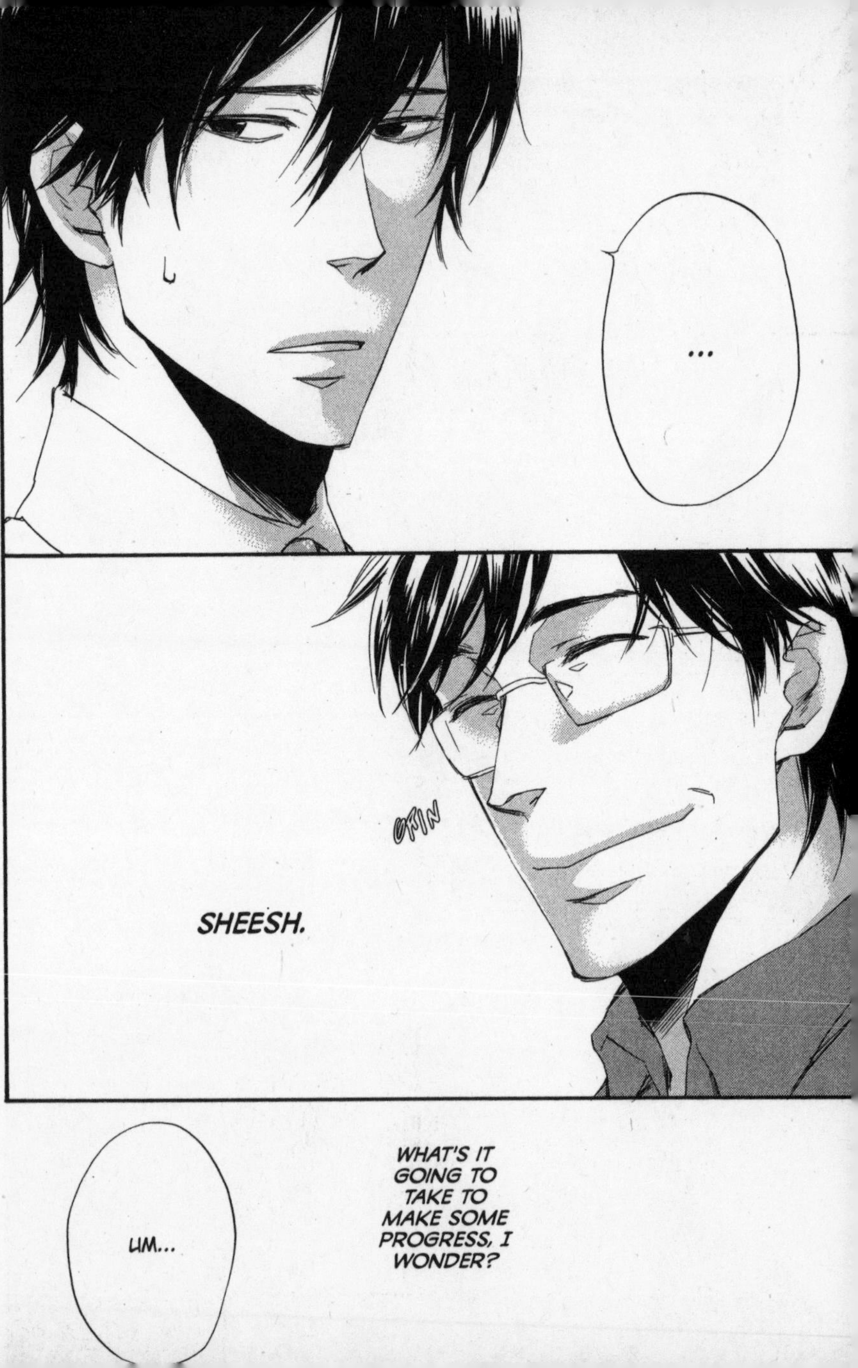
...
GRIN
SHEESH.
WHAT'S IT GOING TO TAKE TO MAKE SOME PROGRESS, I WONDER?
UM...

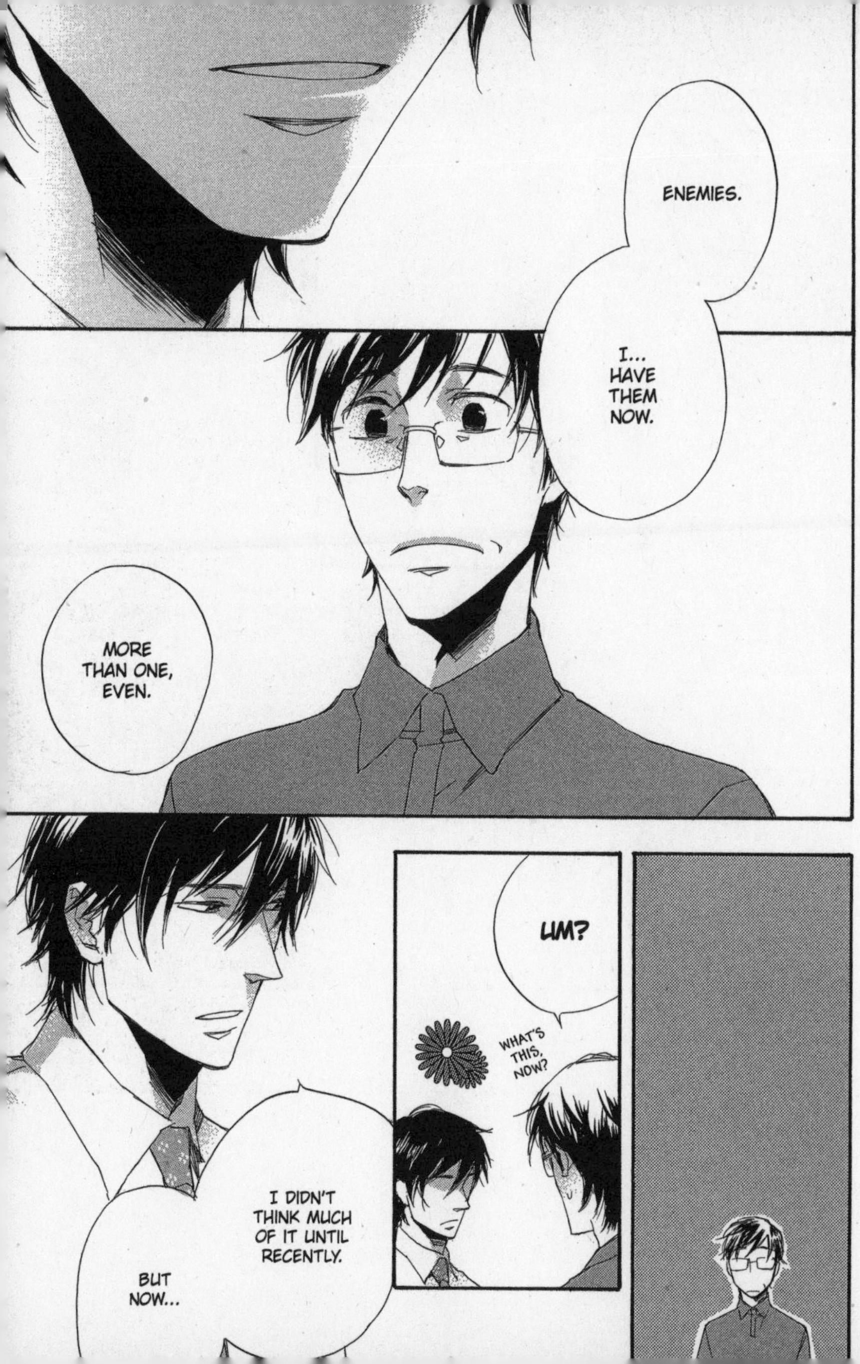
ENEMIES.
I... HAVE THEM NOW.
MORE THAN ONE, EVEN.
UM?
WHAT'S THIS, NOW?
I DIDN'T THINK MUCH OF IT UNTIL RECENTLY.
BUT NOW...

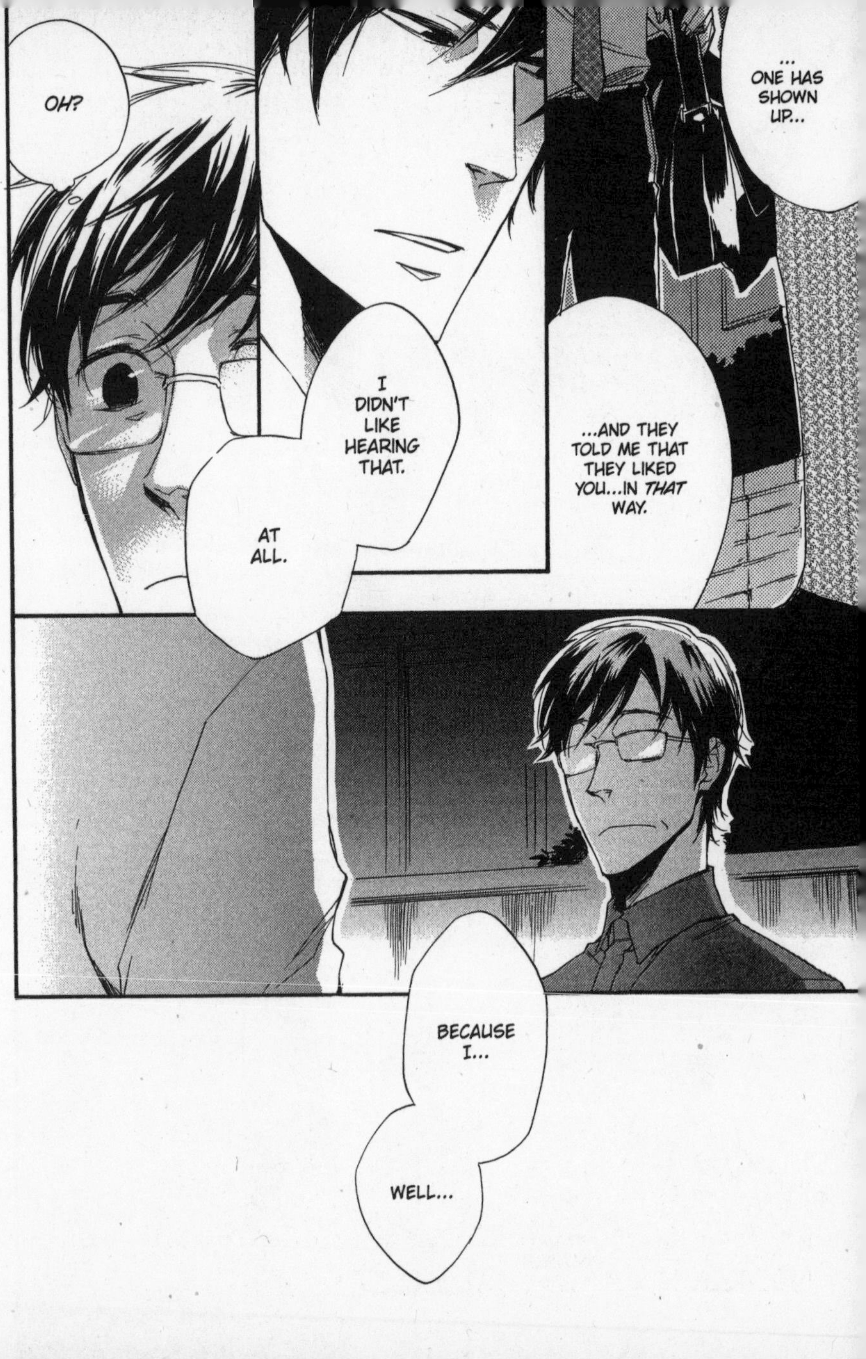
...ONE HAS SHOWN UP...
...AND THEY TOLD ME THAT THEY LIKED YOU...IN *THAT* WAY.
I DIDN'T LIKE HEARING THAT.
AT ALL.
OH?
BECAUSE I...
WELL...

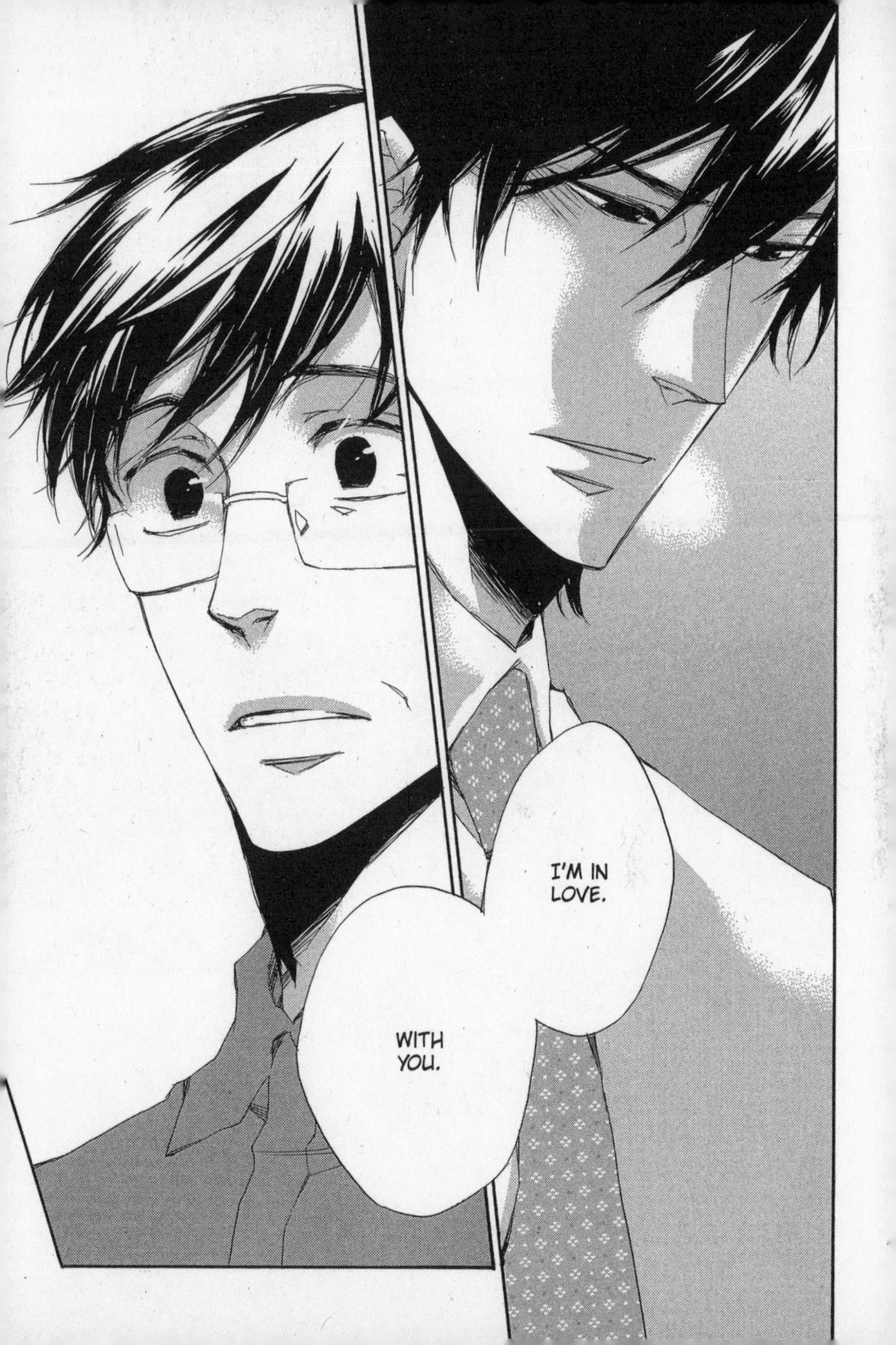
I'M IN LOVE.
WITH YOU.

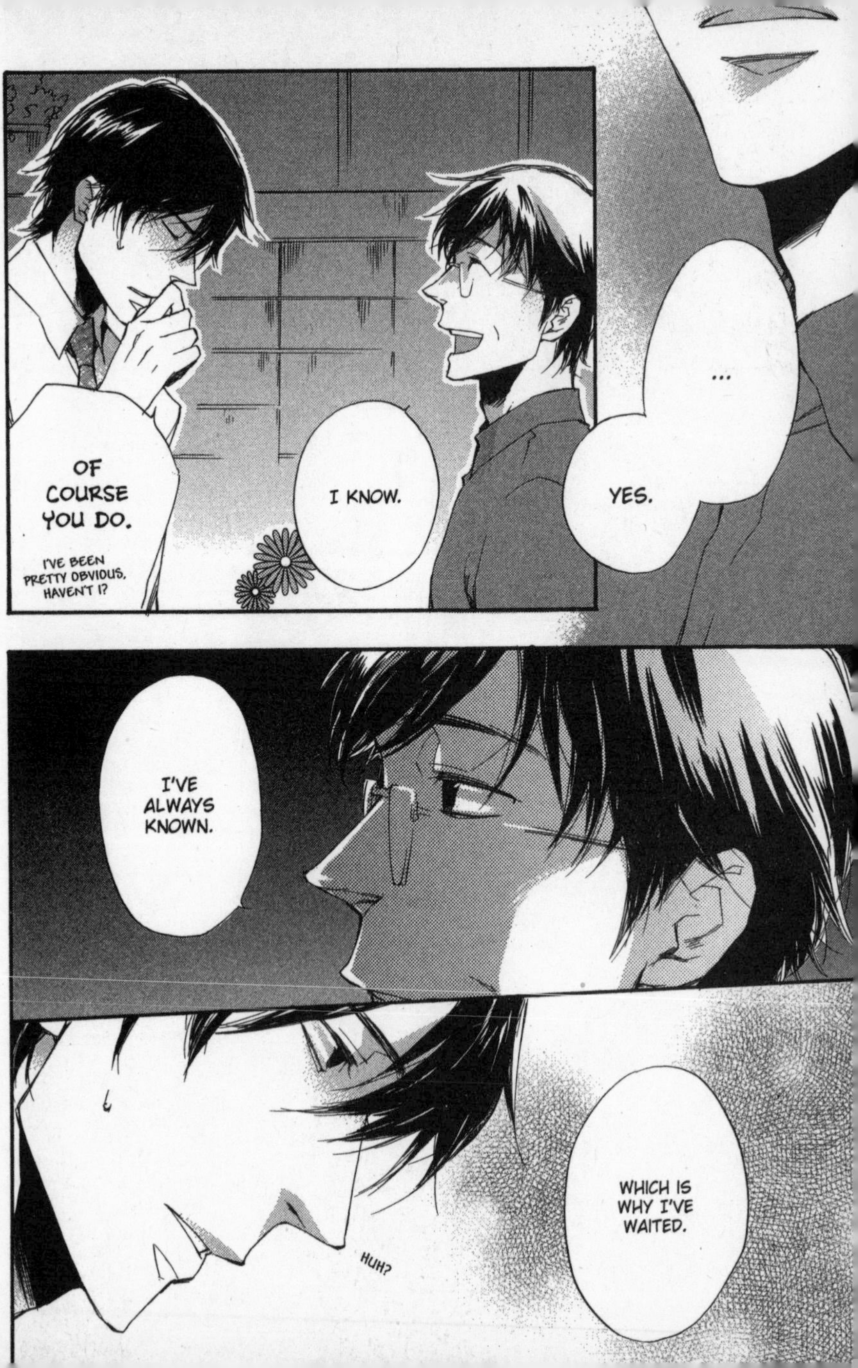
...
YES.
I KNOW.
OF COURSE YOU DO.
I'VE BEEN PRETTY OBVIOUS, HAVEN'T I?
I'VE ALWAYS KNOWN.
WHICH IS WHY I'VE WAITED.
HUH?

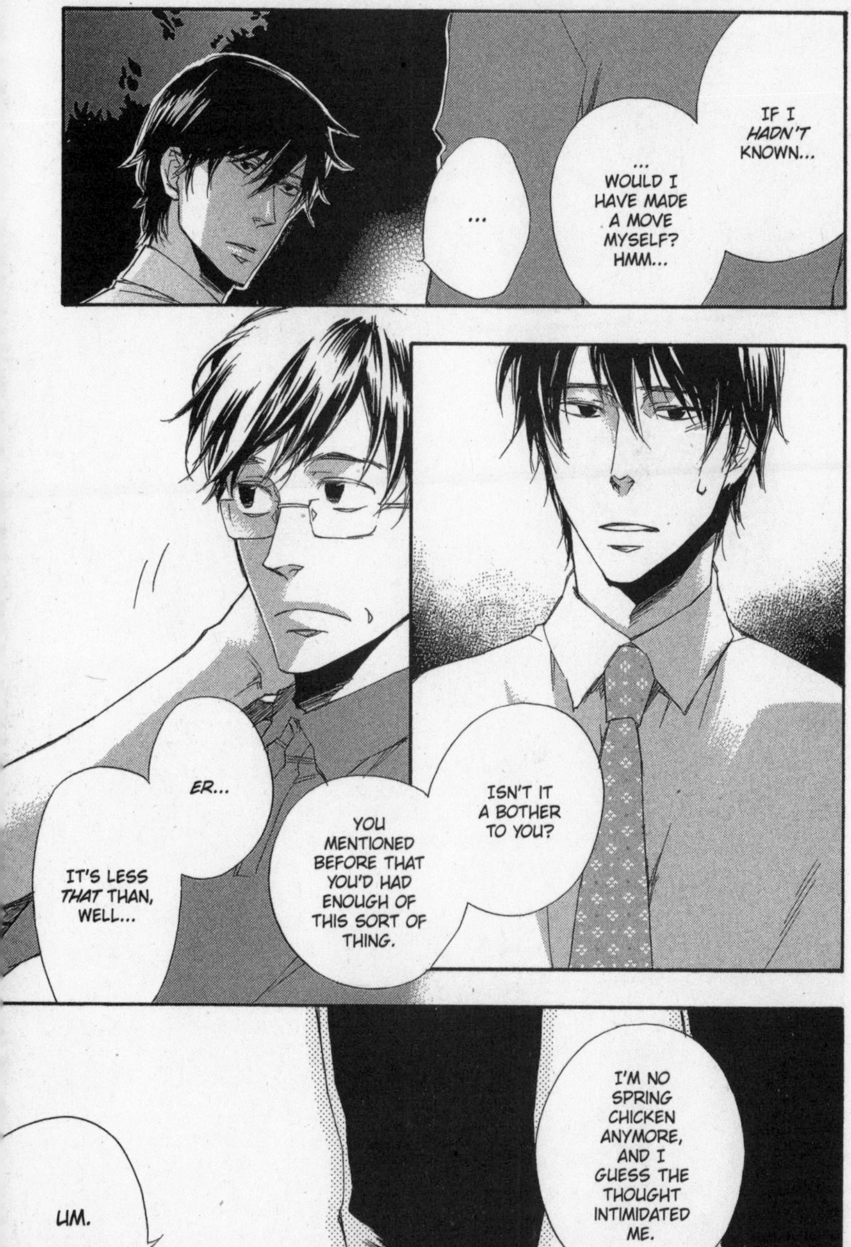
IF I *HADN'T* KNOWN...
... WOULD I HAVE MADE A MOVE MYSELF? HMM...
...
ISN'T IT A BOTHER TO YOU?
YOU MENTIONED BEFORE THAT YOU'D HAD ENOUGH OF THIS SORT OF THING.
ER...
IT'S LESS *THAT* THAN, WELL...
I'M NO SPRING CHICKEN ANYMORE, AND I GUESS THE THOUGHT INTIMIDATED ME.
UM.

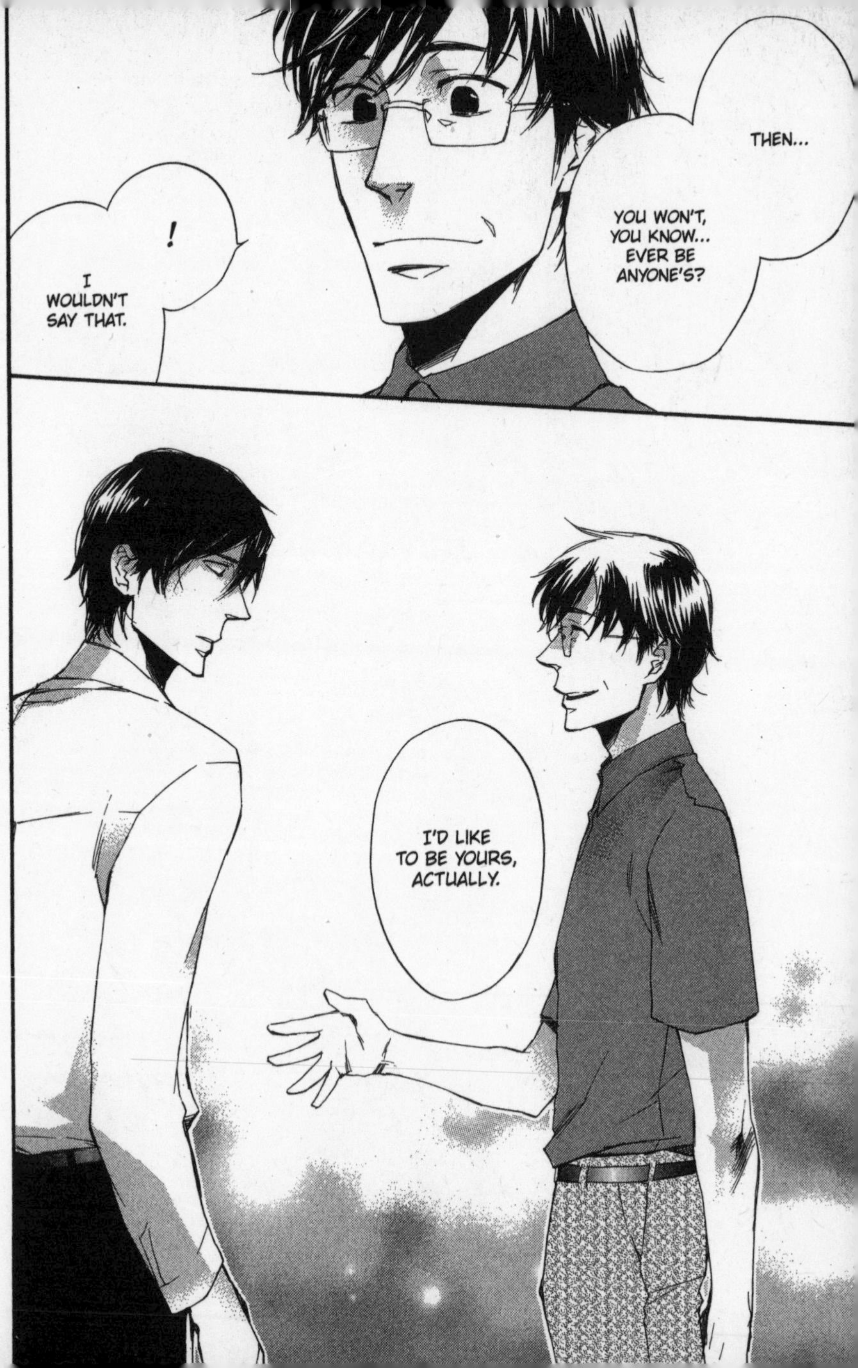
THEN...
YOU WON'T, YOU KNOW... EVER BE ANYONE'S?
!
I WOULDN'T SAY THAT.
I'D LIKE TO BE YOURS, ACTUALLY.

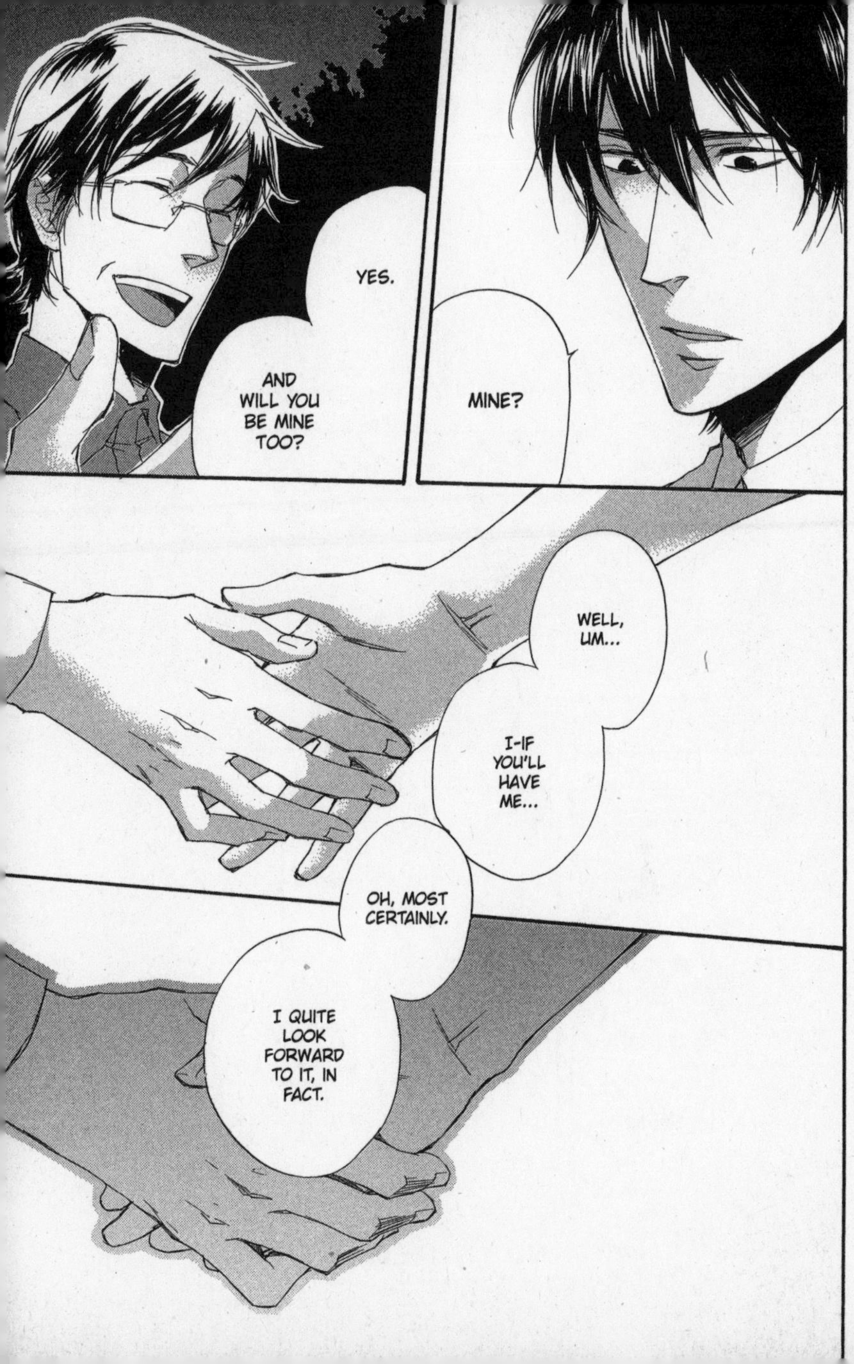
MINE?
YES.
AND WILL YOU BE MINE TOO?
WELL, UM...
I-IF YOU'LL HAVE ME...
OH, MOST CERTAINLY.
I QUITE LOOK FORWARD TO IT, IN FACT.

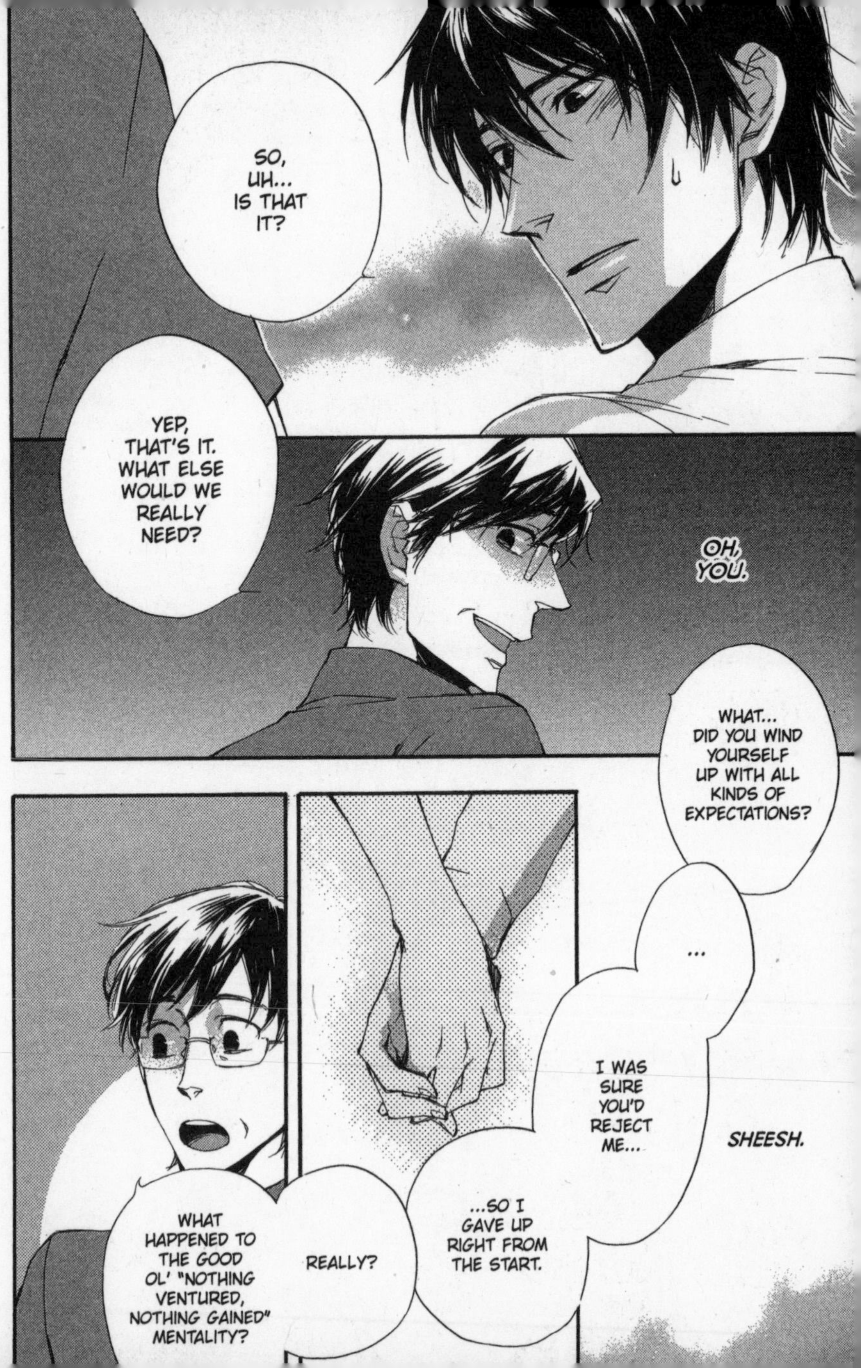
SO, UH... IS THAT IT?
YEP, THAT'S IT. WHAT ELSE WOULD WE REALLY NEED?
OH, YOU.
WHAT... DID YOU WIND YOURSELF UP WITH ALL KINDS OF EXPECTATIONS?
...
SHEESH.
I WAS SURE YOU'D REJECT ME...
...SO I GAVE UP RIGHT FROM THE START.
REALLY?
WHAT HAPPENED TO THE GOOD OL' "NOTHING VENTURED, NOTHING GAINED" MENTALITY?

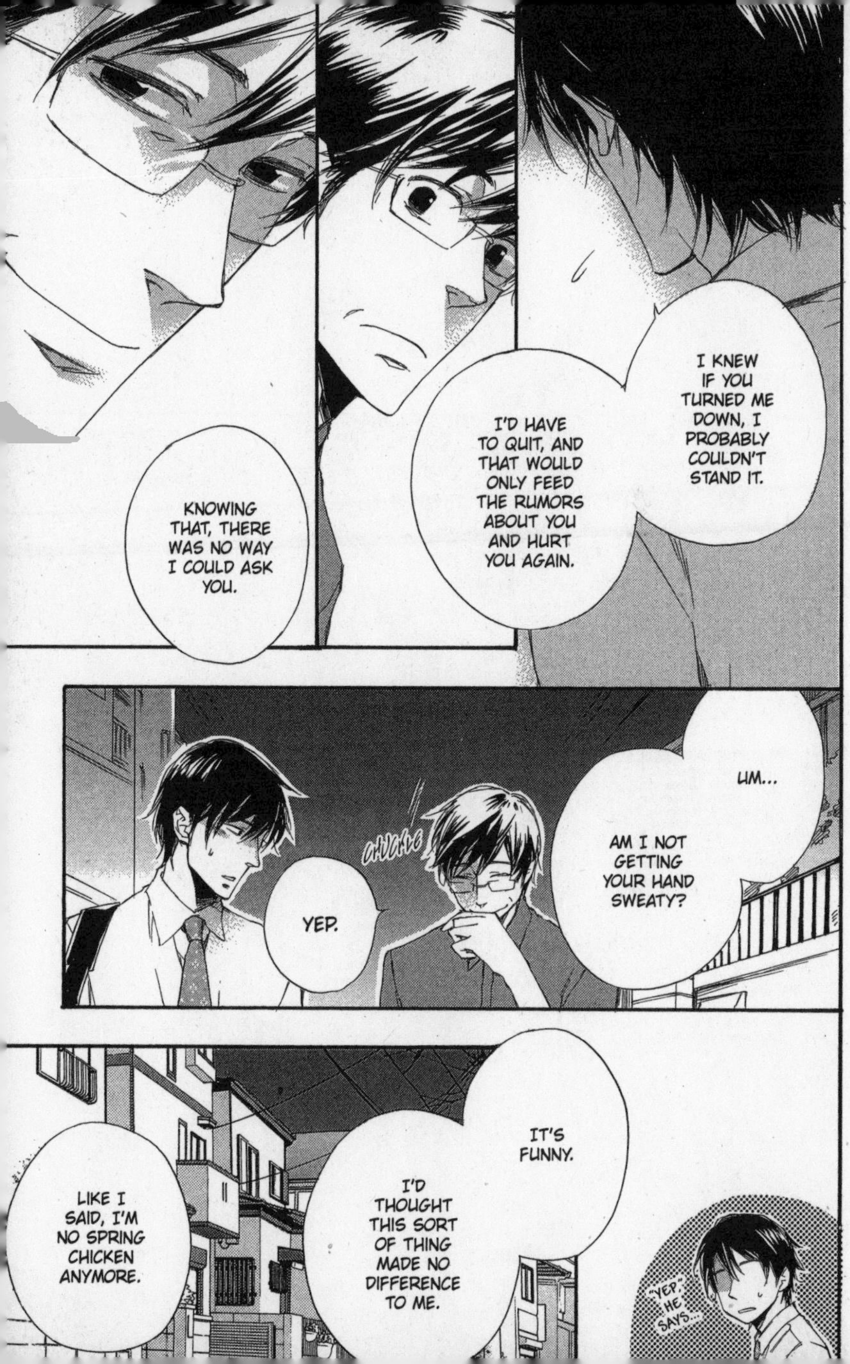
I KNEW IF YOU TURNED ME DOWN, I PROBABLY COULDN'T STAND IT.
I'D HAVE TO QUIT, AND THAT WOULD ONLY FEED THE RUMORS ABOUT YOU AND HURT YOU AGAIN.
KNOWING THAT, THERE WAS NO WAY I COULD ASK YOU.
UM...
AM I NOT GETTING YOUR HAND SWEATY?
YEP.
"YEP," HE SAYS...
IT'S FUNNY.
I'D THOUGHT THIS SORT OF THING MADE NO DIFFERENCE TO ME.
LIKE I SAID, I'M NO SPRING CHICKEN ANYMORE.

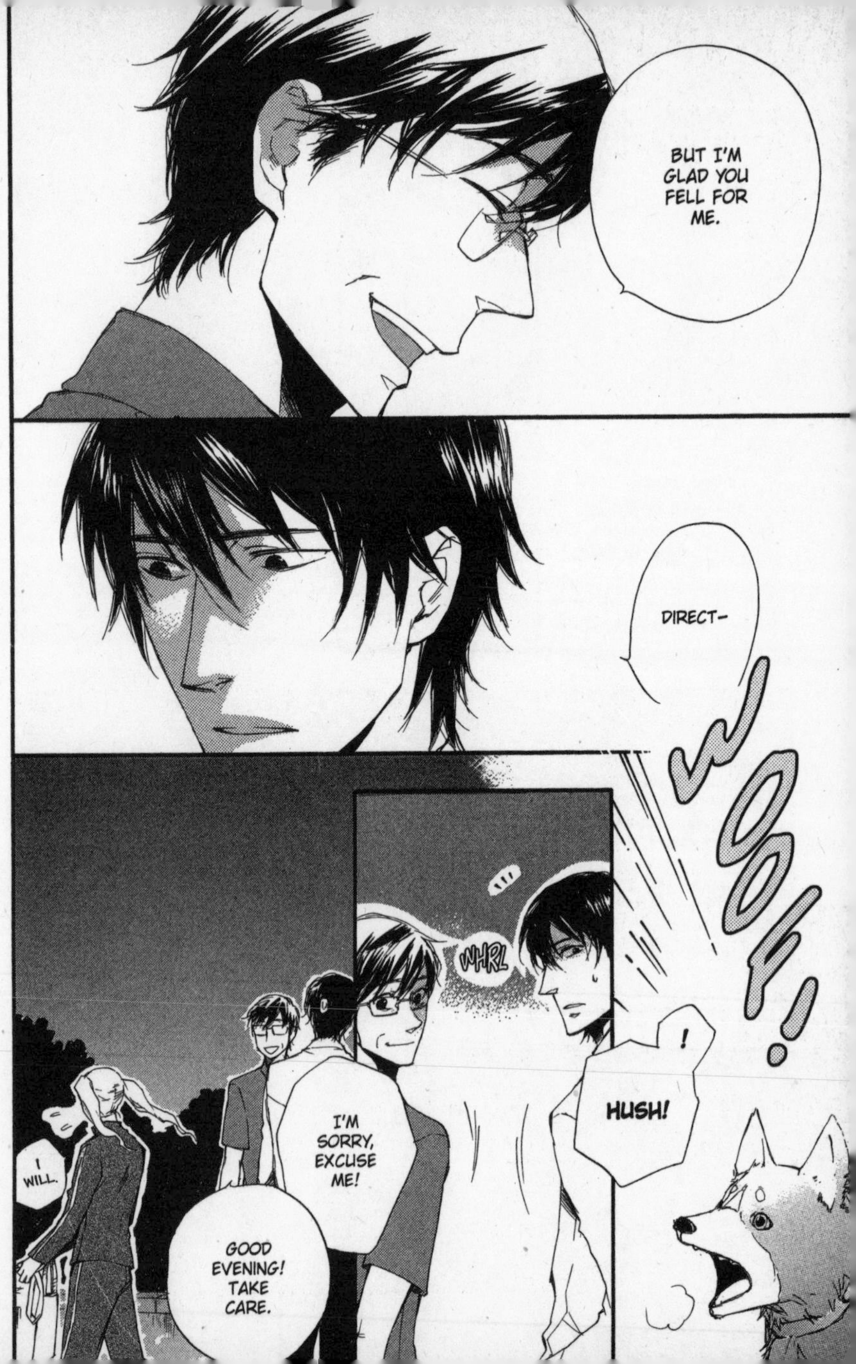
BUT I'M GLAD YOU FELL FOR ME.
DIRECT-
WOOF!!
WHRL
!
HUSH!
I'M SORRY, EXCUSE ME!
GOOD EVENING! TAKE CARE.
I WILL.

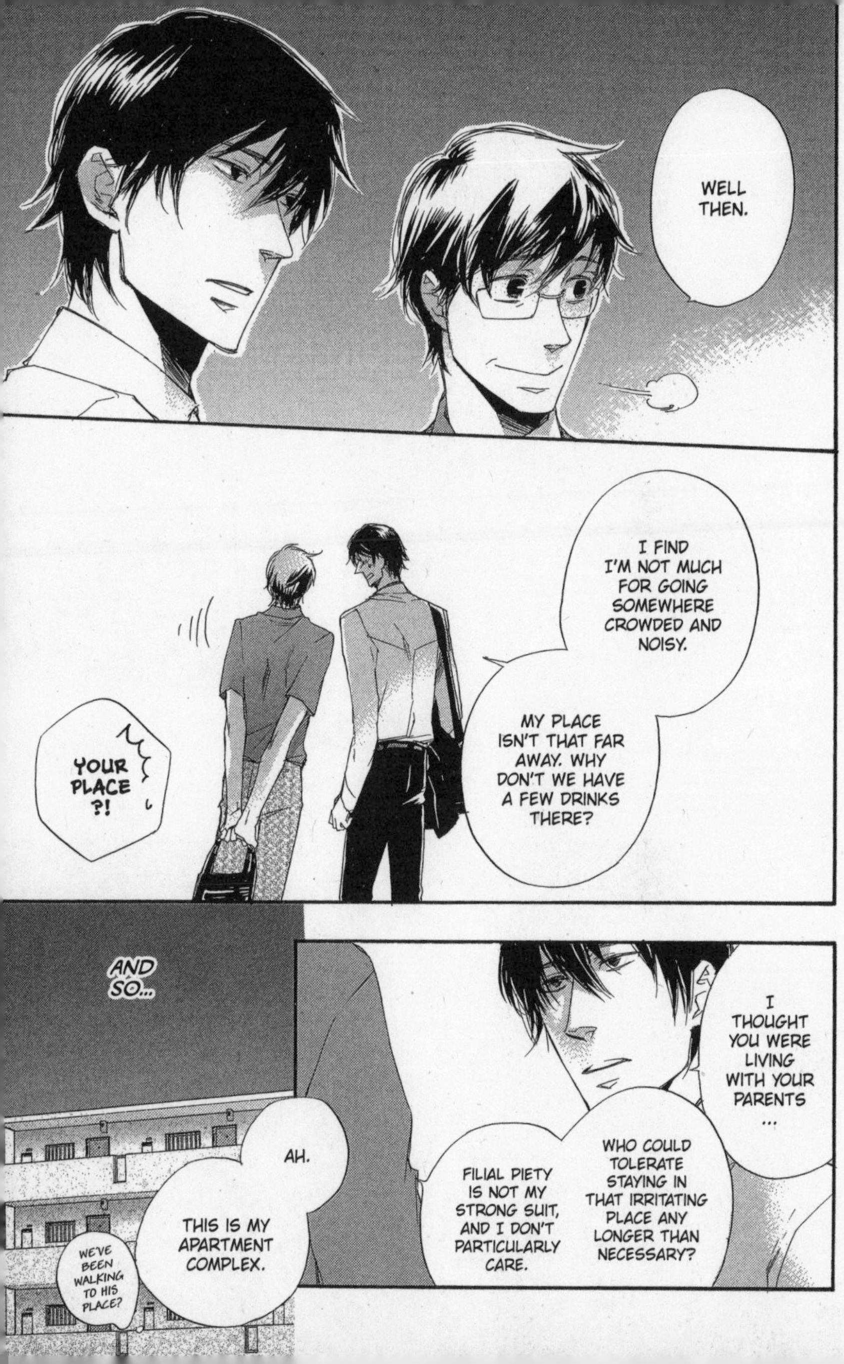
WELL THEN.
I FIND I'M NOT MUCH FOR GOING SOMEWHERE CROWDED AND NOISY.
MY PLACE ISN'T THAT FAR AWAY. WHY DON'T WE HAVE A FEW DRINKS THERE?
YOUR PLACE ?!
I THOUGHT YOU WERE LIVING WITH YOUR PARENTS ...
WHO COULD TOLERATE STAYING IN THAT IRRITATING PLACE ANY LONGER THAN NECESSARY?
FILIAL PIETY IS NOT MY STRONG SUIT, AND I DON'T PARTICULARLY CARE.
AND SO...
AH.
THIS IS MY APARTMENT COMPLEX.
WE'VE BEEN WALKING TO HIS PLACE?

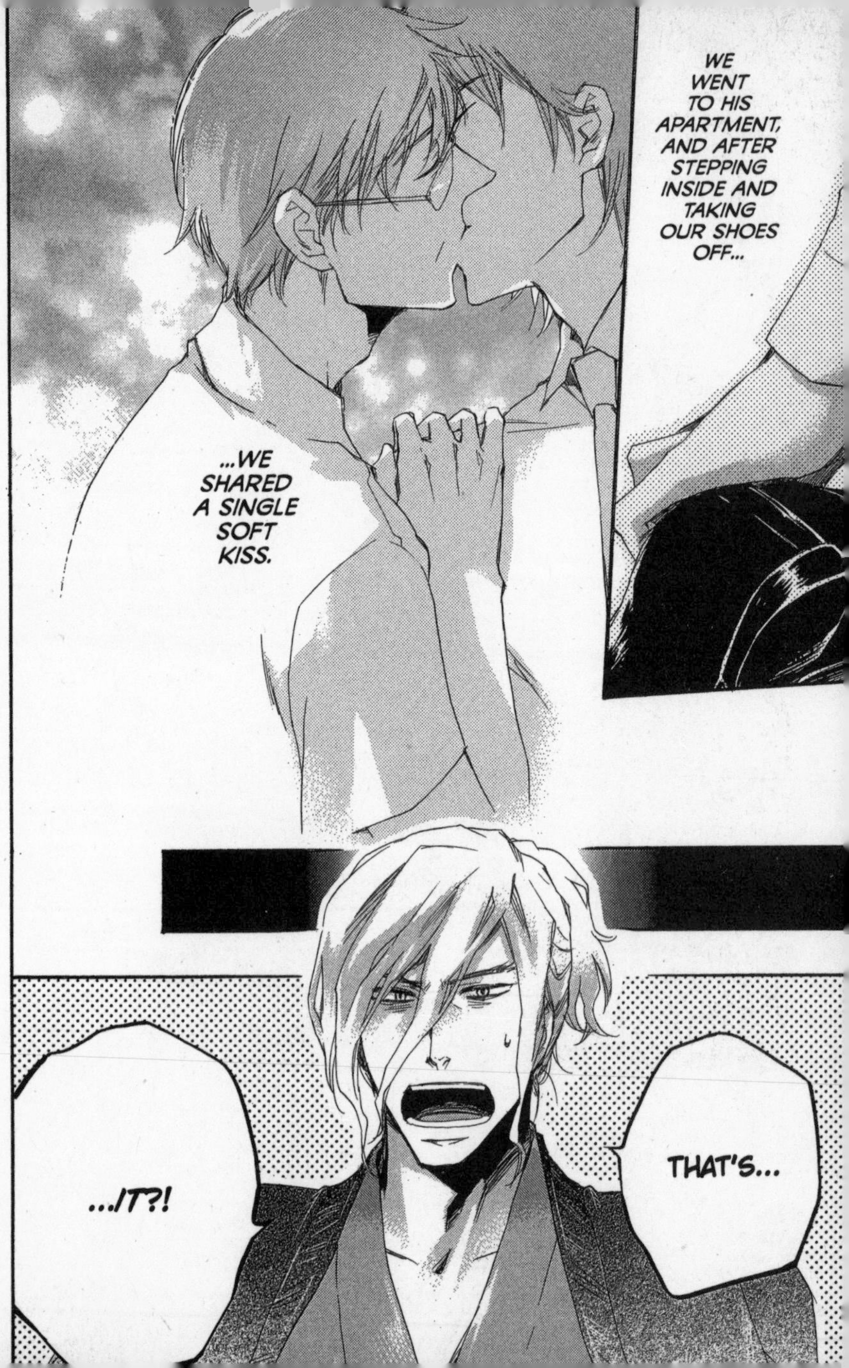
WE WENT TO HIS APARTMENT, AND AFTER STEPPING INSIDE AND TAKING OUR SHOES OFF...
...WE SHARED A SINGLE SOFT KISS.
THAT'S...
...IT?!

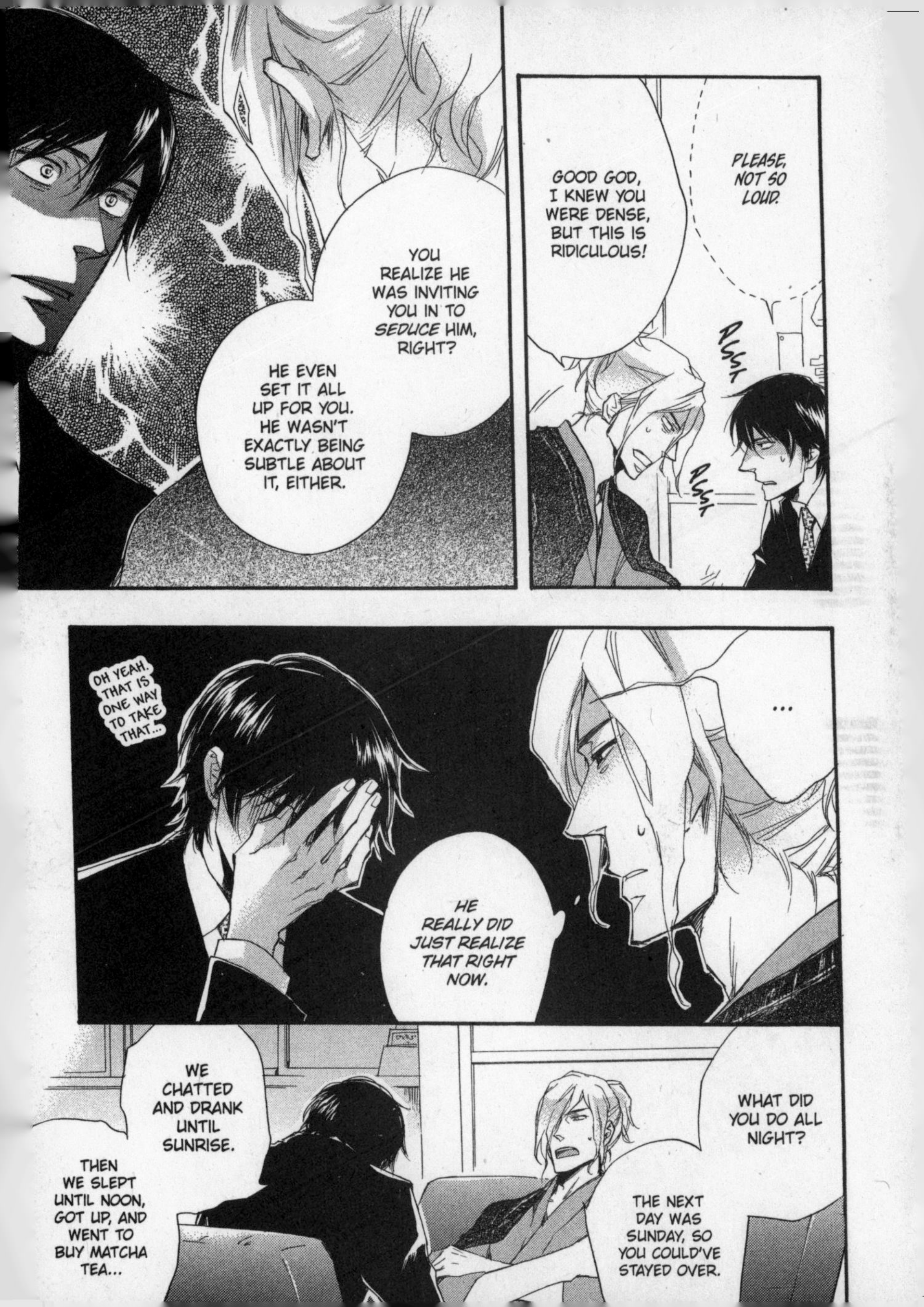
GOOD GOD, I KNEW YOU WERE DENSE, BUT THIS IS RIDICULOUS!
PLEASE, NOT SO LOUD.
YOU REALIZE HE WAS INVITING YOU IN TO SEDUCE HIM, RIGHT?
HE EVEN SET IT ALL UP FOR YOU. HE WASN'T EXACTLY BEING SUBTLE ABOUT IT, EITHER.
...
HE REALLY DID JUST REALIZE THAT RIGHT NOW.
OH YEAH. THAT IS ONE WAY TO TAKE THAT...
WHAT DID YOU DO ALL NIGHT?
WE CHATTED AND DRANK UNTIL SUNRISE.
THEN WE SLEPT UNTIL NOON, GOT UP, AND WENT TO BUY MATCHA TEA...
THE NEXT DAY WAS SUNDAY, SO YOU COULD'VE STAYED OVER.

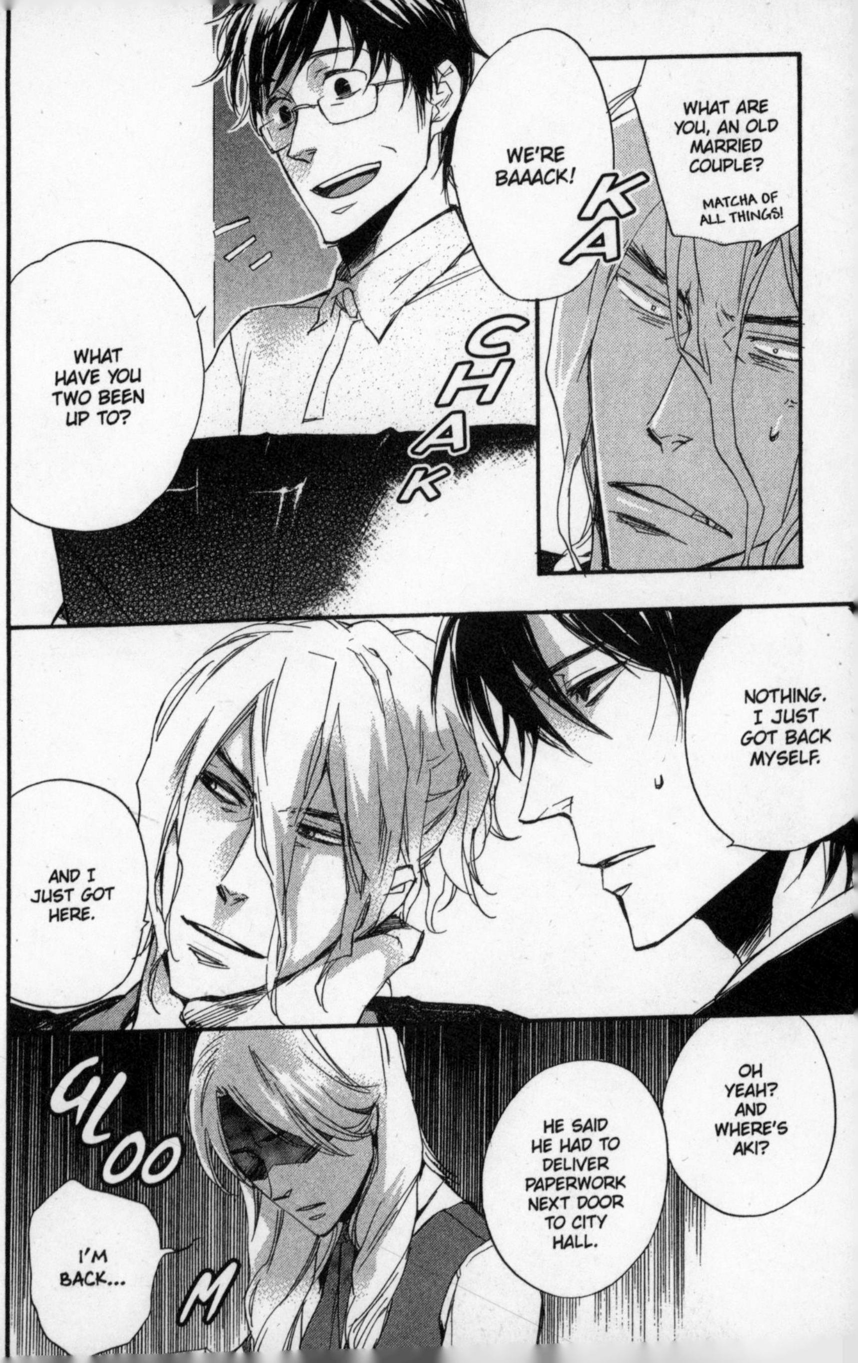
WHAT ARE YOU, AN OLD MARRIED COUPLE?
MATCHA OF ALL THINGS!
KA
CHAK
WE'RE BAAACK!
WHAT HAVE YOU TWO BEEN UP TO?
NOTHING. I JUST GOT BACK MYSELF.
AND I JUST GOT HERE.
OH YEAH? AND WHERE'S AKI?
HE SAID HE HAD TO DELIVER PAPERWORK NEXT DOOR TO CITY HALL.
GLOOM
I'M BACK...

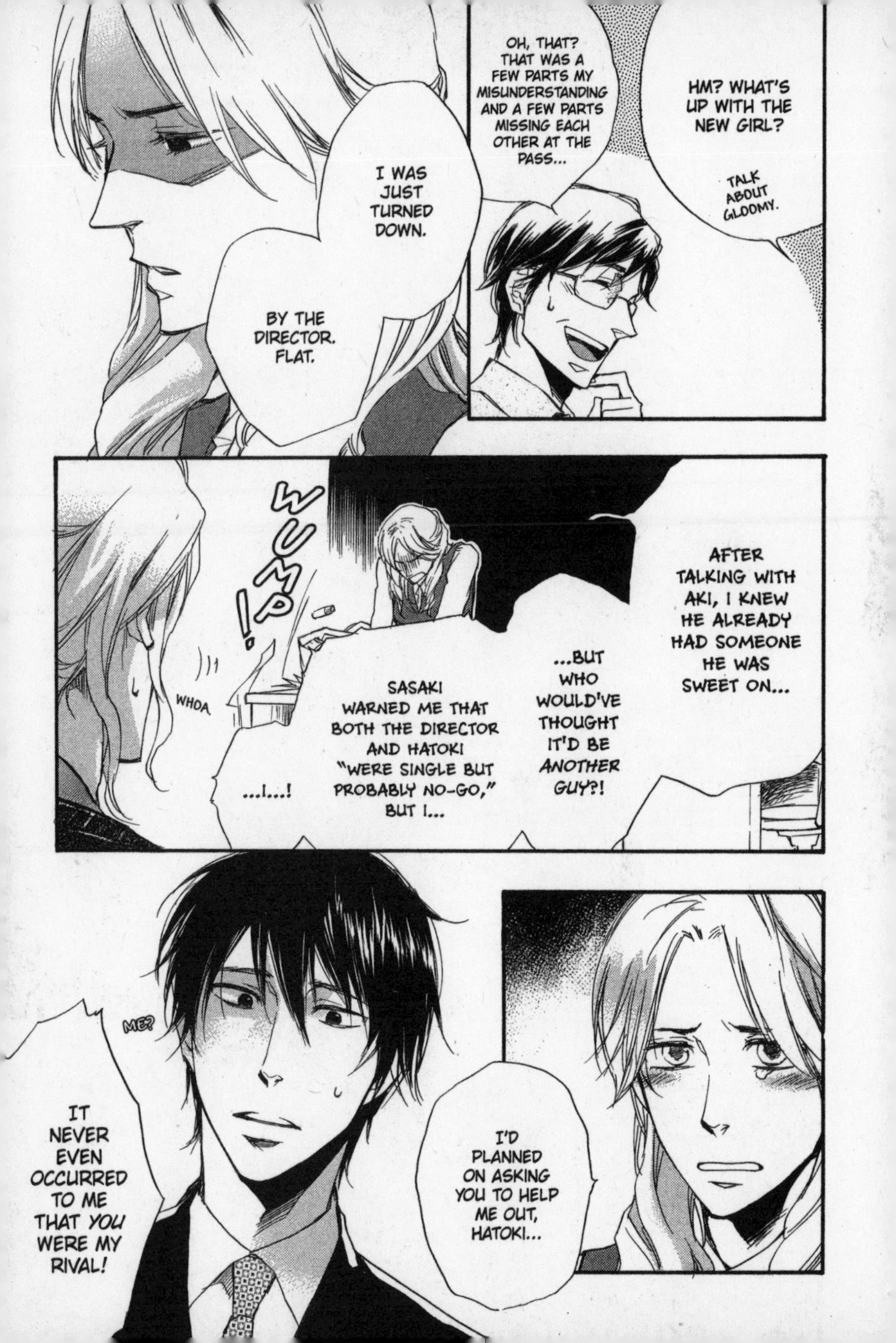
HM? WHAT'S UP WITH THE NEW GIRL?
TALK ABOUT GLOOMY.
OH, THAT? THAT WAS A FEW PARTS MY MISUNDERSTANDING AND A FEW PARTS MISSING EACH OTHER AT THE PASS...
I WAS JUST TURNED DOWN.
BY THE DIRECTOR. FLAT.
AFTER TALKING WITH AKI, I KNEW HE ALREADY HAD SOMEONE HE WAS SWEET ON...
...BUT WHO WOULD'VE THOUGHT IT'D BE *ANOTHER GUY*?!
SASAKI WARNED ME THAT BOTH THE DIRECTOR AND HATOKI "WERE SINGLE BUT PROBABLY NO-GO," BUT I...
...I...!
WUMP!
WHOA
I'D PLANNED ON ASKING YOU TO HELP ME OUT, HATOKI...
ME?
IT NEVER EVEN OCCURRED TO ME THAT *YOU* WERE MY RIVAL!

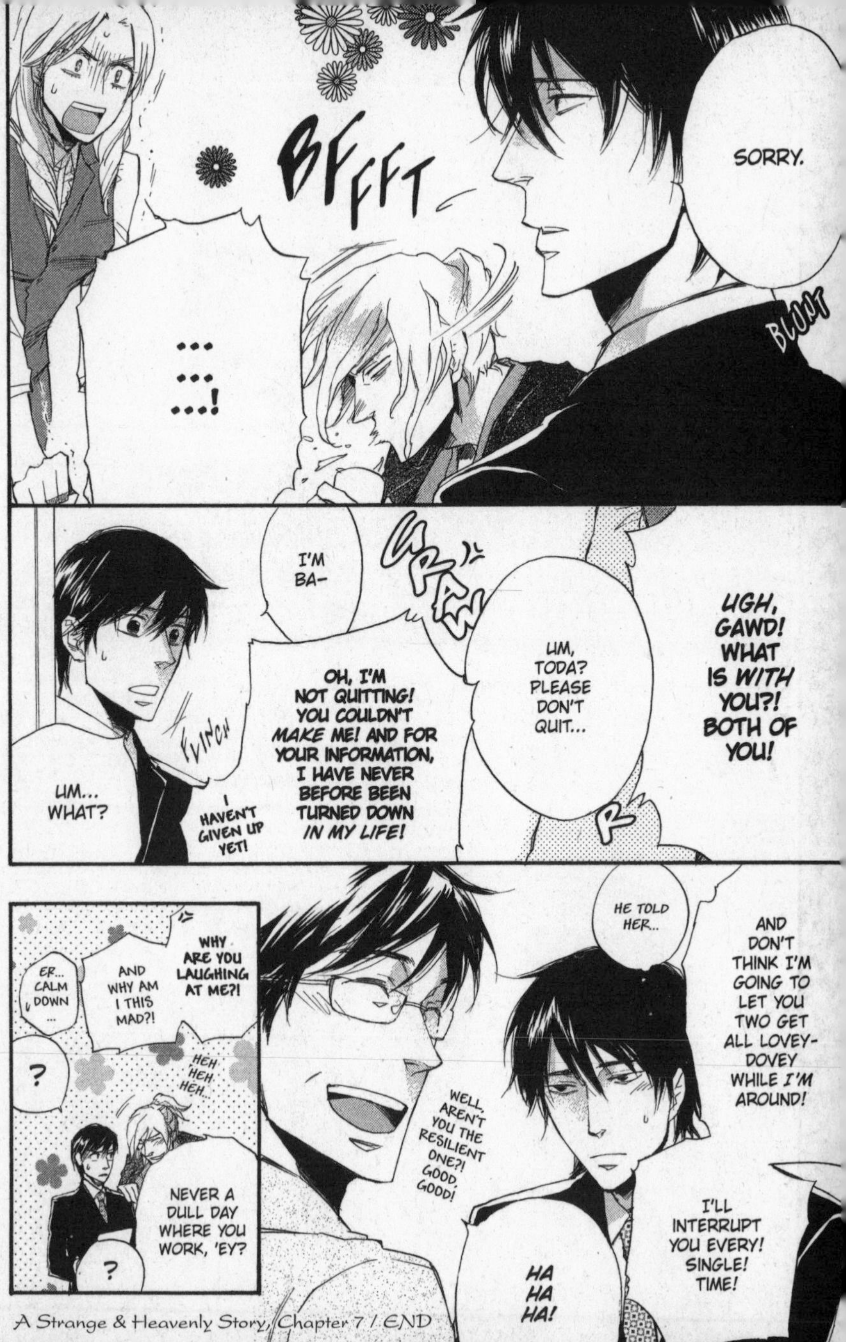
SORRY.
BFFFT
...
...
...!
UGH, GAWD! WHAT IS WITH YOU?! BOTH OF YOU!
R
UM, TODA? PLEASE DON'T QUIT...
I'M BA-
OH, I'M NOT QUITTING! YOU COULDN'T MAKE ME! AND FOR YOUR INFORMATION, I HAVE NEVER BEFORE BEEN TURNED DOWN IN MY LIFE!
I HAVEN'T GIVEN UP YET!
FLINCH
UM... WHAT?
AND DON'T THINK I'M GOING TO LET YOU TWO GET ALL LOVEY-DOVEY WHILE I'M AROUND!
HE TOLD HER...
I'LL INTERRUPT YOU EVERY! SINGLE! TIME!
HA HA HA!
WELL, AREN'T YOU THE RESILIENT ONE?! GOOD, GOOD!
WHY ARE YOU LAUGHING AT ME?!
AND WHY AM I THIS MAD?!
ER... CALM DOWN...
HEH HEH HEH...
?
NEVER A DULL DAY WHERE YOU WORK, 'EY?
?
A Strange & Heavenly Story, Chapter 7 / END

A Strange & Mystifying Story

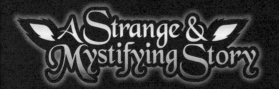

A Strange & Mystifying Story

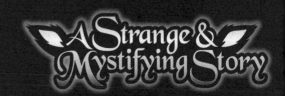

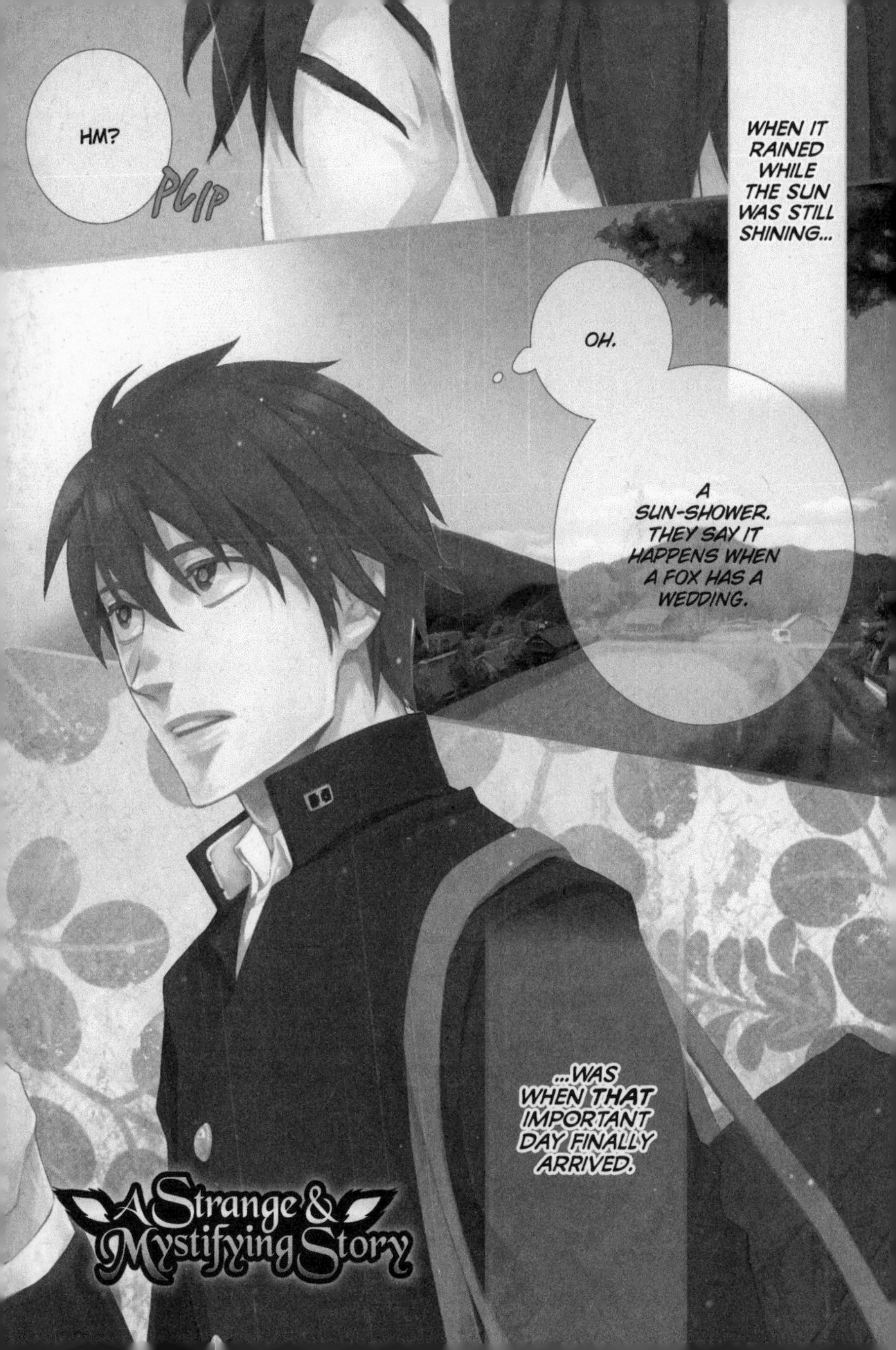
WHEN IT RAINED WHILE THE SUN WAS STILL SHINING...
HM?
PLIP
OH.
A SUN-SHOWER. THEY SAY IT HAPPENS WHEN A FOX HAS A WEDDING.
...WAS WHEN THAT IMPORTANT DAY FINALLY ARRIVED.
A Strange & Mystifying Story

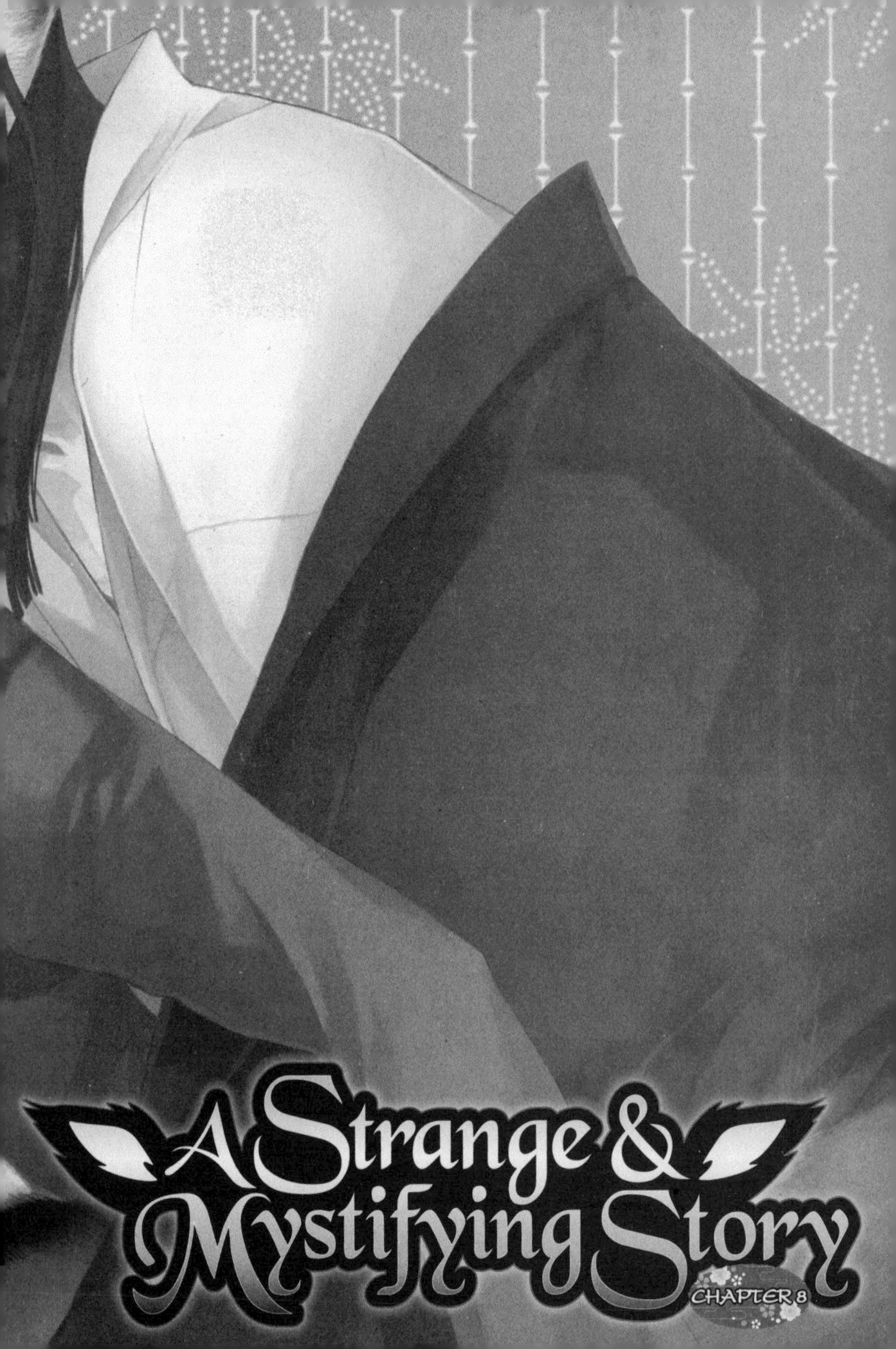
A Strange & Mystifying Story
CHAPTER 8

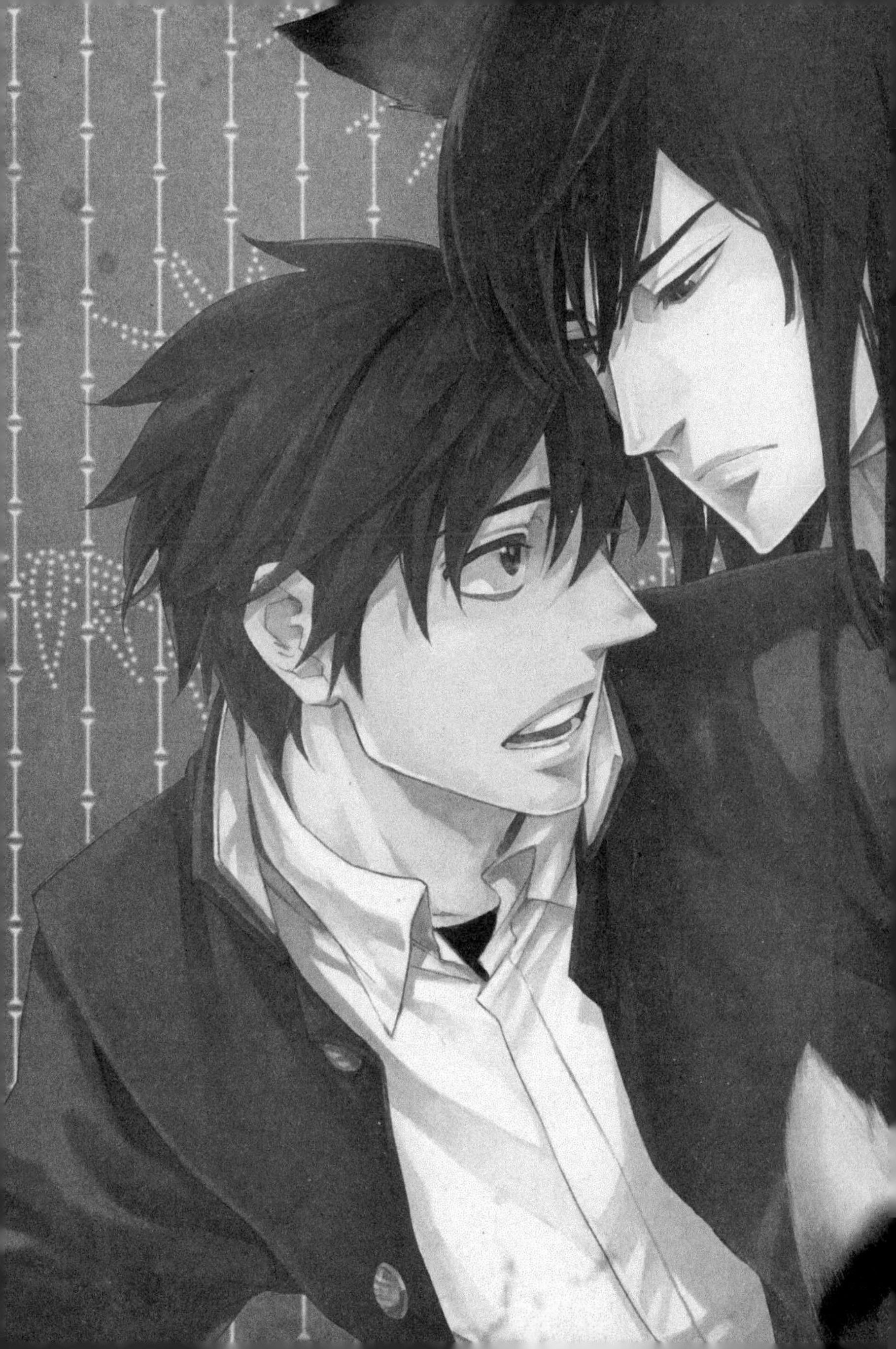

A Strange & Mystifying Story

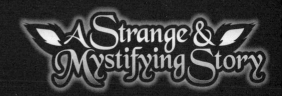

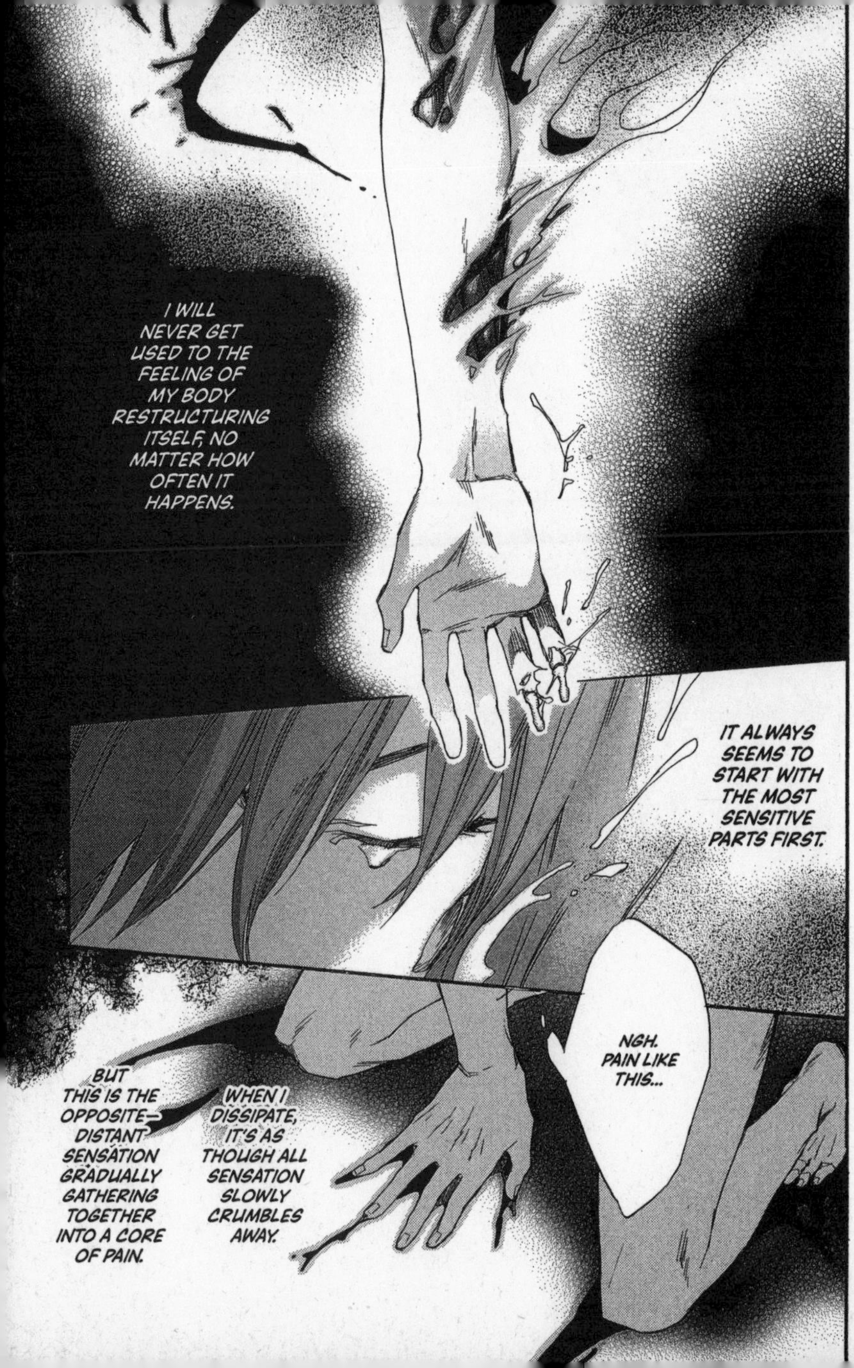
I WILL NEVER GET USED TO THE FEELING OF MY BODY RESTRUCTURING ITSELF, NO MATTER HOW OFTEN IT HAPPENS.
IT ALWAYS SEEMS TO START WITH THE MOST SENSITIVE PARTS FIRST.
NGH. PAIN LIKE THIS...
WHEN I DISSIPATE, IT'S AS THOUGH ALL SENSATION SLOWLY CRUMBLES AWAY.
BUT THIS IS THE OPPOSITE—DISTANT SENSATION GRADUALLY GATHERING TOGETHER INTO A CORE OF PAIN.

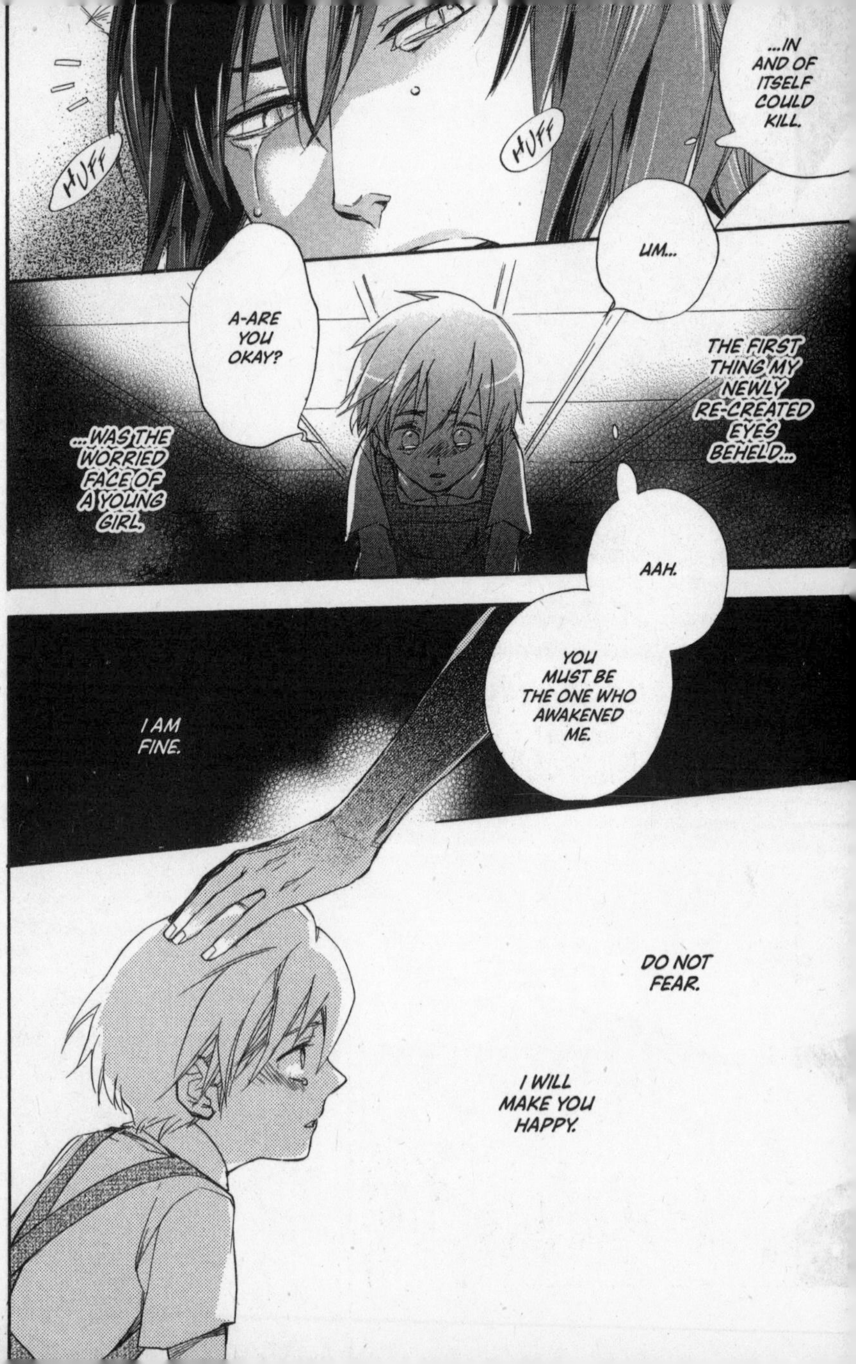
...IN AND OF ITSELF COULD KILL.
HUFF
HUFF
UM...
A-ARE YOU OKAY?
THE FIRST THING MY NEWLY RE-CREATED EYES BEHELD...
...WAS THE WORRIED FACE OF A YOUNG GIRL.
AAH.
YOU MUST BE THE ONE WHO AWAKENED ME.
I AM FINE.
DO NOT FEAR.
I WILL MAKE YOU HAPPY.

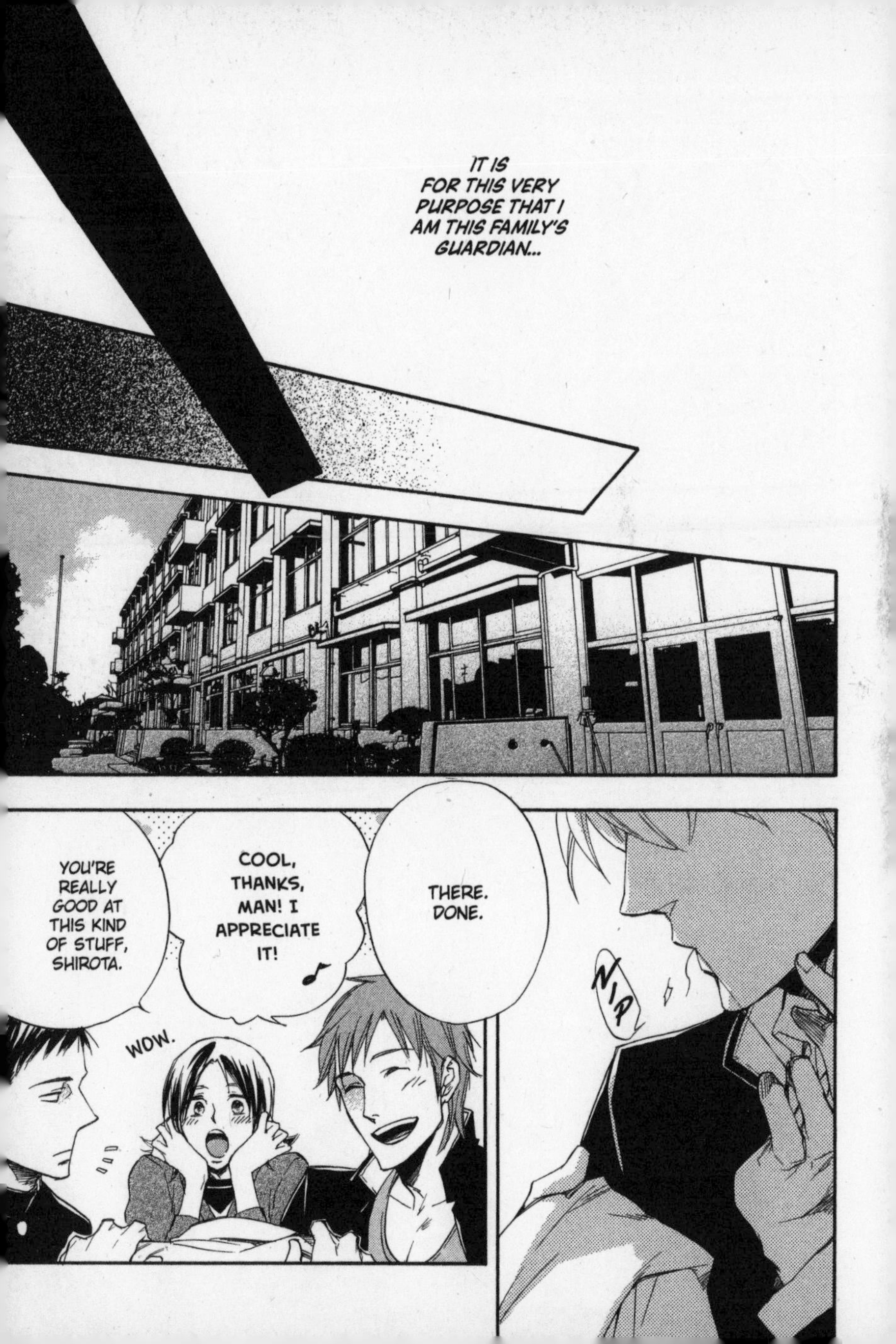
IT IS FOR THIS VERY PURPOSE THAT I AM THIS FAMILY'S GUARDIAN...
NIP
THERE. DONE.
COOL, THANKS, MAN! I APPRECIATE IT!
YOU'RE REALLY GOOD AT THIS KIND OF STUFF, SHIROTA.
WOW.

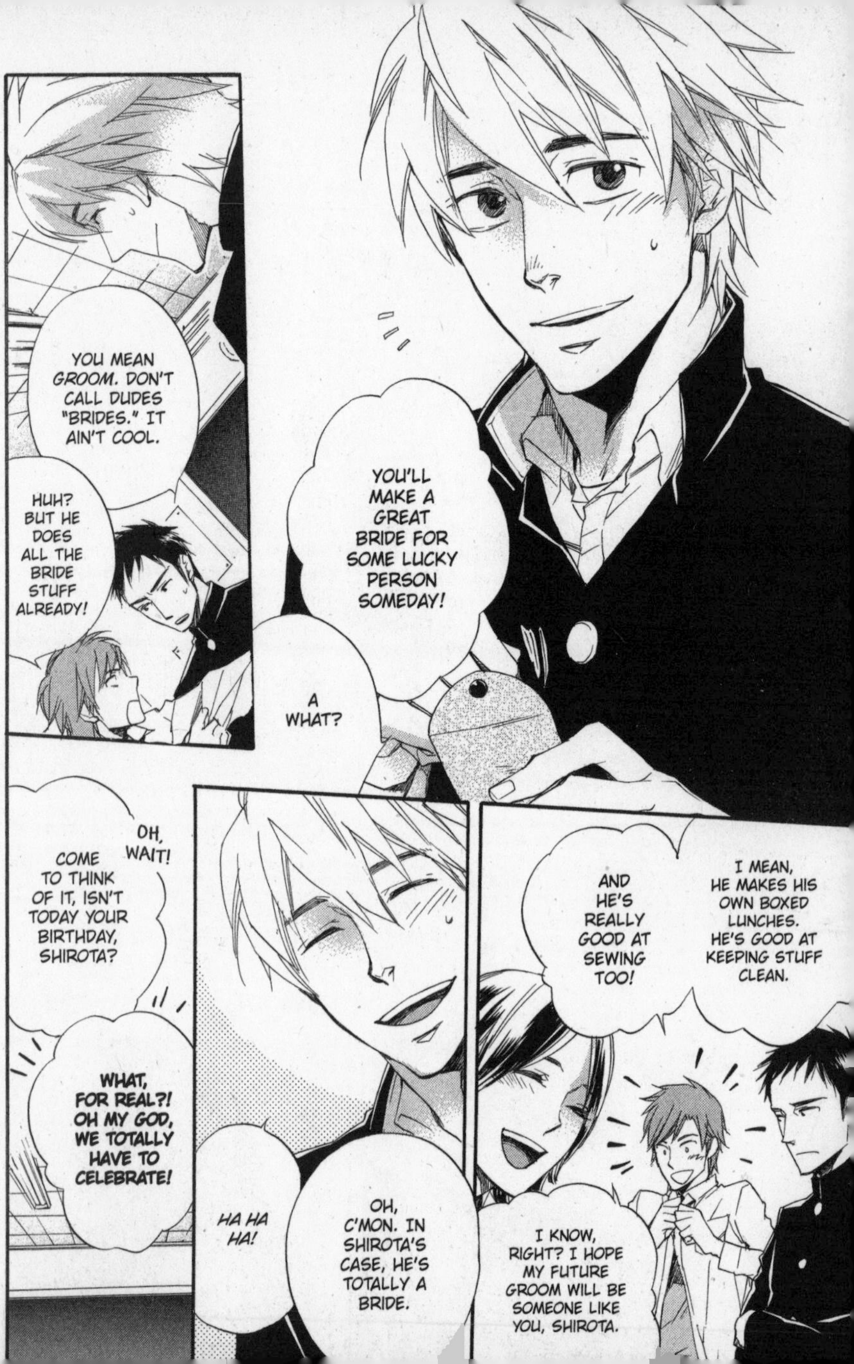
YOU'LL MAKE A GREAT BRIDE FOR SOME LUCKY PERSON SOMEDAY!
A WHAT?
YOU MEAN GROOM. DON'T CALL DUDES "BRIDES." IT AIN'T COOL.
HUH? BUT HE DOES ALL THE BRIDE STUFF ALREADY!
I MEAN, HE MAKES HIS OWN BOXED LUNCHES. HE'S GOOD AT KEEPING STUFF CLEAN.
AND HE'S REALLY GOOD AT SEWING TOO!
I KNOW, RIGHT? I HOPE MY FUTURE GROOM WILL BE SOMEONE LIKE YOU, SHIROTA.
OH, C'MON. IN SHIROTA'S CASE, HE'S TOTALLY A BRIDE.
HA HA HA!
OH, WAIT!
COME TO THINK OF IT, ISN'T TODAY YOUR BIRTHDAY, SHIROTA?
WHAT, FOR REAL?! OH MY GOD, WE TOTALLY HAVE TO CELEBRATE!

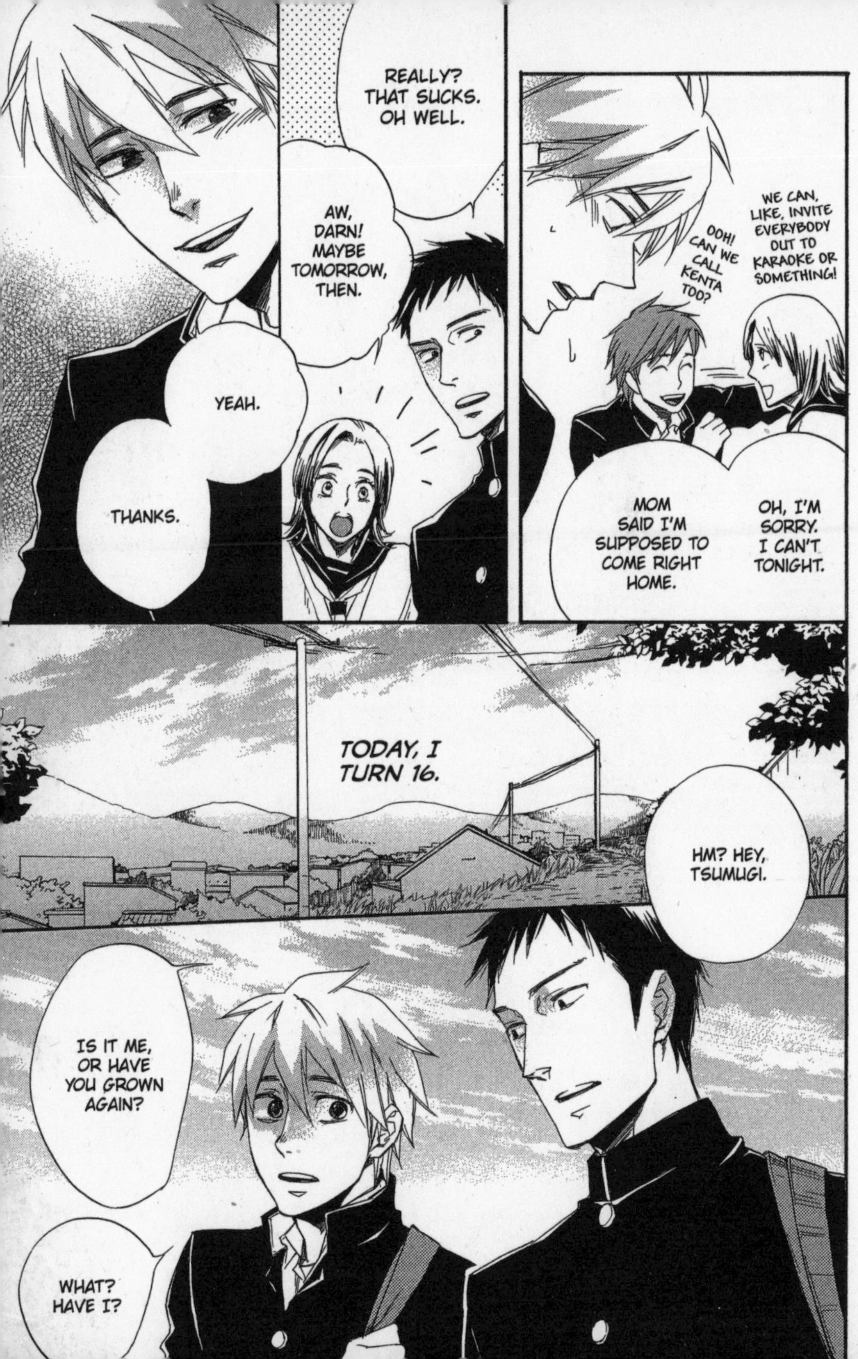
WE CAN, LIKE, INVITE EVERYBODY OUT TO KARAOKE OR SOMETHING!
OOH! CAN WE CALL KENTA TOO?
OH, I'M SORRY. I CAN'T TONIGHT.
MOM SAID I'M SUPPOSED TO COME RIGHT HOME.
REALLY? THAT SUCKS. OH WELL.
AW, DARN! MAYBE TOMORROW, THEN.
YEAH.
THANKS.
TODAY, I TURN 16.
HM? HEY, TSUMUGI.
IS IT ME, OR HAVE YOU GROWN AGAIN?
WHAT? HAVE I?

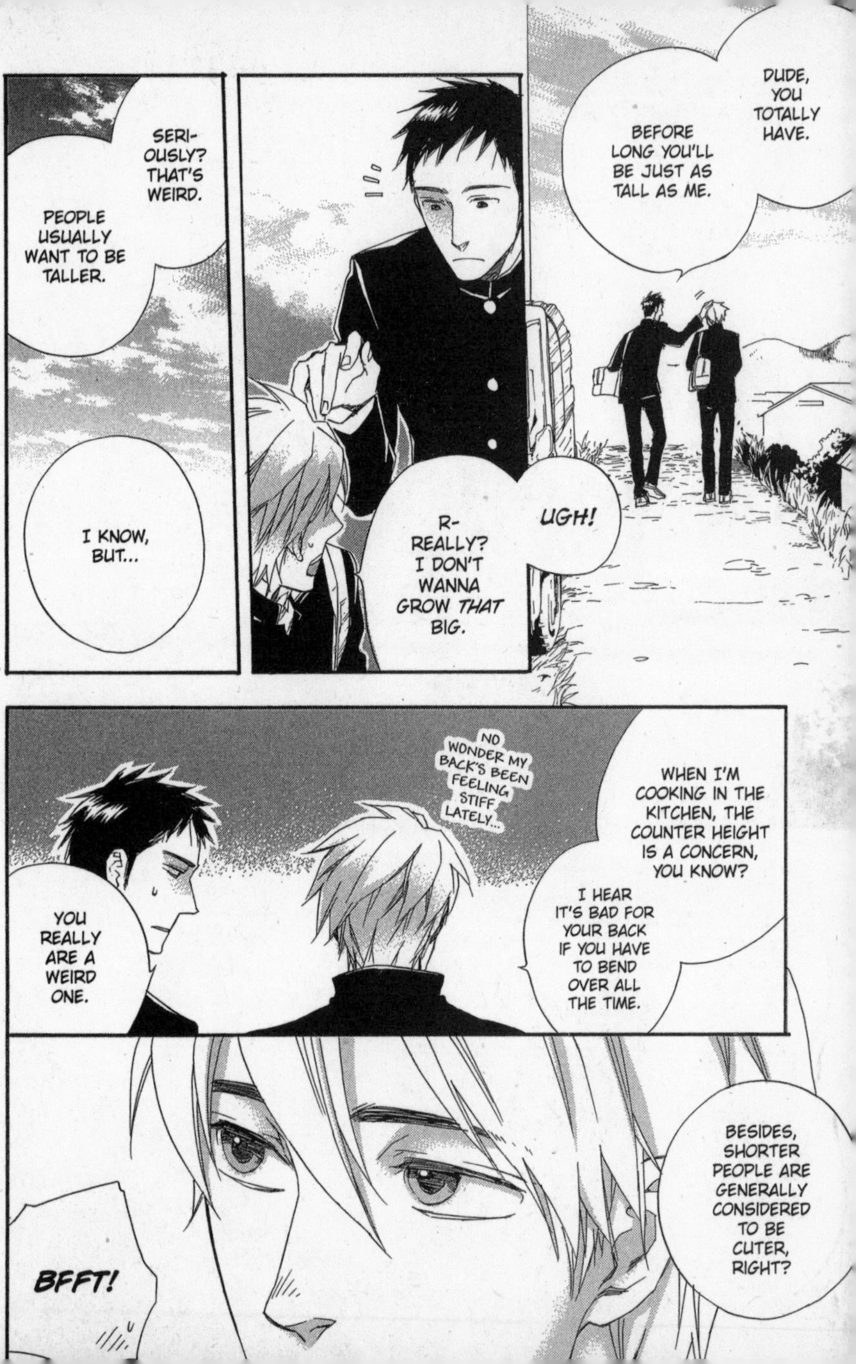
DUDE, YOU TOTALLY HAVE.
BEFORE LONG YOU'LL BE JUST AS TALL AS ME.
UGH!
R-REALLY? I DON'T WANNA GROW *THAT* BIG.
SERI-OUSLY? THAT'S WEIRD.
PEOPLE USUALLY WANT TO BE TALLER.
I KNOW, BUT...
WHEN I'M COOKING IN THE KITCHEN, THE COUNTER HEIGHT IS A CONCERN, YOU KNOW?
I HEAR IT'S BAD FOR YOUR BACK IF YOU HAVE TO BEND OVER ALL THE TIME.
NO WONDER MY BACK'S BEEN FEELING STIFF LATELY...
YOU REALLY ARE A WEIRD ONE.
BESIDES, SHORTER PEOPLE ARE GENERALLY CONSIDERED TO BE CUTER, RIGHT?
BFFT!

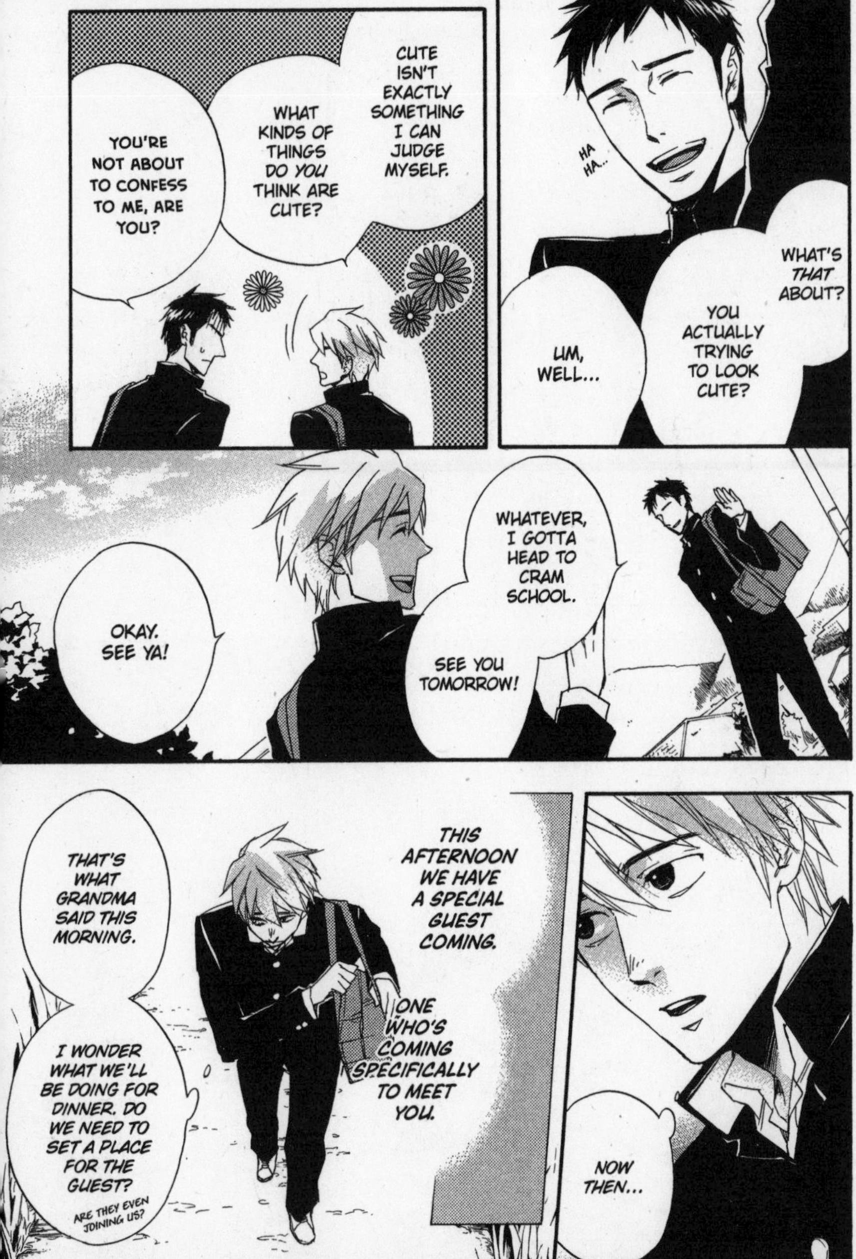
HA HA...
WHAT'S THAT ABOUT?
YOU ACTUALLY TRYING TO LOOK CUTE?
UM, WELL...
CUTE ISN'T EXACTLY SOMETHING I CAN JUDGE MYSELF.
WHAT KINDS OF THINGS DO *YOU* THINK ARE CUTE?
YOU'RE NOT ABOUT TO CONFESS TO ME, ARE YOU?
WHATEVER, I GOTTA HEAD TO CRAM SCHOOL.
SEE YOU TOMORROW!
OKAY. SEE YA!
NOW THEN...
THIS AFTERNOON WE HAVE A SPECIAL GUEST COMING.
ONE WHO'S COMING SPECIFICALLY TO MEET YOU.
THAT'S WHAT GRANDMA SAID THIS MORNING.
I WONDER WHAT WE'LL BE DOING FOR DINNER. DO WE NEED TO SET A PLACE FOR THE GUEST?
ARE THEY EVEN JOINING US?

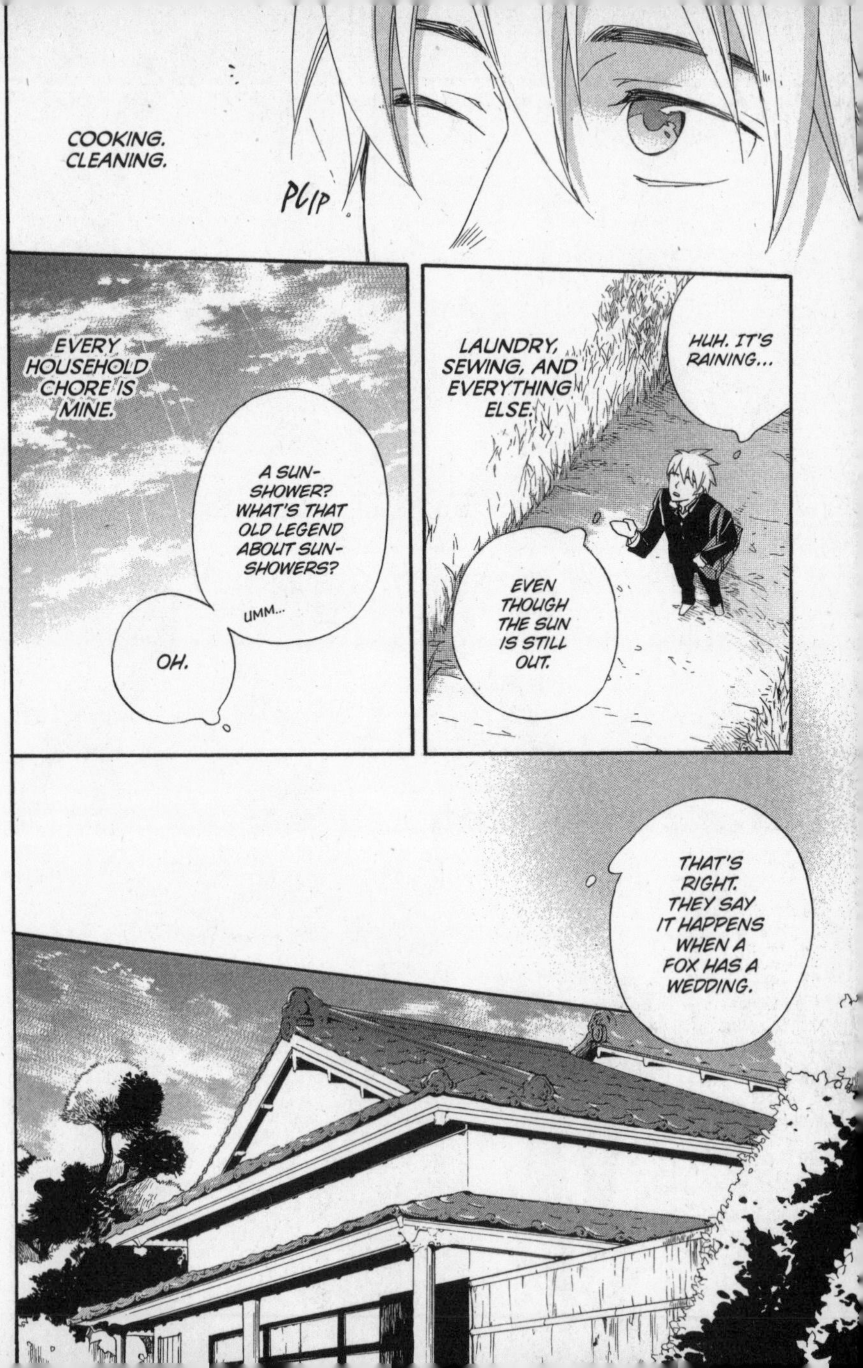
COOKING. CLEANING.
PLIP
HUH. IT'S RAINING...
LAUNDRY, SEWING, AND EVERYTHING ELSE.
EVEN THOUGH THE SUN IS STILL OUT.
EVERY HOUSEHOLD CHORE IS MINE.
A SUN-SHOWER? WHAT'S THAT OLD LEGEND ABOUT SUN-SHOWERS?
UMM...
OH.
THAT'S RIGHT. THEY SAY IT HAPPENS WHEN A FOX HAS A WEDDING.

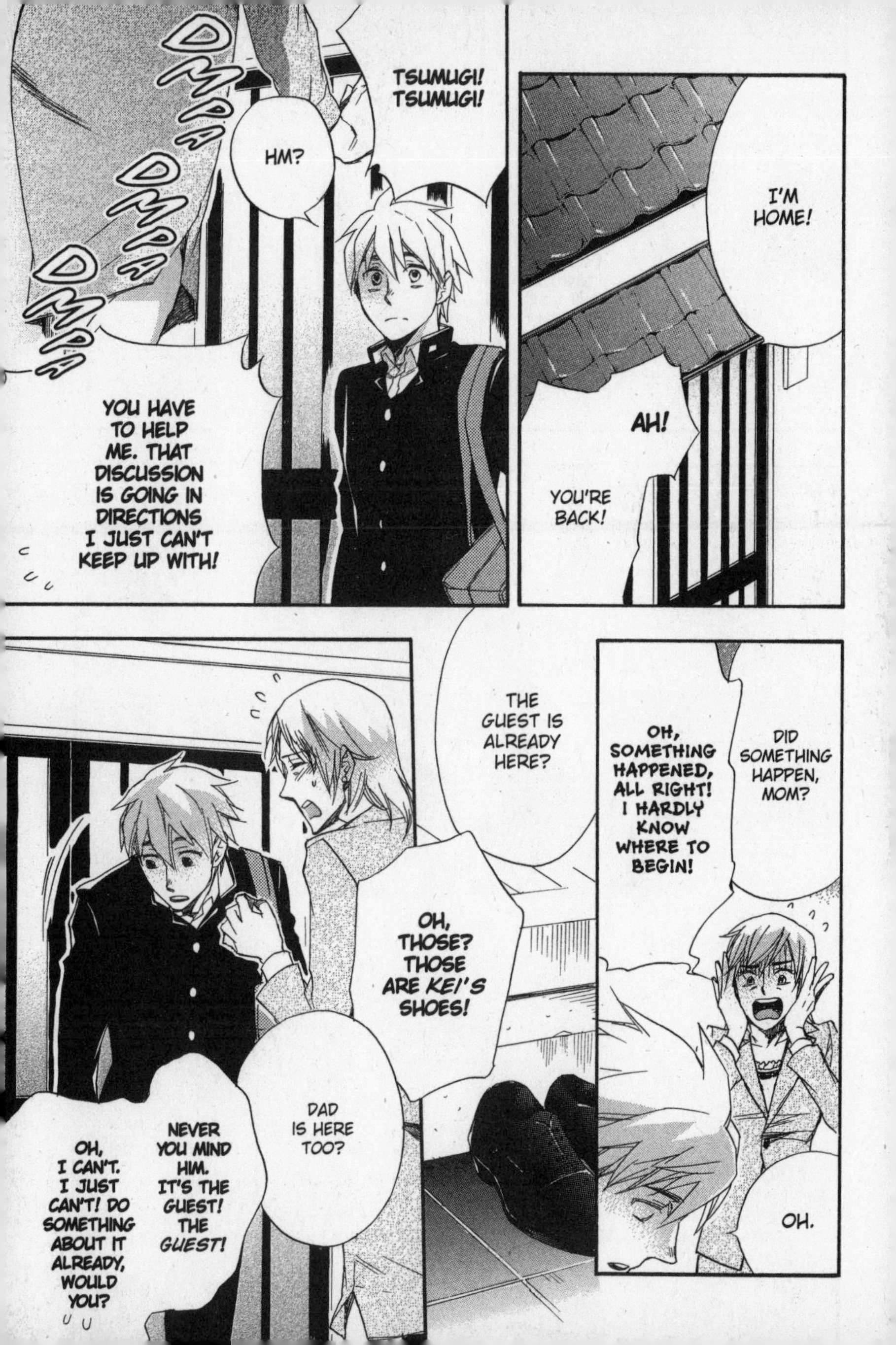
I'M HOME!
AH!
YOU'RE BACK!
TSUMUGI! TSUMUGI!
HM?
DMPA DMPA DMPA DMPA
YOU HAVE TO HELP ME. THAT DISCUSSION IS GOING IN DIRECTIONS I JUST CAN'T KEEP UP WITH!
DID SOMETHING HAPPEN, MOM?
OH, SOMETHING HAPPENED, ALL RIGHT! I HARDLY KNOW WHERE TO BEGIN!
OH.
THE GUEST IS ALREADY HERE?
OH, THOSE? THOSE ARE *KEI'S* SHOES!
DAD IS HERE TOO?
NEVER YOU MIND HIM. IT'S THE GUEST! THE *GUEST!*
OH, I CAN'T. I JUST CAN'T! DO SOMETHING ABOUT IT ALREADY, WOULD YOU?

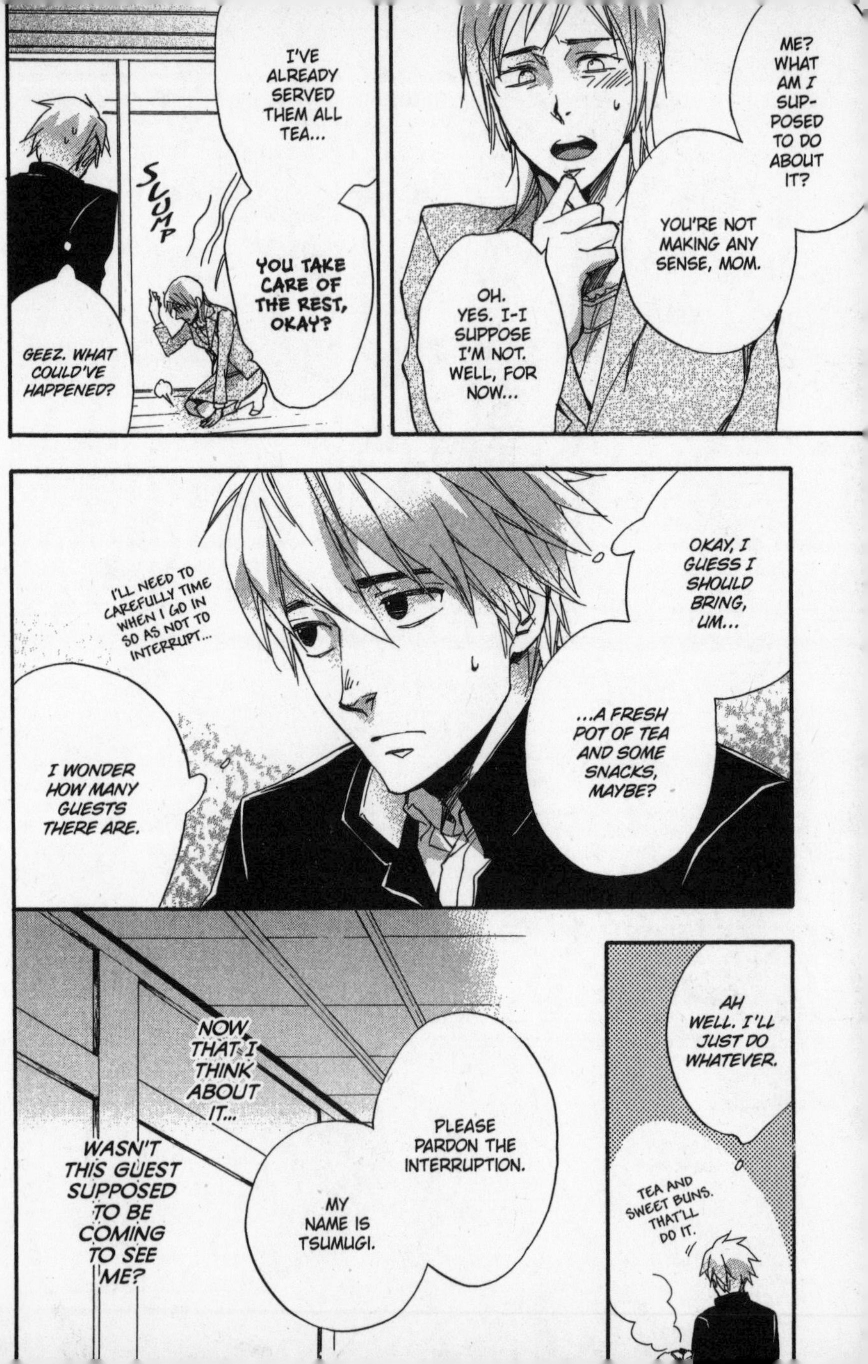
ME? WHAT AM I SUPPOSED TO DO ABOUT IT?
YOU'RE NOT MAKING ANY SENSE, MOM.
OH. YES. I-I SUPPOSE I'M NOT. WELL, FOR NOW...
I'VE ALREADY SERVED THEM ALL TEA...
YOU TAKE CARE OF THE REST, OKAY?
SLUMP
GEEZ. WHAT COULD'VE HAPPENED?
OKAY, I GUESS I SHOULD BRING, UM...
...A FRESH POT OF TEA AND SOME SNACKS, MAYBE?
I'LL NEED TO CAREFULLY TIME WHEN I GO IN SO AS NOT TO INTERRUPT...
I WONDER HOW MANY GUESTS THERE ARE.
AH WELL. I'LL JUST DO WHATEVER.
TEA AND SWEET BUNS. THAT'LL DO IT.
PLEASE PARDON THE INTERRUPTION.
MY NAME IS TSUMUGI.
NOW THAT I THINK ABOUT IT...
WASN'T THIS GUEST SUPPOSED TO BE COMING TO SEE ME?

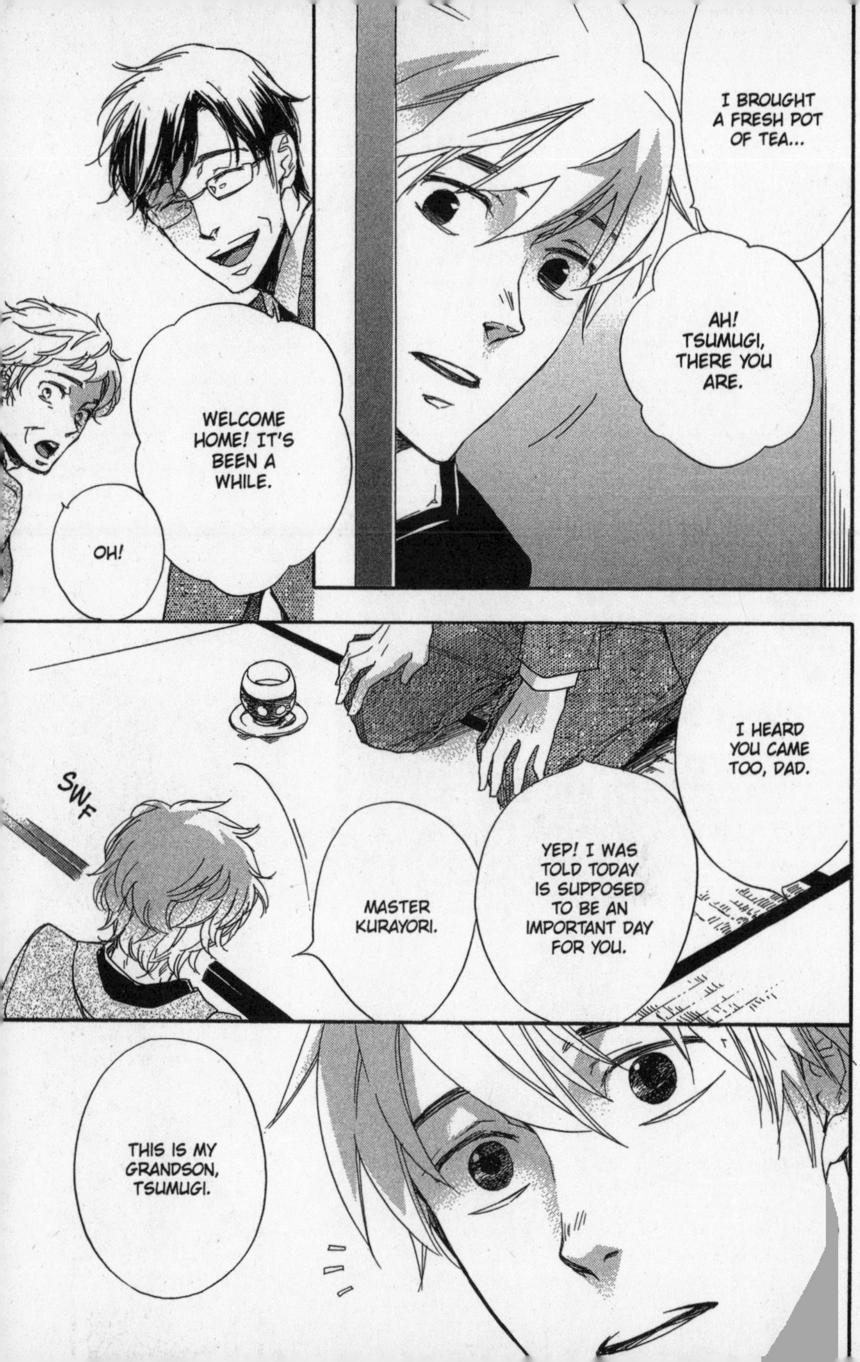
I BROUGHT A FRESH POT OF TEA...
AH! TSUMUGI, THERE YOU ARE.
WELCOME HOME! IT'S BEEN A WHILE.
OH!
I HEARD YOU CAME TOO, DAD.
YEP! I WAS TOLD TODAY IS SUPPOSED TO BE AN IMPORTANT DAY FOR YOU.
MASTER KURAYORI.
SWF
THIS IS MY GRANDSON, TSUMUGI.

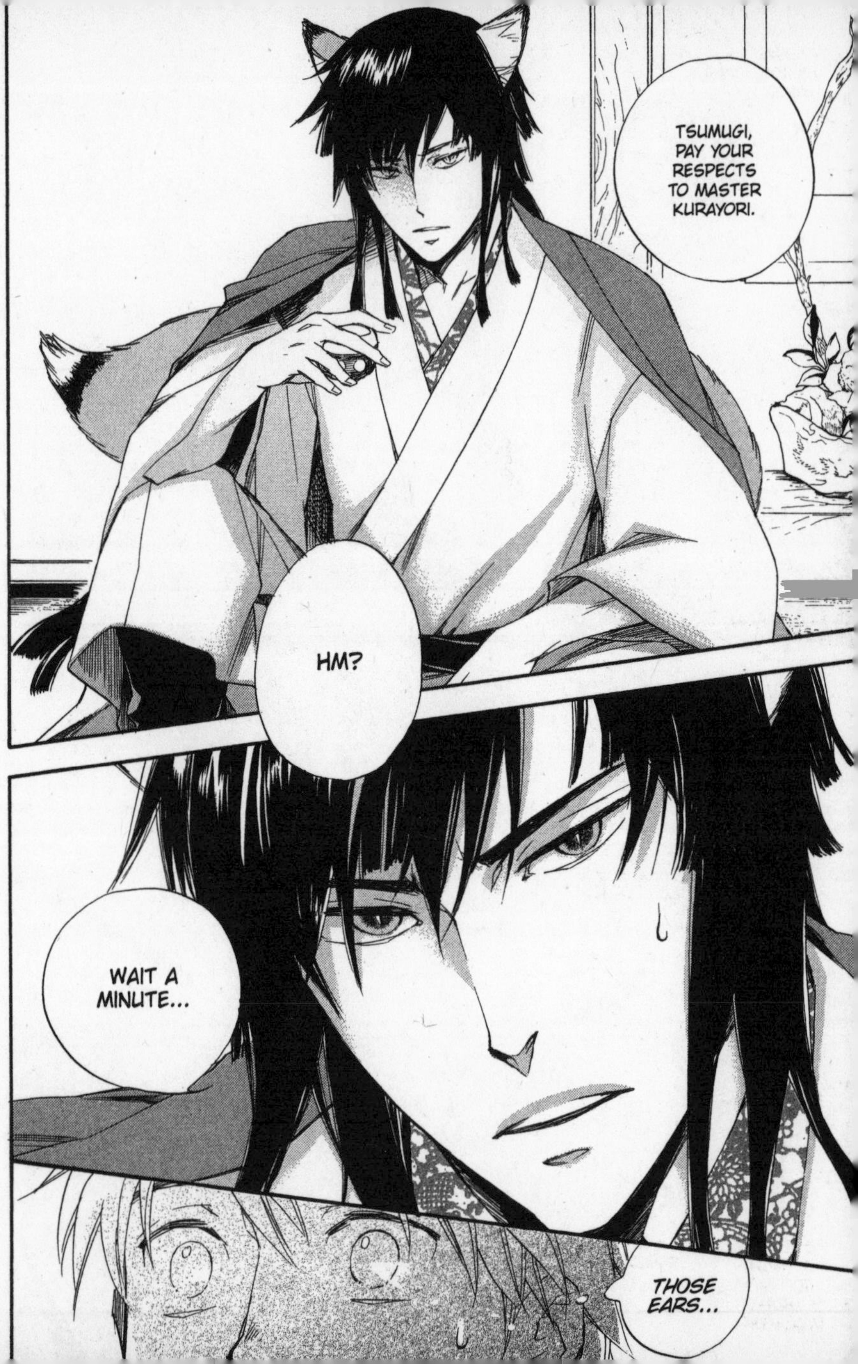
TSUMUGI, PAY YOUR RESPECTS TO MASTER KURAYORI.
HM?
WAIT A MINUTE...
THOSE EARS...

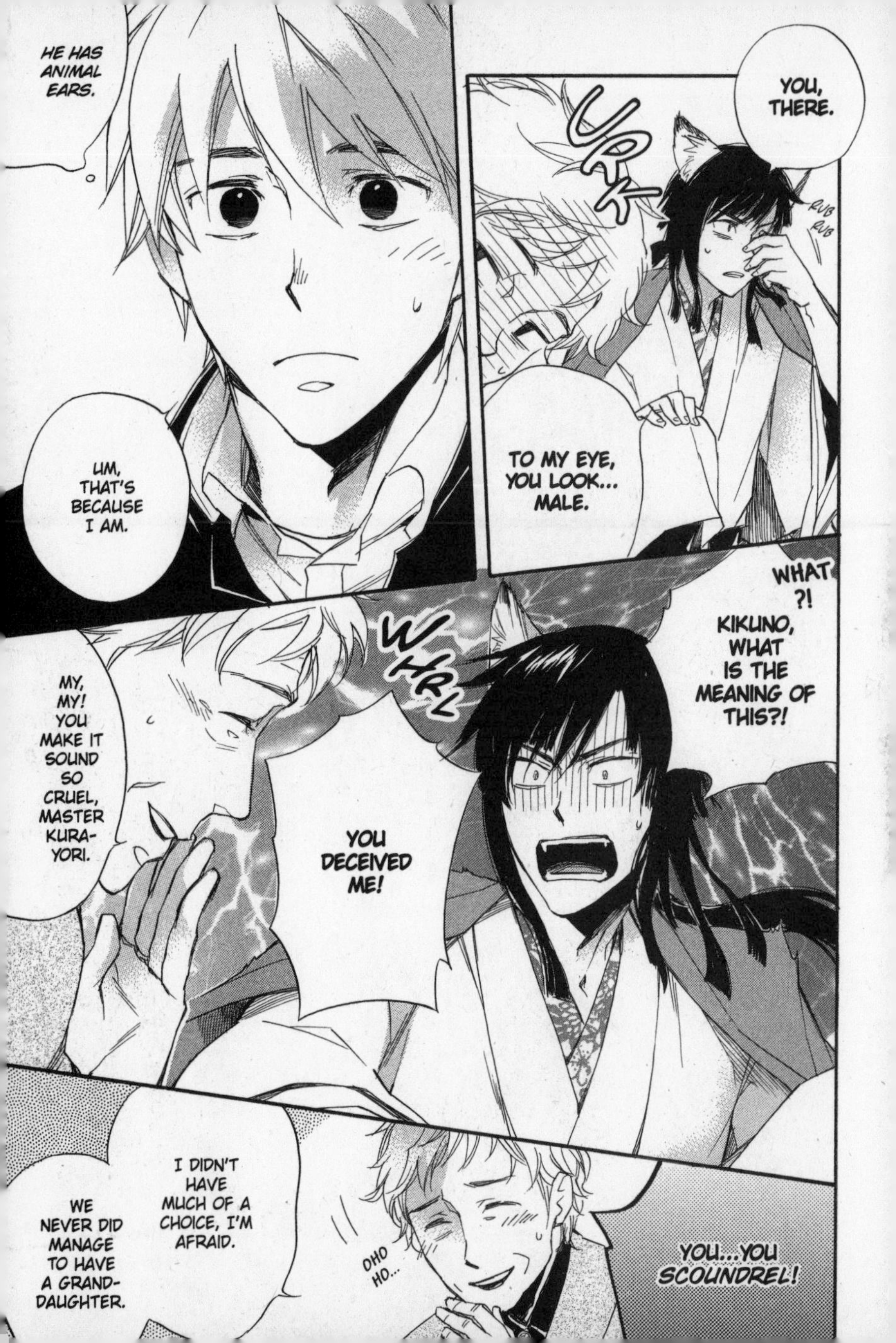
YOU, THERE.
URK
RUB RUB
TO MY EYE, YOU LOOK... MALE.
HE HAS ANIMAL EARS.
UM, THAT'S BECAUSE I AM.
WHAT?!
KIKUNO, WHAT IS THE MEANING OF THIS?!
WHRL
YOU DECEIVED ME!
MY, MY! YOU MAKE IT SOUND SO CRUEL, MASTER KURA-YORI.
YOU...YOU SCOUNDREL!
OHO HO...
I DIDN'T HAVE MUCH OF A CHOICE, I'M AFRAID.
WE NEVER DID MANAGE TO HAVE A GRAND-DAUGHTER.

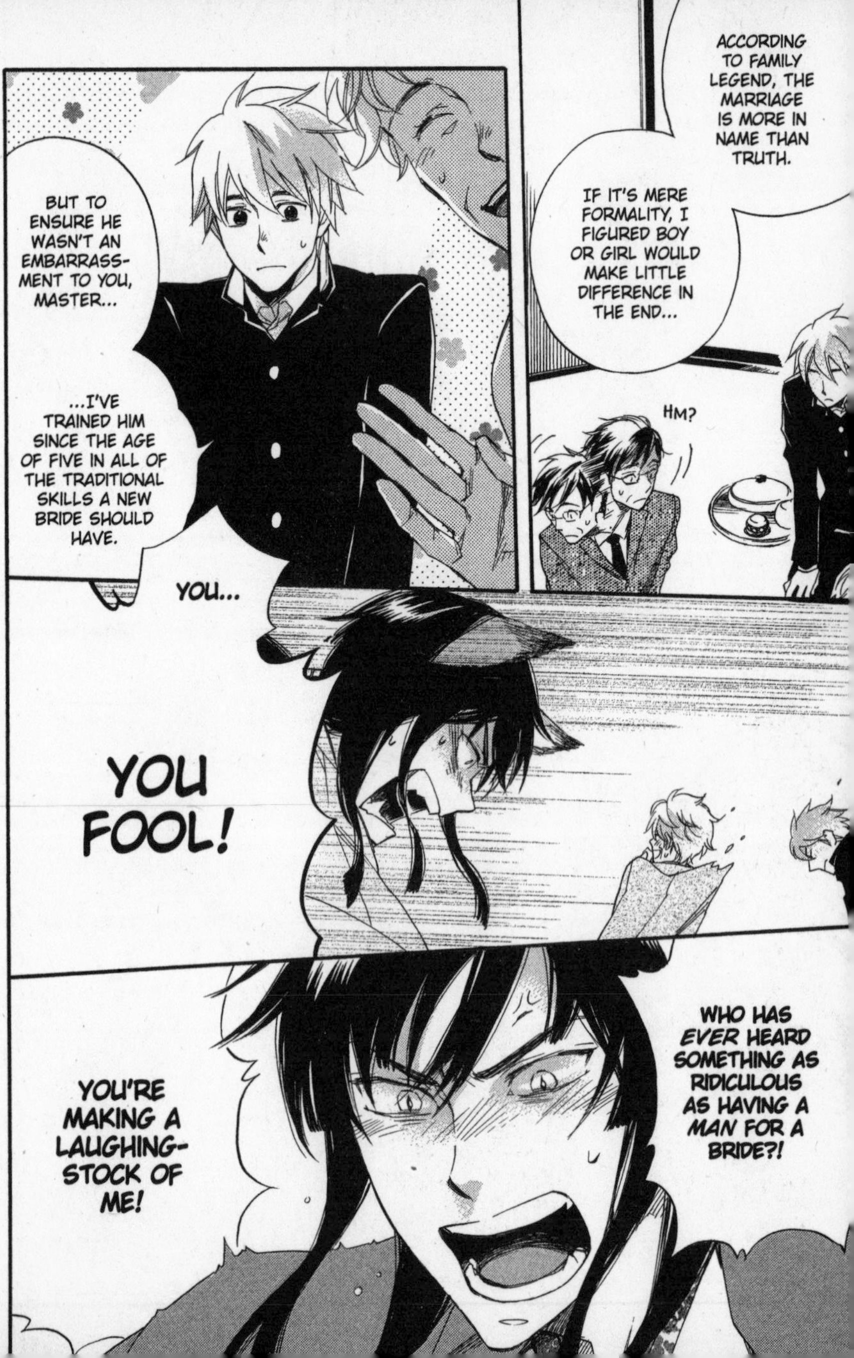
ACCORDING TO FAMILY LEGEND, THE MARRIAGE IS MORE IN NAME THAN TRUTH.
IF IT'S MERE FORMALITY, I FIGURED BOY OR GIRL WOULD MAKE LITTLE DIFFERENCE IN THE END...
HM?
BUT TO ENSURE HE WASN'T AN EMBARRASS-MENT TO YOU, MASTER...
...I'VE TRAINED HIM SINCE THE AGE OF FIVE IN ALL OF THE TRADITIONAL SKILLS A NEW BRIDE SHOULD HAVE.
YOU...
YOU FOOL!
WHO HAS *EVER* HEARD SOMETHING AS RIDICULOUS AS HAVING A *MAN* FOR A BRIDE?!
YOU'RE MAKING A LAUGHING-STOCK OF ME!

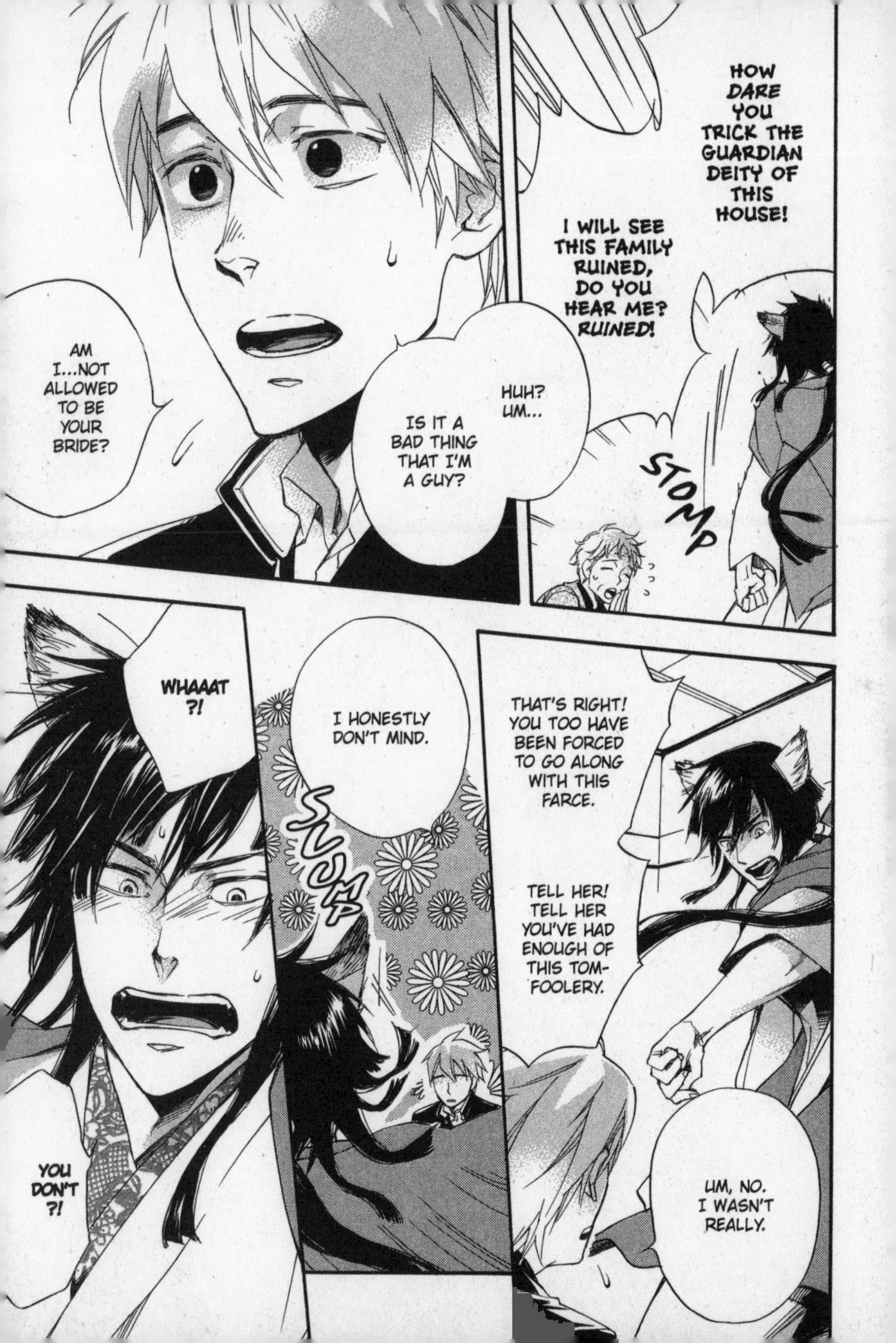
HOW DARE YOU TRICK THE GUARDIAN DEITY OF THIS HOUSE!
I WILL SEE THIS FAMILY RUINED, DO YOU HEAR ME? RUINED!
STOMP
HUH? UM...
IS IT A BAD THING THAT I'M A GUY?
AM I...NOT ALLOWED TO BE YOUR BRIDE?
THAT'S RIGHT! YOU TOO HAVE BEEN FORCED TO GO ALONG WITH THIS FARCE.
TELL HER! TELL HER YOU'VE HAD ENOUGH OF THIS TOM-FOOLERY.
UM, NO. I WASN'T REALLY.
I HONESTLY DON'T MIND.
SLUMP
WHAAAT ?!
YOU DON'T ?!

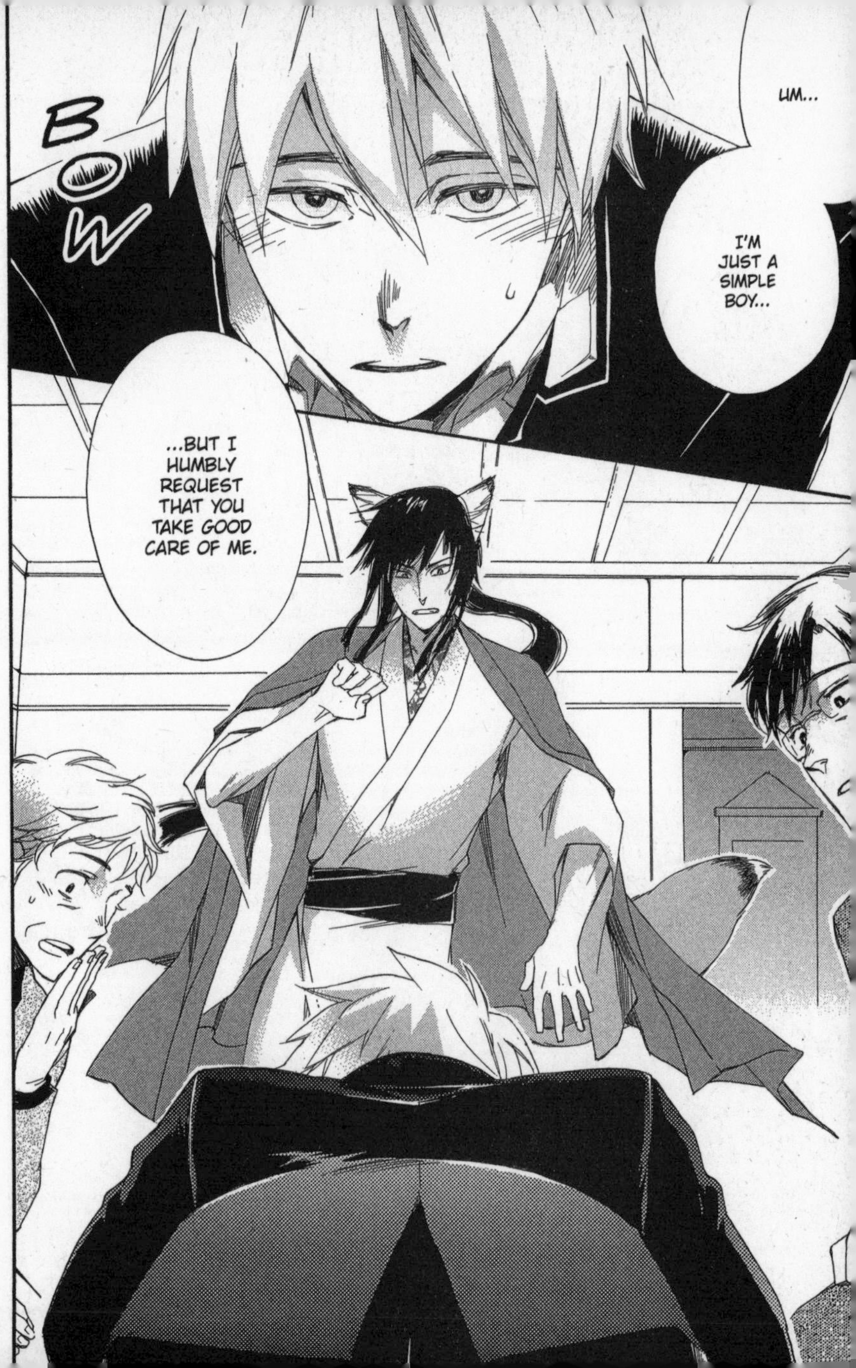
UM...
I'M JUST A SIMPLE BOY...
BOW
...BUT I HUMBLY REQUEST THAT YOU TAKE GOOD CARE OF ME.

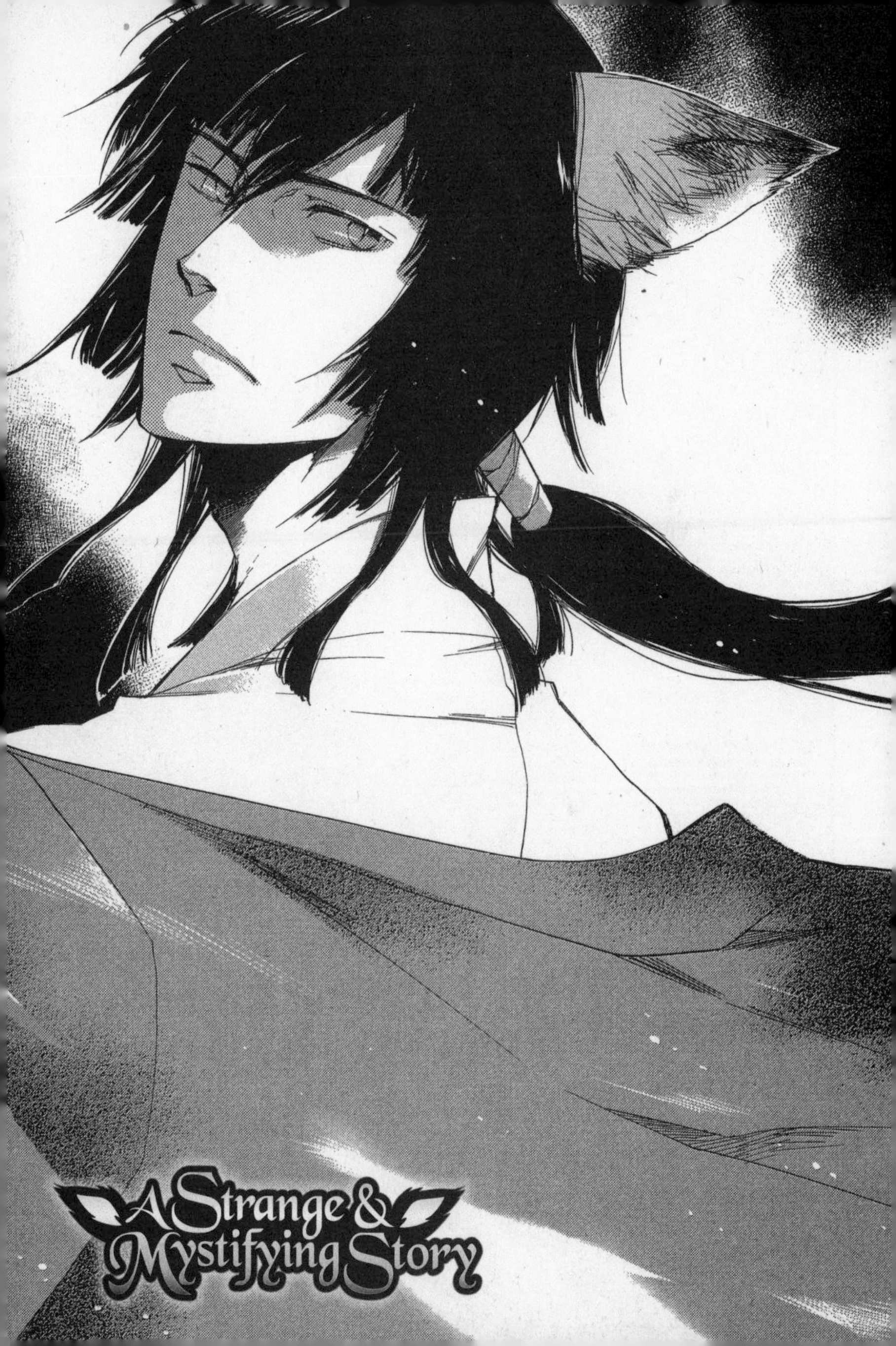
A Strange & Mystifying Story

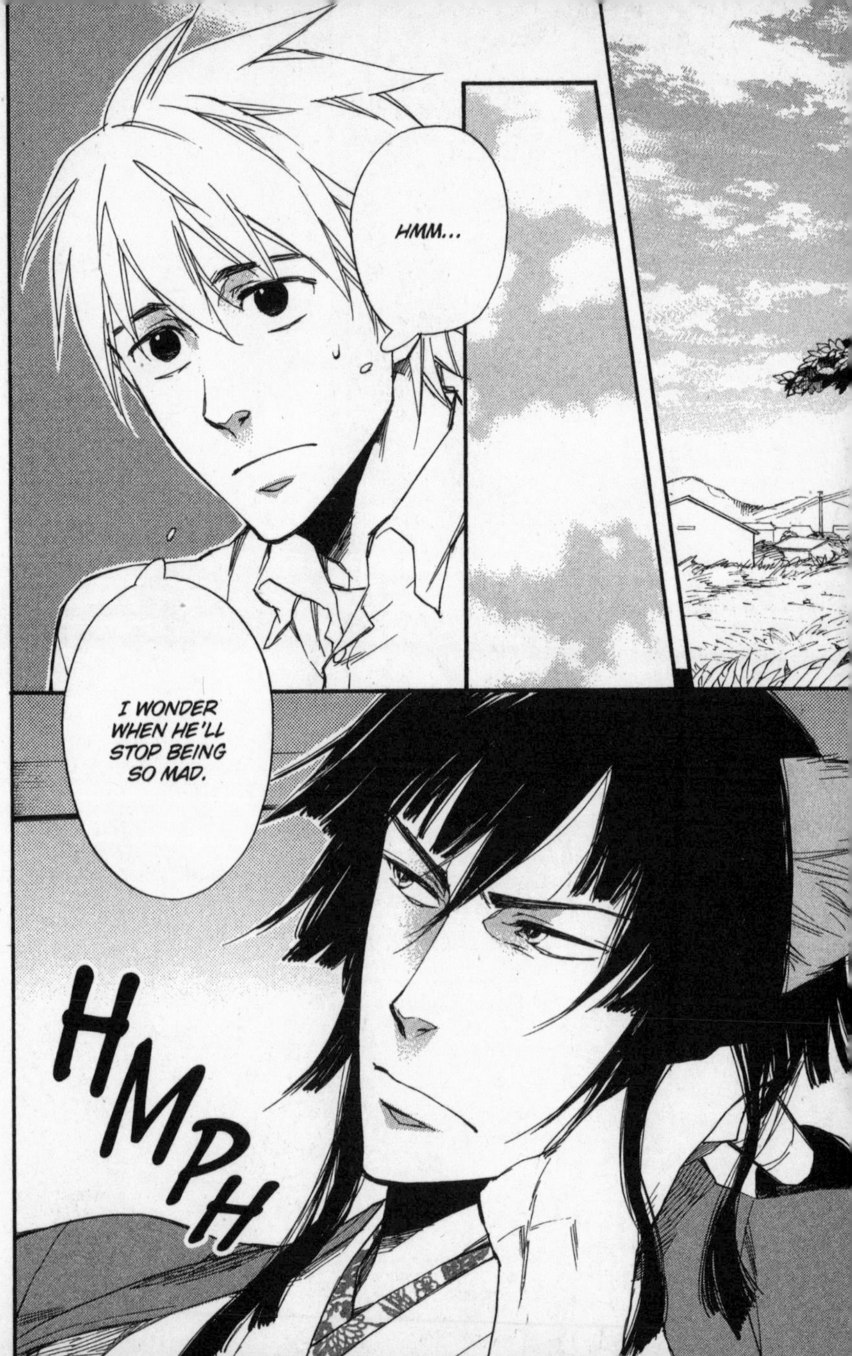
HMM...
I WONDER WHEN HE'LL STOP BEING SO MAD.
HMPH

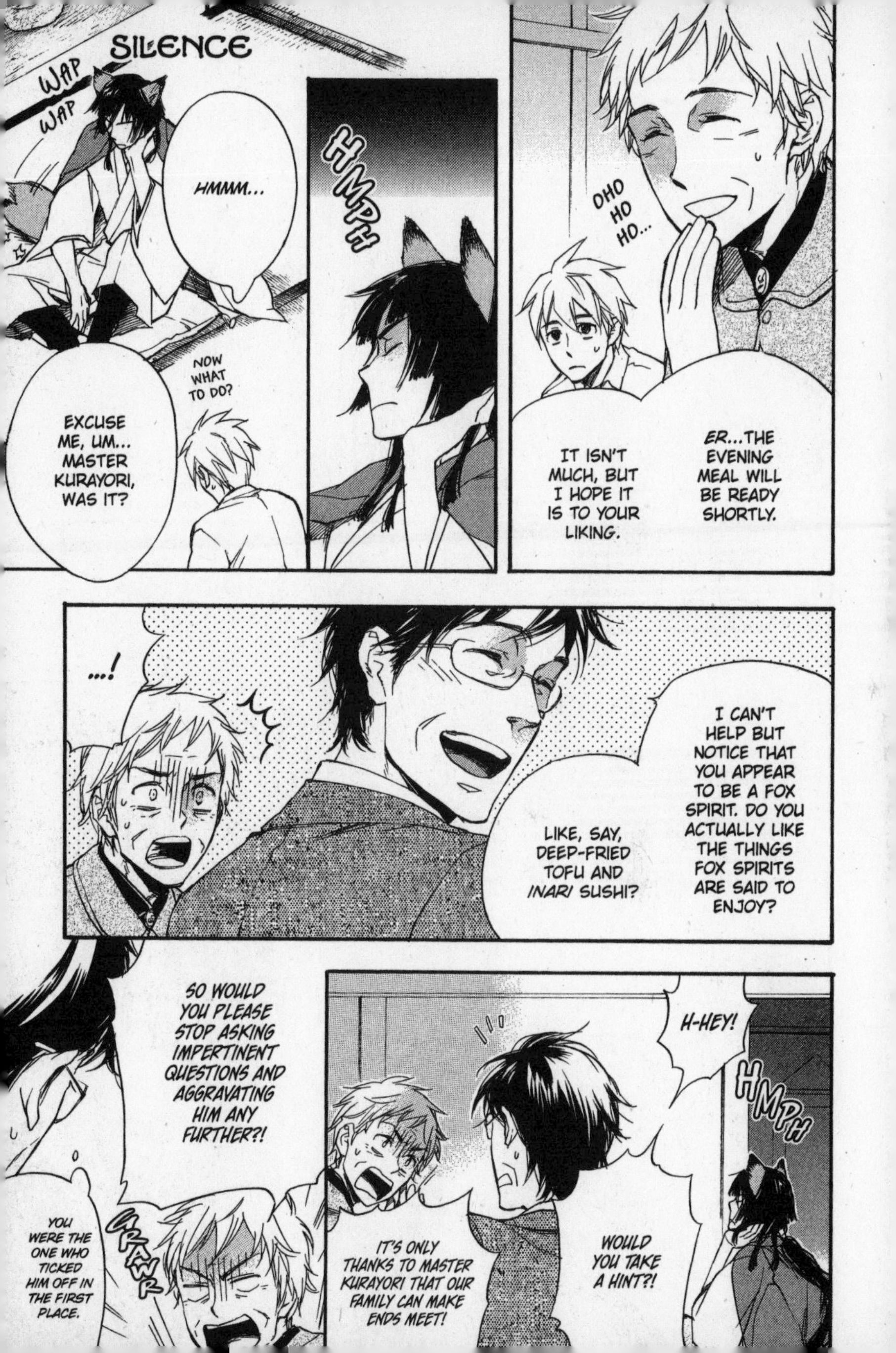
ER...THE EVENING MEAL WILL BE READY SHORTLY.
IT ISN'T MUCH, BUT I HOPE IT IS TO YOUR LIKING.
OHO HO HO...
HMPH
SILENCE
HMMM...
WAP WAP
NOW WHAT TO DO?
EXCUSE ME, UM... MASTER KURAYORI, WAS IT?
I CAN'T HELP BUT NOTICE THAT YOU APPEAR TO BE A FOX SPIRIT. DO YOU ACTUALLY LIKE THE THINGS FOX SPIRITS ARE SAID TO ENJOY?
LIKE, SAY, DEEP-FRIED TOFU AND INARI SUSHI?
...!
H-HEY!
HMPH
WOULD YOU TAKE A HINT?!
IT'S ONLY THANKS TO MASTER KURAYORI THAT OUR FAMILY CAN MAKE ENDS MEET!
SO WOULD YOU PLEASE STOP ASKING IMPERTINENT QUESTIONS AND AGGRAVATING HIM ANY FURTHER?!
YOU WERE THE ONE WHO TICKED HIM OFF IN THE FIRST PLACE.

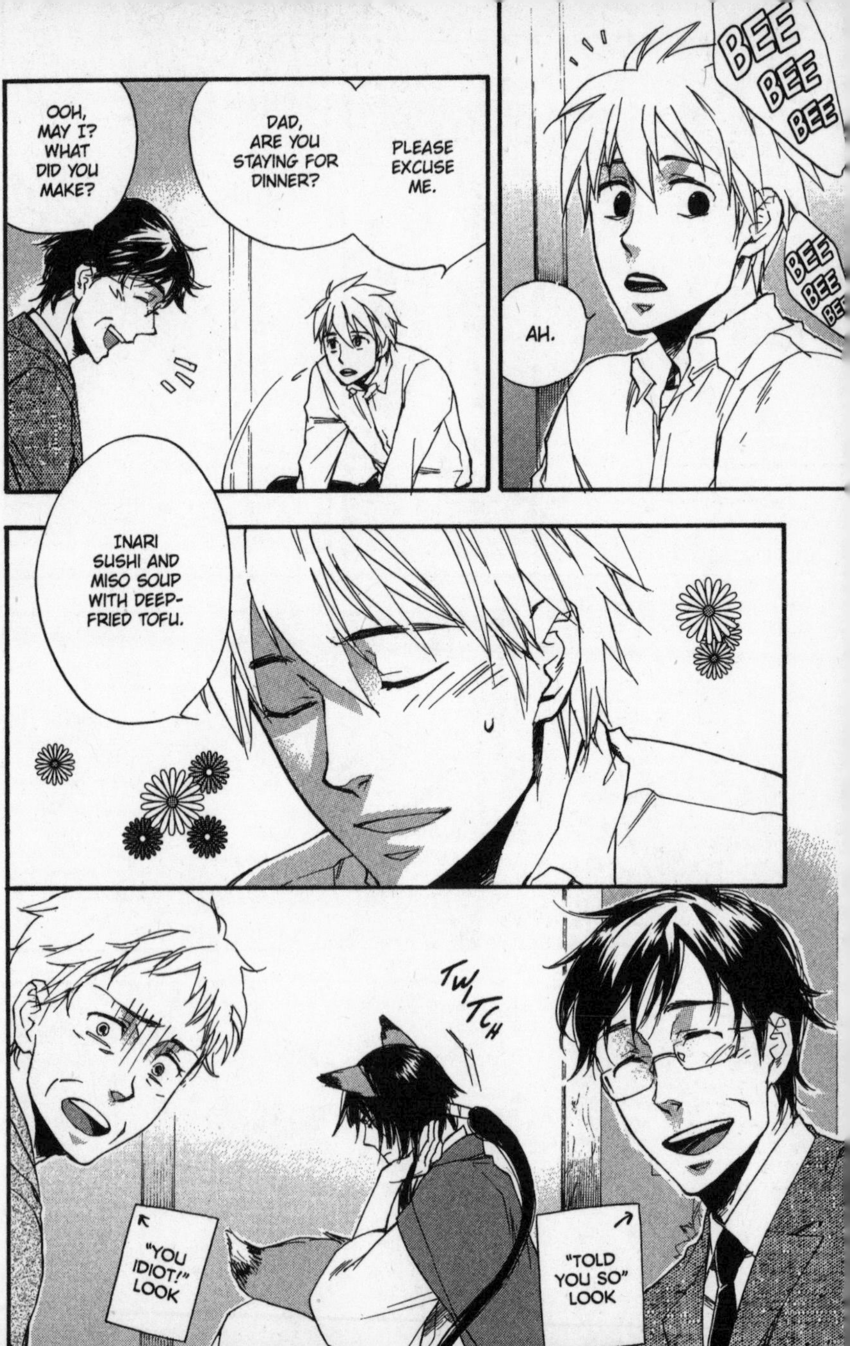
BEE BEE BEE
BEE BEE BE
AH.
PLEASE EXCUSE ME.
DAD, ARE YOU STAYING FOR DINNER?
OOH, MAY I? WHAT DID YOU MAKE?
INARI SUSHI AND MISO SOUP WITH DEEP-FRIED TOFU.
TWITCH
"TOLD YOU SO" LOOK
"YOU IDIOT!" LOOK

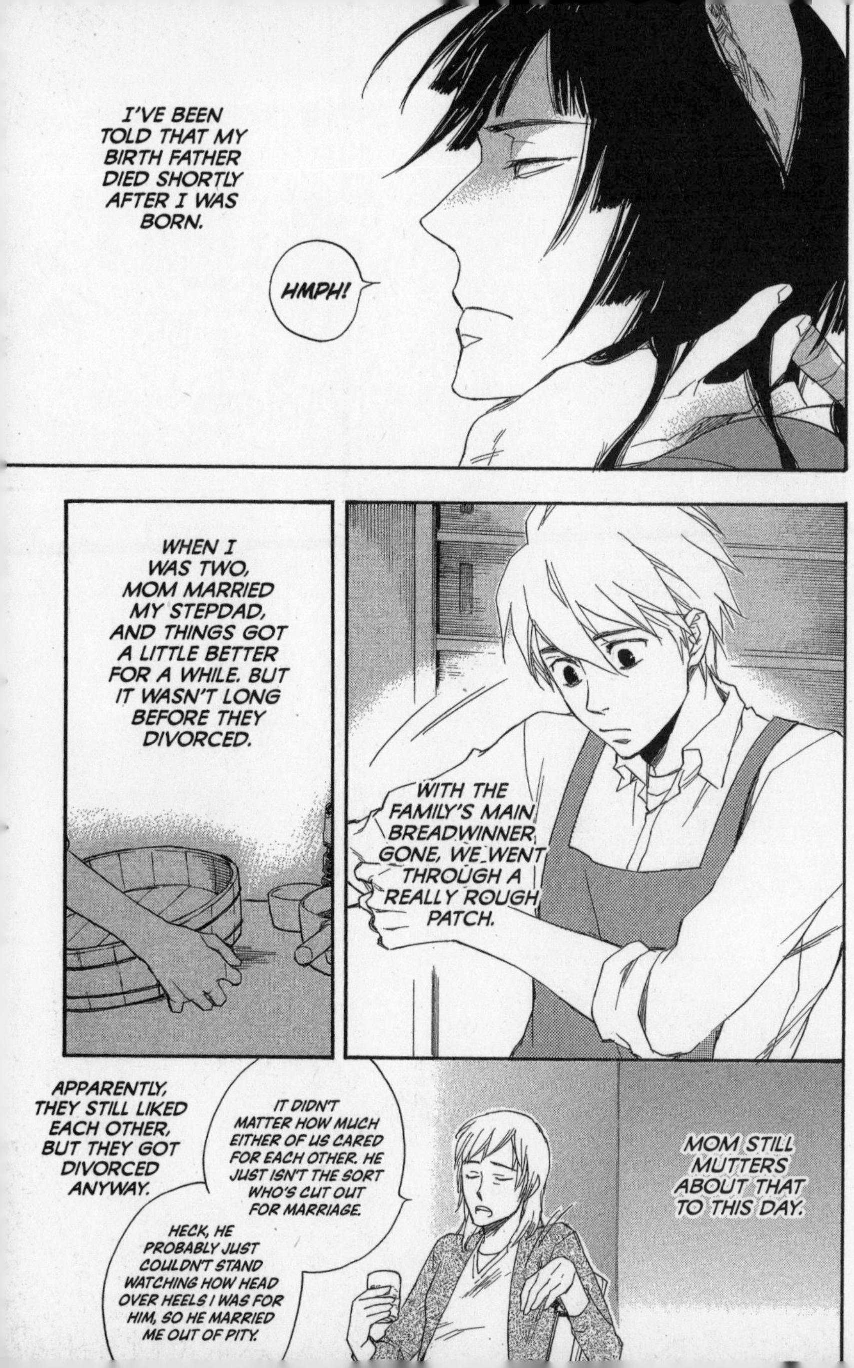
I'VE BEEN TOLD THAT MY BIRTH FATHER DIED SHORTLY AFTER I WAS BORN.
HMPH!
WHEN I WAS TWO, MOM MARRIED MY STEPDAD, AND THINGS GOT A LITTLE BETTER FOR A WHILE. BUT IT WASN'T LONG BEFORE THEY DIVORCED.
WITH THE FAMILY'S MAIN BREADWINNER GONE, WE WENT THROUGH A REALLY ROUGH PATCH.
APPARENTLY, THEY STILL LIKED EACH OTHER, BUT THEY GOT DIVORCED ANYWAY.
IT DIDN'T MATTER HOW MUCH EITHER OF US CARED FOR EACH OTHER. HE JUST ISN'T THE SORT WHO'S CUT OUT FOR MARRIAGE.
HECK, HE PROBABLY JUST COULDN'T STAND WATCHING HOW HEAD OVER HEELS I WAS FOR HIM, SO HE MARRIED ME OUT OF PITY.
MOM STILL MUTTERS ABOUT THAT TO THIS DAY.

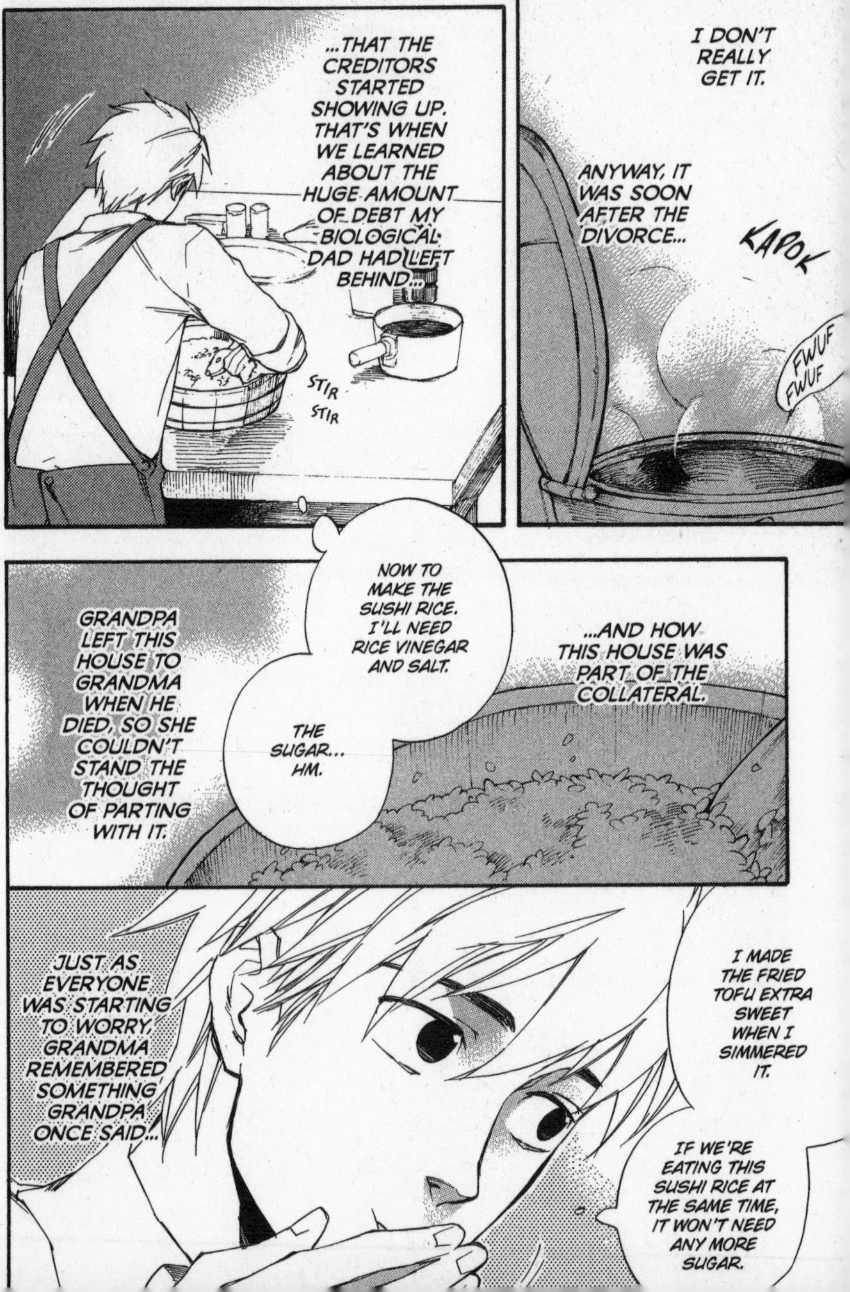
I DON'T REALLY GET IT.
ANYWAY, IT WAS SOON AFTER THE DIVORCE...
KAPOK
FWUF FWUF
...THAT THE CREDITORS STARTED SHOWING UP. THAT'S WHEN WE LEARNED ABOUT THE HUGE AMOUNT OF DEBT MY BIOLOGICAL DAD HAD LEFT BEHIND...
STIR STIR
...AND HOW THIS HOUSE WAS PART OF THE COLLATERAL.
NOW TO MAKE THE SUSHI RICE. I'LL NEED RICE VINEGAR AND SALT.
THE SUGAR... HM.
GRANDPA LEFT THIS HOUSE TO GRANDMA WHEN HE DIED, SO SHE COULDN'T STAND THE THOUGHT OF PARTING WITH IT.
I MADE THE FRIED TOFU EXTRA SWEET WHEN I SIMMERED IT.
IF WE'RE EATING THIS SUSHI RICE AT THE SAME TIME, IT WON'T NEED ANY MORE SUGAR.
JUST AS EVERYONE WAS STARTING TO WORRY, GRANDMA REMEMBERED SOMETHING GRANDPA ONCE SAID...

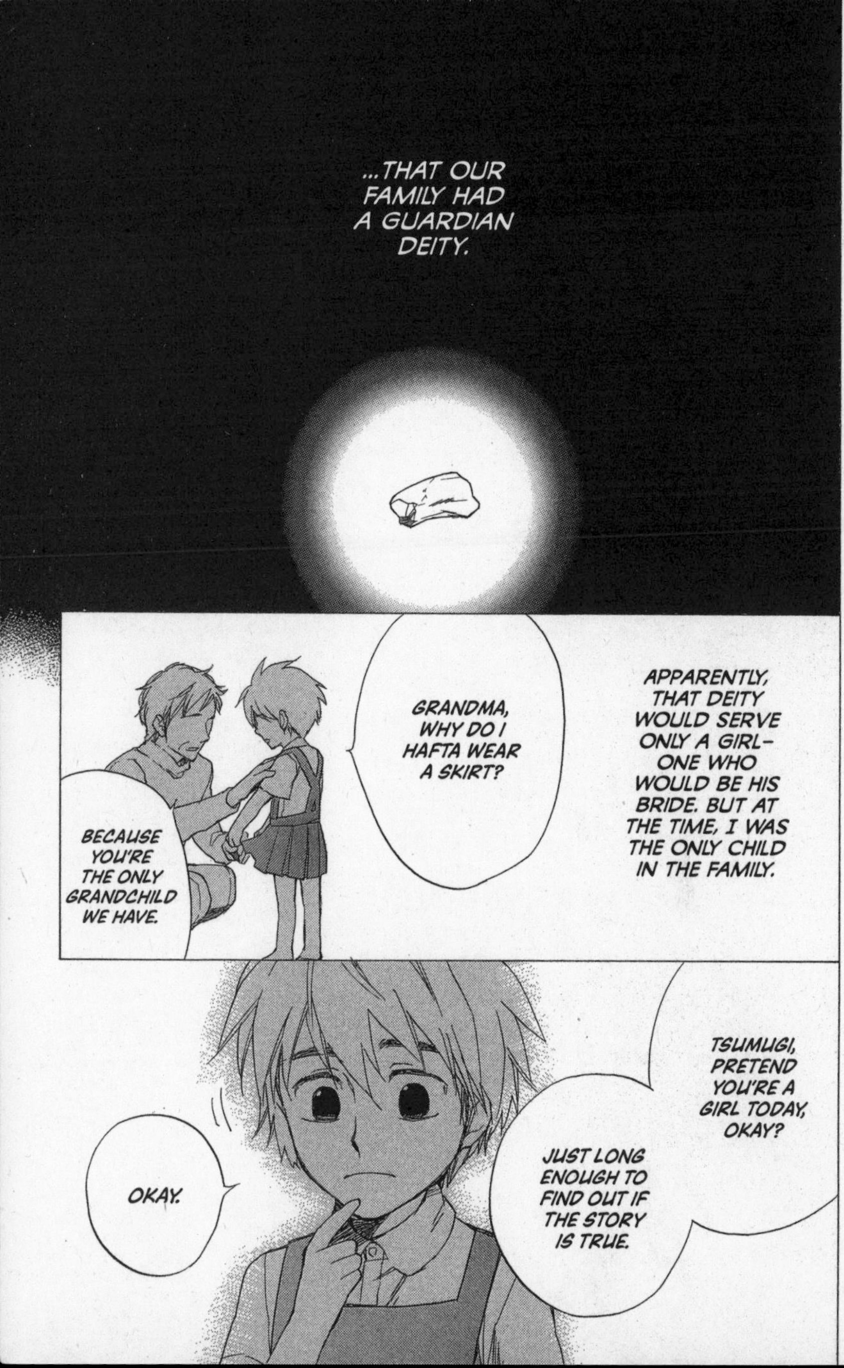
...THAT OUR FAMILY HAD A GUARDIAN DEITY.
APPARENTLY, THAT DEITY WOULD SERVE ONLY A GIRL— ONE WHO WOULD BE HIS BRIDE. BUT AT THE TIME, I WAS THE ONLY CHILD IN THE FAMILY.
GRANDMA, WHY DO I HAFTA WEAR A SKIRT?
BECAUSE YOU'RE THE ONLY GRANDCHILD WE HAVE.
TSUMUGI, PRETEND YOU'RE A GIRL TODAY, OKAY?
JUST LONG ENOUGH TO FIND OUT IF THE STORY IS TRUE.
OKAY.

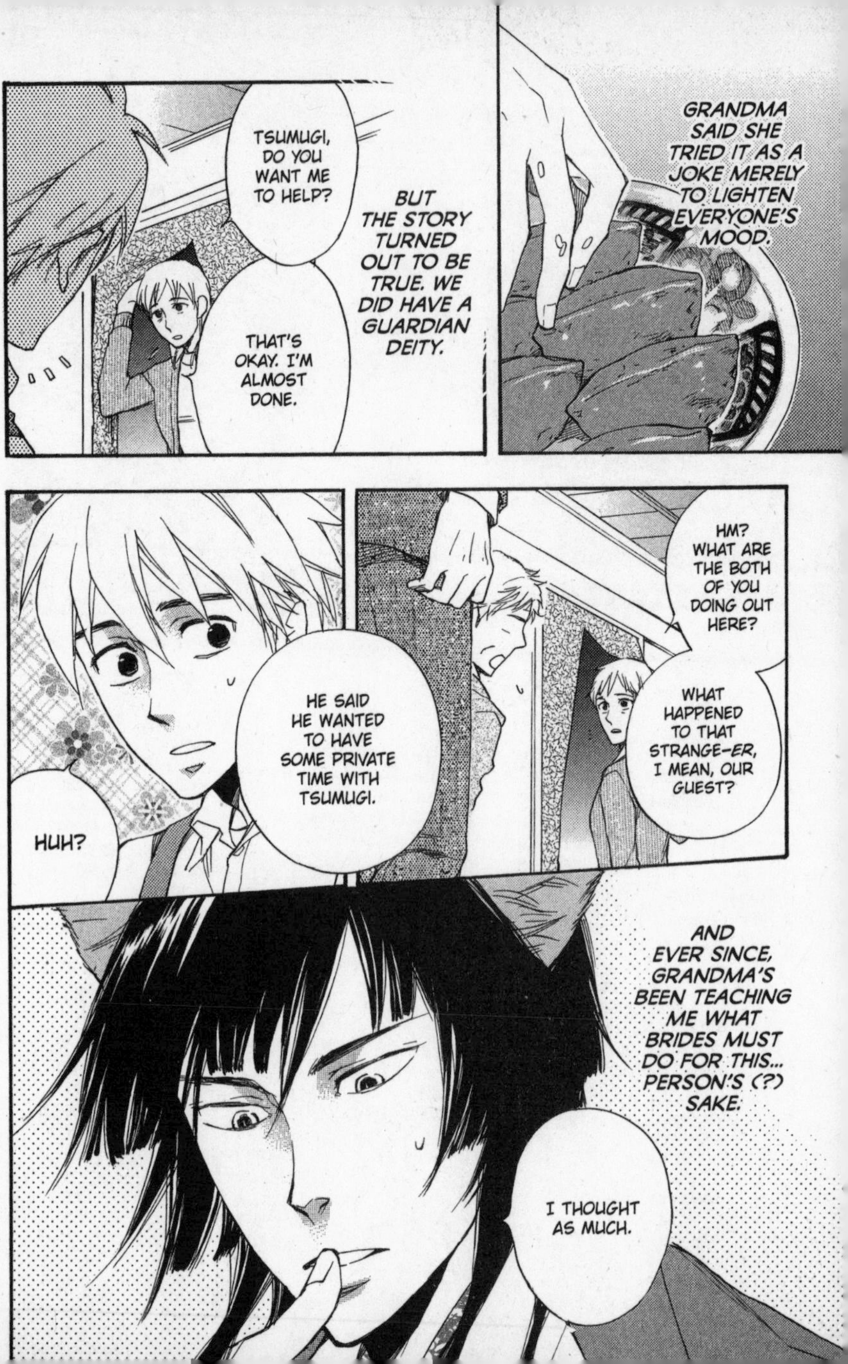
GRANDMA SAID SHE TRIED IT AS A JOKE MERELY TO LIGHTEN EVERYONE'S MOOD.
BUT THE STORY TURNED OUT TO BE TRUE. WE DID HAVE A GUARDIAN DEITY.
TSUMUGI, DO YOU WANT ME TO HELP?
THAT'S OKAY. I'M ALMOST DONE.
HM? WHAT ARE THE BOTH OF YOU DOING OUT HERE?
WHAT HAPPENED TO THAT STRANGE-ER, I MEAN, OUR GUEST?
HE SAID HE WANTED TO HAVE SOME PRIVATE TIME WITH TSUMUGI.
HUH?
AND EVER SINCE, GRANDMA'S BEEN TEACHING ME WHAT BRIDES MUST DO FOR THIS... PERSON'S (?) SAKE.
I THOUGHT AS MUCH.

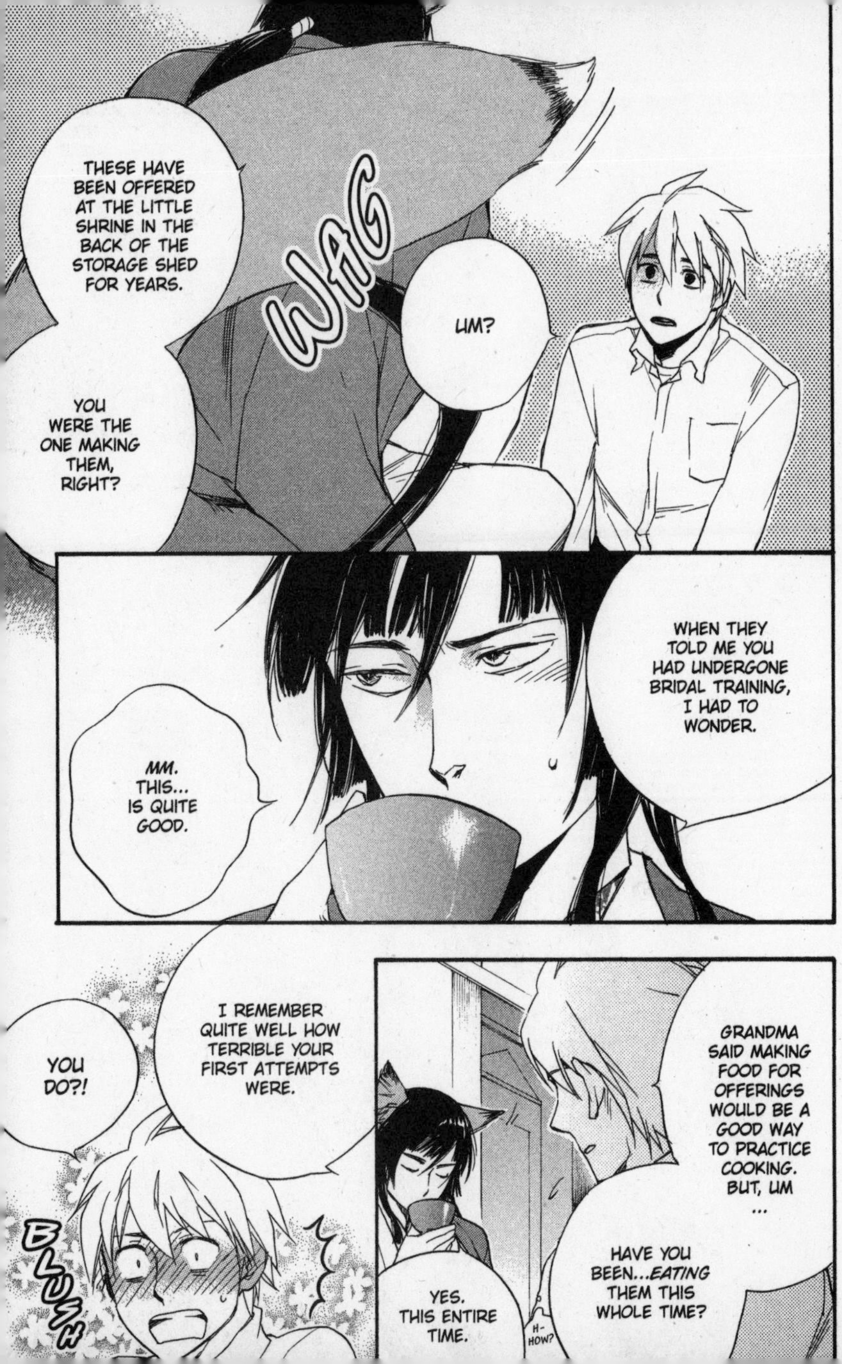
THESE HAVE BEEN OFFERED AT THE LITTLE SHRINE IN THE BACK OF THE STORAGE SHED FOR YEARS.
WAG
UM?
YOU WERE THE ONE MAKING THEM, RIGHT?
WHEN THEY TOLD ME YOU HAD UNDERGONE BRIDAL TRAINING, I HAD TO WONDER.
MM. THIS... IS QUITE GOOD.
GRANDMA SAID MAKING FOOD FOR OFFERINGS WOULD BE A GOOD WAY TO PRACTICE COOKING. BUT, UM ...
HAVE YOU BEEN...*EATING* THEM THIS WHOLE TIME?
YES. THIS ENTIRE TIME.
H-HOW?
I REMEMBER QUITE WELL HOW TERRIBLE YOUR FIRST ATTEMPTS WERE.
YOU DO?!
BLUSH

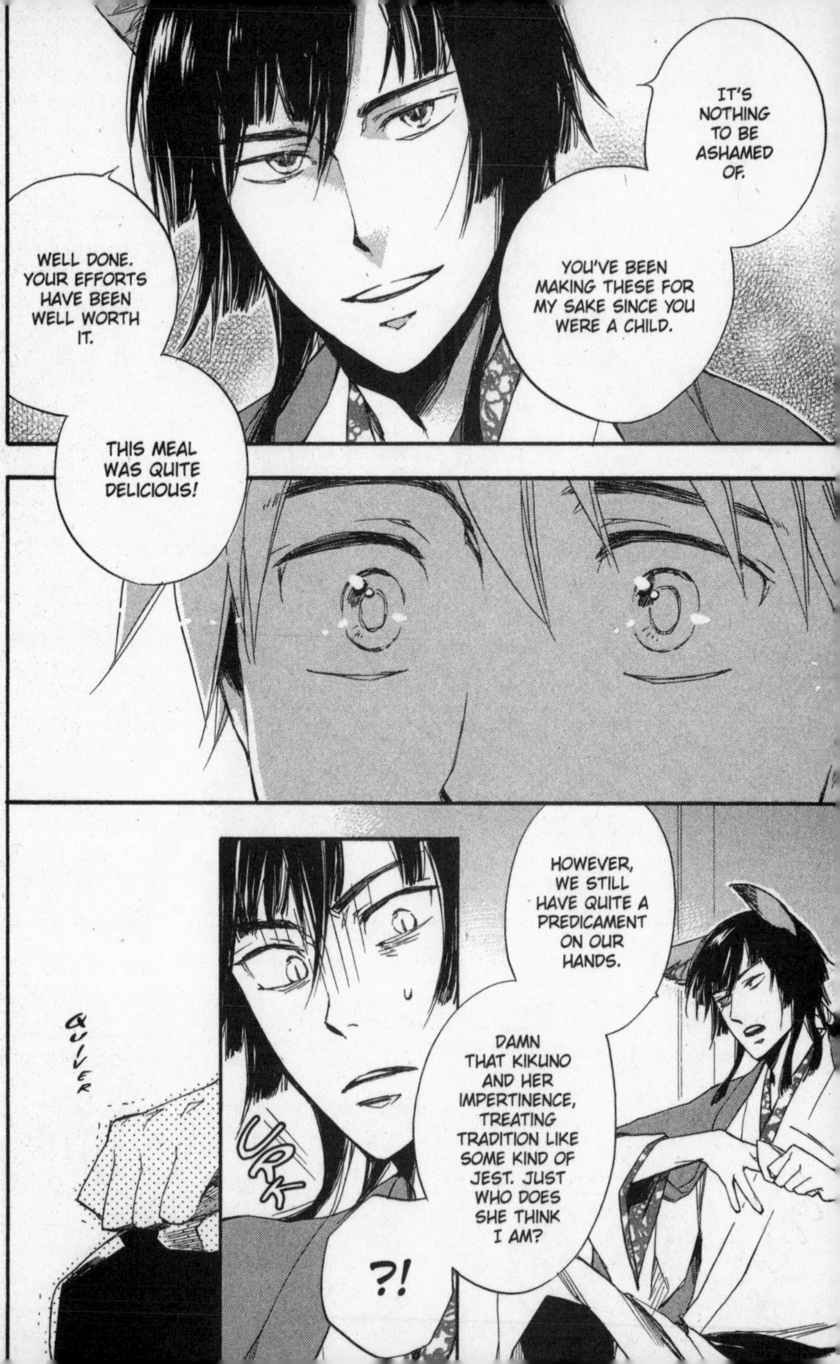
IT'S NOTHING TO BE ASHAMED OF.
YOU'VE BEEN MAKING THESE FOR MY SAKE SINCE YOU WERE A CHILD.
WELL DONE. YOUR EFFORTS HAVE BEEN WELL WORTH IT.
THIS MEAL WAS QUITE DELICIOUS!
HOWEVER, WE STILL HAVE QUITE A PREDICAMENT ON OUR HANDS.
DAMN THAT KIKUNO AND HER IMPERTINENCE, TREATING TRADITION LIKE SOME KIND OF JEST. JUST WHO DOES SHE THINK I AM?
?!
URK
QUIVER

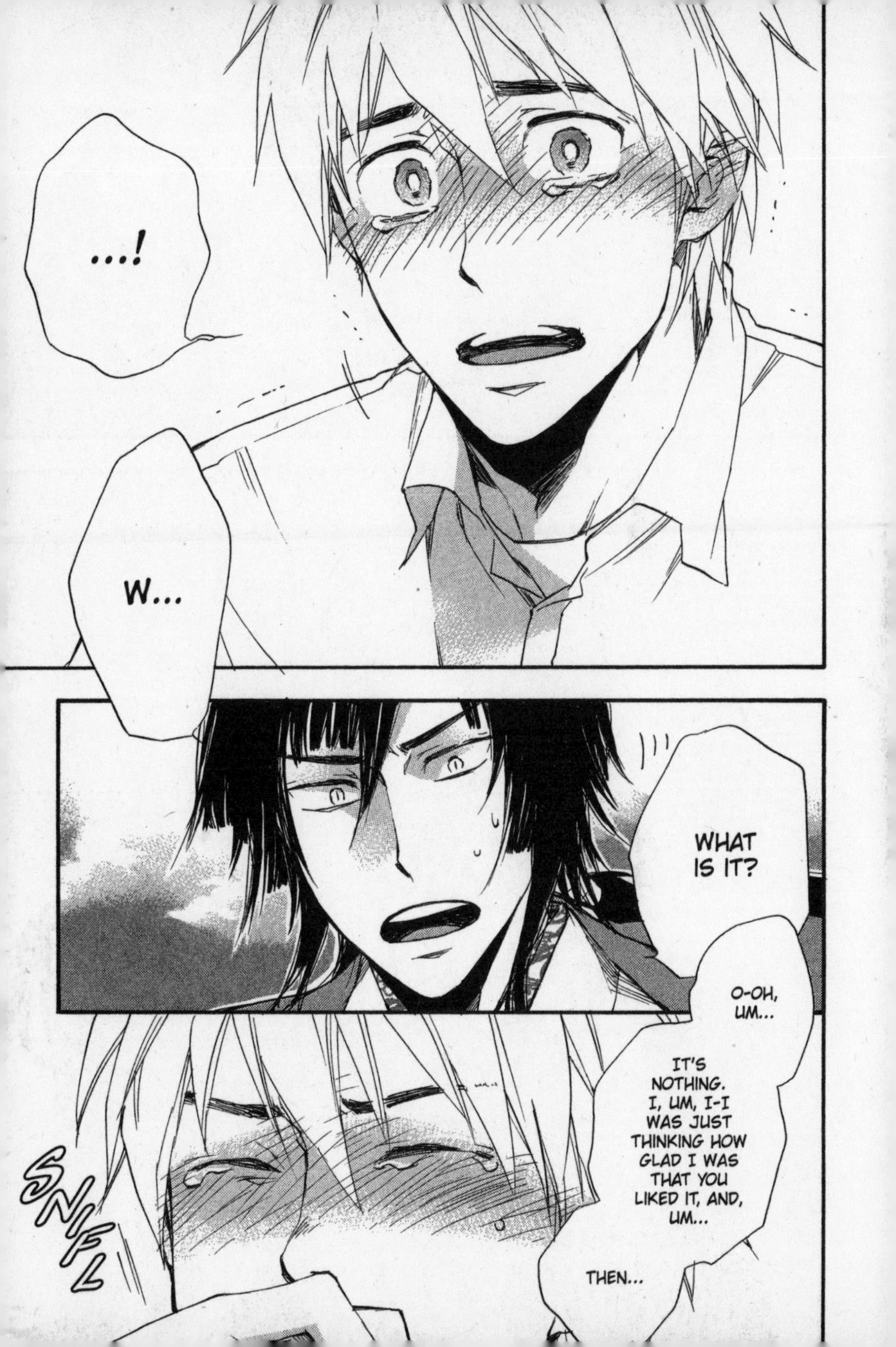
...!
W...
WHAT IS IT?
O-OH, UM...
IT'S NOTHING. I, UM, I-I WAS JUST THINKING HOW GLAD I WAS THAT YOU LIKED IT, AND, UM...
THEN...
SNIFL

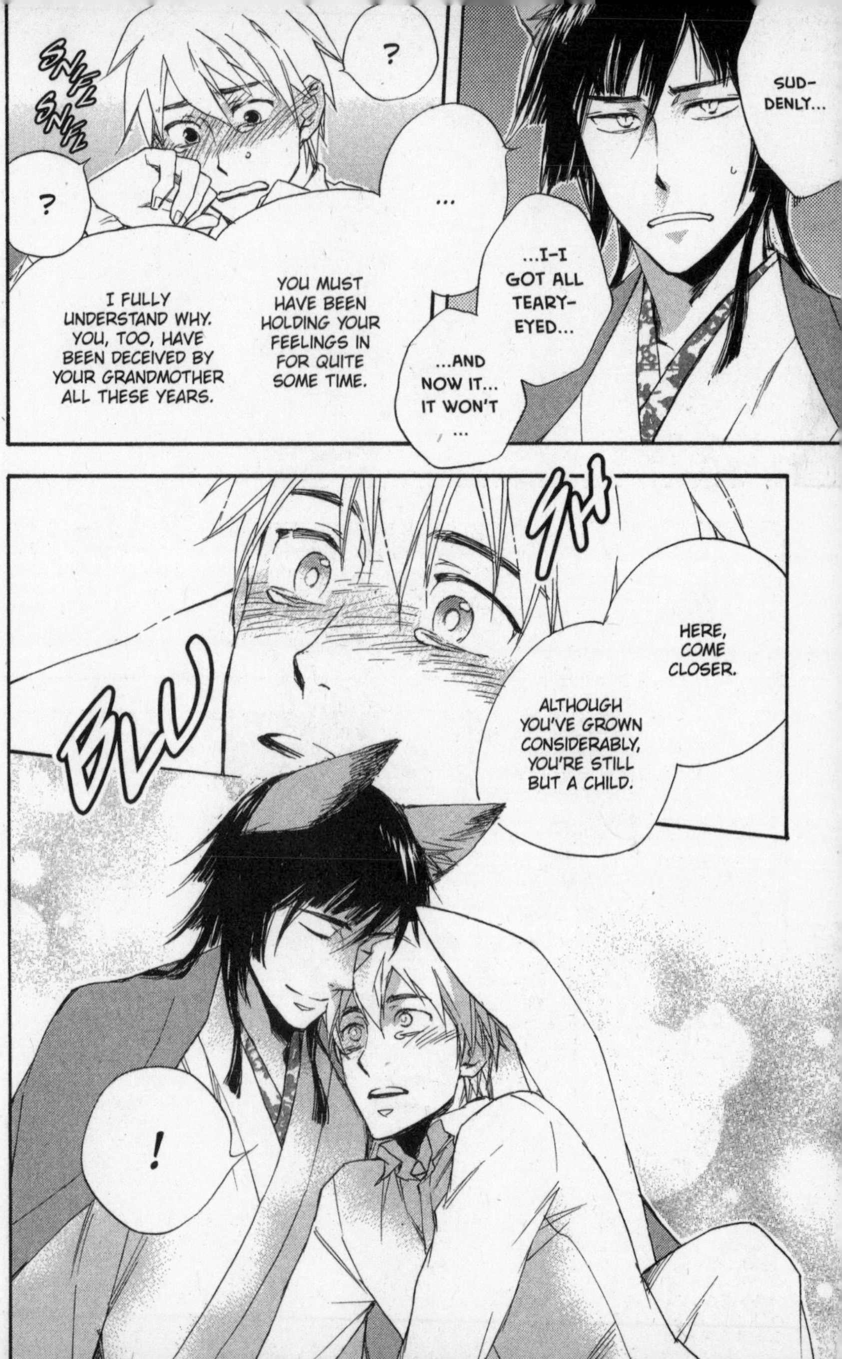
SUD-DENLY...
...I-I GOT ALL TEARY-EYED...
...AND NOW IT... IT WON'T ...
?
...
YOU MUST HAVE BEEN HOLDING YOUR FEELINGS IN FOR QUITE SOME TIME.
?
I FULLY UNDERSTAND WHY. YOU, TOO, HAVE BEEN DECEIVED BY YOUR GRANDMOTHER ALL THESE YEARS.
HERE, COME CLOSER.
ALTHOUGH YOU'VE GROWN CONSIDERABLY, YOU'RE STILL BUT A CHILD.
BLU
!

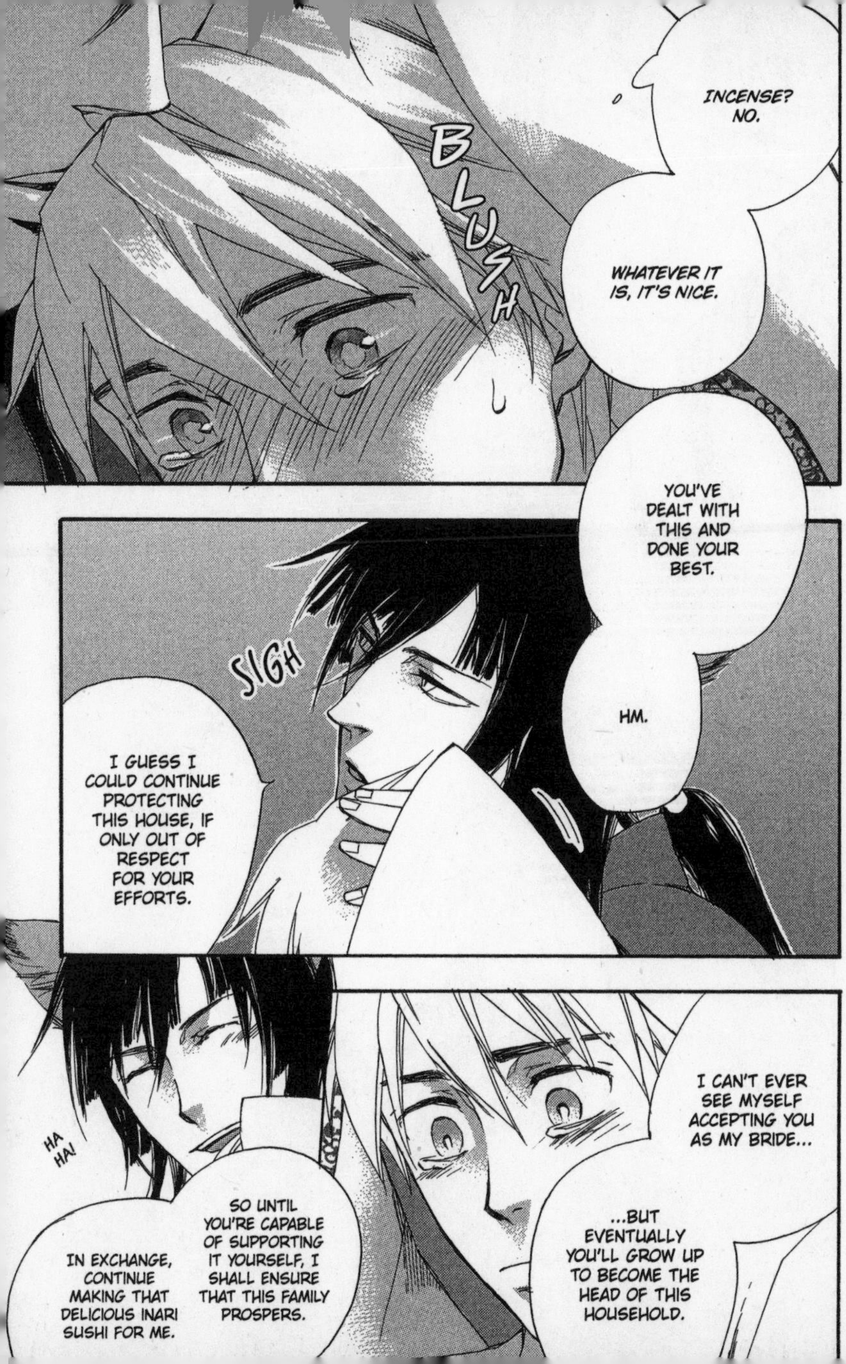
INCENSE? NO.
BLUSH
WHATEVER IT IS, IT'S NICE.
YOU'VE DEALT WITH THIS AND DONE YOUR BEST.
HM.
SIGH
I GUESS I COULD CONTINUE PROTECTING THIS HOUSE, IF ONLY OUT OF RESPECT FOR YOUR EFFORTS.
I CAN'T EVER SEE MYSELF ACCEPTING YOU AS MY BRIDE...
...BUT EVENTUALLY YOU'LL GROW UP TO BECOME THE HEAD OF THIS HOUSEHOLD.
SO UNTIL YOU'RE CAPABLE OF SUPPORTING IT YOURSELF, I SHALL ENSURE THAT THIS FAMILY PROSPERS.
IN EXCHANGE, CONTINUE MAKING THAT DELICIOUS INARI SUSHI FOR ME.
HA HA!

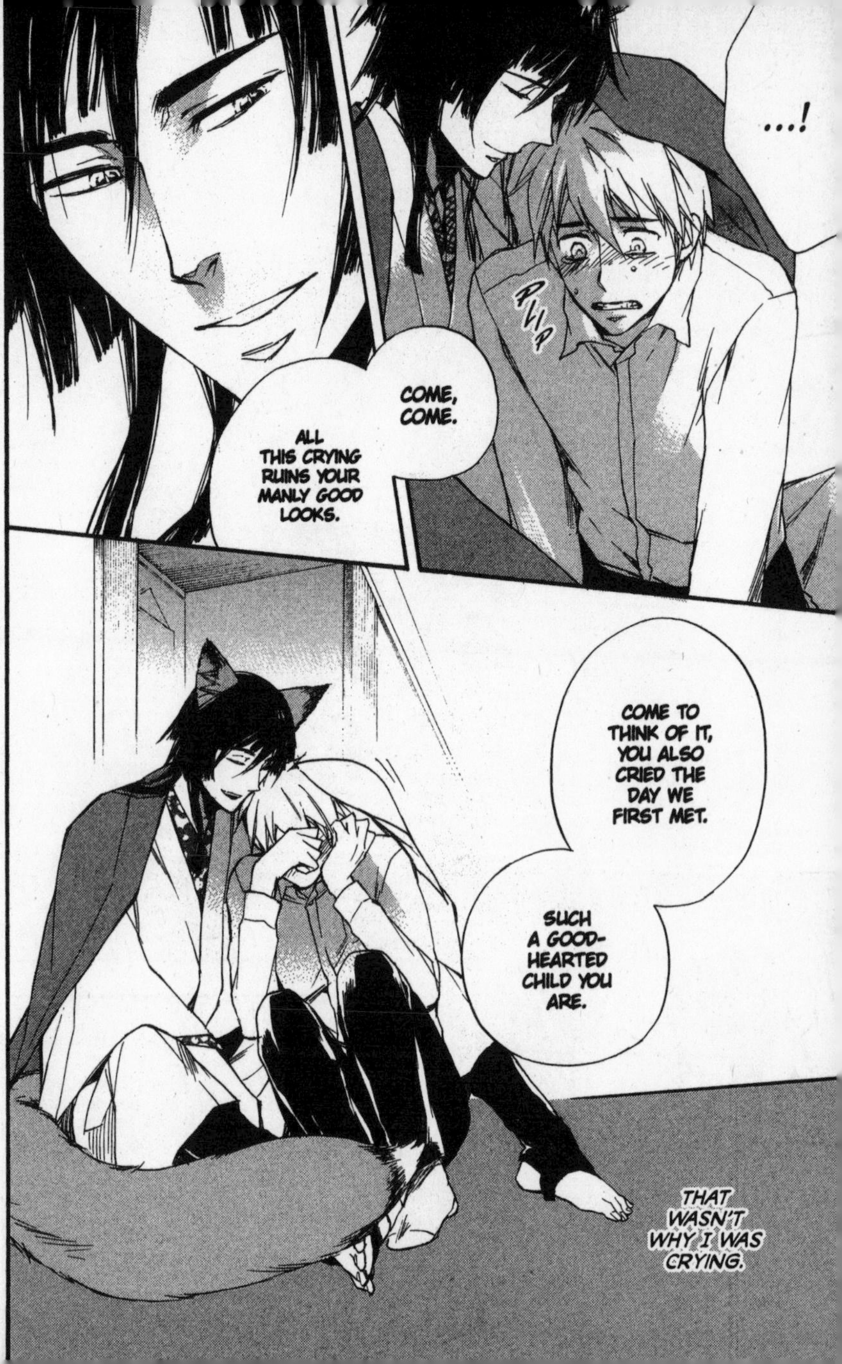
...!
RRIP
COME, COME.
ALL THIS CRYING RUINS YOUR MANLY GOOD LOOKS.
COME TO THINK OF IT, YOU ALSO CRIED THE DAY WE FIRST MET.
SUCH A GOOD-HEARTED CHILD YOU ARE.
THAT WASN'T WHY I WAS CRYING.

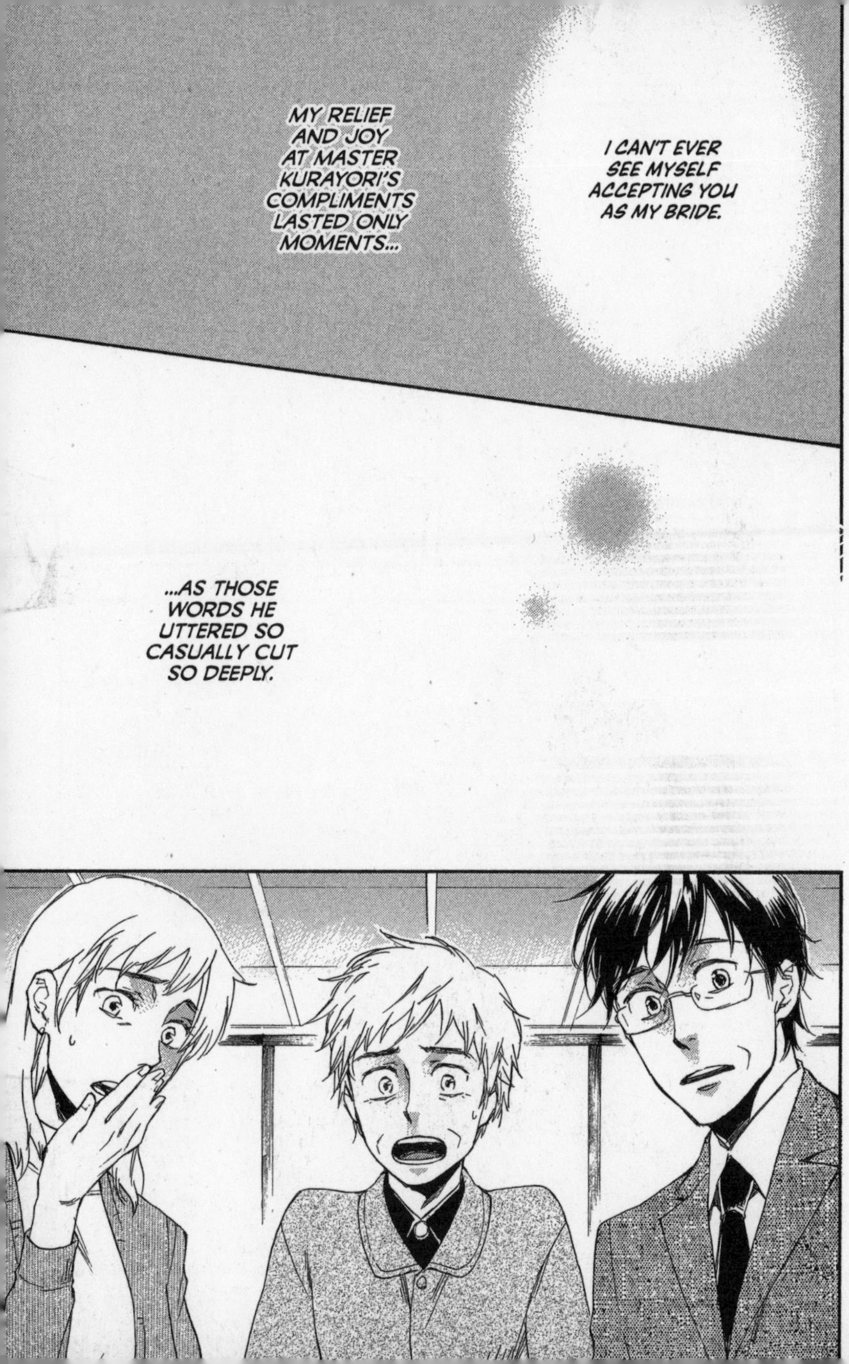
I CAN'T EVER SEE MYSELF ACCEPTING YOU AS MY BRIDE.
MY RELIEF AND JOY AT MASTER KURAYORI'S COMPLIMENTS LASTED ONLY MOMENTS...
...AS THOSE WORDS HE UTTERED SO CASUALLY CUT SO DEEPLY.

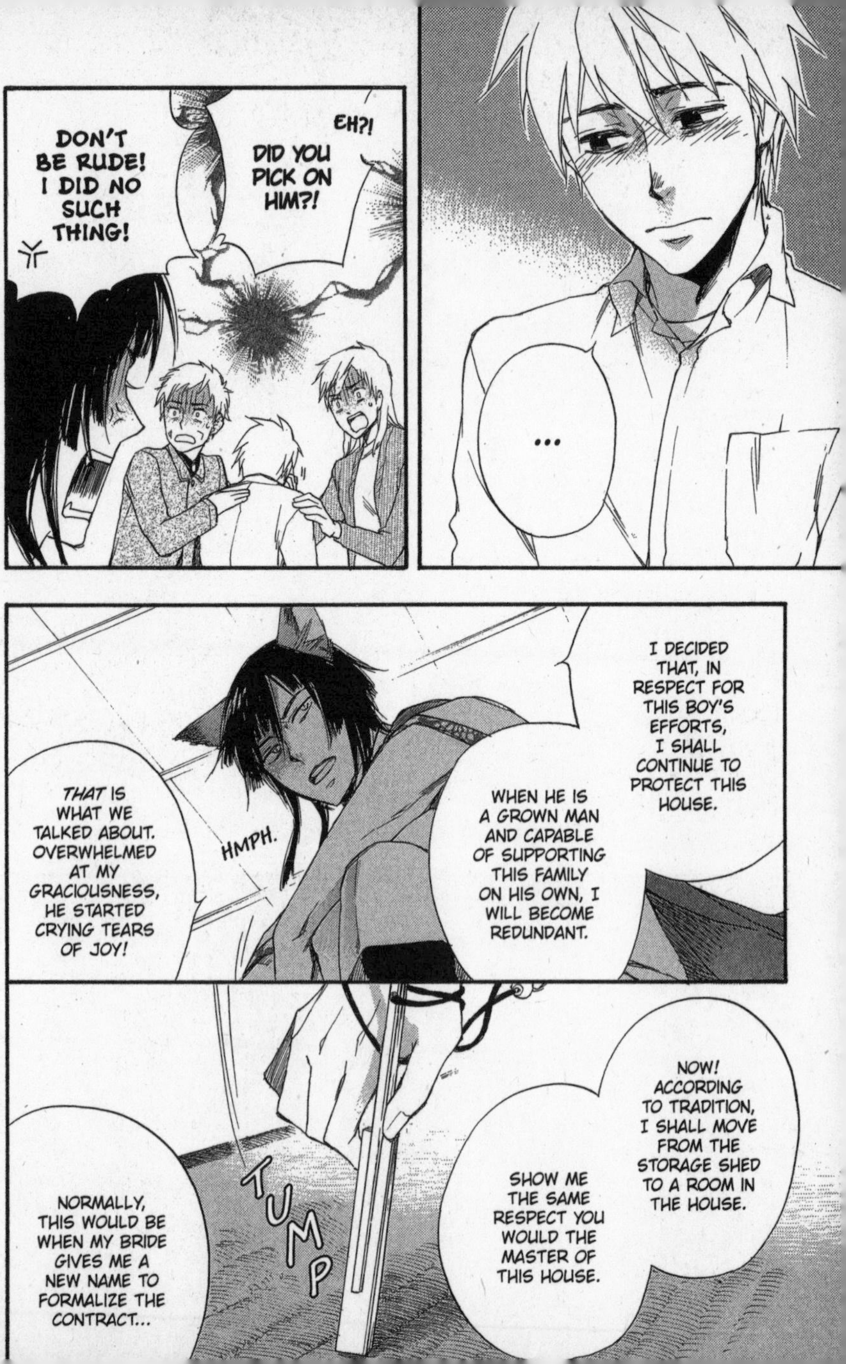
...
EH?!
DID YOU PICK ON HIM?!
DON'T BE RUDE! I DID NO SUCH THING!
I DECIDED THAT, IN RESPECT FOR THIS BOY'S EFFORTS, I SHALL CONTINUE TO PROTECT THIS HOUSE.
WHEN HE IS A GROWN MAN AND CAPABLE OF SUPPORTING THIS FAMILY ON HIS OWN, I WILL BECOME REDUNDANT.
HMPH.
THAT IS WHAT WE TALKED ABOUT. OVERWHELMED AT MY GRACIOUSNESS, HE STARTED CRYING TEARS OF JOY!
NOW! ACCORDING TO TRADITION, I SHALL MOVE FROM THE STORAGE SHED TO A ROOM IN THE HOUSE.
SHOW ME THE SAME RESPECT YOU WOULD THE MASTER OF THIS HOUSE.
TUMP
NORMALLY, THIS WOULD BE WHEN MY BRIDE GIVES ME A NEW NAME TO FORMALIZE THE CONTRACT...

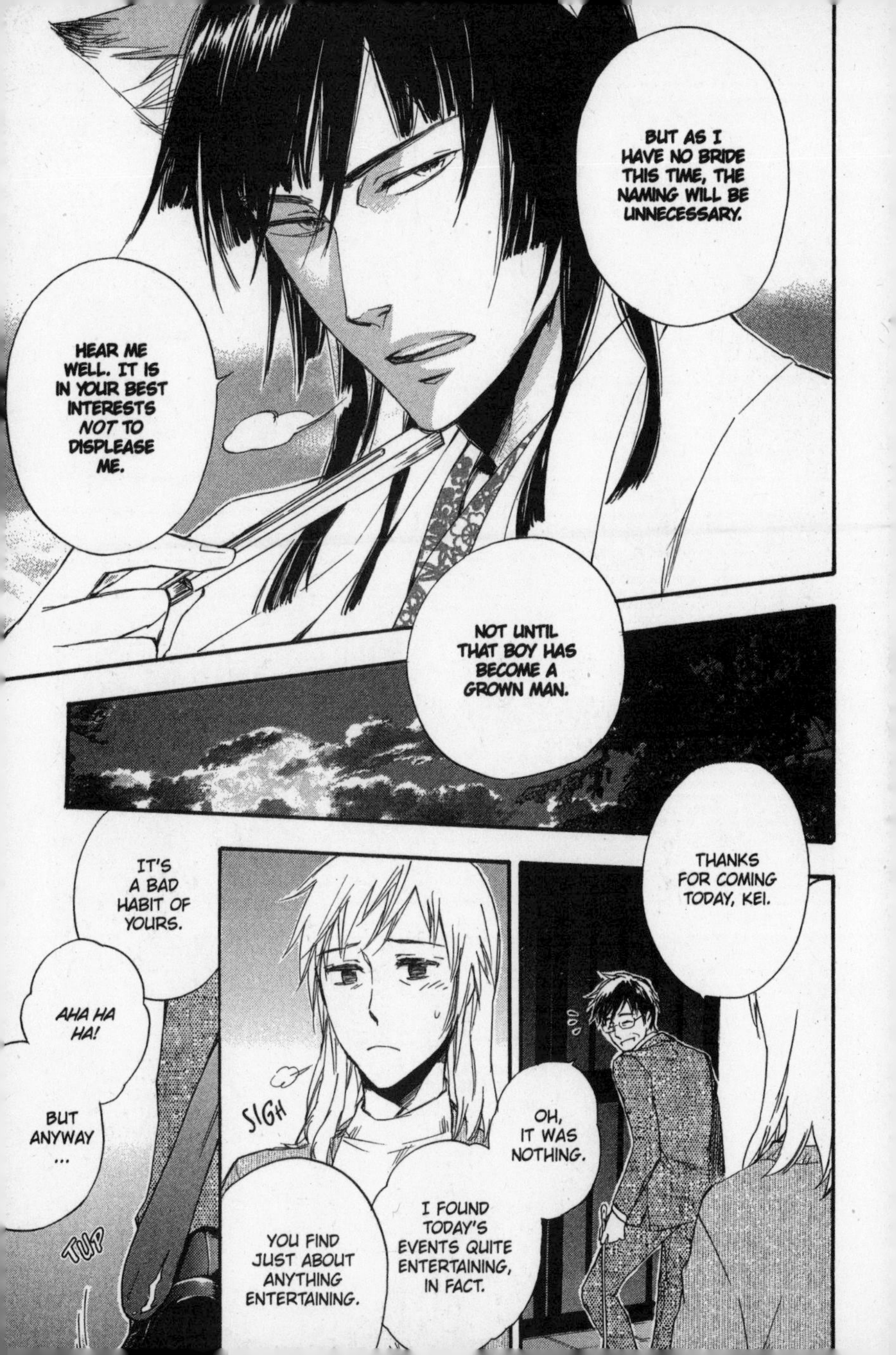
BUT AS I HAVE NO BRIDE THIS TIME, THE NAMING WILL BE UNNECESSARY.
HEAR ME WELL. IT IS IN YOUR BEST INTERESTS *NOT* TO DISPLEASE ME.
NOT UNTIL THAT BOY HAS BECOME A GROWN MAN.
THANKS FOR COMING TODAY, KEI.
OH, IT WAS NOTHING.
I FOUND TODAY'S EVENTS QUITE ENTERTAINING, IN FACT.
SIGH
YOU FIND JUST ABOUT ANYTHING ENTERTAINING.
IT'S A BAD HABIT OF YOURS.
AHA HA HA!
BUT ANYWAY ...
TUP

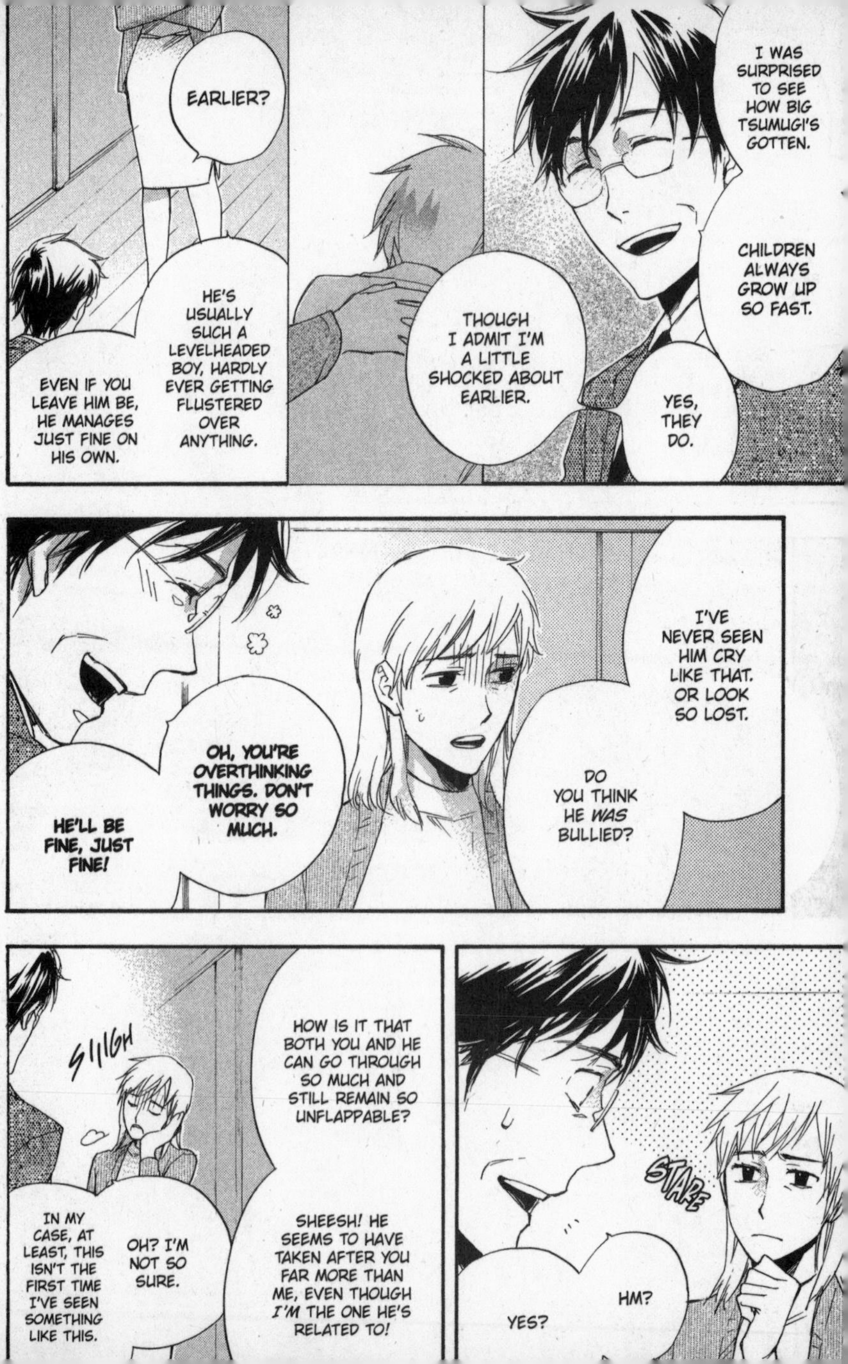
I WAS SURPRISED TO SEE HOW BIG TSUMUGI'S GOTTEN.
CHILDREN ALWAYS GROW UP SO FAST.
YES, THEY DO.
THOUGH I ADMIT I'M A LITTLE SHOCKED ABOUT EARLIER.
EARLIER?
HE'S USUALLY SUCH A LEVELHEADED BOY, HARDLY EVER GETTING FLUSTERED OVER ANYTHING.
EVEN IF YOU LEAVE HIM BE, HE MANAGES JUST FINE ON HIS OWN.
I'VE NEVER SEEN HIM CRY LIKE THAT. OR LOOK SO LOST.
DO YOU THINK HE *WAS* BULLIED?
OH, YOU'RE OVERTHINKING THINGS. DON'T WORRY SO MUCH.
HE'LL BE FINE, JUST FINE!
STARE
HM?
YES?
HOW IS IT THAT BOTH YOU AND HE CAN GO THROUGH SO MUCH AND STILL REMAIN SO UNFLAPPABLE?
SIIIGH
SHEESH! HE SEEMS TO HAVE TAKEN AFTER YOU FAR MORE THAN ME, EVEN THOUGH *I'M* THE ONE HE'S RELATED TO!
OH? I'M NOT SO SURE.
IN MY CASE, AT LEAST, THIS ISN'T THE FIRST TIME I'VE SEEN SOMETHING LIKE THIS.

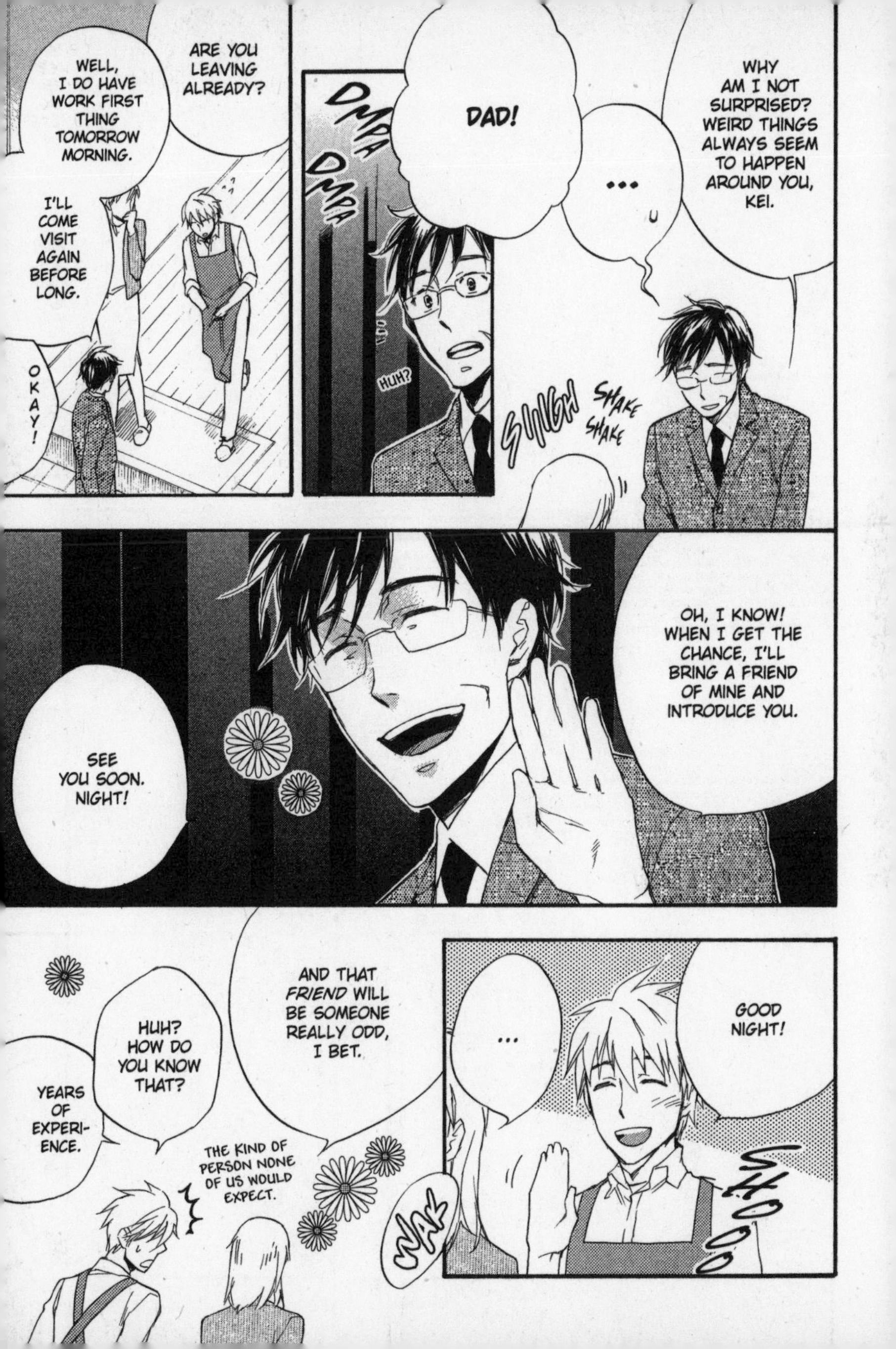
WHY AM I NOT SURPRISED? WEIRD THINGS ALWAYS SEEM TO HAPPEN AROUND YOU, KEI.
...
SIGH
SHAKE SHAKE
DAD!
DMPA DMPA
HUH?
ARE YOU LEAVING ALREADY?
WELL, I DO HAVE WORK FIRST THING TOMORROW MORNING.
I'LL COME VISIT AGAIN BEFORE LONG.
OKAY!
OH, I KNOW! WHEN I GET THE CHANCE, I'LL BRING A FRIEND OF MINE AND INTRODUCE YOU.
SEE YOU SOON. NIGHT!
GOOD NIGHT!
...
SHOOOO
WAK
AND THAT *FRIEND* WILL BE SOMEONE REALLY ODD, I BET.
HUH? HOW DO YOU KNOW THAT?
YEARS OF EXPERIENCE.
THE KIND OF PERSON NONE OF US WOULD EXPECT.

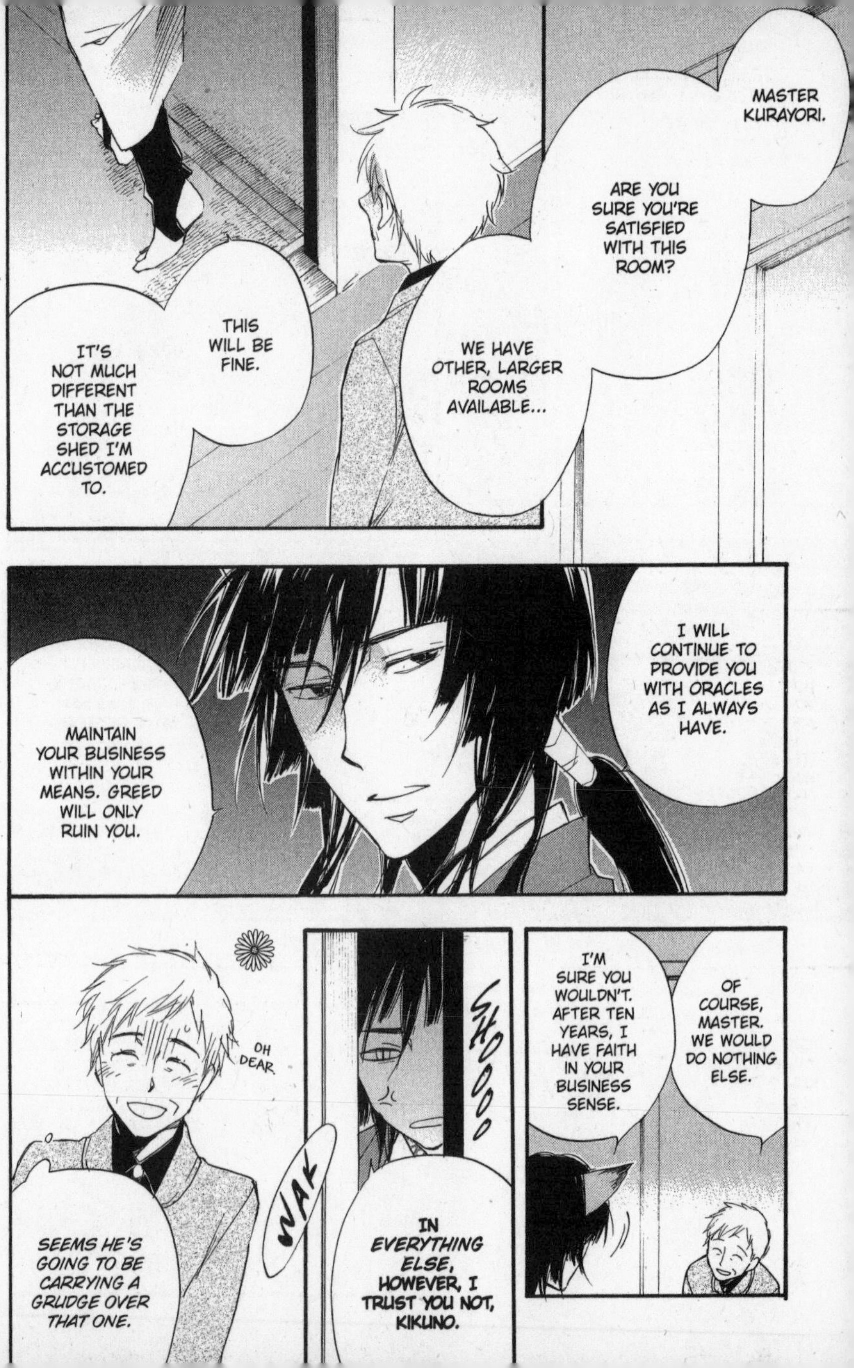
MASTER KURAYORI.
ARE YOU SURE YOU'RE SATISFIED WITH THIS ROOM?
WE HAVE OTHER, LARGER ROOMS AVAILABLE...
THIS WILL BE FINE.
IT'S NOT MUCH DIFFERENT THAN THE STORAGE SHED I'M ACCUSTOMED TO.
I WILL CONTINUE TO PROVIDE YOU WITH ORACLES AS I ALWAYS HAVE.
MAINTAIN YOUR BUSINESS WITHIN YOUR MEANS. GREED WILL ONLY RUIN YOU.
OF COURSE, MASTER. WE WOULD DO NOTHING ELSE.
I'M SURE YOU WOULDN'T. AFTER TEN YEARS, I HAVE FAITH IN YOUR BUSINESS SENSE.
SHOOOO
IN EVERYTHING ELSE, HOWEVER, I TRUST YOU NOT, KIKUNO.
WAK
OH DEAR.
SEEMS HE'S GOING TO BE CARRYING A GRUDGE OVER THAT ONE.

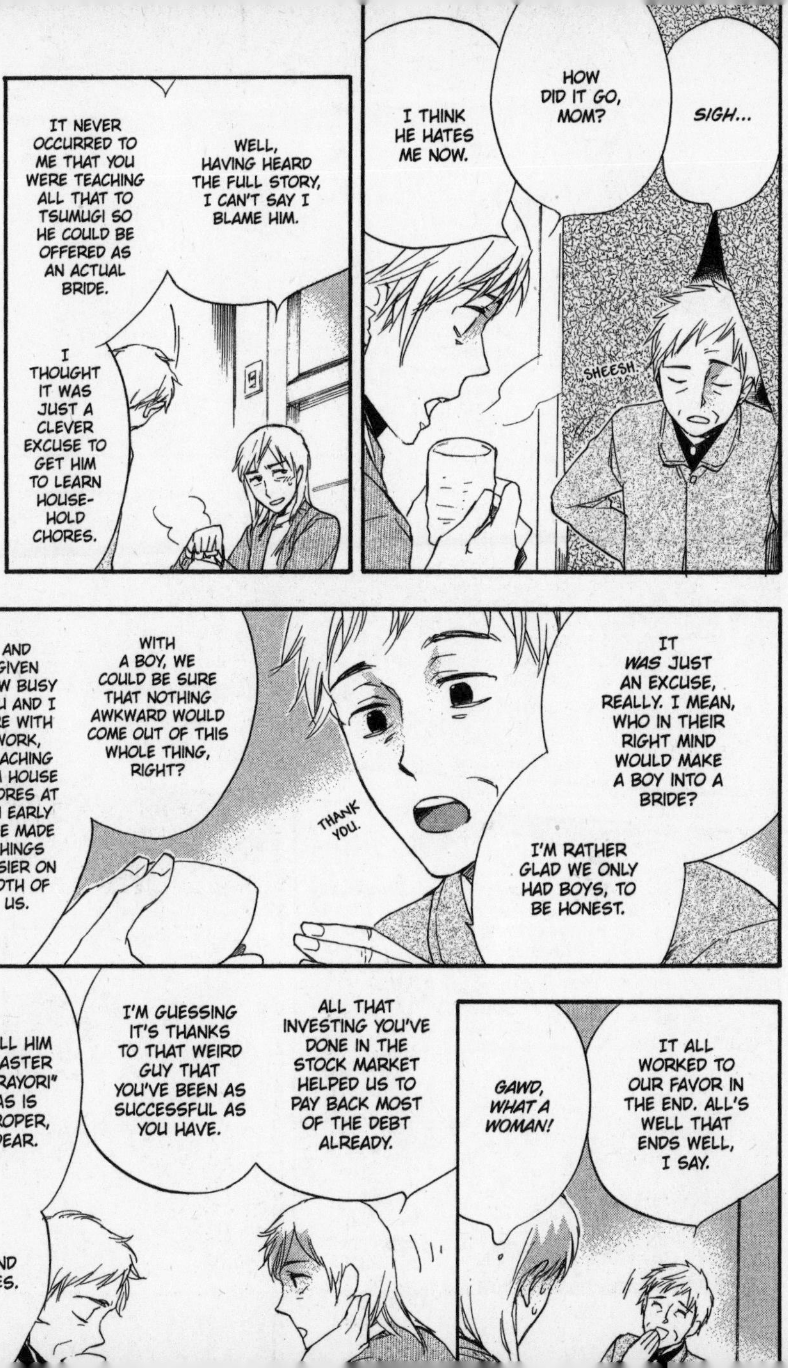
SIGH...
HOW DID IT GO, MOM?
I THINK HE HATES ME NOW.
SHEESH.
WELL, HAVING HEARD THE FULL STORY, I CAN'T SAY I BLAME HIM.
IT NEVER OCCURRED TO ME THAT YOU WERE TEACHING ALL THAT TO TSUMUGI SO HE COULD BE OFFERED AS AN ACTUAL BRIDE.
I THOUGHT IT WAS JUST A CLEVER EXCUSE TO GET HIM TO LEARN HOUSE-HOLD CHORES.
IT *WAS* JUST AN EXCUSE, REALLY. I MEAN, WHO IN THEIR RIGHT MIND WOULD MAKE A BOY INTO A BRIDE?
I'M RATHER GLAD WE ONLY HAD BOYS, TO BE HONEST.
THANK YOU.
WITH A BOY, WE COULD BE SURE THAT NOTHING AWKWARD WOULD COME OUT OF THIS WHOLE THING, RIGHT?
AND GIVEN HOW BUSY YOU AND I ARE WITH WORK, TEACHING HIM HOUSE CHORES AT AN EARLY AGE MADE THINGS EASIER ON BOTH OF US.
IT ALL WORKED TO OUR FAVOR IN THE END. ALL'S WELL THAT ENDS WELL, I SAY.
GAWD, WHAT A WOMAN!
ALL THAT INVESTING YOU'VE DONE IN THE STOCK MARKET HELPED US TO PAY BACK MOST OF THE DEBT ALREADY.
I'M GUESSING IT'S THANKS TO THAT WEIRD GUY THAT YOU'VE BEEN AS SUCCESSFUL AS YOU HAVE.
CALL HIM "MASTER KURAYORI" AS IS PROPER, DEAR.
AND YES.

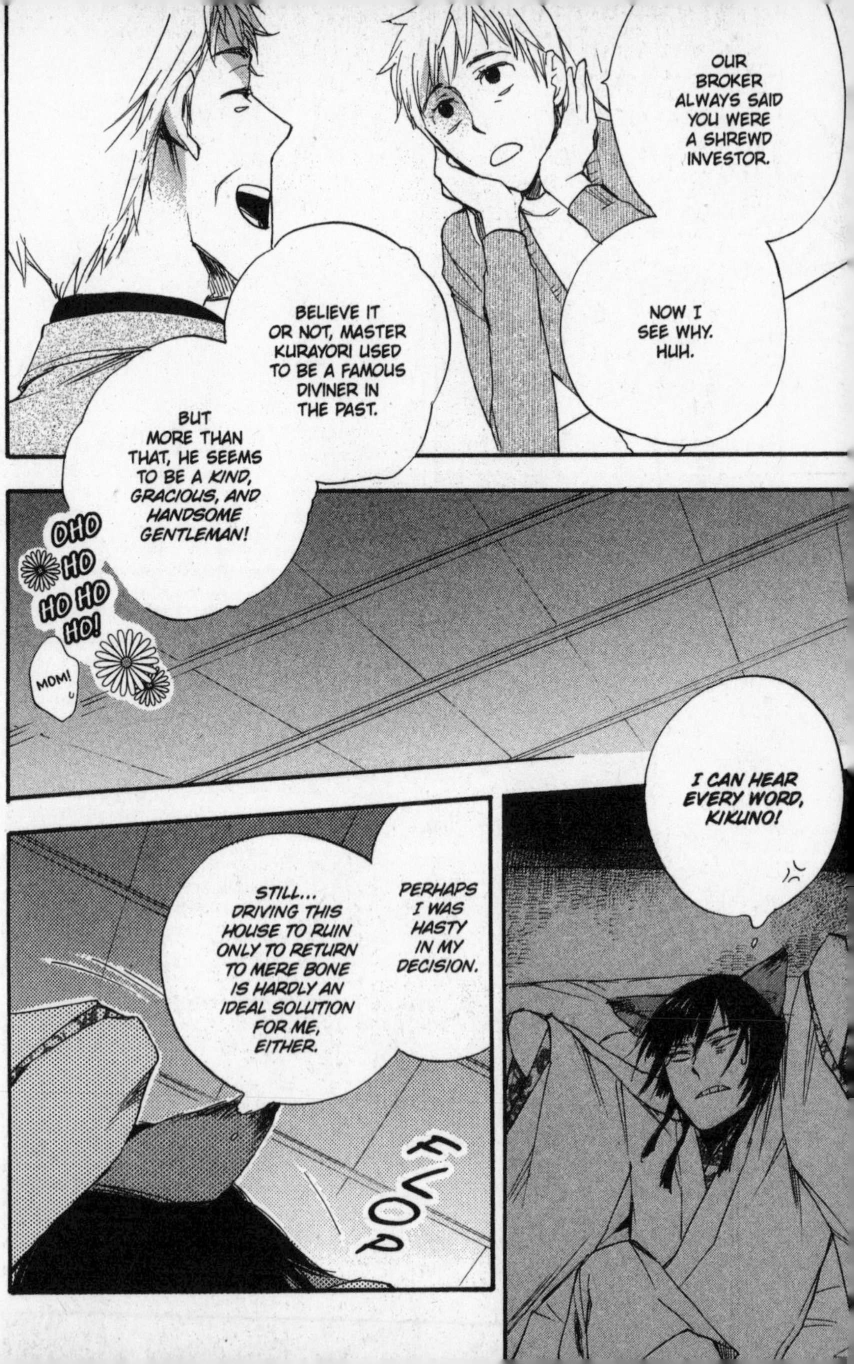
OUR BROKER ALWAYS SAID YOU WERE A SHREWD INVESTOR.
NOW I SEE WHY. HUH.
BELIEVE IT OR NOT, MASTER KURAYORI USED TO BE A FAMOUS DIVINER IN THE PAST.
BUT MORE THAN THAT, HE SEEMS TO BE A *KIND*, GRACIOUS, AND HANDSOME GENTLEMAN!
OHO HO HO HO HO!
MOM!
I CAN HEAR EVERY WORD, KIKUNO!
PERHAPS I WAS HASTY IN MY DECISION.
STILL... DRIVING THIS HOUSE TO RUIN ONLY TO RETURN TO MERE BONE IS HARDLY AN IDEAL SOLUTION FOR ME, EITHER.
FLOP

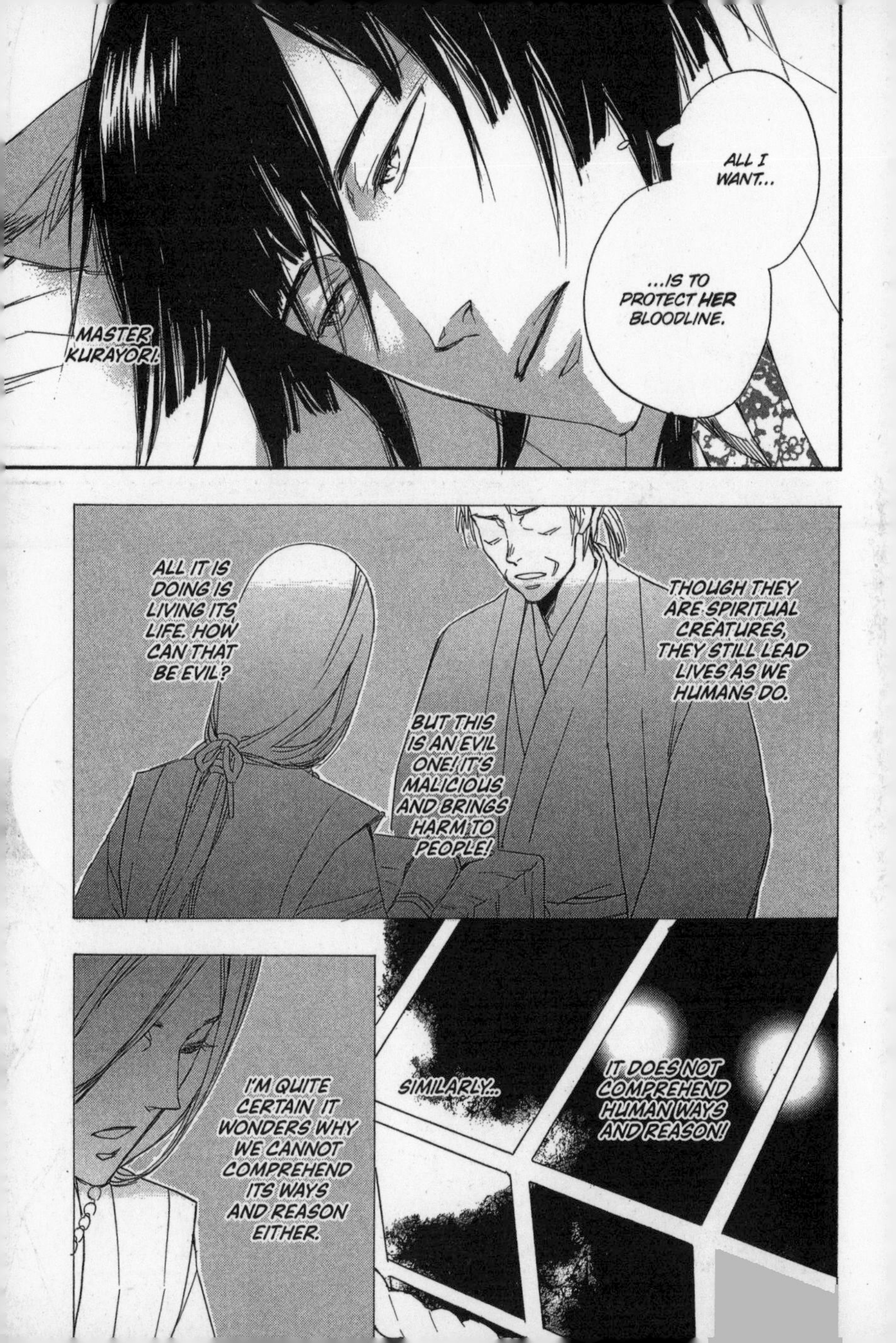
ALL I WANT...
...IS TO PROTECT HER BLOODLINE.
MASTER KURAYORI.
THOUGH THEY ARE SPIRITUAL CREATURES, THEY STILL LEAD LIVES AS WE HUMANS DO.
ALL IT IS DOING IS LIVING ITS LIFE. HOW CAN THAT BE EVIL?
BUT THIS IS AN EVIL ONE! IT'S MALICIOUS AND BRINGS HARM TO PEOPLE!
IT DOES NOT COMPREHEND HUMAN WAYS AND REASON!
SIMILARLY...
I'M QUITE CERTAIN IT WONDERS WHY WE CANNOT COMPREHEND ITS WAYS AND REASON EITHER.

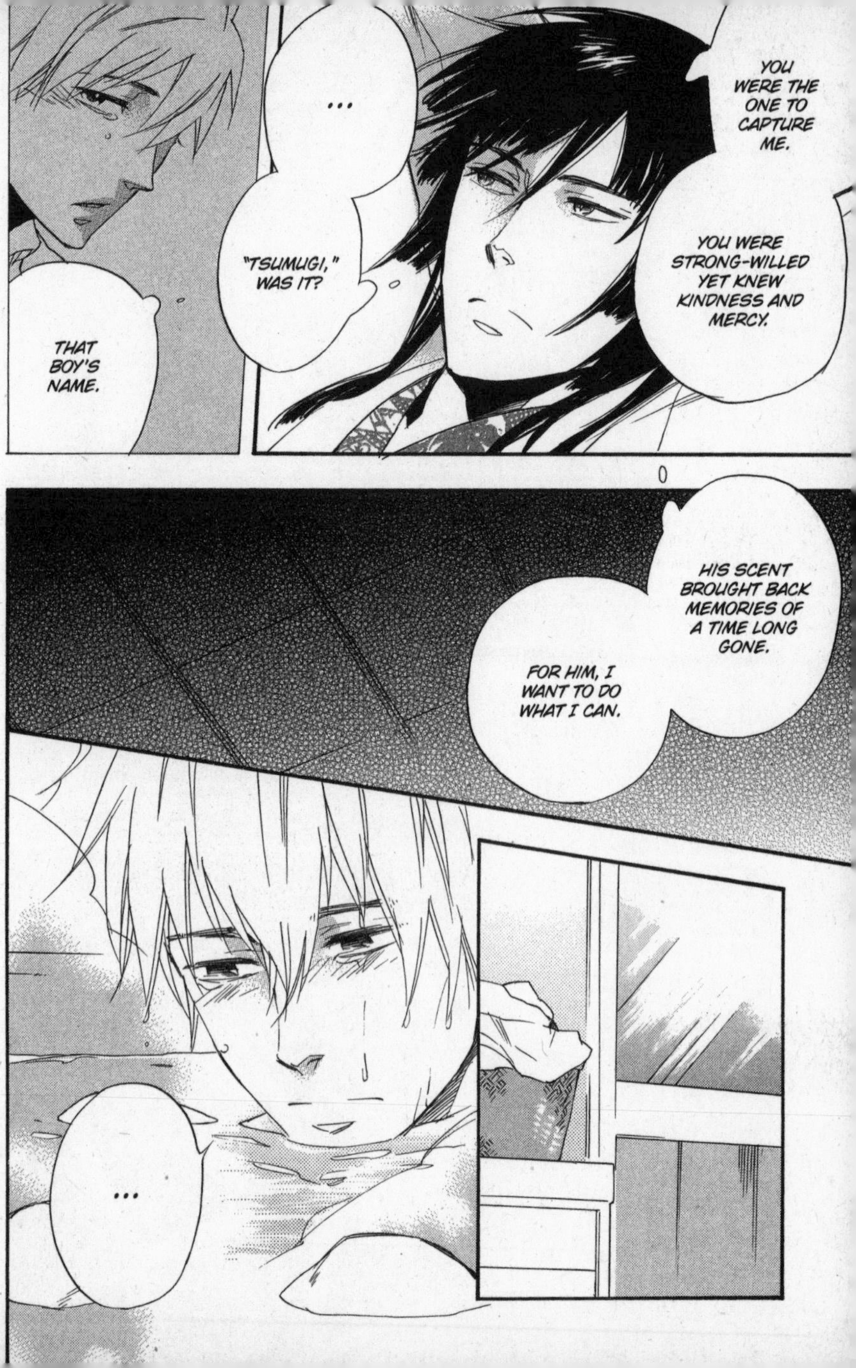
YOU WERE THE ONE TO CAPTURE ME.
YOU WERE STRONG-WILLED YET KNEW KINDNESS AND MERCY.
...
"TSUMUGI," WAS IT?
THAT BOY'S NAME.
HIS SCENT BROUGHT BACK MEMORIES OF A TIME LONG GONE.
FOR HIM, I WANT TO DO WHAT I CAN.
...

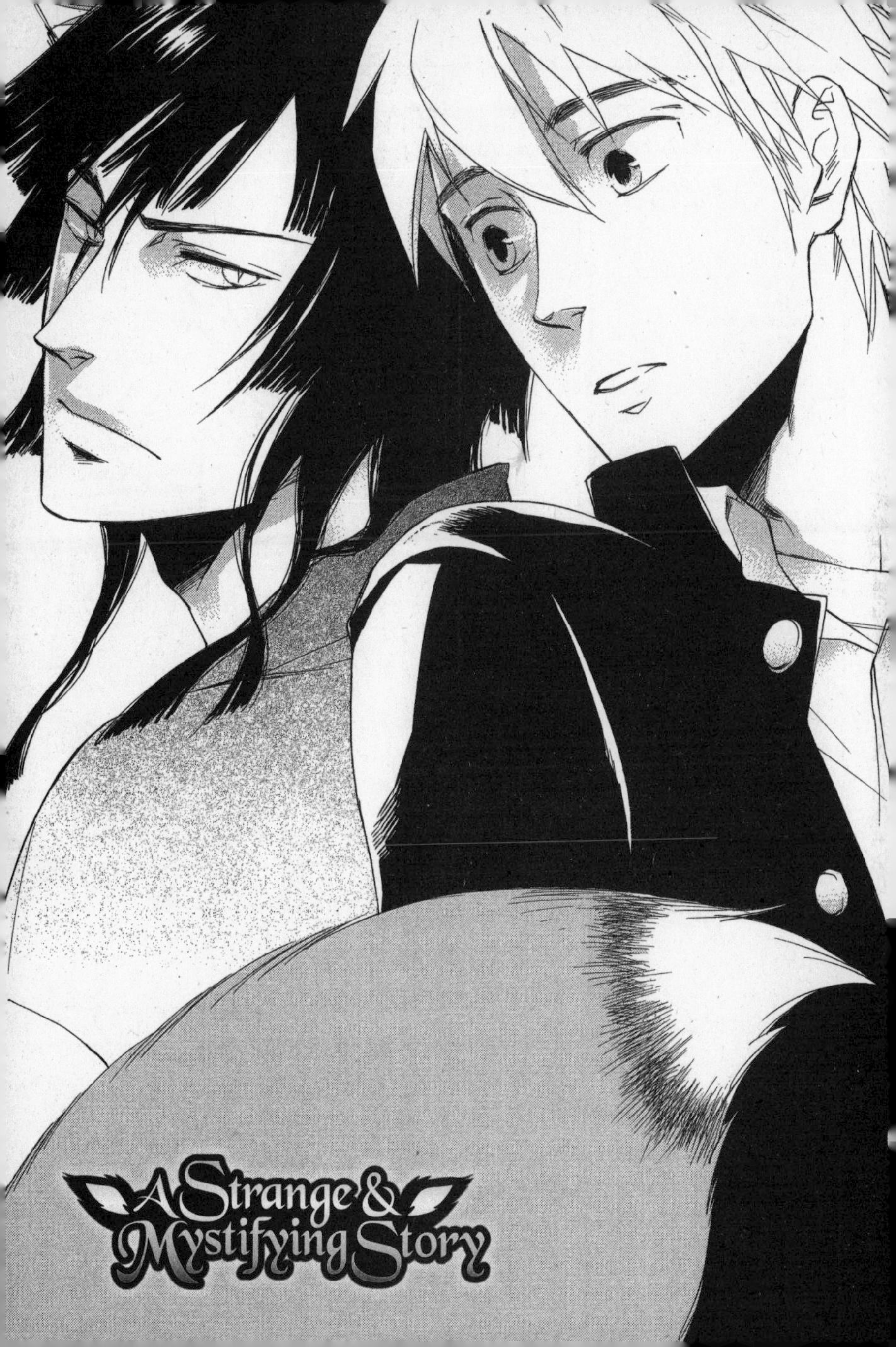
A Strange &
Mystifying Story

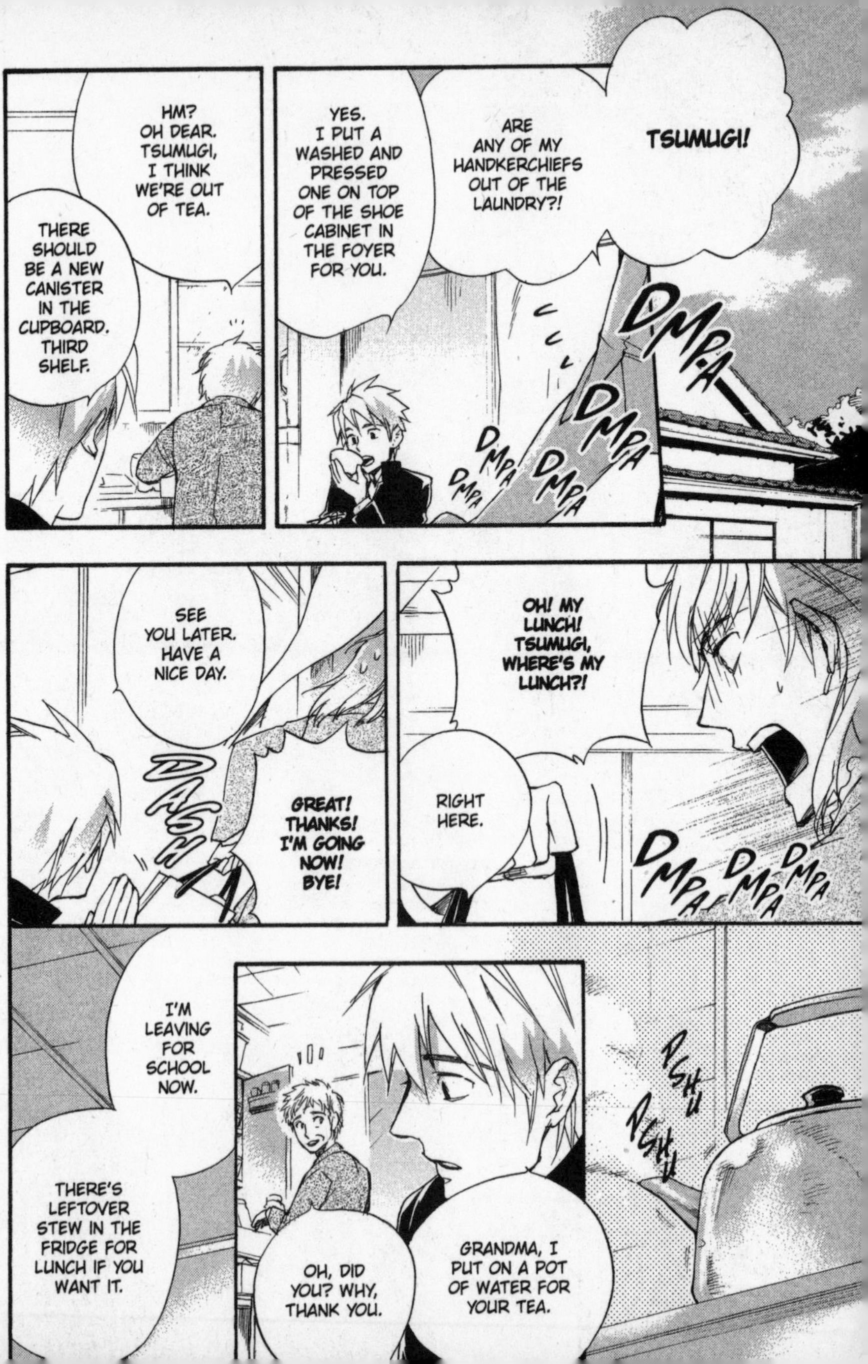
TSUMUGI!
ARE ANY OF MY HANDKERCHIEFS OUT OF THE LAUNDRY?!
DMPA DMPA DMPA DMPA DMPA
YES. I PUT A WASHED AND PRESSED ONE ON TOP OF THE SHOE CABINET IN THE FOYER FOR YOU.
HM? OH DEAR. TSUMUGI, I THINK WE'RE OUT OF TEA.
THERE SHOULD BE A NEW CANISTER IN THE CUPBOARD. THIRD SHELF.
OH! MY LUNCH! TSUMUGI, WHERE'S MY LUNCH?!
RIGHT HERE.
DMPA DMPA DMPA
GREAT! THANKS! I'M GOING NOW! BYE!
SEE YOU LATER. HAVE A NICE DAY.
DASH
GRANDMA, I PUT ON A POT OF WATER FOR YOUR TEA.
OH, DID YOU? WHY, THANK YOU.
PSHU PSHU
I'M LEAVING FOR SCHOOL NOW.
THERE'S LEFTOVER STEW IN THE FRIDGE FOR LUNCH IF YOU WANT IT.

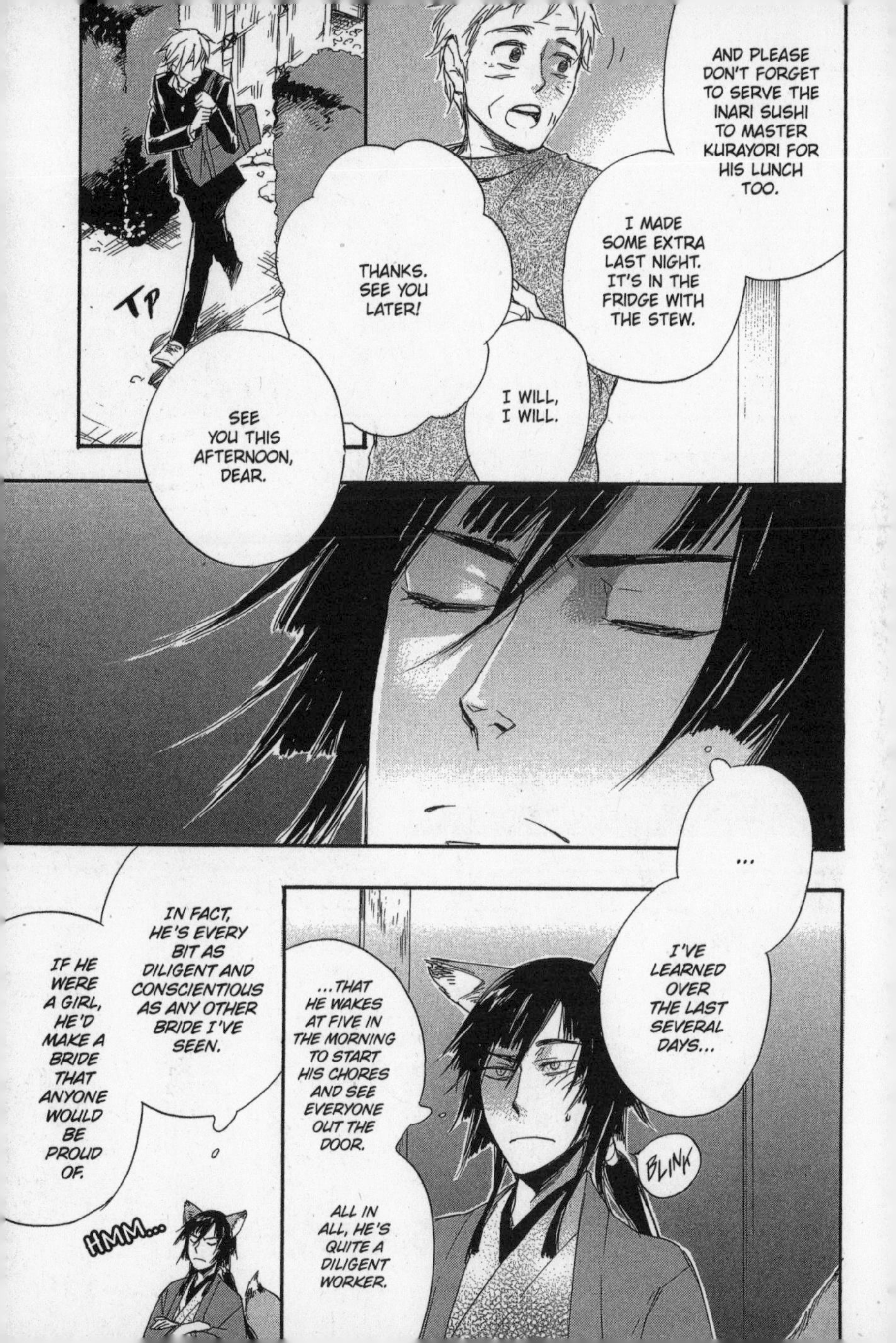
AND PLEASE DON'T FORGET TO SERVE THE INARI SUSHI TO MASTER KURAYORI FOR HIS LUNCH TOO.
I MADE SOME EXTRA LAST NIGHT. IT'S IN THE FRIDGE WITH THE STEW.
I WILL, I WILL.
THANKS. SEE YOU LATER!
TP
SEE YOU THIS AFTERNOON, DEAR.
...
I'VE LEARNED OVER THE LAST SEVERAL DAYS...
...THAT HE WAKES AT FIVE IN THE MORNING TO START HIS CHORES AND SEE EVERYONE OUT THE DOOR.
BLINK
ALL IN ALL, HE'S QUITE A DILIGENT WORKER.
IN FACT, HE'S EVERY BIT AS DILIGENT AND CONSCIENTIOUS AS ANY OTHER BRIDE I'VE SEEN.
IF HE WERE A GIRL, HE'D MAKE A BRIDE THAT ANYONE WOULD BE PROUD OF.
HMM...

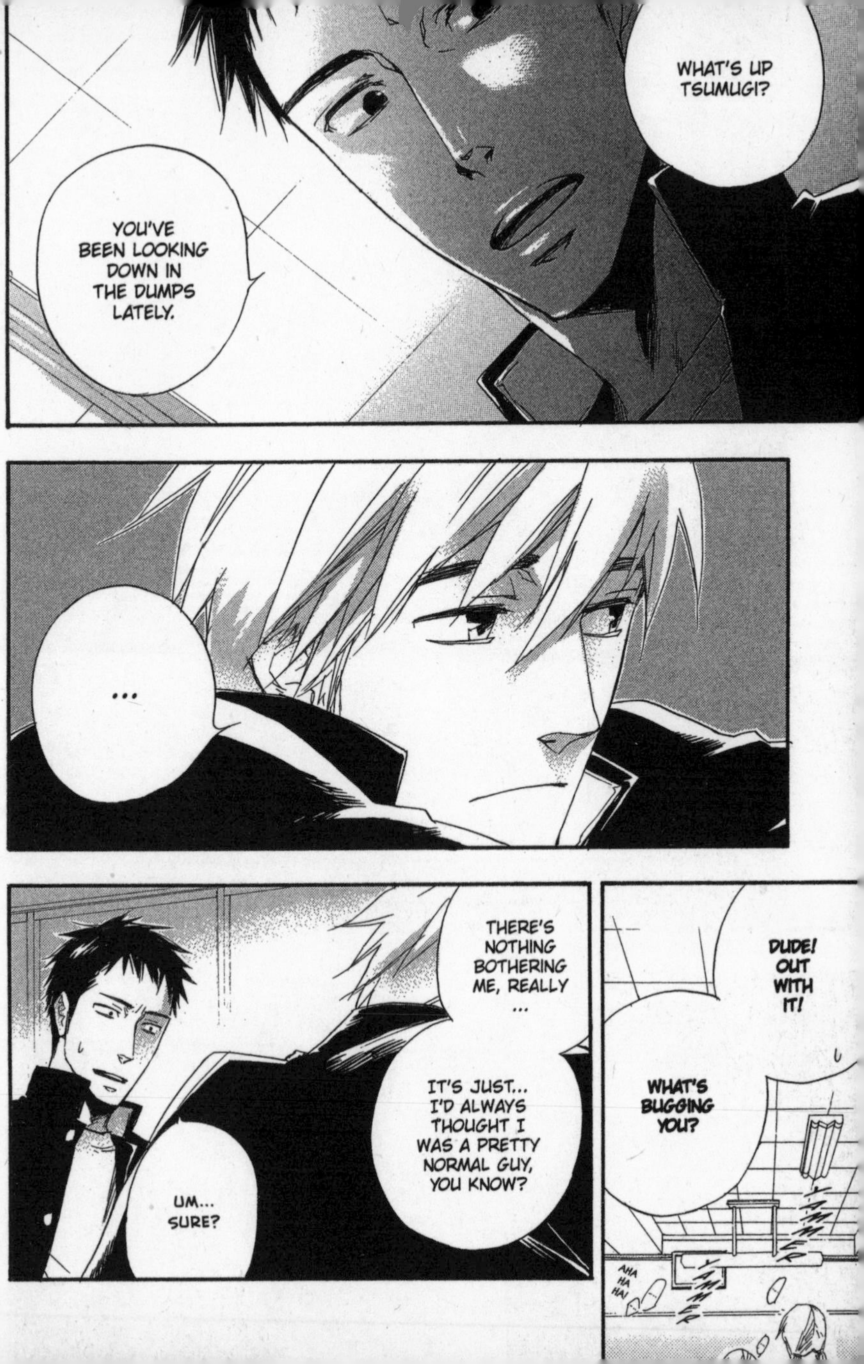
WHAT'S UP TSUMUGI?
YOU'VE BEEN LOOKING DOWN IN THE DUMPS LATELY.
...
DUDE! OUT WITH IT!
WHAT'S BUGGING YOU?
YAMMER
YAMMER
AHA HA HA!
THERE'S NOTHING BOTHERING ME, REALLY ...
IT'S JUST... I'D ALWAYS THOUGHT I WAS A PRETTY NORMAL GUY, YOU KNOW?
UM... SURE?

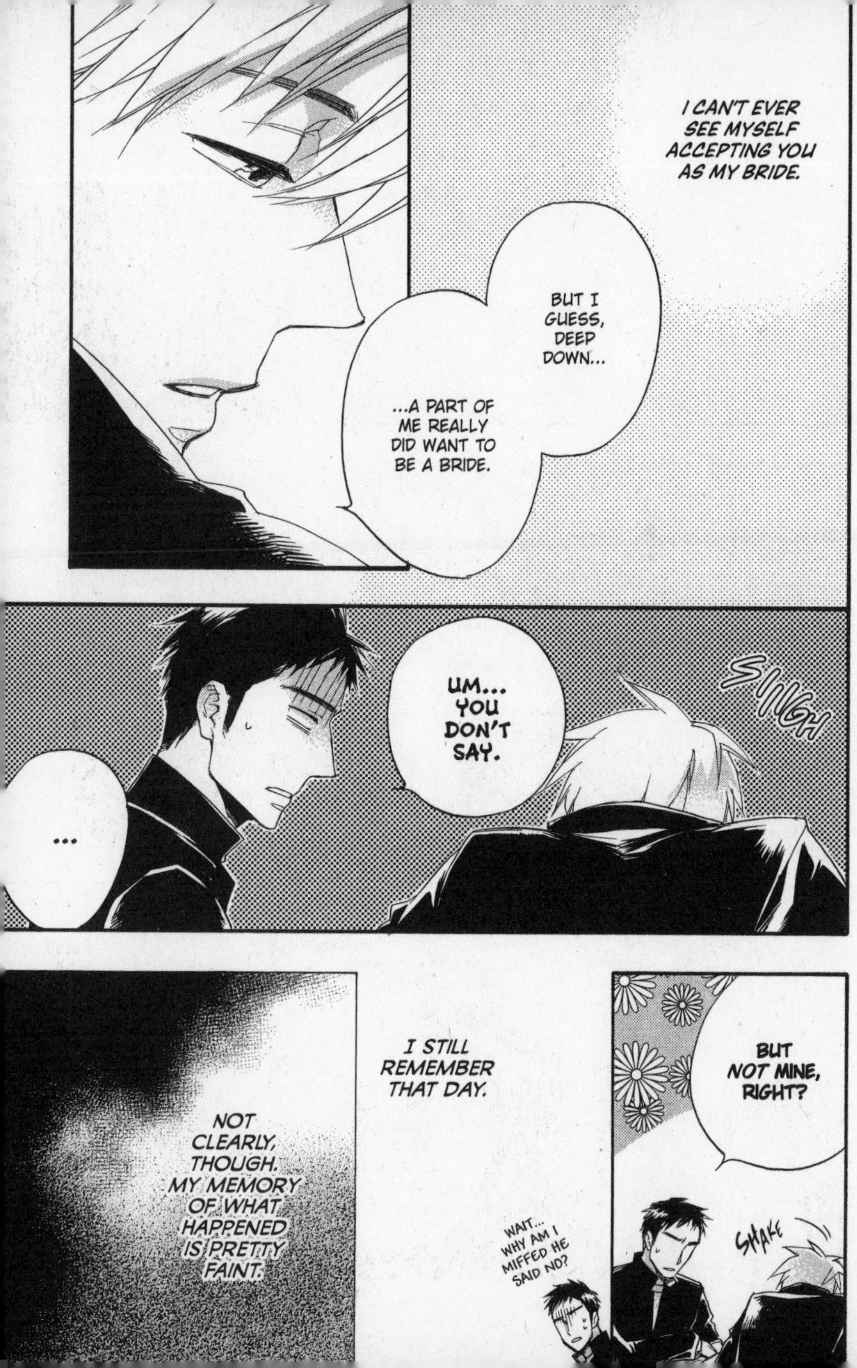
I CAN'T EVER SEE MYSELF ACCEPTING YOU AS MY BRIDE.
BUT I GUESS, DEEP DOWN...
...A PART OF ME REALLY DID WANT TO BE A BRIDE.
SIIGH
UM... YOU DON'T SAY.
...
BUT NOT MINE, RIGHT?
SHAKE
WAIT... WHY AM I MIFFED HE SAID NO?
I STILL REMEMBER THAT DAY.
NOT CLEARLY, THOUGH. MY MEMORY OF WHAT HAPPENED IS PRETTY FAINT.

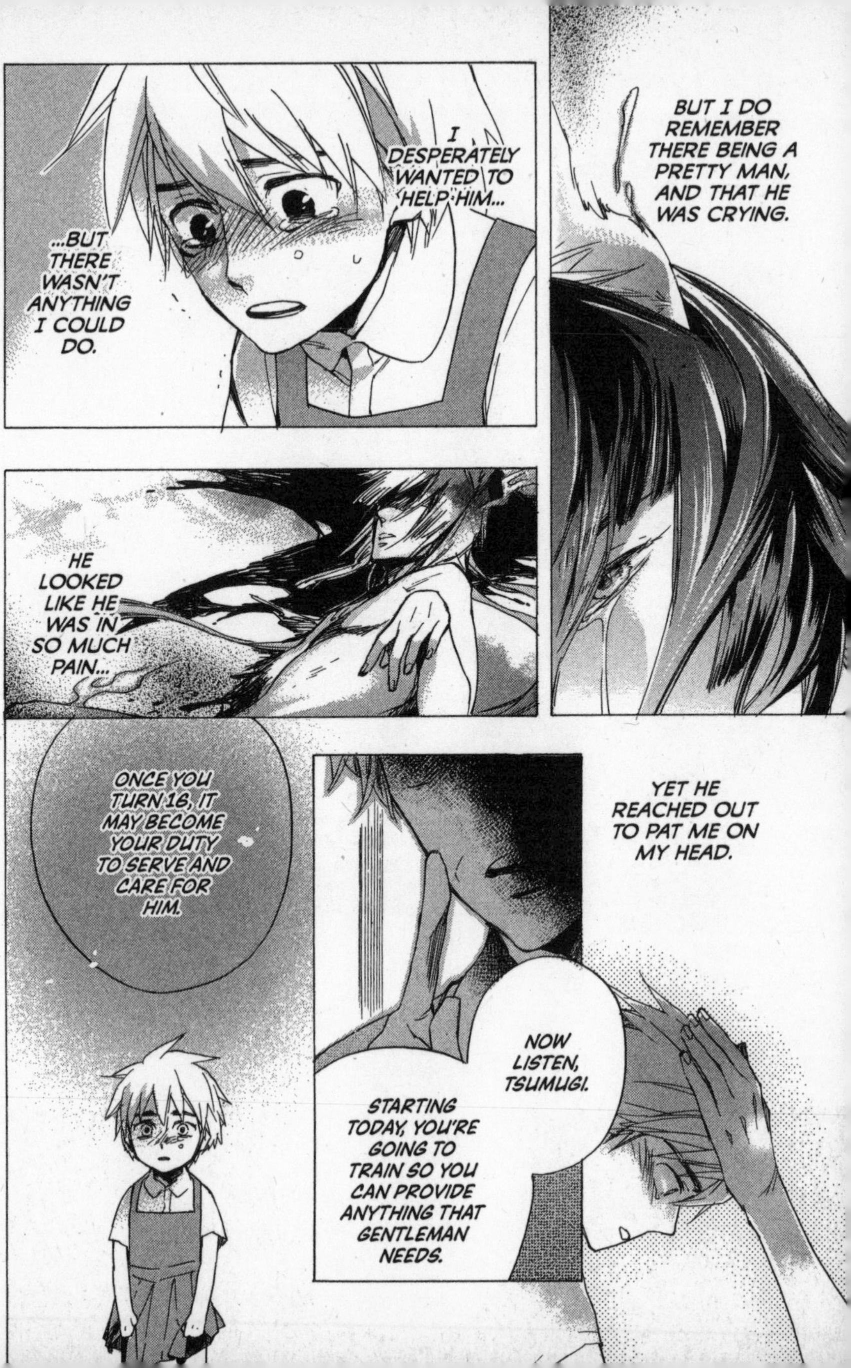
BUT I DO REMEMBER THERE BEING A PRETTY MAN, AND THAT HE WAS CRYING.
I DESPERATELY WANTED TO HELP HIM...
...BUT THERE WASN'T ANYTHING I COULD DO.
HE LOOKED LIKE HE WAS IN SO MUCH PAIN...
YET HE REACHED OUT TO PAT ME ON MY HEAD.
NOW LISTEN, TSUMUGI.
STARTING TODAY, YOU'RE GOING TO TRAIN SO YOU CAN PROVIDE ANYTHING THAT GENTLEMAN NEEDS.
ONCE YOU TURN 16, IT MAY BECOME YOUR DUTY TO SERVE AND CARE FOR HIM.

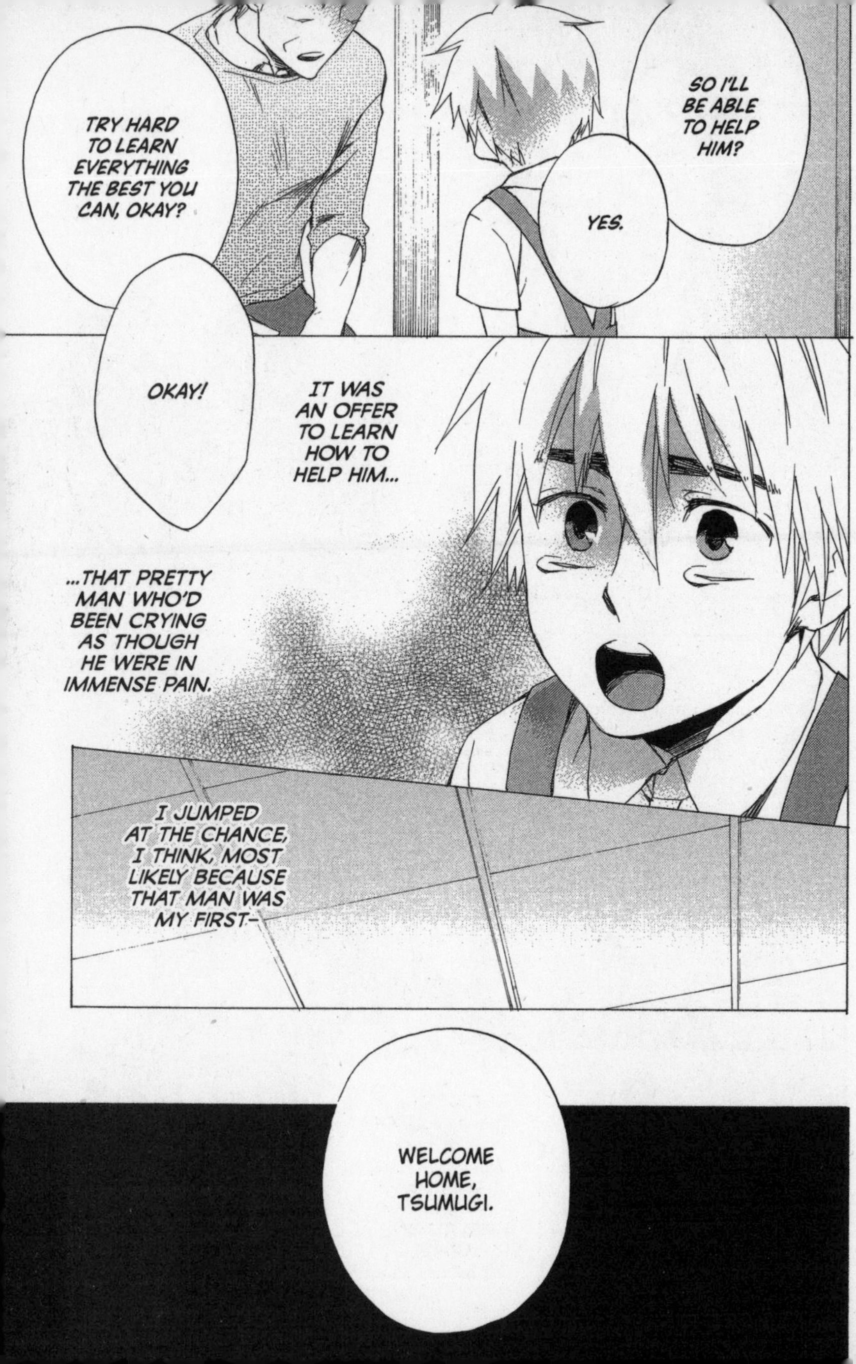
SO I'LL BE ABLE TO HELP HIM?
YES.
TRY HARD TO LEARN EVERYTHING THE BEST YOU CAN, OKAY?
OKAY!
IT WAS AN OFFER TO LEARN HOW TO HELP HIM...
...THAT PRETTY MAN WHO'D BEEN CRYING AS THOUGH HE WERE IN IMMENSE PAIN.
I JUMPED AT THE CHANCE, I THINK, MOST LIKELY BECAUSE THAT MAN WAS MY FIRST-
WELCOME HOME, TSUMUGI.

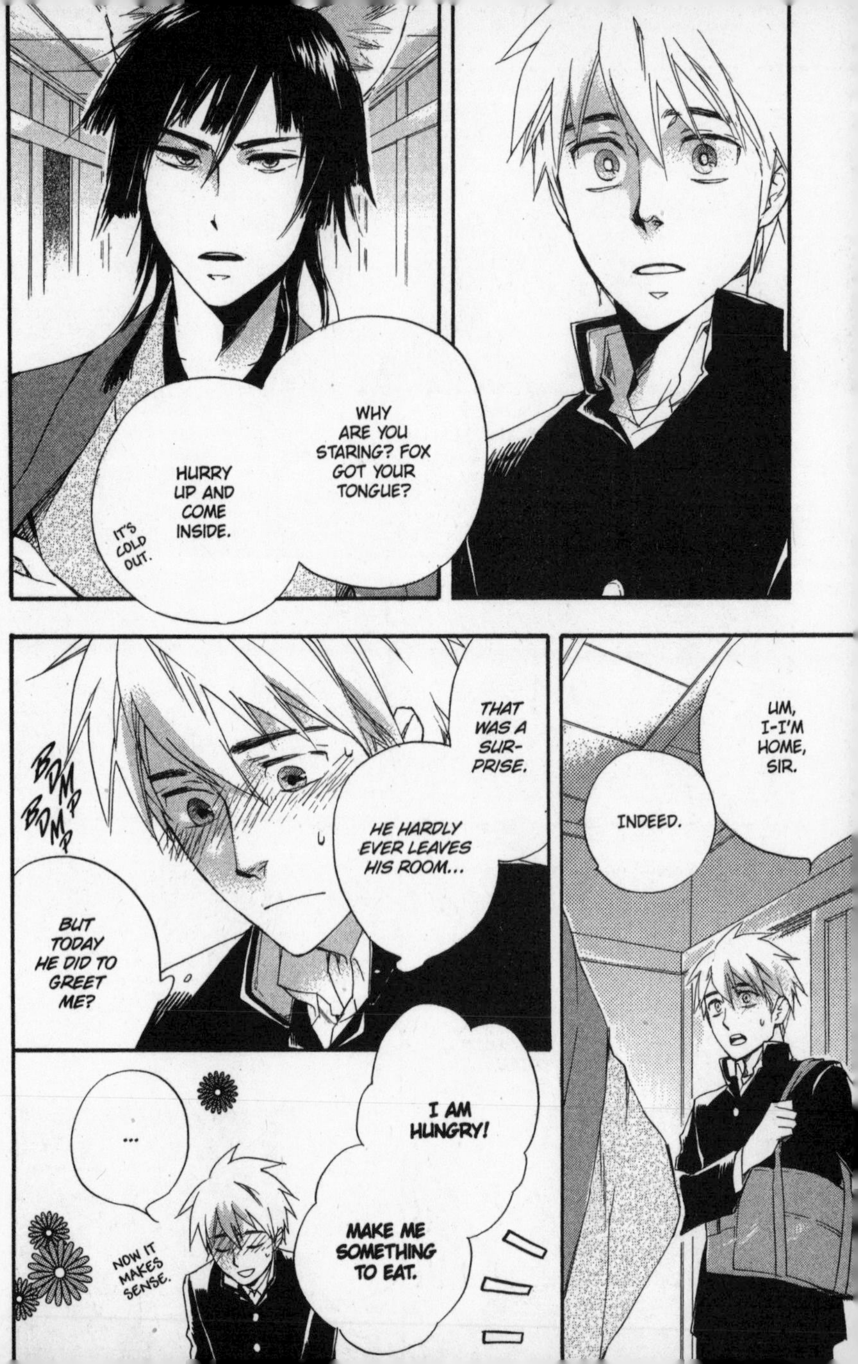
WHY ARE YOU STARING? FOX GOT YOUR TONGUE?
HURRY UP AND COME INSIDE.
IT'S COLD OUT.
UM, I-I'M HOME, SIR.
INDEED.
THAT WAS A SURPRISE.
HE HARDLY EVER LEAVES HIS ROOM...
BDMP BDMP
BUT TODAY HE DID TO GREET ME?
I AM HUNGRY!
MAKE ME SOMETHING TO EAT.
...
NOW IT MAKES SENSE.

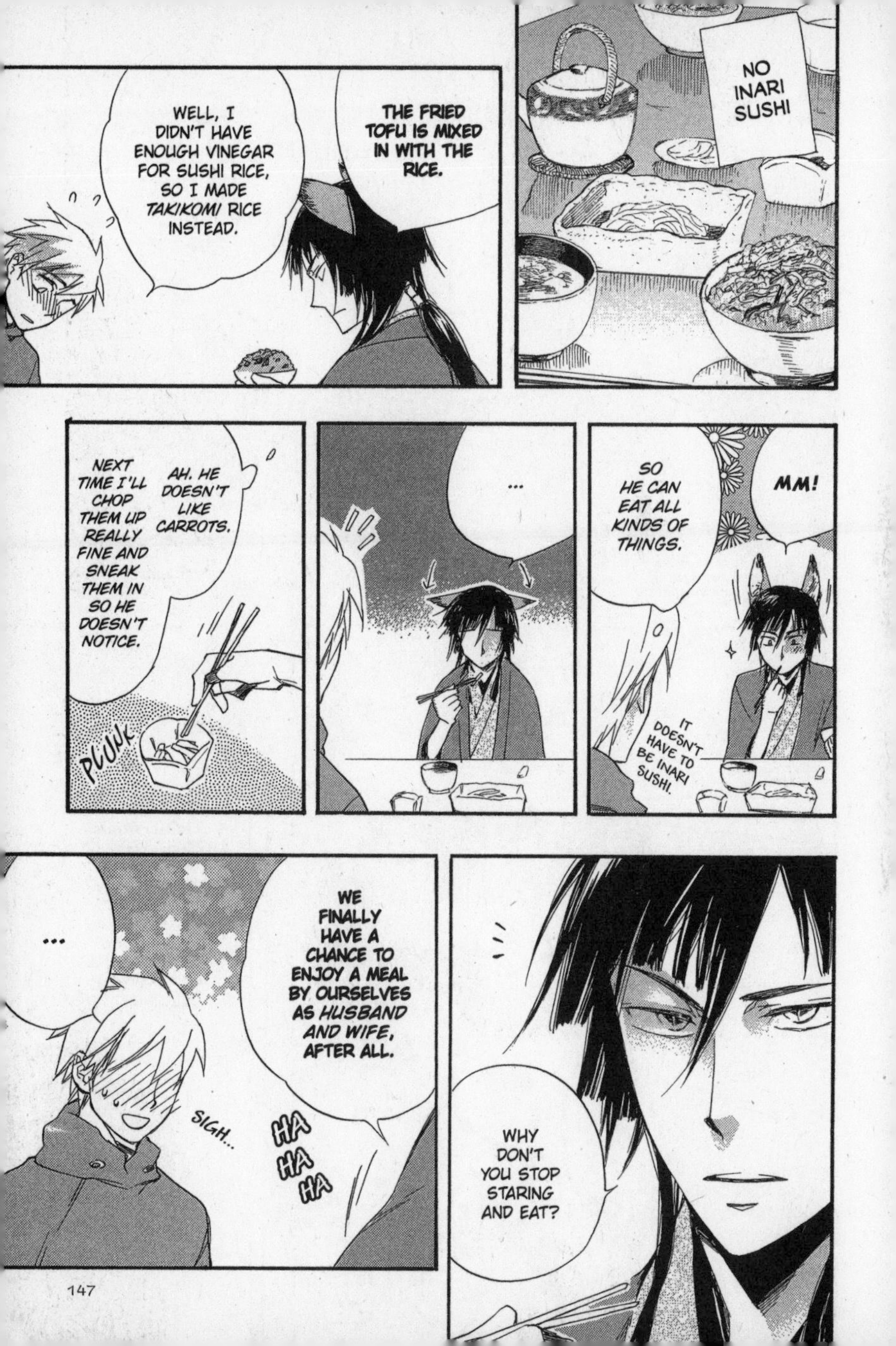
NO INARI SUSHI
THE FRIED TOFU IS MIXED IN WITH THE RICE.
WELL, I DIDN'T HAVE ENOUGH VINEGAR FOR SUSHI RICE, SO I MADE *TAKIKOMI* RICE INSTEAD.
MM!
SO HE CAN EAT ALL KINDS OF THINGS.
IT DOESN'T HAVE TO BE INARI SUSHI.
...
AH. HE DOESN'T LIKE CARROTS.
NEXT TIME I'LL CHOP THEM UP REALLY FINE AND SNEAK THEM IN SO HE DOESN'T NOTICE.
PLUNK
WHY DON'T YOU STOP STARING AND EAT?
WE FINALLY HAVE A CHANCE TO ENJOY A MEAL BY OURSELVES AS *HUSBAND AND WIFE*, AFTER ALL.
HA HA HA
SIGH...
...

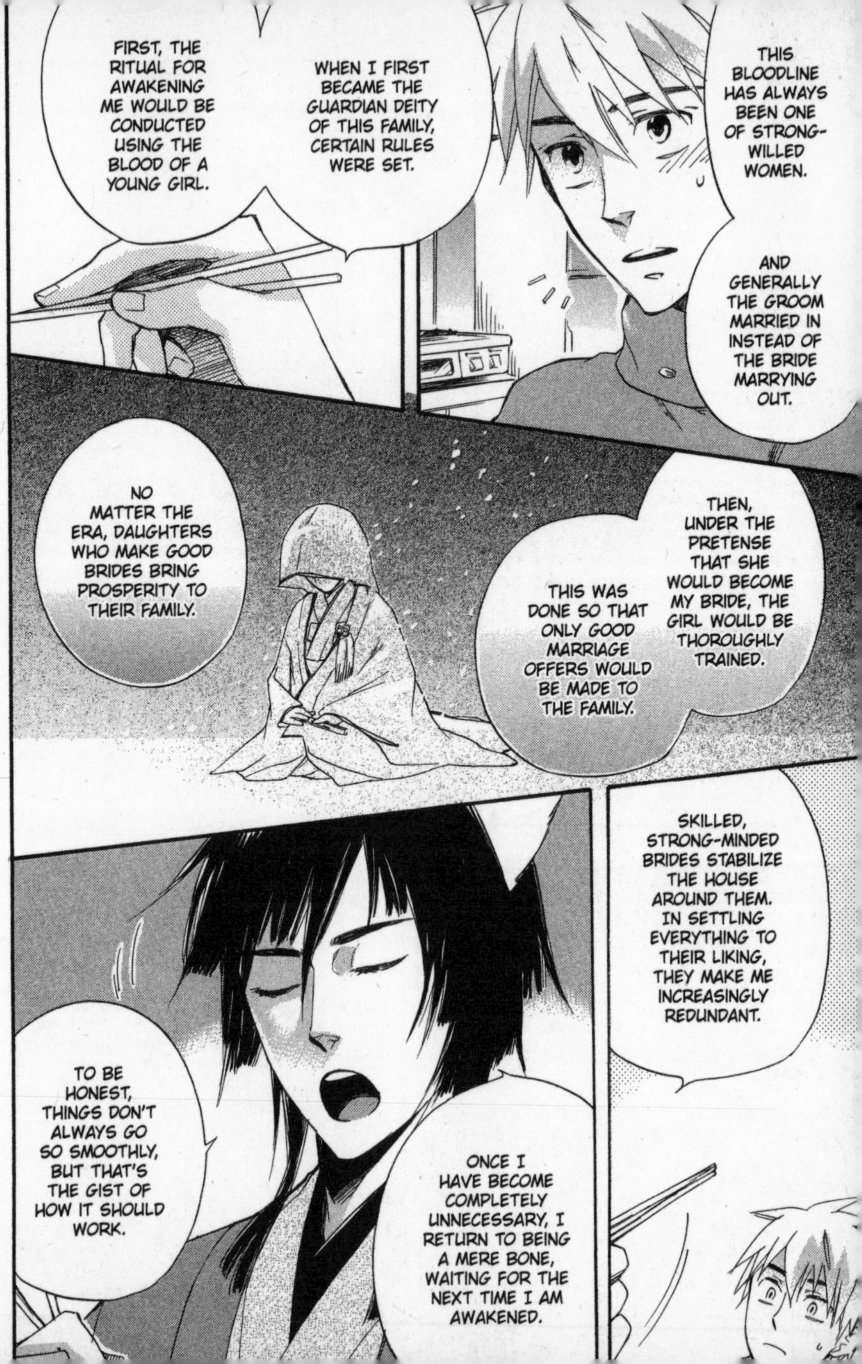
THIS BLOODLINE HAS ALWAYS BEEN ONE OF STRONG-WILLED WOMEN.
AND GENERALLY THE GROOM MARRIED IN INSTEAD OF THE BRIDE MARRYING OUT.
WHEN I FIRST BECAME THE GUARDIAN DEITY OF THIS FAMILY, CERTAIN RULES WERE SET.
FIRST, THE RITUAL FOR AWAKENING ME WOULD BE CONDUCTED USING THE BLOOD OF A YOUNG GIRL.
THEN, UNDER THE PRETENSE THAT SHE WOULD BECOME MY BRIDE, THE GIRL WOULD BE THOROUGHLY TRAINED.
THIS WAS DONE SO THAT ONLY GOOD MARRIAGE OFFERS WOULD BE MADE TO THE FAMILY.
NO MATTER THE ERA, DAUGHTERS WHO MAKE GOOD BRIDES BRING PROSPERITY TO THEIR FAMILY.
SKILLED, STRONG-MINDED BRIDES STABILIZE THE HOUSE AROUND THEM. IN SETTLING EVERYTHING TO THEIR LIKING, THEY MAKE ME INCREASINGLY REDUNDANT.
ONCE I HAVE BECOME COMPLETELY UNNECESSARY, I RETURN TO BEING A MERE BONE, WAITING FOR THE NEXT TIME I AM AWAKENED.
TO BE HONEST, THINGS DON'T ALWAYS GO SO SMOOTHLY, BUT THAT'S THE GIST OF HOW IT SHOULD WORK.

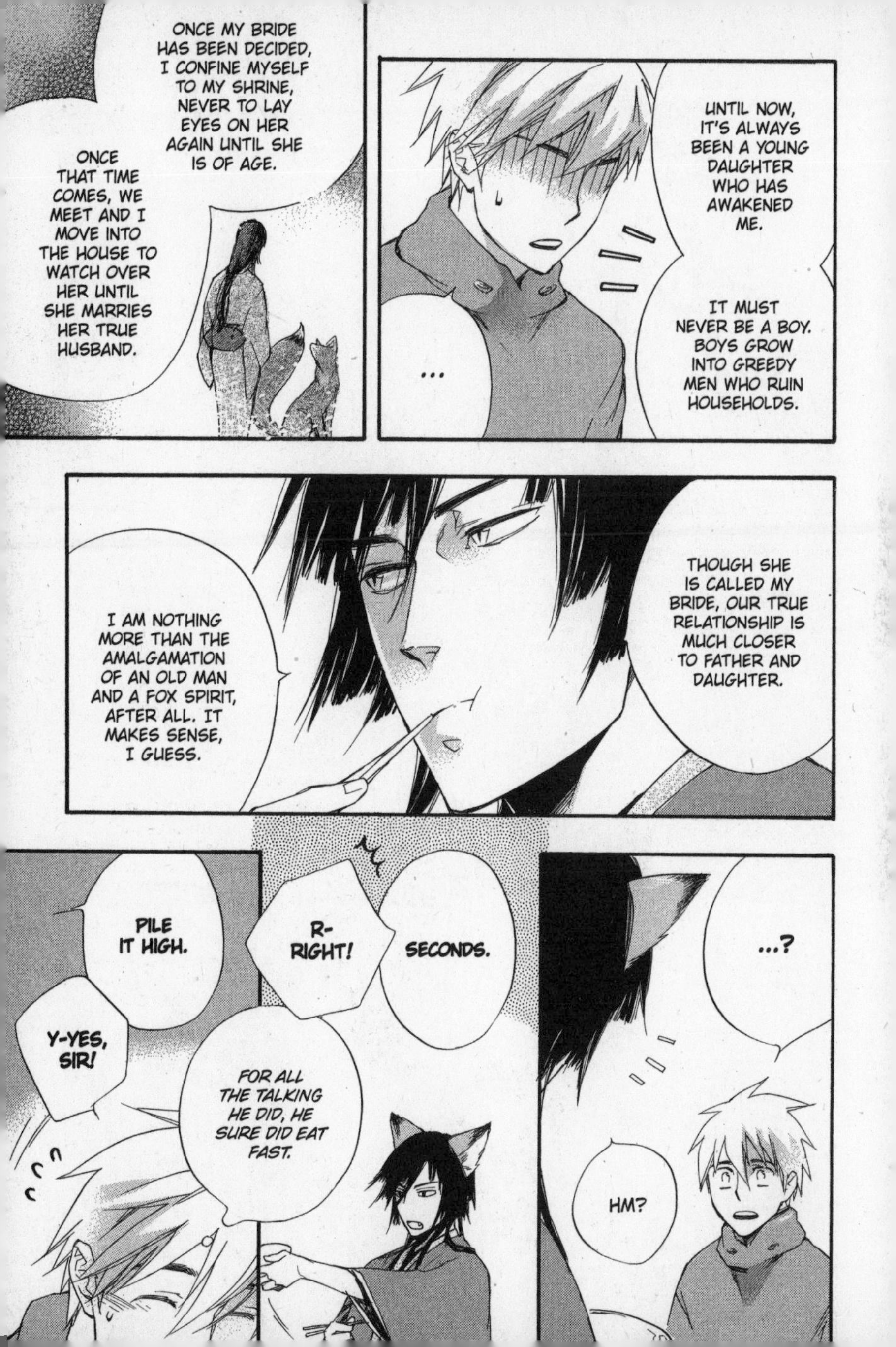
UNTIL NOW, IT'S ALWAYS BEEN A YOUNG DAUGHTER WHO HAS AWAKENED ME.
IT MUST NEVER BE A BOY. BOYS GROW INTO GREEDY MEN WHO RUIN HOUSEHOLDS.
...
ONCE MY BRIDE HAS BEEN DECIDED, I CONFINE MYSELF TO MY SHRINE, NEVER TO LAY EYES ON HER AGAIN UNTIL SHE IS OF AGE.
ONCE THAT TIME COMES, WE MEET AND I MOVE INTO THE HOUSE TO WATCH OVER HER UNTIL SHE MARRIES HER TRUE HUSBAND.
THOUGH SHE IS CALLED MY BRIDE, OUR TRUE RELATIONSHIP IS MUCH CLOSER TO FATHER AND DAUGHTER.
I AM NOTHING MORE THAN THE AMALGAMATION OF AN OLD MAN AND A FOX SPIRIT, AFTER ALL. IT MAKES SENSE, I GUESS.
...?
HM?
SECONDS.
R-RIGHT!
PILE IT HIGH.
Y-YES, SIR!
FOR ALL THE TALKING HE DID, HE SURE DID EAT FAST.

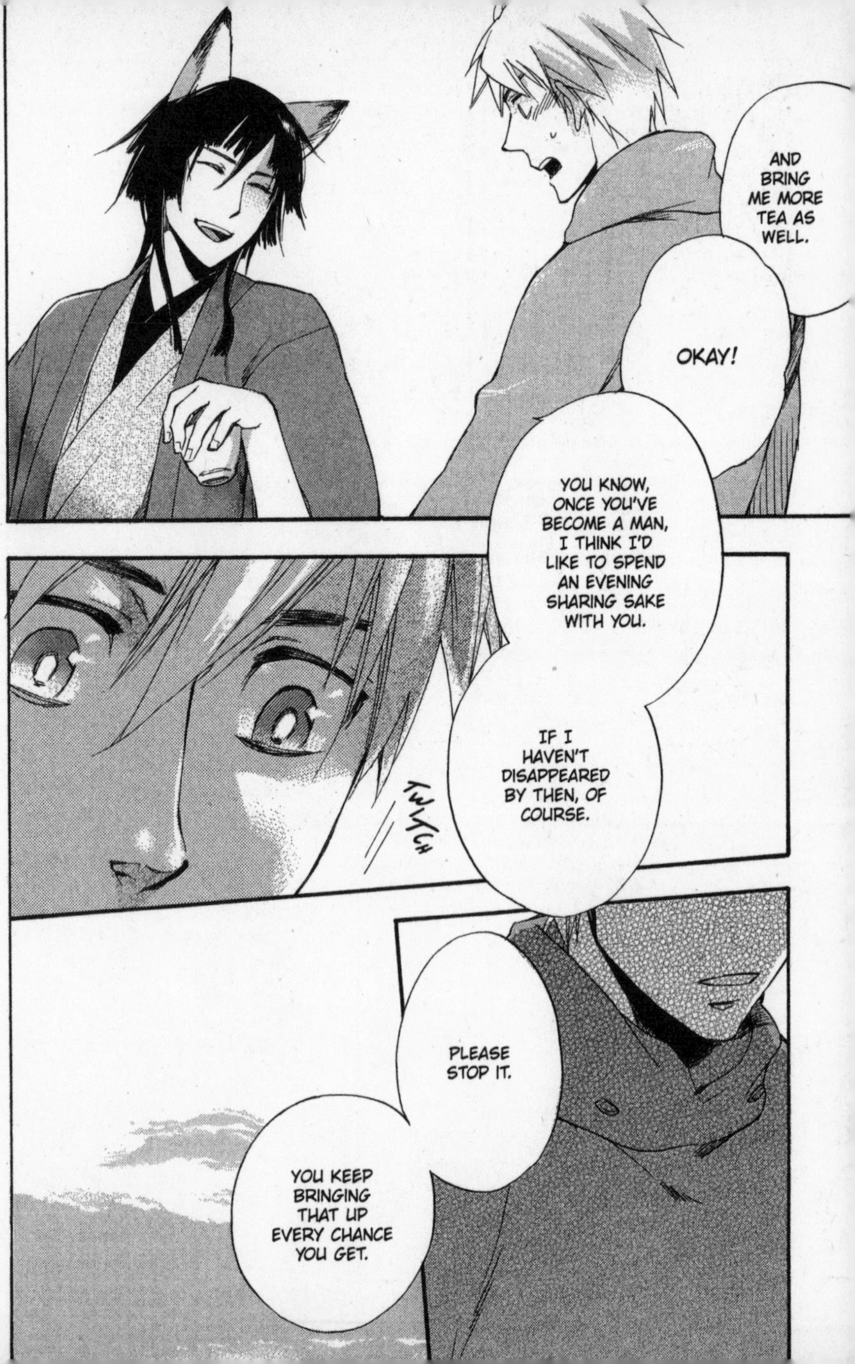
AND BRING ME MORE TEA AS WELL.
OKAY!
YOU KNOW, ONCE YOU'VE BECOME A MAN, I THINK I'D LIKE TO SPEND AN EVENING SHARING SAKE WITH YOU.
IF I HAVEN'T DISAPPEARED BY THEN, OF COURSE.
TWITCH
PLEASE STOP IT.
YOU KEEP BRINGING THAT UP EVERY CHANCE YOU GET.

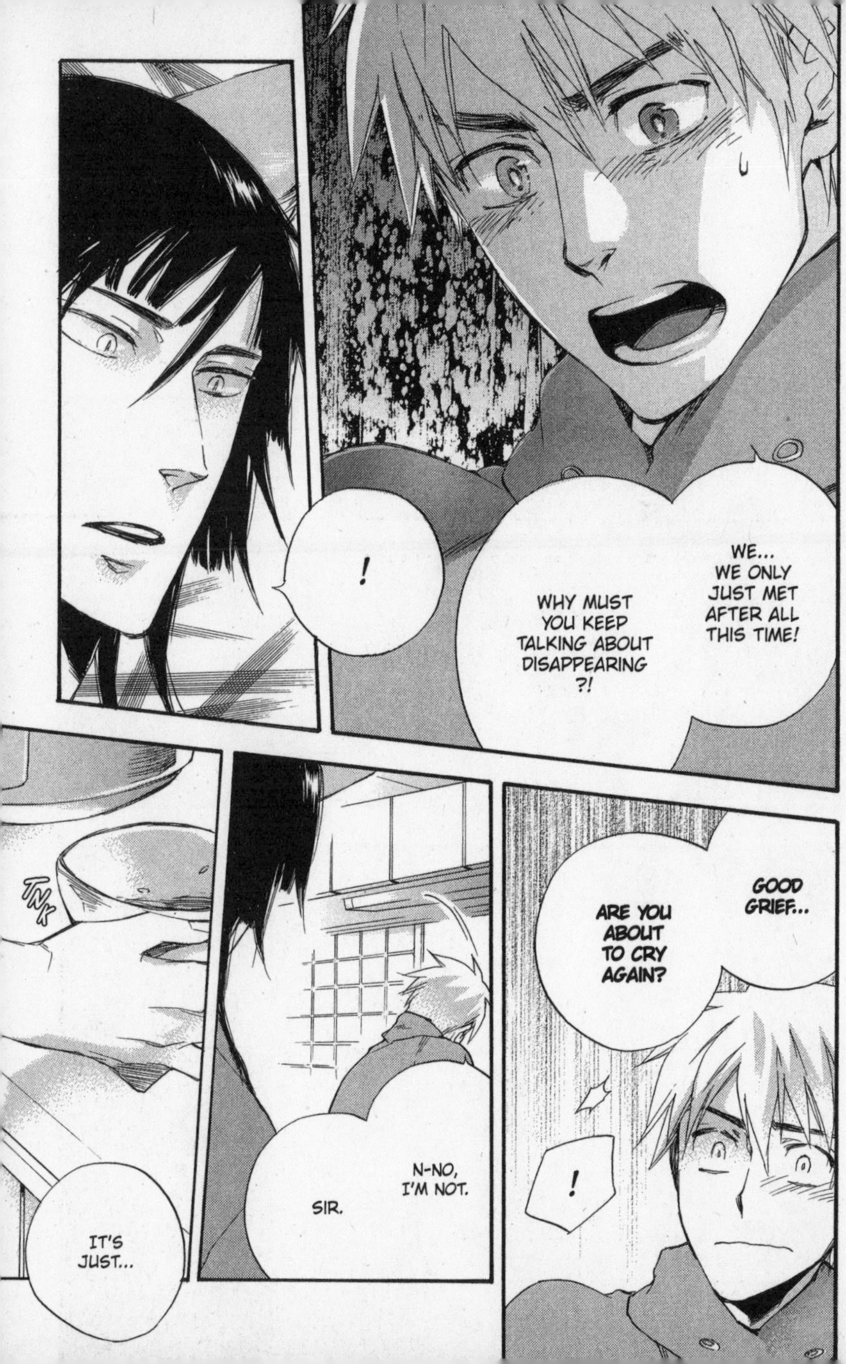
WE... WE ONLY JUST MET AFTER ALL THIS TIME!
WHY MUST YOU KEEP TALKING ABOUT DISAPPEARING ?!
!
GOOD GRIEF...
ARE YOU ABOUT TO CRY AGAIN?
!
N-NO, I'M NOT.
SIR.
TNK
IT'S JUST...

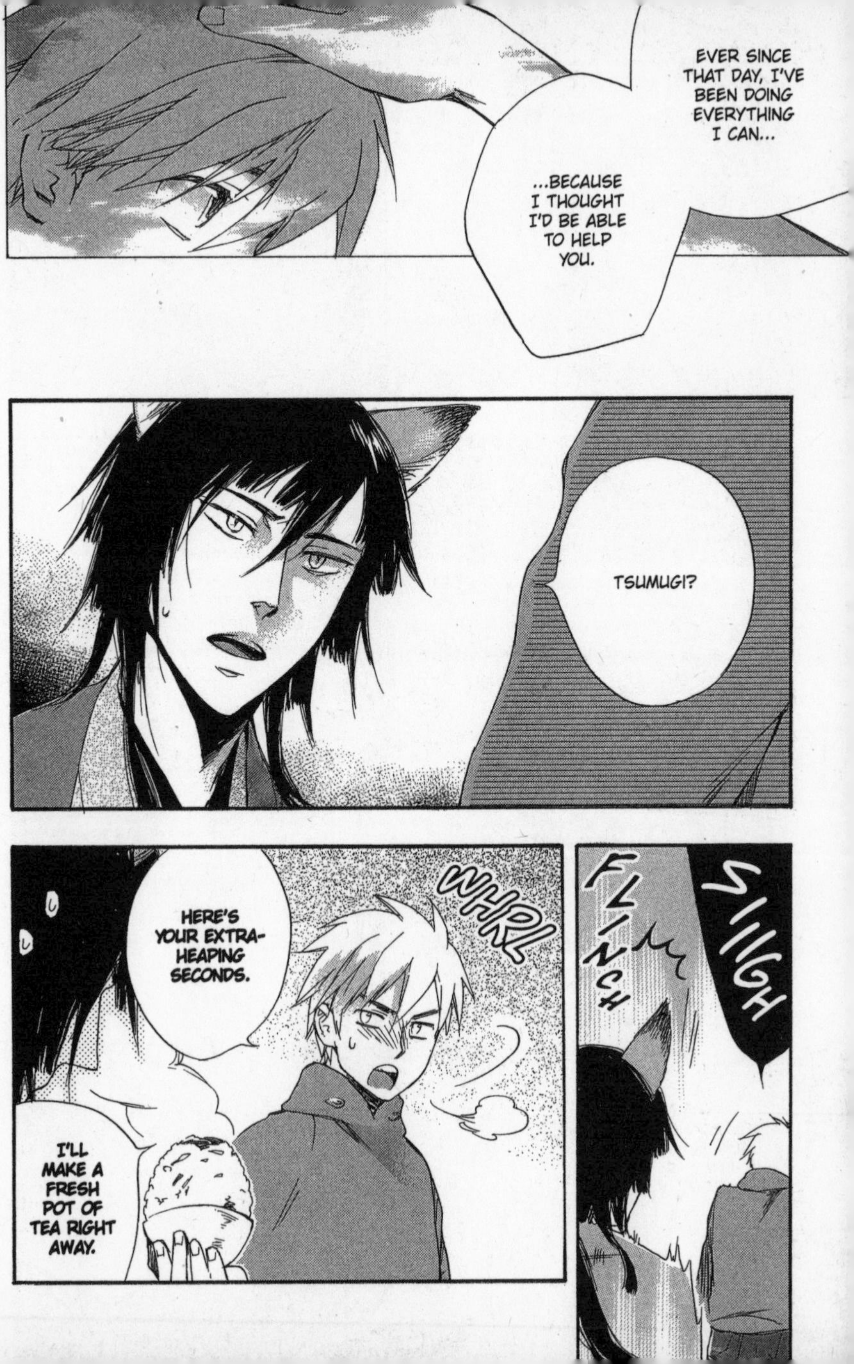
EVER SINCE THAT DAY, I'VE BEEN DOING EVERYTHING I CAN...
...BECAUSE I THOUGHT I'D BE ABLE TO HELP YOU.
TSUMUGI?
SIIIGH
FLINCH
WHRL
HERE'S YOUR EXTRA-HEAPING SECONDS.
I'LL MAKE A FRESH POT OF TEA RIGHT AWAY.

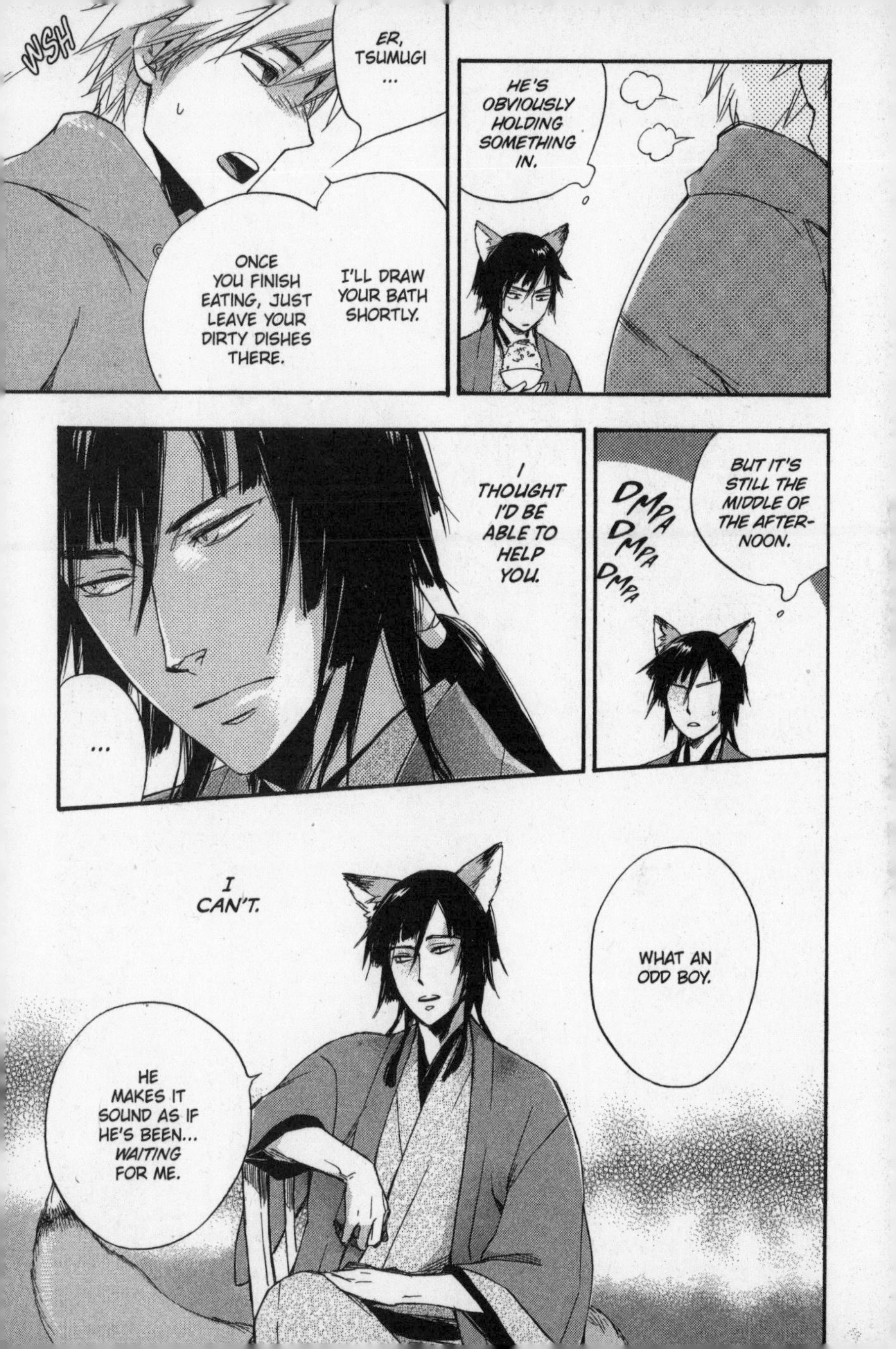
HE'S OBVIOUSLY HOLDING SOMETHING IN.
ER, TSUMUGI ...
WSH
I'LL DRAW YOUR BATH SHORTLY.
ONCE YOU FINISH EATING, JUST LEAVE YOUR DIRTY DISHES THERE.
BUT IT'S STILL THE MIDDLE OF THE AFTER-NOON.
DMPA DMPA DMPA
I THOUGHT I'D BE ABLE TO HELP YOU.
...
WHAT AN ODD BOY.
I CAN'T.
HE MAKES IT SOUND AS IF HE'S BEEN... WAITING FOR ME.

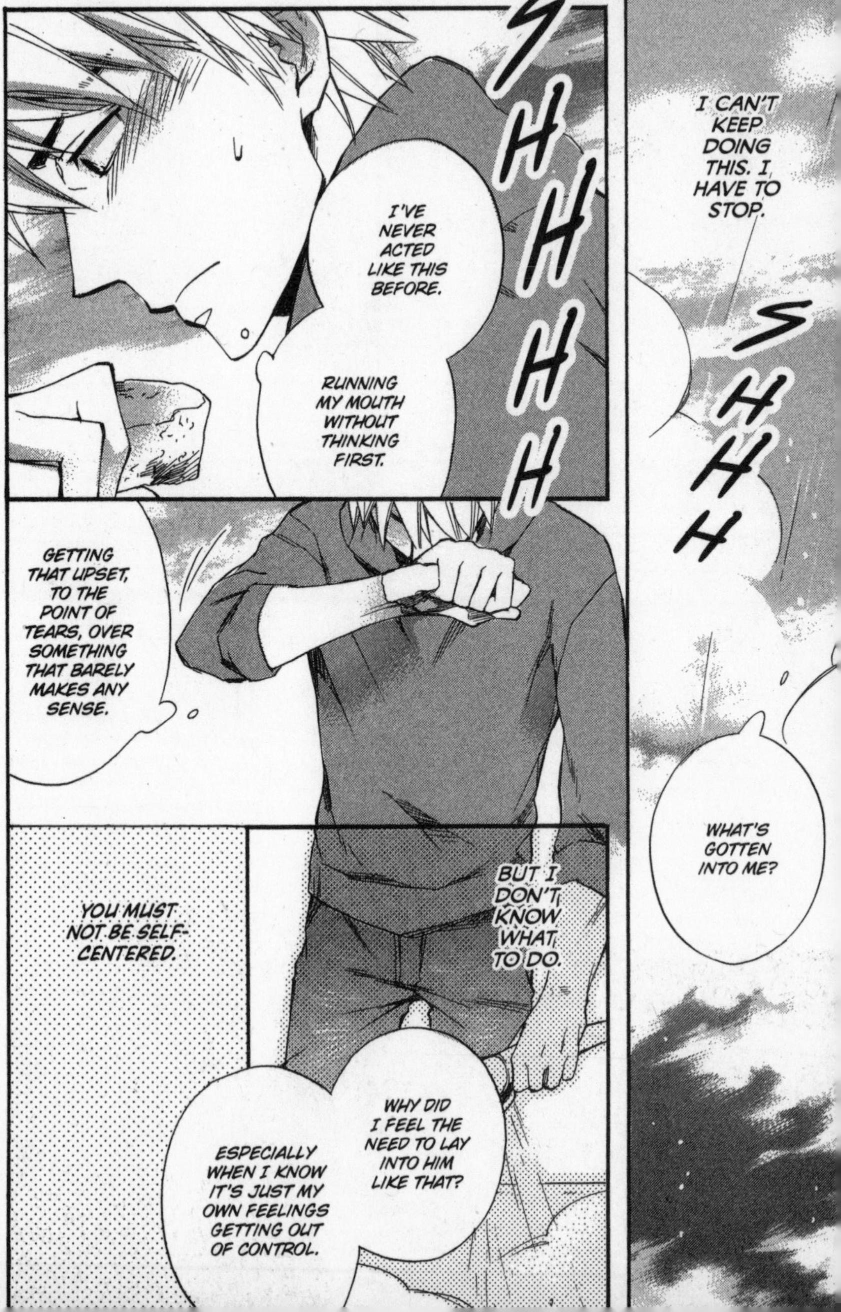
I CAN'T KEEP DOING THIS. I HAVE TO STOP.
SHHHH
WHAT'S GOTTEN INTO ME?
SHHHHH
I'VE NEVER ACTED LIKE THIS BEFORE.
RUNNING MY MOUTH WITHOUT THINKING FIRST.
GETTING THAT UPSET, TO THE POINT OF TEARS, OVER SOMETHING THAT BARELY MAKES ANY SENSE.
BUT I DON'T KNOW WHAT TO DO.
WHY DID I FEEL THE NEED TO LAY INTO HIM LIKE THAT?
ESPECIALLY WHEN I KNOW IT'S JUST MY OWN FEELINGS GETTING OUT OF CONTROL.
YOU MUST NOT BE SELF-CENTERED.

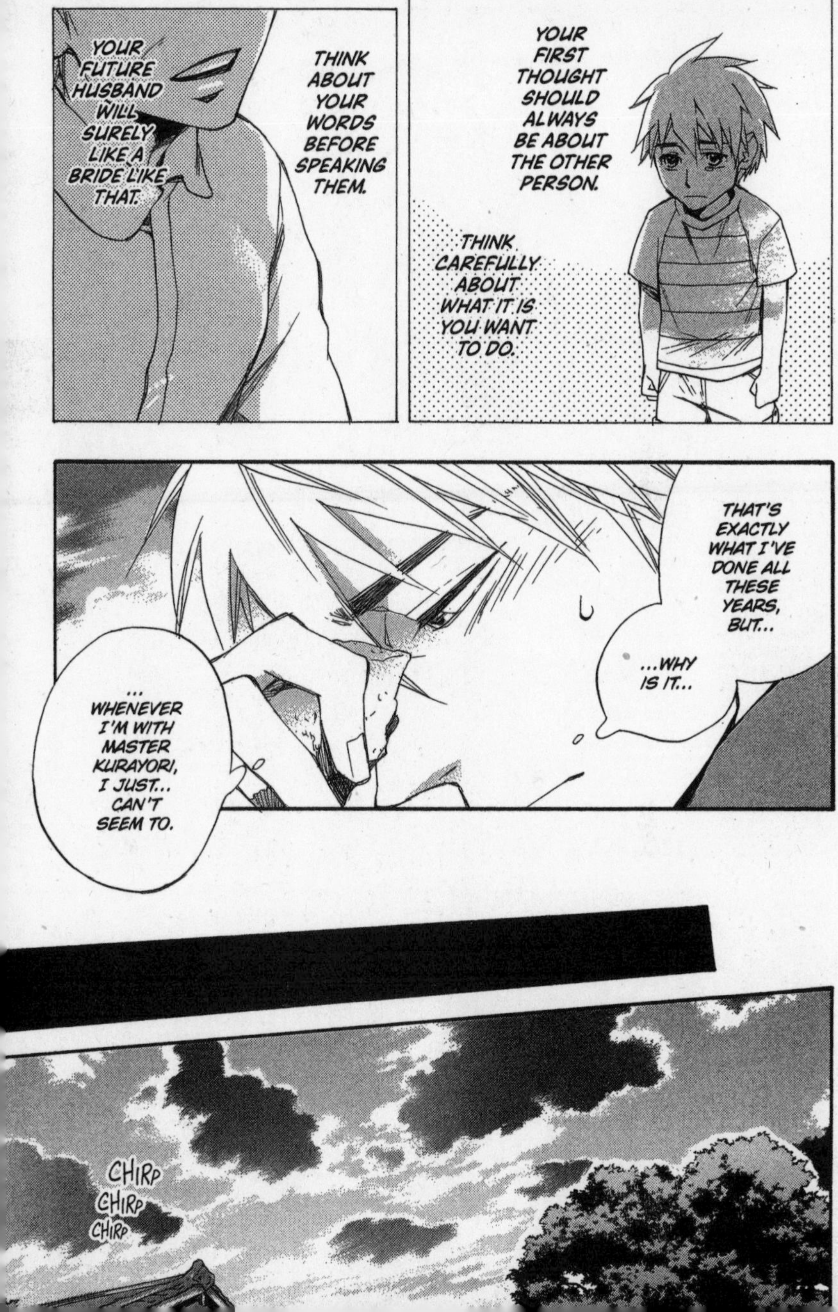
YOUR FIRST THOUGHT SHOULD ALWAYS BE ABOUT THE OTHER PERSON.
THINK CAREFULLY ABOUT WHAT IT IS YOU WANT TO DO.
THINK ABOUT YOUR WORDS BEFORE SPEAKING THEM.
YOUR FUTURE HUSBAND WILL SURELY LIKE A BRIDE LIKE THAT.
THAT'S EXACTLY WHAT I'VE DONE ALL THESE YEARS, BUT...
...WHY IS IT...
...WHENEVER I'M WITH MASTER KURAYORI, I JUST... CAN'T SEEM TO.
CHIRP
CHIRP
CHIRP

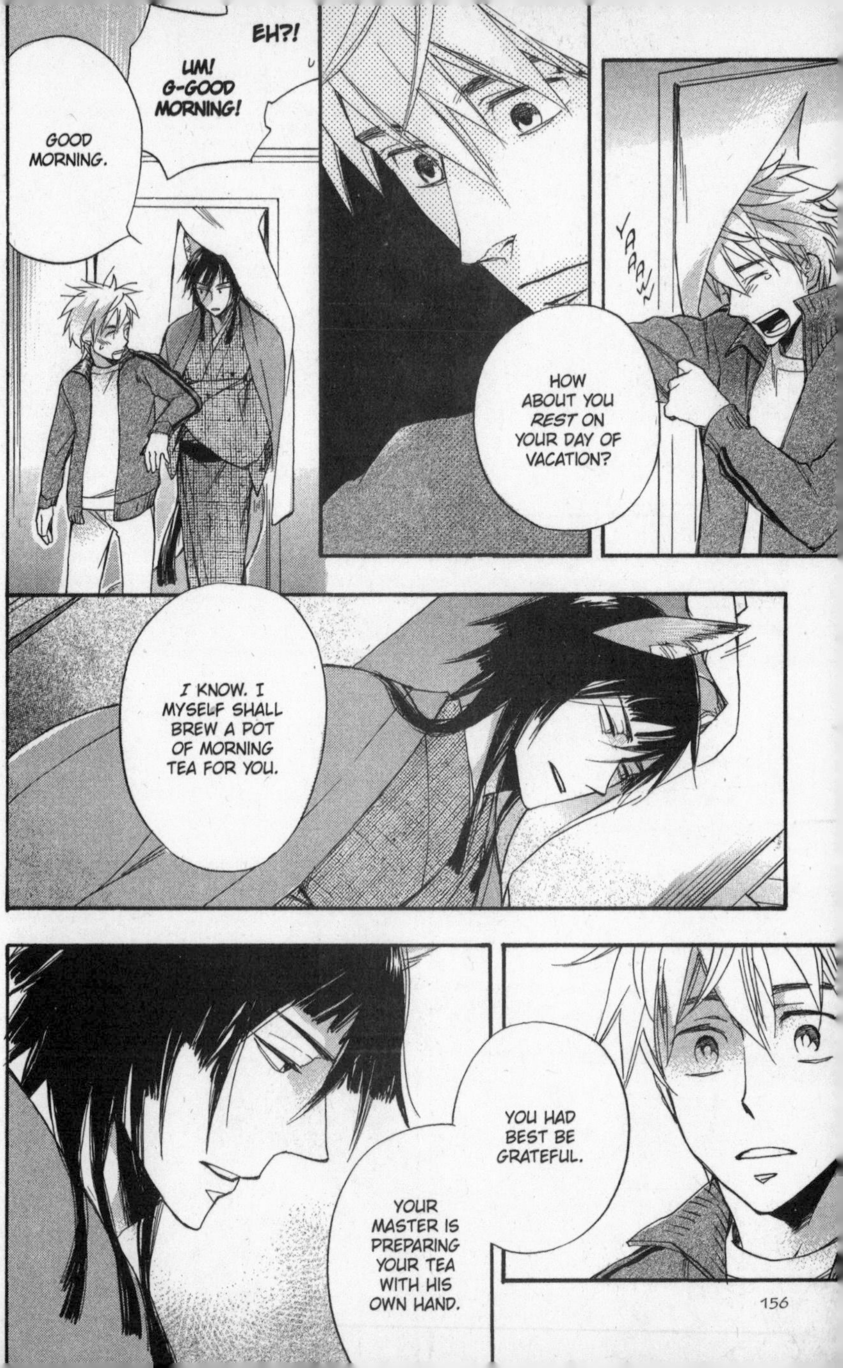

YAAAWN
HOW ABOUT YOU *REST* ON YOUR DAY OF VACATION?
EH?!
UM! G-GOOD MORNING!
GOOD MORNING.
I KNOW. I MYSELF SHALL BREW A POT OF MORNING TEA FOR YOU.
YOU HAD BEST BE GRATEFUL.
YOUR MASTER IS PREPARING YOUR TEA WITH HIS OWN HAND.

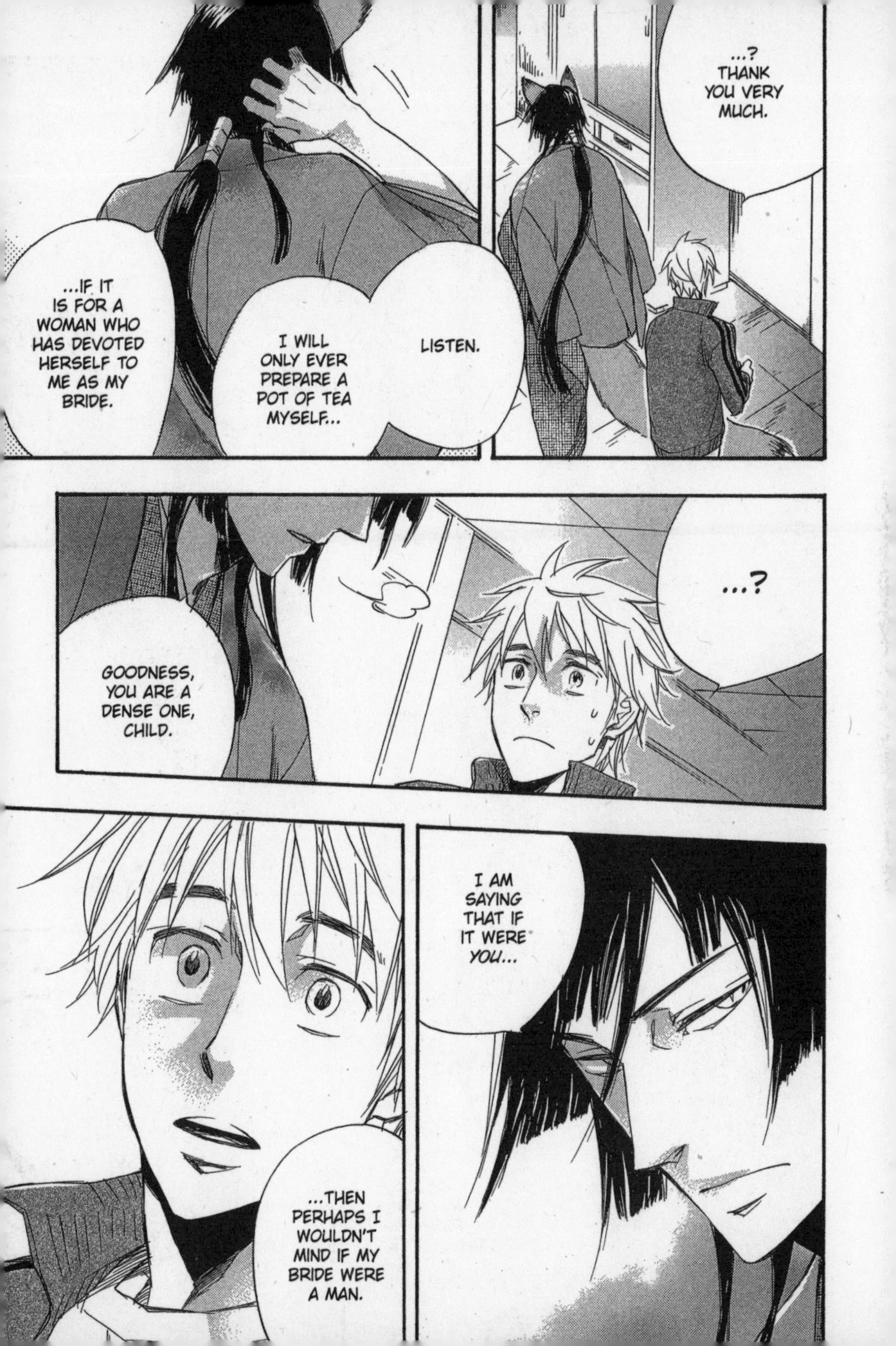
...? THANK YOU VERY MUCH.
LISTEN.
I WILL ONLY EVER PREPARE A POT OF TEA MYSELF...
...IF IT IS FOR A WOMAN WHO HAS DEVOTED HERSELF TO ME AS MY BRIDE.
...?
GOODNESS, YOU ARE A DENSE ONE, CHILD.
I AM SAYING THAT IF IT WERE *YOU*...
...THEN PERHAPS I WOULDN'T MIND IF MY BRIDE WERE A MAN.

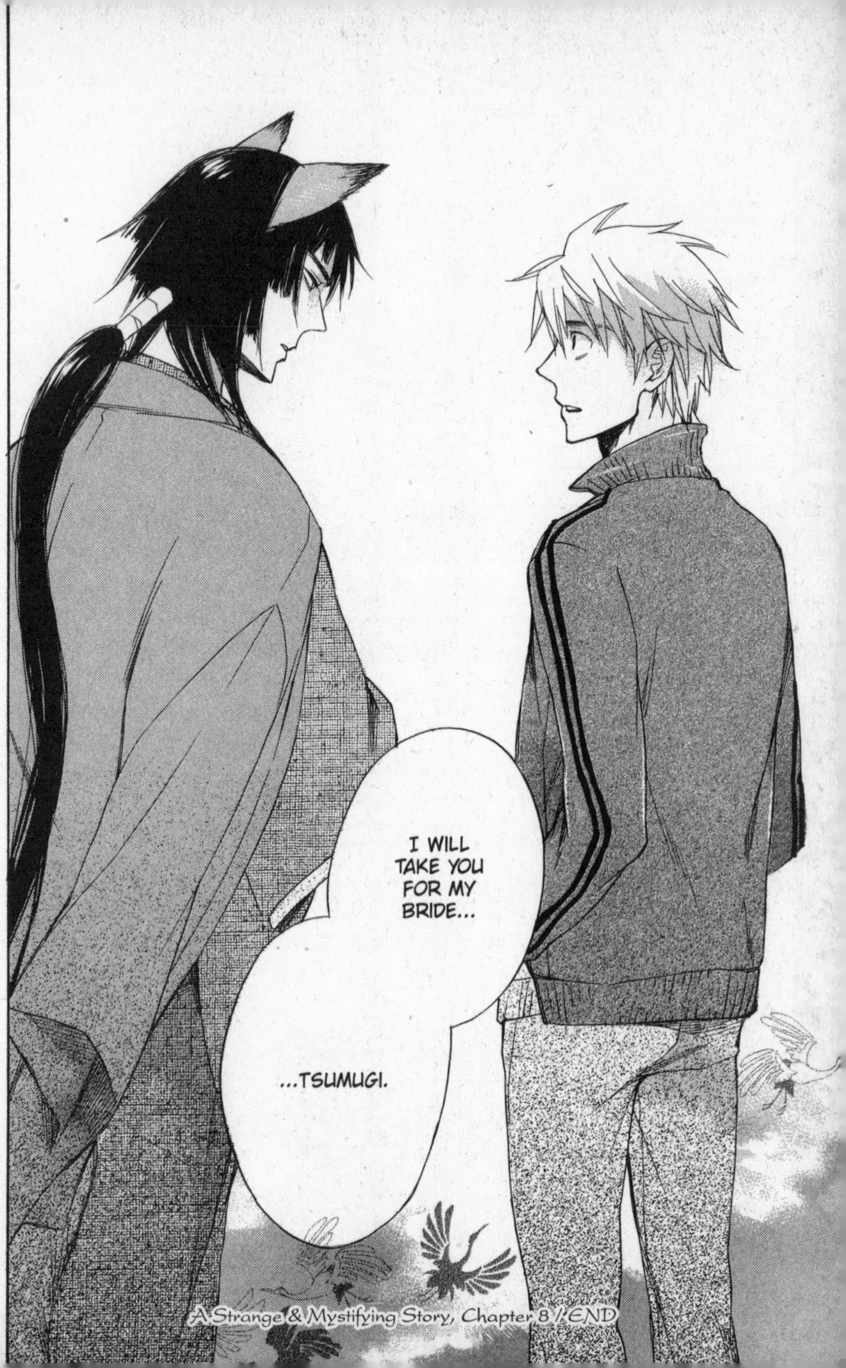
I WILL TAKE YOU FOR MY BRIDE...
...TSUMUGI.
A Strange & Mystifying Story, Chapter 8 / END

A Strange & Mystifying Story

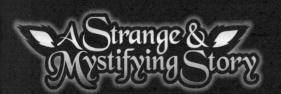

A Strange & Mystifying Story

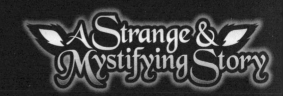

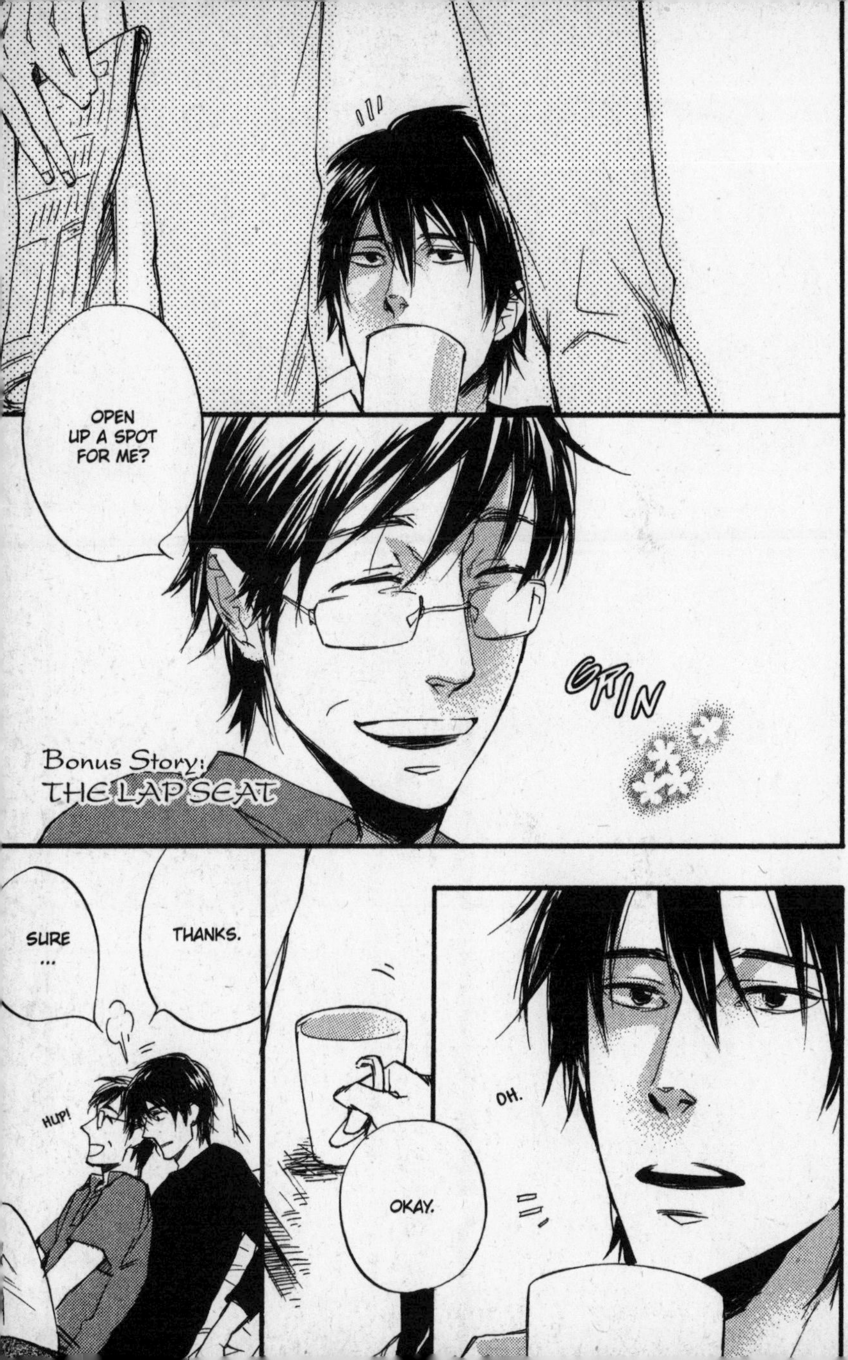
OPEN UP A SPOT FOR ME?
GRIN
Bonus Story:
THE LAP SEAT
OH.
OKAY.
THANKS.
SURE ...
HUP!

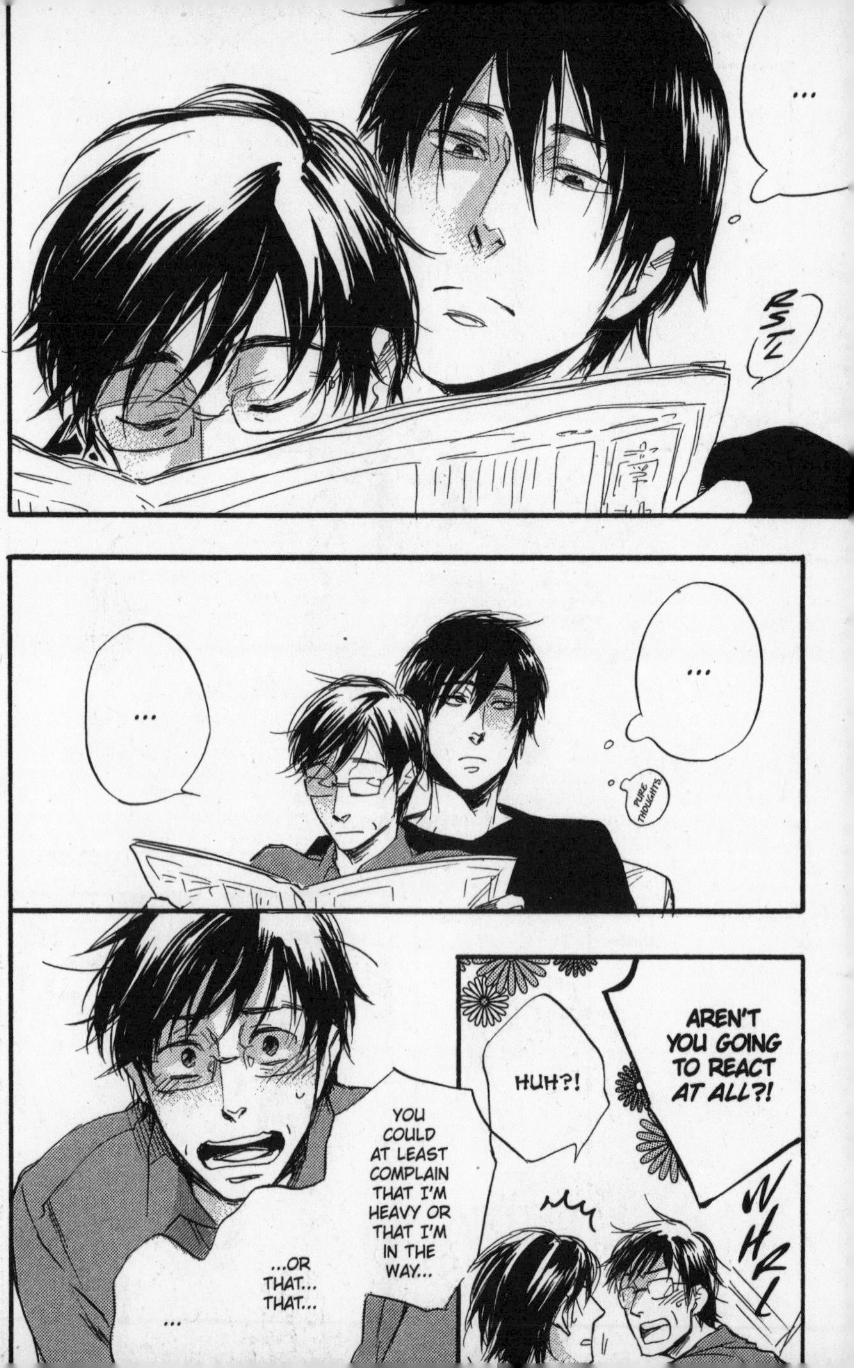
...
...
PURE THOUGHTS
...
AREN'T YOU GOING TO REACT AT ALL?!
HUH?!
WHRL
YOU COULD AT LEAST COMPLAIN THAT I'M HEAVY OR THAT I'M IN THE WAY...
...OR THAT... THAT...
...

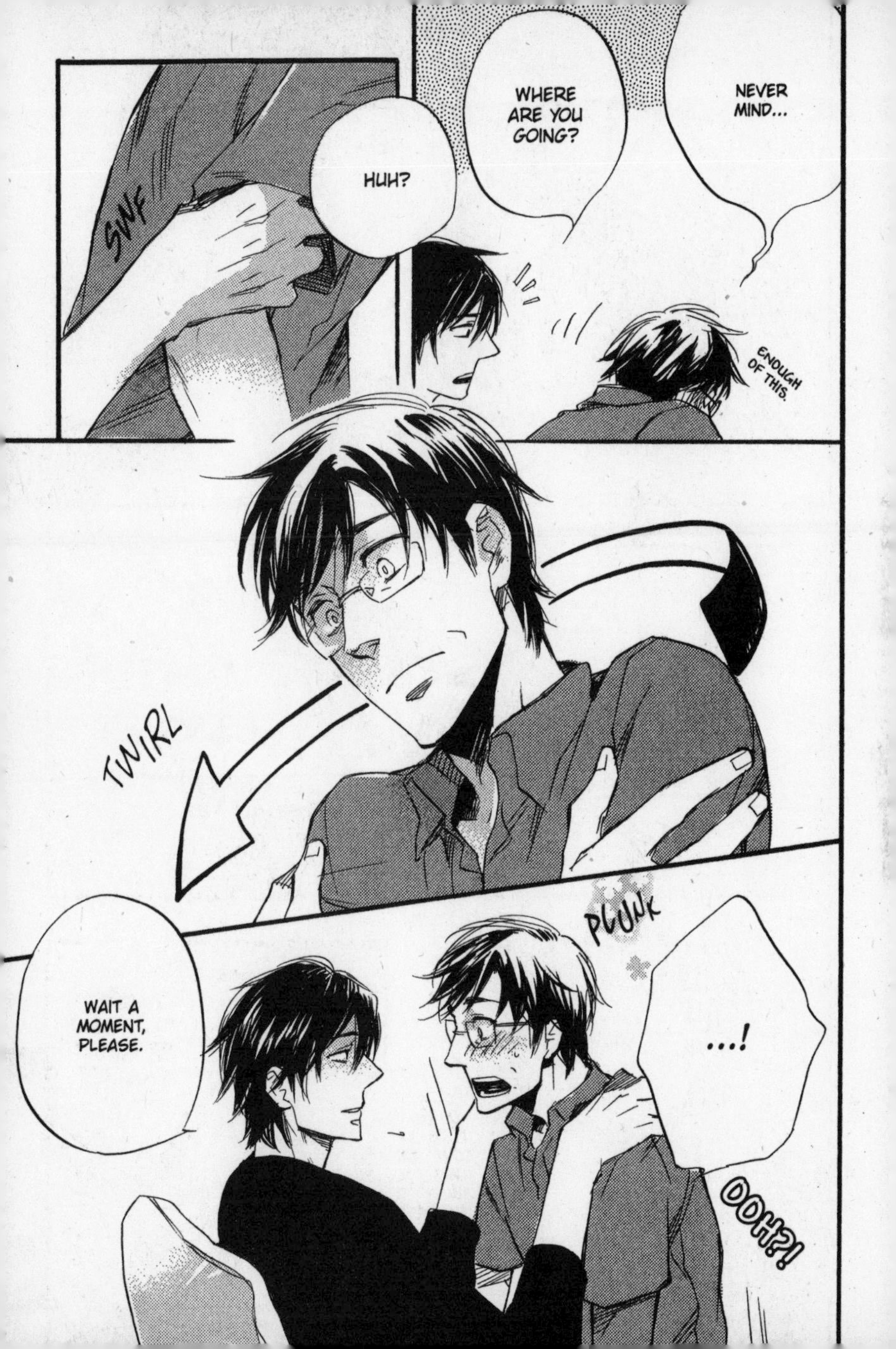
NEVER MIND...
WHERE ARE YOU GOING?
ENOUGH OF THIS.
HUH?
SNF
TWIRL
...!
PLUNK
OOH?!
WAIT A MOMENT, PLEASE.

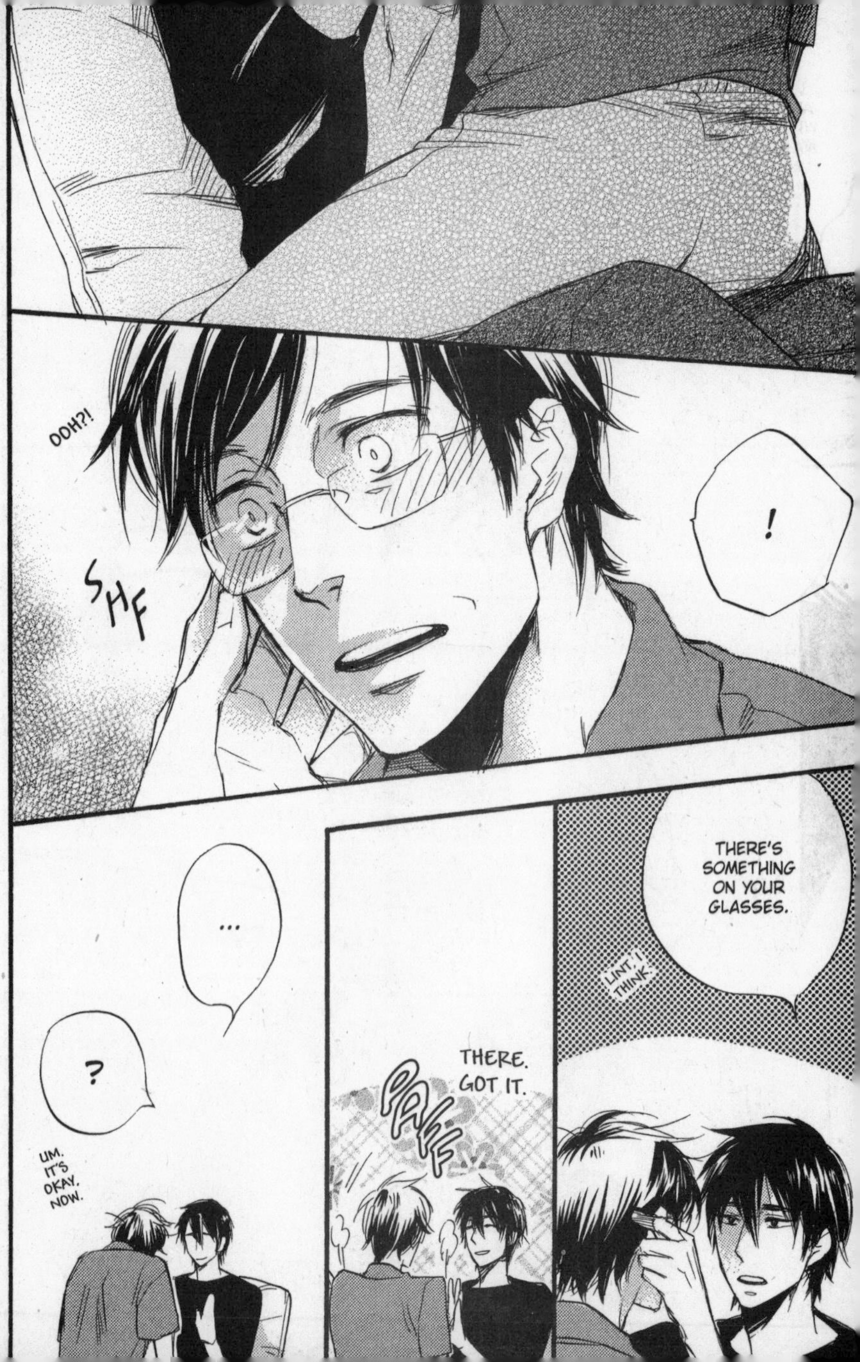
!
OOH?!
SHF
THERE'S SOMETHING ON YOUR GLASSES.
LINT, I THINK.
PAFF
THERE. GOT IT.
...
?
UM. IT'S OKAY. NOW.

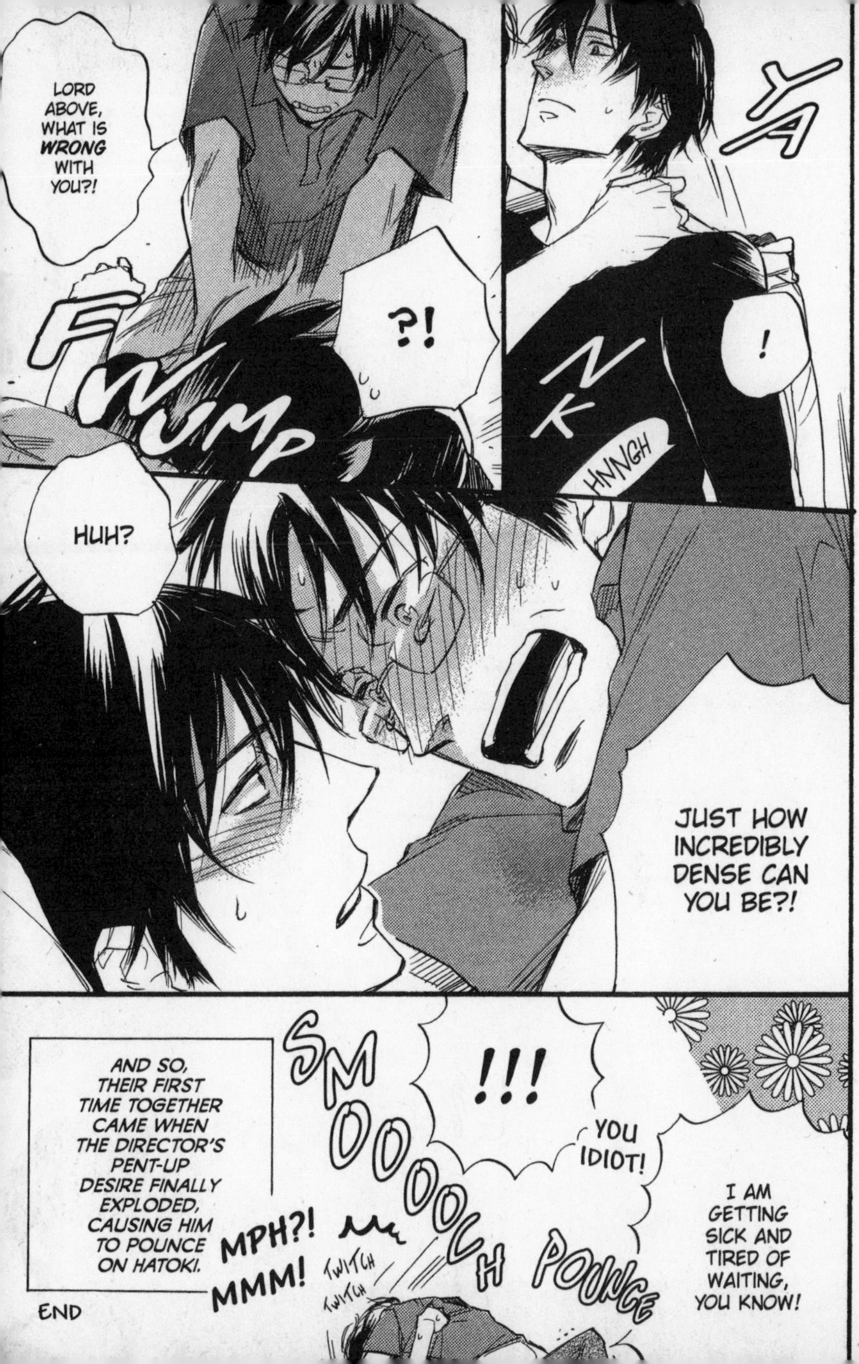
YANK
!
HNNGH
LORD ABOVE, WHAT IS **WRONG** WITH YOU?!
?!
FWUMP
HUH?
JUST HOW INCREDIBLY DENSE CAN YOU BE?!
I AM GETTING SICK AND TIRED OF WAITING, YOU KNOW!
YOU IDIOT!
!!!
SMOOOOOCH
POUNCE
TWITCH TWITCH
MPH?! MMM!
AND SO, THEIR FIRST TIME TOGETHER CAME WHEN THE DIRECTOR'S PENT-UP DESIRE FINALLY EXPLODED, CAUSING HIM TO POUNCE ON HATOKI.
END

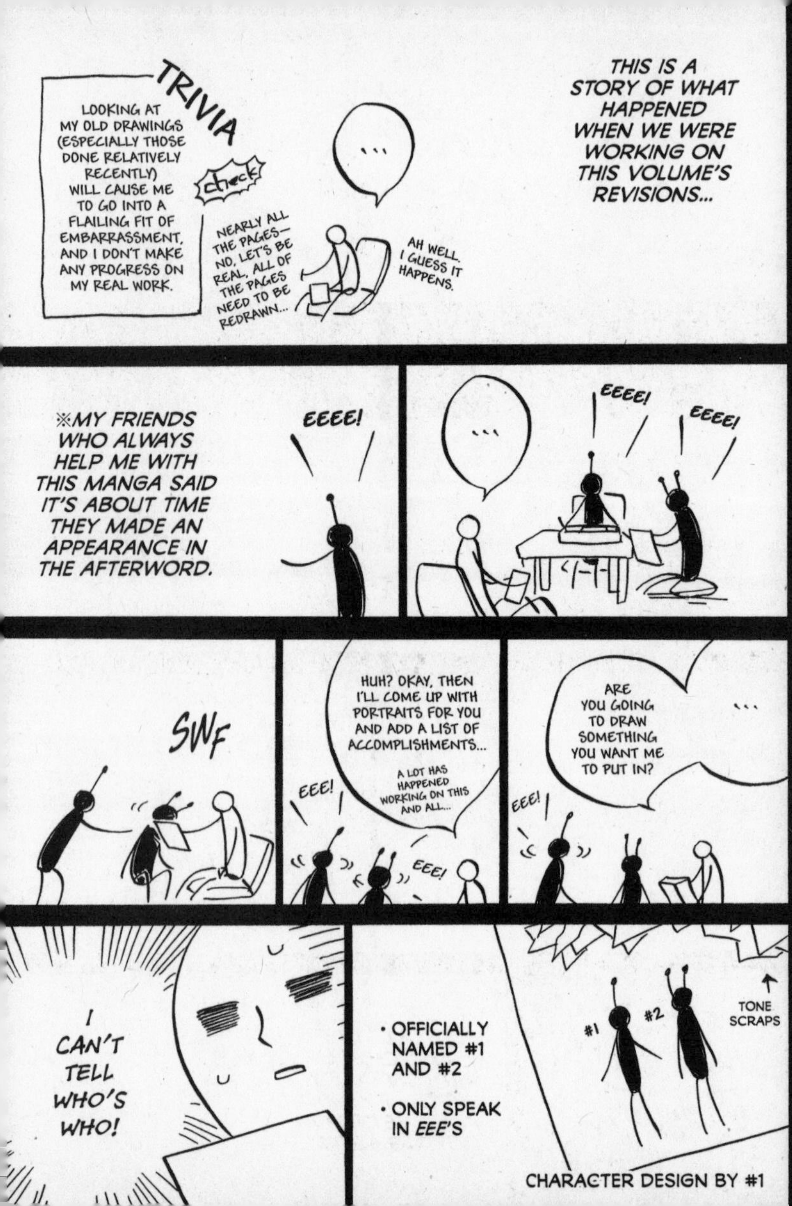
THIS IS A STORY OF WHAT HAPPENED WHEN WE WERE WORKING ON THIS VOLUME'S REVISIONS...
...
AH WELL, I GUESS IT HAPPENS.
NEARLY ALL THE PAGES—NO, LET'S BE REAL, ALL OF THE PAGES NEED TO BE REDRAWN...
check
TRIVIA
LOOKING AT MY OLD DRAWINGS (ESPECIALLY THOSE DONE RELATIVELY RECENTLY) WILL CAUSE ME TO GO INTO A FLAILING FIT OF EMBARRASSMENT, AND I DON'T MAKE ANY PROGRESS ON MY REAL WORK.
...
EEEE!
EEEE!
EEEE!
※MY FRIENDS WHO ALWAYS HELP ME WITH THIS MANGA SAID IT'S ABOUT TIME THEY MADE AN APPEARANCE IN THE AFTERWORD.
...
ARE YOU GOING TO DRAW SOMETHING YOU WANT ME TO PUT IN?
EEE!
HUH? OKAY, THEN I'LL COME UP WITH PORTRAITS FOR YOU AND ADD A LIST OF ACCOMPLISHMENTS...
A LOT HAS HAPPENED WORKING ON THIS AND ALL...
EEE!
EEE!
SWF
TONE SCRAPS
#2
#1
• OFFICIALLY NAMED #1 AND #2
• ONLY SPEAK IN EEE'S
CHARACTER DESIGN BY #1
I CAN'T TELL WHO'S WHO!

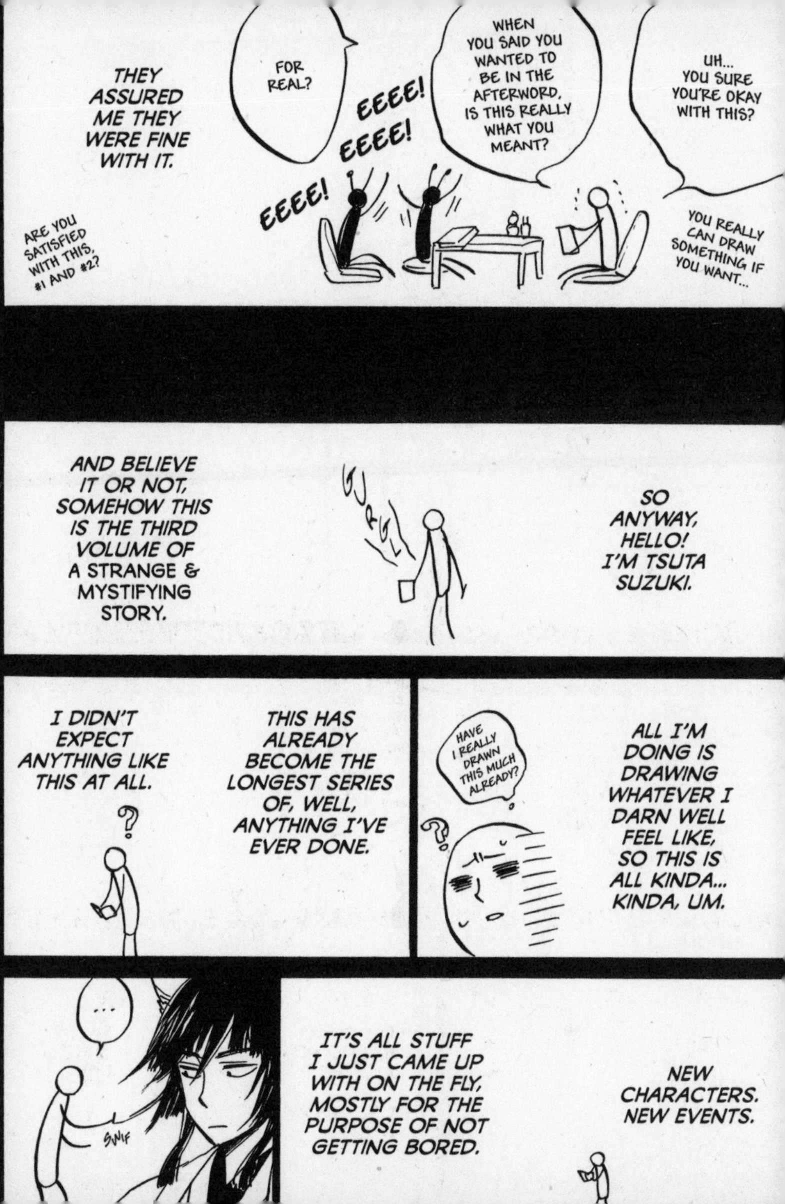
UH... YOU SURE YOU'RE OKAY WITH THIS?
YOU REALLY CAN DRAW SOMETHING IF YOU WANT...
WHEN YOU SAID YOU WANTED TO BE IN THE AFTERWORD, IS THIS REALLY WHAT YOU MEANT?
EEEE!
EEEE!
EEEE!
FOR REAL?
THEY ASSURED ME THEY WERE FINE WITH IT.
ARE YOU SATISFIED WITH THIS, #1 AND #2?
SO ANYWAY, HELLO! I'M TSUTA SUZUKI.
AND BELIEVE IT OR NOT, SOMEHOW THIS IS THE THIRD VOLUME OF A STRANGE & MYSTIFYING STORY.
ALL I'M DOING IS DRAWING WHATEVER I DARN WELL FEEL LIKE, SO THIS IS ALL KINDA... KINDA, UM.
HAVE I REALLY DRAWN THIS MUCH ALREADY?
THIS HAS ALREADY BECOME THE LONGEST SERIES OF, WELL, ANYTHING I'VE EVER DONE.
I DIDN'T EXPECT ANYTHING LIKE THIS AT ALL.
NEW CHARACTERS. NEW EVENTS.
IT'S ALL STUFF I JUST CAME UP WITH ON THE FLY, MOSTLY FOR THE PURPOSE OF NOT GETTING BORED.
...
SNIF

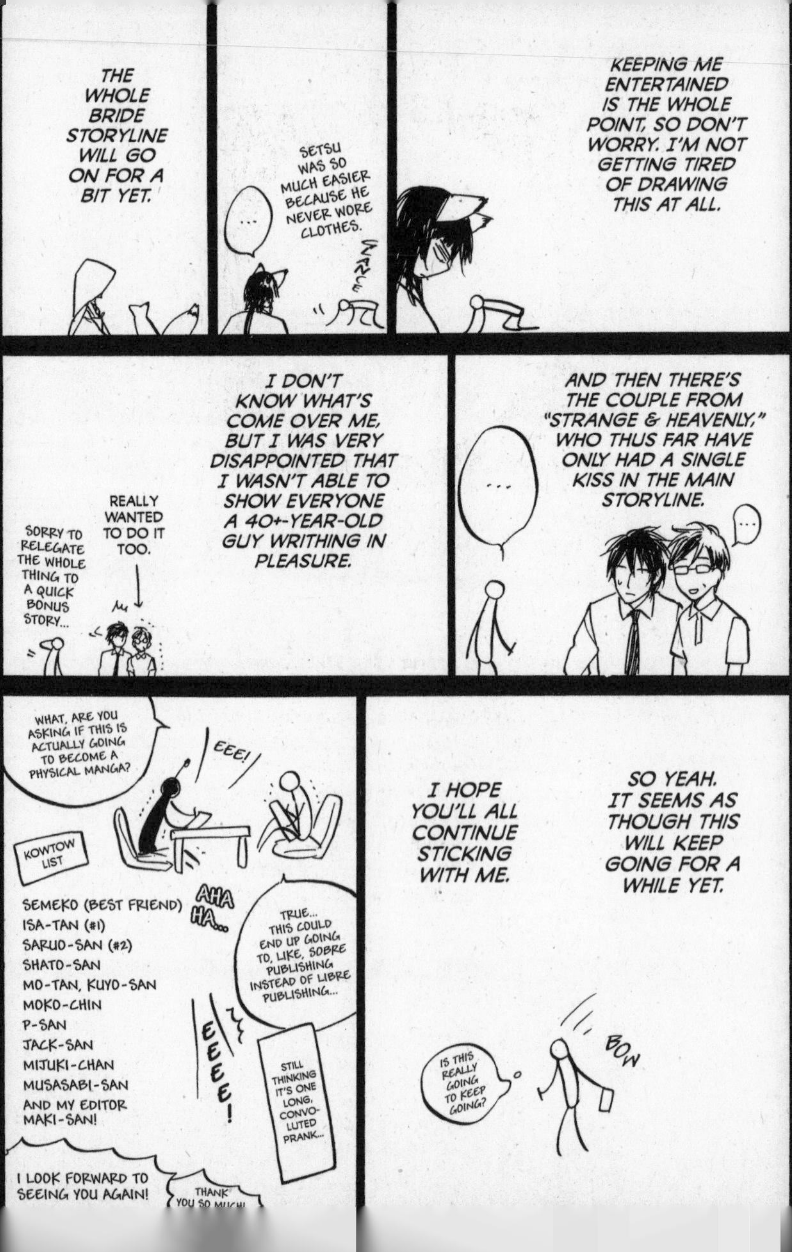
KEEPING ME ENTERTAINED IS THE WHOLE POINT, SO DON'T WORRY. I'M NOT GETTING TIRED OF DRAWING THIS AT ALL.
SETSU WAS SO MUCH EASIER BECAUSE HE NEVER WORE CLOTHES.
...
THE WHOLE BRIDE STORYLINE WILL GO ON FOR A BIT YET.
AND THEN THERE'S THE COUPLE FROM "STRANGE & HEAVENLY," WHO THUS FAR HAVE ONLY HAD A SINGLE KISS IN THE MAIN STORYLINE.
...
...
I DON'T KNOW WHAT'S COME OVER ME, BUT I WAS VERY DISAPPOINTED THAT I WASN'T ABLE TO SHOW EVERYONE A 40+-YEAR-OLD GUY WRITHING IN PLEASURE.
REALLY WANTED TO DO IT TOO.
SORRY TO RELEGATE THE WHOLE THING TO A QUICK BONUS STORY...
SO YEAH. IT SEEMS AS THOUGH THIS WILL KEEP GOING FOR A WHILE YET.
I HOPE YOU'LL ALL CONTINUE STICKING WITH ME.
IS THIS REALLY GOING TO KEEP GOING?
BOW
WHAT, ARE YOU ASKING IF THIS IS ACTUALLY GOING TO BECOME A PHYSICAL MANGA?
EEE!
KOWTOW LIST
AHAHA...
TRUE... THIS COULD END UP GOING TO, LIKE, SOBRE PUBLISHING INSTEAD OF LIBRE PUBLISHING...
SEMEKO (BEST FRIEND)
ISA-TAN (#1)
SARUO-SAN (#2)
SHATO-SAN
MO-TAN, KUYO-SAN
MOKO-CHIN
P-SAN
JACK-SAN
MIJUKI-CHAN
MUSASABI-SAN
AND MY EDITOR MAKI-SAN!
EEEE!
STILL THINKING IT'S ONE LONG, CONVO-LUTED PRANK...
I LOOK FORWARD TO SEEING YOU AGAIN!
THANK YOU SO MUCH!

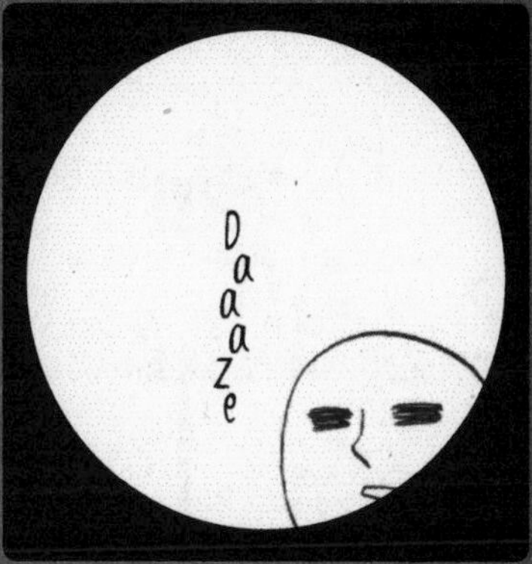
Daaaze

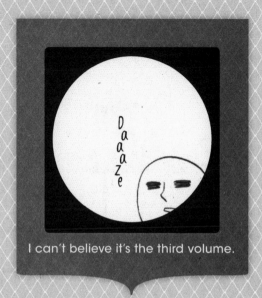

I can't believe it's the third volume.

About the Author

This is **Tsuta Suzuki's** second English-language release, with her first being *Your Story I've Known*. Formerly working under the name "Yogore," she has also published *doujinshi* (independent comics) under the circle name "Muddy Pool." Born a Sagittarius in Shikoku, Japan on December 3rd, she has an A blood type and currently resides in Kyoto.

A Strange & Mystifying Story
Volume 3
SuBLime Manga Edition

Story and Art by **Tsuta Suzuki**

Translation—**Adrienne Beck**
Touch-Up Art and Lettering—**Bianca Pistillo**
Cover and Graphic Design—**Julian [JR] Robinson**
Editor—**Jennifer LeBlanc**

libre

Printed in the U.S.A.

Published by SuBLime Manga
P.O. Box 77010
San Francisco, CA 94107

10 9 8 7 6 5 4 3 2 1
First printing, May 2018

M
MATURE

PARENTAL ADVISORY
A STRANGE & MYSTIFYING STORY is rated M for Mature and is recommended for mature readers. This volume contains graphic imagery and mature themes.

SUBLIME

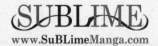

www.SuBLimeManga.com